SILHOUETTES AND SHADOWS

PART 1

Real Deal Press/J R Martin Media Inc
jrmar2039@gmail.com

www.jrmartinmedia.com
FIRST EDITION

Book Design Real Deal Press

Cover Design and Layout Aaron J Martin

Ordering Information:
Quantity sales. Special discounts are available on quantity purchases by corporations, associations, and others. For details, contact the "Special Sales Department" at the e-mail address above.

Silhouettes and Shadows James R Martin.
ISBN: 979-8-9875933-1-8

pb/01280123revING

SILHOUETTES AND SHADOWS

*"HUMANITY FOLLOWS THE EARTH;
EARTH FOLLOWS THE UNIVERSE."*

A Novel

James R. Martin

Real Deal Press Orlando Florida

Also by James R Martin

Screenplays

2076 Olympiad

Studio A

Wrapped In Steel

Fired-Up

Books

Create Documentary Films, Videos and Multimedia

Actuality Interviewing and Listening

Documentary Directing and Storytelling

Listen Learn Share

Office and Home Tai Chi - Yue Zhang Translator/
Editor English Edition

The Shaolin Temple Story - Shi Yongxin
Translator/Writer, Editor English Edition

Yishan Cheng

CHAPTER ONE

....

"Hollowed out, a lump of clay makes a pot. Where the pot is not is where it's useful. The profit in what may be is in using what is not." --Dao De Jing

Paul Arroyo gets up from his director's chair and stands next to the cameraman. He raises a frustrated eyebrow, indicating he is unhappy with how this scene is going. In some ways, he regrets that his company signed a contract to create a series of films based on popular romance novels. The screenplays came directly from the publisher. The studio can usually turn out the sixty-minute episodic series films in four weeks for digital streaming. From the beginning, Paul isn't too excited about the project. He decides to try to elevate the genre with classic cinematic concepts. He recently concluded that there is only so much you can do with these screenplays. He continuously learns something from every project.

"Let's do one more take of that shot and a close-up of Barbara reacting. Then take a break," Paul tells the 1st Assistant Director (1st AD). The crew prepares to do another take.

Paul's mind drifts as they do the retake. He remembers his father asked him to come by the garage today. Paul is anxious to see what is going on. He knows his parents, Raoul Sr. and Marcella, have been working on a high-priority project and keeping the details secret. We can't talk about it on the phone stuff. Paul is used to his parents coming up with new inventions. He does not anticipate how this discovery will come to change his life. His focus returns to the present. Checking his watch, he finds it is 4:00 p.m. Time to wrap for the day.

The "garage" is a vast hangar building, one of several that comprises the Arroyo Aerospace engineering and manufacturing center. Paul's mother, Marcella, has always been a tinkerer. She and Raoul Sr., Paul's father, build amazing things in the garage. The couple has accumulated a fortune inventing devices and unique parts for NASA and the aerospace industry. It is a mom-and-pop operation; they like it this way.

The setting Florida sun replaces the afternoon downpour of rain as Paul walks to his garage and a small collection of cars. He knows which car he wants to drive this afternoon. He slides into one of his favorites, a silver 1993 RX-7 twin-turbo, pushes a button to turn it on, puts it into gear, and drives off with a barely audible low-pitched hum and no exhaust sound. It sounds like the stock rotary engine with which Mazda equipped the car. However, Paul's father long ago modified the rotary engine. They rebuilt the engine in the Arroyo Aerospace facility, where most of their experimental work is done. The engine is no longer conventionally turbocharged. It runs on electricity, not gasoline. The only thing in common with the old rotary engine is that it still only has three moving parts. Turbocharging is now electric. Another Arroyo innovation is smaller, lighter-weight batteries able to hold a much larger charge than anyone, including Tesla, has been able to invent.

On his way to meet his father, Paul drives past the solar panels and wind turbines on the private road between his studio and his parents' property. The family owns a ranch and raises horses and some cattle. The large garden provides lots of fresh vegetables and other crops in season. The ranch property also houses Arroyo Aerospace buildings and businesses. The Arroyos have an extensive network of customers and friends in the aerospace engineering and technology industries. Over many years their reputation for innovation and solving problems quietly spread among other innovators. Their company name can be found on some very impressive contact lists. They design and fabricate everything from one-of-a-kind silicon chips to parts for space shuttles. They choose to keep a low profile and stay a private company.

Paul is the fourth of eight children in the Arroyo family. About six feet tall and dark-complected, he resembles his father in looks and height. He didn't join the family business; he became a filmmaker, producer/writer, and director of some of Hollywood's recently successful films. Paul believes he probably just got lucky as a certain percentage of the worldwide audience got tired of watching zombies ripping off heads or comic book action heroes flying around. They currently enjoy a plot, romance, and a happy ending that does not seem contrived. A romantic at heart Paul enjoys exploring the emotional side of relationships.

When Paul returns from studying film in Europe, Raoul Sr. and Marcella finance his first movie in 2004, costing $877,000. He writes, directs, and produces a romantic coming-of-age story at twenty-five. That film ends up netting him about four hundred million to date. Paul doesn't believe in sequels; he likes to tell new stories in the same genre. You can never tell when a character from another story will turn up in one of his films. Some critics label them movie soaps. For a while, he turns out a new epic every six to eight months. The films make money on TV, and cable runs, home rentals, and sales are equal to the box-office revenue. Over a few years, his movies net his studio billions of dollars. Paul is happy living in Florida near family and friends and, for now, making short sixty-minute films for digital streaming. His time is his own since he is an independent producer. He also invests in film projects by other filmmakers and producers.

Paul follows his parent's example creating a low profile for his business. Paul Arroyo Studios is family run. A small staff runs the day-to-day operations. His sister Annie manages the studio, and his brother Bill handles the accounting and legal work through his law firm. The studio and back lot are on two hundred acres of land not far from Orlando, Disney World, and Universal Studios. Talented production people are living in the Orlando area. Even though buying the tract of land is expensive, he purchased it because the property is adjacent to his parent's land. Paul and his parents own a valuable chuck of Brevard County near the headwaters of the St. John River.

Since the two Arroyo properties are adjacent, they built a private road to join them. The road has straightaways, curves, and unique places with solar panels and a few wind turbines to drive around. The now electric Mazda has a dual drive transmission which can act as a manual or automatic drive. Paul eases the car into top gear as he comes out of the seven palms loop and onto a straight-a-way. He watches the speedometer quickly move to 170 mph as the vehicle's front end begins to feel like it might go airborne. He slows down.

"Great engine and drive train," he said out loud. "The only thing I can't do is fly."

Arroyo Aerospace holds patents on all the engine parts they create. To keep their work private, they patent various parts for purposes that are not necessarily intended. His father, Raoul Sr. said, "the major car builders aren't ready for Arroyo Aerospace electric engines. Nor are they ready for the paint material that coats the entire body of the automobile conducting solar energy to storage cells that power the engine."

The paint is a spin-off of the coatings used on stealth bombers and Swedish submarine coning towers to reduce, absorb, or eliminate radar detection. It still has some of its original properties. The car body is a thin, lightweight material that is as hard as zircon carbide but more flexible. Stronger than steel. The main ingredient is sand, which is very plentiful in Florida. It resists heat better than the tiles used on the space shuttle. The material molds into any shape using a 3D printer. Marcella developed ceramic material and the paint in the "garage." They replicated several of Paul's collection cars and a dozen others, primarily for their other children and practical use. Paul's collection of cars and other family vehicles are not always what they appear. What seems to be a stock sports car or SUV has accessories the manufacturer does not include.

Outside immediate family members, only Paul's girlfriend, Stacy, knows about the car modifications. Stacy works with one of the local members of Congress as an aide; she runs his Florida office. She and Paul attended the same schools and grew up together in Central Florida. They both are graduates of Cocoa Beach High and UCF. The Arroyos consider her one of the family. Paul and Stacy have a long-term intimate relationship. They have been in love all their lives. Stacy is Paul's biggest fan and confidant. He trusts her judgment in all matters.

Paul pulls alongside his older brother Sam's aging 1973 "VW Thing" parked in front of the office area for Arroyo Aerospace. Sam bought the Thing from someone in South Florida who kept it on his yacht for many years. Sam restores it for short runs around the beach and to the Arroyo ranch. He owns a marina and some fishing boats in Port Canaveral. His field is engineering, ship design, and marine technologies. Sam is an engineering marvel in his own right. He can make most anything function mechanically. He works in the family business whenever he is needed.

"Maybe Raoul Sr. will modify the 'Thing,'" Paul imagines. Although he knows Sam likes it just as it is."

Paul's phone rings on the car's speakers before he turns off the engine. "Better drive around to the back," his mother's voice said in a friendly manner, and is gone. Marcella Arroyo, Paul's mother, never minces words. Paul drives around the large hangar to the back of the building.

He stops in front of a standard-size two-car garage overshadowed by a 747-size hangar behind it. One of several large hangars lined up along the private airstrip. A tower, satellite dish, and radar dome can also be seen. The strip has all the latest features, including a radar beacon and runway lights for night landings. Commercial planes never land here. Only the Arroyo Aerospace corporate jet, turboprop Cesena, and some delivery planes. Occasionally visitors or customers flew to the ranch. Many Arroyo siblings learned to fly and have a pilot's license.

A large double door slides back, allowing Paul to drive into the hangar and park where his father directs him.

Paul Arroyo resembles his father even though he is two inches taller. Pau's beard is still dark, whereas Raoul Arroyo Sr. has a head of silver hair and salt and pepper beard. He looks young for his age. He keeps in shape by swimming, walking, and Tai Chi exercises. The entire family learned Tai Chi many years ago. They practice together whenever possible.

Raoul Sr. and his family are native Floridians in the most far-reaching sense. Raoul Sr. traces his ancestors back to Captain Emilio de Gonzales Arroyo, who came with his family to St. Augustine from Spain in 1671. An architect and engineer of the time, he helps to build Castillo de San Marcos, the fortress still guarding the port in St. Augustine. Captain Arroyo manages to get a land grant for some property deeper in the interior of Florida. Ultimately the family arranges to move there, making deals with the indigenous population of Seminole people. This arrangement to share the land and pay the Seminole in kind for land worked out well until the British came along and started fighting with most of the indigenous people and Spanish settlers. Many of the British are either pirates or traders looking for slaves. Some English and Scottish settlers move into the area. The Arroyo family manages to stay in place, arranging marriages with certain British families and indigenous peoples.

Raoul Arroyo Sr. began his career as a mechanical engineer. He is always at the forefront as technology evolves, inventing state-of-the-art devices that involve multiple emerging technologies. He never stops studying and learning.

"How are you, son?" His father asks him in a tone that tells Paul to be prepared for anything.

"I'm doing fine. Where's mom? I noticed Sam's 'Thing' outside. Where is he?"

"He came over last night; he's with your mother. Before we join them, I need to take you for a ride," he said, pointing to a minivan. Originally a '93 Toyota Previa, it has been dramatically customized inside and out.

"Something new? Must be special," Paul said. Raoul Sr. motioned his son to follow him. Paul got into the minivan beside his father. The interior doesn't look much different than before. Over the years, more and more gauges and dials have materialized. The interior looks like a science lab for automobiles.

"Put your seat belt on," Raoul Sr. instructs his son.

Paul buckles up as his father shifts the van into drive. The vehicle effortlessly floats forward.

"So that's it, you've made the motor instant on. There's no lurch or power surge. It feels like we're floating. Are we going out?"

"Not going out. We're floating up!"

Raoul Sr. eases a second lever on the center floor console forward. It looks like a joystick for a video game. Before Paul realizes it, they gently move away from the hangar's floor. Up and toward the opposite end of the building. At the same time, he notices what looks like a gyroscope, a new gauge, and an altimeter are now installed.

"We're going up. Are we flying? I don't believe it."

"Sorry can't take you outside during the daylight. Best that no one sees an unidentified flying van. We fly at night and only on our property," Raoul Sr. said.

"Marcella and I are calling a meeting of the immediate family. Tamara will be here. Everyone except for Sharon, who can't come because she's in Australia and because we did not invite her. All will be here by next weekend. We have to make some decisions." Paul looks at his father for a few seconds. "Can't wait to hear what you have in mind. This is a revolutionary invention. What is it? How does it work?"

"It's just the tip of the iceberg. We'll explain it all soon," Raoul Sr. replies. Along with Carlos, Raoul Jr., and Sam, your mother and I have been working on this idea for a while, so she will help explain it."

Paul knows why Sharon is not invited. They are a tight nit family, and it hurts them to exclude anyone from family decisions. In everyone's opinion, Sharon Arroyo has gone over to the "dark side." She went away to a Christian University where she decided to get a bachelor's degree in Christian theology. No one has a problem with that. However, from that point, she seems brainwashed with right-wing evangelical religious beliefs laced with antiquated ideas about race. She becomes anti-science, which for her parents is hard to understand. Her political views become very conservative. She gets involved in right-wing politics, campaigning for a man who is as far from evangelical Christian principles as anyone can be. Every encounter with her and her family members becomes painful to the other person. Over time family members start avoiding her and her e-mails full of conspiracy theories, anti-vaccine theories, and racist remarks about the President of the country. In 2016 there were repeated crazy accusations about a female presidential candidate. Once the election was over in 2017, Sharon landed a job with the new Republican administration. Marcella and Raoul Sr. believe she cannot be trusted with knowledge of this family project since she might leak it to that administration.

That evening, on his way back to his home near the studio, Paul tries to imagine what his parents will do with this ability to defy gravity. Will they build flying cars? When he gets home, he finds Sam there waiting for him.

"Sorry I missed you at the ranch; I had to run an errand. How do you like the flying van?" Sam asked.

"Awesome, how does it work?"

"Remember when we used to go surfing, riding the waves? It's kind of like that. I'll let our genius parents and other siblings explain all that," Sam said. "I want to talk to you about some ideas we can bring up at this family meeting."

"Ideas?" Paul said.

"Yeah, like flying very high, maybe visiting the moon or Mars,"

"High-flying ideas. Okay, sounds interesting. I'm all ears," Paul said.

"First, let's take a ride. I parked over here by the side of the building," Sam said, putting his arm around Paul's shoulder as he led the way.

"I guess today's my day for taking rides," Paul replies resignedly.

Before Paul can ask why he notices the tear-shaped sports car size object sitting in front of them. "What's this?" he asks in a whisper.

"I've been consulting for a while on their project. I wanted to build a test vehicle. Marcella helped write programs for the large-format 3d printer. We printed all the parts and assembled them around their new drive. It's a two-seater with a night vision monitor and GPS. I call it Galaxy Zero. It has landing pods on the bottom, no wheels. Otherwise, bare bones."

They walk over and raise the gull-wing doors on each side of the prototype.

"Get in, and we'll take a short ride. Don't worry. It is not made to go very high. I'm sure it will help you understand the potential," Sam said.

They lower themselves into the prototype's low-slung seats. The dashboard is a console with a seventeen-inch screen in the middle, a gyroscope, and some gauges, including an altimeter. Below that on the floor console is a joystick and some buttons.

"There's no steering wheel," Paul said.

"No wheels either," Sam replied. "Everything works off the center console and joystick. It's like a game console. Using the joystick and its knob, we can go in any direction at any angle, up or down. We can also hover in neutral once we're airborne. I've got two petals on the floor for acceleration and breaking. This is a prototype. Things will change. We are just testing the drive system right now. Are you ready?"

Paul nodded affirmatively. "Let's go."

Paul and Sam pull down the doors. Sam pushes a button on the dashboard console. The screen lights up with a view of the nighttime exterior and a GPS grid. It is too dark to see out the front window.

"So, we're going to fly by what we see on the screen," Paul said, sounding slightly worried.

"Don't worry, I've been practicing," Sam said as he floated Galaxy Zero off the ground and gently rose about fifty feet. "We'll stay on the property and not go any higher."

"This could be a prototype for a flying car," Paul said as they moved forward.

"You're right. However, the inventors don't think the world is ready for flying cars," Sam said. "They have their sights on the solar system."

"Yes, I got that impression talking to them this afternoon after I rode in the minivan.

Paul is impressed at how effortlessly Galaxy Zero flies. Sam moves it in various directions as they circle the property. Sam accelerates from a neutral position to a high speed at one point. The rapid acceleration pushes Paul back in his seat.

"Wow, feels like zero to 200 mph in a few seconds."

"I'm sure we can do better than that. I can take this tiny ship up to a high altitude at twice the speed of sound. I won't do that. First, I don't want to be spotted on the horizon by anyone, and second, this ship is not constructed for speed and high altitude. Anyway, the sonic boom might wake the neighbors."

"Well, it seems like the prototype works. I'll buy one and invest in the startup," Paul declares.

"Sam laughs, "I'm going to head back to the hangar, put this guy away. Then drive you back to your place, where we can continue our conversation."

"Great, I've got a couple of cold beers in the fridge."

CHAPTER TWO

....

Time washes across the universe like waves on the beach, never stopping, day and night, moving in and out, gently, slowly, then massive, angry, and overwhelming. Spontaneously, as if the cosmos needed to take a breath, there's a momentary lull, the rushing sound of the surf hesitates for a split second, and there's a great silent sigh. At that moment, many realities merge, lives begin and end, fortunes are made and lost, and the universe is explored and washed away. Small white sand crabs, the only witnesses, scurry down holes in the wet sand.

In the florescent twilight of an operating room, Joshua Bennett bends over a patient with wires leading to various monitoring devices. The patient's face is a mass of right-wing militia group tattoos. Josh's gray eyes peer over the surgical mask stuck to his dark beard. The steady humming sound of a cardiac monitor grows in intensity as his forty-seven-year-old dreaming mind tries to reconcile the fact that he isn't a medical doctor. What is he doing here? The patient is dead. Abruptly he reaches down and thumps the man's chest several times. The machine begins to emit a pulsing sound. The man's heart is beating louder and louder.

Josh stares in amazement. The man opens his eyes as the beeping from the heart machine monitor continues. Gasping as his waking consciousness returns, Josh escapes the dream reality. He reaches for the beeping sound of a watch alarm on the nightstand beside the bed. Adrienne, sleeping next to Josh, is awake but quickly returns to sleep.

The dream fades quickly, leaving only a few shrill notes in Josh's short-term memory. Dreams, random musing of the mind, or messages from the subconscious? Over the years, he recognized the difference between paranoid flight or fight thinking and actual threats. One day, looking out a window and staring at nothing, he remembers how his mother went to the window, lifting one slat of the blind to look at the street outside. He realizes that his mother did this by constantly checking on the neighbors or activity in the area. The window shades were down, blinds closed, and curtains were drawn so no one could see into the house. Her habit became worse over time. Standing at a window, he realizes that somehow, he can also be moved unconsciously to paranoid thinking. He learns to recognize fearful thinking and actions. The trick is to know when these feelings are present. Meditation and mindfulness help him with what the Buddhist sutras call "monkey talk" in one's mind. So many people are not aware of the incessant chatter in their minds.

"Is there a message hidden in the dream? Perhaps it is a module in the mind dramatizing his anxiety with certain issues at work. Maybe it is delusional projections of imagined fear, or maybe it is the anchovy pizza from last night," Josh thinks. The room is dark, but he can feel the presence of his wife, Adrienne, still asleep on the other side of the bed. "Time to get moving," he thinks as he heads for the bathroom. Soon he is almost ready for his morning run. First, he stretches and sits for a few minutes in meditation. Daily meditation and mindfulness are a part of his everyday life. He focuses on his breathing, the rising and falling of his abdomen, or the movement of air through his nostrils. He listens to his body's natural breathing without trying to control it.

Josh grew up in Bucks County, Pennsylvania, near New Hope. His father, Nathan, is a lawyer in New York City. His mother, Irma, is a talented artist who works from their home while Josh is growing up. Living close to New Hope, with its galleries and artists, is essential to her. The New Hope area is his father's easy commute to New York City. Josh finishes high school at sixteen and receives his bachelor's degree by the time he is 19. Against his parent's wishes, he joins the army with a four-year enlistment and a chance to attend Officer Candidate School. He completes officer training and is recruited into communication security. Several months later, he worked in the American Embassy in England as a First Lieutenant assistant to Colonel Goldman, the military liaison. While in London, he travels in England and Europe with the Colonel. Josh attends functions and events at the embassy, where he meets several famous people, including physicist Anthony Hawkins. At this point, he decides what he desires to do in life. He is interested in science. When he finishes military service, he stays in England and earns his master's degree at Cambridge in Theoretical Physics.

Shortly after returning from England, Josh's parents are killed in a car accident. He feels the loss deeply. He never thought about them dying. They are both only sixty years old and healthy at the time of the accident. He inherits the house in Bucks County and money that is sheltered in ways that make him financially independent and able to live comfortably. He appreciates the inheritance. He feels guilty that he is alive and they are not. He mourns their loss for many years. He became interested in Buddhist philosophy around this time. His parents were not religious. Growing up, he studied Judaism and different Judeo-Christian religions. He read the Old Testament Bible as if it were a novel. When his parents passed away, he found that Buddhism comforted him from a philosophical point of view. Many of its tenants make sense. In particular, the notion that there is no self. No little controller inside his head telling him what to do. There appears to be a blending of what is science today and practical philosophy in Buddhism. Reading the sutras gives him insight into many questions about his life and death. Josh believes there is a connection between modern scientific theories and Buddhist philosophy.

He meditates and practices Buddhist Mindfulness. He visits China and Shaolin Temple, a Buddhist monastery known for Kung Fu, where Ch'an Buddhism begins. Ch'an Buddhism migrated to Japan and became Zen

Buddhism. He stays at Shaolin Temple for a year. The Kung Fu he practices is more exercise than defensive martial arts. He learns Chinese and studies the Shurangama Sutra with the monks. The Abbot of the monastery gives him a wooden prayer bead bracelet that he still wears.

Josh met Adrienne in 2004 in Philadelphia while working on his Ph.D. in molecular physics at the University of Pennsylvania. Adrienne and Josh both live in Central City, Philadelphia. Adrienne has recently received her master's in communication. She lands a job working for Stackle Associates, an up-and-coming advertising and public relations agency in Philadelphia. Adrienne is a native Philadelphian. Her family moved there from Jamaica two generations before she was born. Adrienne's parents work in education. Her father is an administrator, and her mother is a teacher.

Adrienne has been dating very little since starting the new job. She spends her time working and learning the new position. The agency has offices in New York City and Philly. She needs to commute to New York City occasionally. She began taking a course in photography two nights a week at the Philadelphia College of Art because she wanted to know more about photography for her work. She has always had an interest in photography. One weekend, she meets Josh at the Philadelphia Museum of Art while viewing a unique retrospective of photographs drawn from the historic Edward Steichen Family of Man Exhibit.

Josh visits the museum often. In good weather, there are places outside to meditate. Inside the museum, he finds it relaxing to contemplate the work exhibited mindfully. No thoughts or judgment, only being there in the present moment with the art. Entering a new photography exhibit, he remembers seeing the photographs in a book titled "The Family of Man." Looking around, he spots Adrienne working her way around the room. He begins viewing from the opposite end, moving around the room toward her. He thinks she is attractive and interesting. Adrienne notes his entrance and movement. He is a decent-looking guy, and she wants to see what he does when they inevitably meet.

Ultimately, Josh finds himself next to Adrienne in front of the famous Migrant Mother photograph by Dorothea Lange. Adrienne is there in the present moment with the photograph. After a minute or two, they can't help talking about the picture.

"Very famous photograph," Josh said softly, breaking the silence.

Adrienne has been waiting for him to say something. She nods her head affirmatively. "Yes, we're so used to seeing color photographs. This picture takes on an abstract quality in black and white."

"I believe the government paid Dorothea Lange to take some pictures during the great depression. This is one of them."

"Are you interested in photography?"

"Yes, I used to develop my film and do some printing. I went on excursions with a couple of friends to different places around the area, taking pictures."

"I'm taking a photography course at Philadelphia College of Art, where we do some darkroom stuff—learning a lot. I like the tactile feel of working with the film and printing. Everything is going digital and Photoshop these days," Adrienne said."

"What got you interested in studying photography?"

"I'm working in advertising and public relations, and I thought I should know more about the graphic arts. Are you involved in the arts?"

"Although I have a great appreciation for the arts, no. I'm getting my Ph.D. in Molecular Physics at the University of Pennsylvania," Josh said quickly, hoping she wouldn't just walk away. Many women he meets almost immediately change the subject of the conversation once he tells them what he is doing.

"You study the physical and structural properties of molecules. What made you decide on this field?"

Surprised that she is interested in the field, Josh smiles, "I'm fascinated by the notion that these bodies we exist in are walking universes on their own. Molecules are the building blocks of biological creatures like us and everything. Molecules are where it all begins."

"Yes," Adrienne replies, "I've always been intrigued by the notion that we are sentient, seemingly conscious, biological creatures, yet we might be part of some bigger organism. You can't help but wonder where we fit in this huge universe around us."

Josh and Adrienne introduce themselves. Their conversation continues while they finish touring the exhibit. There is an easy, natural rapport between them. Living in Center City, they both walked to the museum. Without hesitation, they walk back down the parkway together, still finding the conversation and company compelling. They decide to stop for dinner before parting and agreeing to meet again.

Finishing his meditation Josh heads out for his morning run. There are big billowy clouds stacked up in the distance. The sun rises behind these clouds, making it appear that a vast range of mountains has replaced part of the city. The morning traffic moves along, unaware that some of the town has vanished. It is late February, almost spring in Central Florida. Sixty-five degrees this morning at 6:30 a.m. He jogs slowly down the alley behind the townhouses, where he meets George Gallagher, a neighbor. Josh begins to speak but stops when a man on a bicycle passes by them.

"Hey, can I talk to you about something?" Josh whispers after the bicycle rider passes. George's confusion is evident from his best-inherited, quizzical Irish frown. He is curious enough to follow without protest. They cross the street and head north along the path around Lake Baldwin. It is early, and not many runners, walkers, or cyclists are out yet.

Josh and George live in similar homes on the same street. Over the last few years, they built a casual friendship based on living near each other and morning runs. At first, like many men, they only discuss sports, politics, real estate values, and work. George is a general practice law firm lawyer that mainly does civil and litigation work.

Running is Josh's favorite exercise. He isn't sure if he is addicted to the activity or enjoys it. He knows it keeps him in shape and alleviates some of the stress he is experiencing working on the research grant at the University.

When he runs alone, he uses the time to meditate and feel the Qui moving in his body. Josh looks over his shoulder to see if anyone is nearby before speaking.

"What I'm going to tell you is in absolute confidence. You're a lawyer. You know what that means?"

"Okay. So, what's her name?" George jokes, "I'm not sure 'client privilege' applies unless you're a paying client. We won't worry about that yet."

"This is serious, George; you know we have a grant, and I've been working on a special top-secret project at UCF for the last six months or so."

George nods his awareness. "Christ, you got that grad student, what's-her-name, Tamara, pregnant; I don't do paternity suits."

George knows Josh well enough to understand he doesn't fool around. George enjoys teasing because it bugs Josh.

"He never stops," Josh thinks, "he can't help it; to him, it's friendly banter."

"No, you just chase ambulances," Josh said. "Tamara Arroyo is not a grad student anymore, she got her Ph.D. a year ago, and nothing is going on between us except work and professional friendship. I know you don't think that's possible between men and women!"

"George, listen, let's knock off the wisecracks. This is important. The project I'm working on is a spin-off of the old 'Star Wars Initiative.' I've been doing the primary development for a cloaking device," Josh said.

"What are you talking about? I thought you were working on molecular structure or something. Anyway, I thought the 'Star Wars' space weapon program was to shoot down missiles somehow from space. Didn't it die along with Reagan many years ago?"

"Forty-five's administration secretly brought it back when he invented the Space Force. My experiments involve altering molecular structures so that surfaces don't reflect light in the frequencies visible to humans. Perhaps something that can be incorporated into a fabric or metal."

"I thought you were into biological stuff?"

"Yes. I am also interested in how molecular structures exist in non-biological materials like metal and ceramics. Also, how the effect of biological agents might alter them. I have always had a side interest in metallurgy. I thought we would work on the molecular structure of various alloys."

"Whatever. Why are you telling me all this if it's so secret?"

"This project is funded by the Pentagon and CIA, who have an agent on site. A month ago, we received a memo from someone in the current administration who works for the Pentagon or CIA. The memo says they reviewed our experiments and want us to try our formula on a living animal. Then they send us a rabbit! I am not happy, but I think we'll experiment to show this is not a good idea."

"Two weeks ago, we sprayed the rabbit with a formula we are testing on metal and ceramic objects. I'm not even sure exactly what it contained finally. The rabbit becomes cloaked for thirty seconds until we wash it off. The spray formula should not have affected a biological surface like fur and skin. Everything we do is recorded, so now they want to come to see the rabbit. They are also talking about sending us monkeys."

George laughed, "How the hell do you think this stuff up so early in the morning, and I'm here listening."

"This is no joke, George. I'm a researcher and a teacher. They sent me a request to step up the project. They want us to try this experiment again. Maybe you have some ideas from a legal standpoint?"

"You understood all this going in, didn't you?"

"No, there is nothing in our grant proposal about experimenting on biological living things. It all starts with the notion I've had that we've always relied on mechanical development, not biochemistry. We and every living creature are molecular creations. I've been exploring molecular structure, the basic building blocks of our... I figure it will look good at the university if I apply for a grant. I have some ideas, and the next thing I know, the government is dumping big bucks on us. I think it will be a chance to follow up on some of my theories. I can apply them to study the molecular structure of metals and other materials, not human or animal cell structures. Tamara and I have the basic spray formula in our notes. What we used on the rabbit differs from what is entered into the database."

Josh finally had George's full attention.

"So now you want out?"

"This government administration is strange. This president said he wants to be in office for life, like a king! Once they have the formula, I can do nothing to prevent them from selling it to the highest bidder. I think Tamara will be okay with just deleting our notes. I told them it was too soon to try anything. I will figure out how to get out of this and stop this line of experimentation. I want someone to be aware of what I'm involved in. If I should suddenly disappear, end up killed in some car accident, or don't show up for a run one morning, I want you to start looking for me."

George still isn't sure if Josh is putting him on or not. "What can happen to you? Don't you think you're overreacting?

"When I began work on this project, they had the FBI check me out for a security clearance. One day an FBI agent comes to see me. He mentions that he's checking you out as well because we run together and that he considers you, how did he put it, 'not good company,' because you have what he insinuates are liberal lefty leanings."

"They checked me out! That's an invasion of privacy."

"Don't worry. I told him you are all talk, just another yuppie driving a German car. The next day I received a visit from another agent. He has an envelope. Among the contents is a list of the organizations you support, a few pictures of us running, and you and some woman. I'm sure it wasn't your ex-wife."

This information came as no surprise to Josh. Over time, during their morning runs, he's heard about George's exploits.

George is speechless, his anger rising.

"Why didn't you tell me? What woman is it?"

"They told me not to divulge anything they discuss with me. Now you know, so watch your step. At the time, you were still married. Halfway across a designated crosswalk, Josh looks up in time to see a car driven by a woman talking on a mobile phone coming directly toward them at 30 mph. He nudges George, and they jump to the side as she whizzes through the crosswalk and the stop sign. They each head back to their respective homes after the run.

"You don't have to do anything right now," Josh said as they parted. I want someone to know."

"Okay, I get it," George said, still annoyed about being spied on.

CHAPTER THREE

....

I have explored reality's shadows where
all paths merge and fade into shades of gray.

Arno Cameron's earliest memories are of his father coming home from work with black soot on his work clothing. His father is a steelworker. He works at U.S. Steel's blast furnace facility. The local black church employs his mother. She handles all the administrative tasks for the minister and church. The area of Southeast Chicago they live in is known as the Bush. A fence separates the Bush from the vast U.S. Steel mill property. The neighborhood is mixed ethnically. There are many Polish, Mexican, African American, and other ethnic groups living in the area. Most residents have a least one family member working in the mills. It takes many years before a union steelworker of any ethnic group can count on employment year-round in this working-class neighborhood. Arno's father is one of the early black members of United Steel Workers Local 65

Arno attends public schools in the area. His mother teaches him to read at an early age and impresses on him the need to do well in school if he wants a better life. He becomes an avid reader with high comprehension. He knows he wants out of the neighborhood. Living there now means he must get along with the others his age. Like most kids, he wants to fit in. It is challenging to survive if you are not a group member. In high school, he gets involved in sports and the school newspaper. The newspaper's faculty advisor takes an interest in Arno and pushes him to keep his grades high. This results in Arno qualifying for a scholarship to a state university. Working part-time, he can afford to share an apartment with a couple of other students near the university campus. This takes him out of the neighborhood. He decides he wants to study law. He earns a scholarship to attend the University of Chicago Law School. He is the only black student at the time to get into this law school.

Arno pushes open the heavy security door to the dark laboratory and enters. He hears a rustle coming from a nearby cage. In the crowded lab, lit only by security lights and computer monitors, his 6' 2" frame seems awkward. "Why did I ever join the CIA? I could have gone into private law practice or been corporate council." Major law firms offered him a good starting salary to join their firm when he finished law school. Doing some research, he finds no other African Americans in the firm. He gets the feeling they want him as their token black associate. By joining the CIA, he thought he'd have a chance to do something different. Maybe one day, but now he had to hang around these researchers, snoop around, and play bureaucratic games like the recent meeting in Washington with his liaison, Ms. Virginia Walton. She was appointed to her position by the current administration in 2017 to oversee special projects. She is not a CIA agent, just a civilian with political connections. A political appointee. Since the current administration took control, politically influenced people have taken over the agency. Walton seems to have her political agenda.

He runs the meeting over in his mind as he walks across the lab. How he sat at the end of the conference table, playing along with her absurd game. "What a bunch of crap. She sits there like a zombie at the end of the table, trying to look like she's in charge. No make-up, stringy brown hair, ugly suit. She looks like she hasn't been in the sun for a year or two."

"The rabbit has no adverse side effects, in your judgment," she asks as if she was mailing the words down to the other end of the table.

Arno detects that she speaks another language, perhaps Russian. He's tempted to see if he can get her to reply to a few words in that language. "Not the time or place for that," he decides. He wants to say, "In my judgment, how the hell would I know? I'm not a researcher," of course, he does not. "The rabbit seems healthy enough from what I hear," he said matter-of-factly.

"We want to visit the project. I'm going to send someone to help you. Tighten up security. Nothing gets out about this. See if you can get Bennett to accelerate the process."

"Accelerate your ass," he thought as he gathered his papers and left the room. Still, talking in his head, "You think these academic people jump when I walk in the door? The dam bunny only appeared cloaked for thirty seconds. I'll be glad when this project is over."

Present reality again replaces Arno's head talk as he switches on a desk lamp. He can see the face of Josh Bennett, his wife Adrienne, and their two children staring up at him as he checks Josh's appointments for the coming week. Nothing of note as usual.

Arno gets along well with Josh and his associate Tamara Arroyo. They occasionally have lunch or a drink after work. He and his friend Deborah have dinner with Josh and Adrienne a few times. They all share a dim view of the current president and his administration, so their conversations might venture into the country's political realities.

Arno once told them that "until recently, the agency considered itself apolitical philosophically." Although in practice, it is difficult to stay out of politics when the head of the agency changes with each new administration. Even so, the rank-and-file career people stay on course doing their jobs regardless of who is in the White House. The current administration behaves like all the intelligence agencies must pledge loyalty to the president and his administration, not the country and constitution. Morale is low because of this kind of pressure. The president behaves like he is a divine monarch. Everyone must pledge loyalty to him. "

CHAPTER FOUR

....

"Each day presents myriad choices, each leading to a different reality, yet we proceed as if we know where we're going."

Weekday mornings are a rush at the Bennett's. A joint effort on the part of Adrienne and Josh to get everyone's day started. This morning Josh listens to the weather for the day and bits of news as he drinks his coffee. "Breaking News" interrupts the weather forecast. Another domestic right-wing terrorist attack somewhere. Josh turns off the television. He can check the weather on his phone. He watches Lauren, age ten, and Morgan, age twelve, eat breakfast.

Morgan is growing taller each day. He does well in school, and he needs more educational challenges. He has many friends at school. His hobbies are collecting certain comic books and playing games on his phone. Josh doesn't bug him about all the time playing games on or off the phone since his grades are excellent. He does encourage him to find interest in other things like music and art. Lauren is a cute, pretentious ten-year-old girl who looks like she will grow up to resemble her mother. She also does well in school and is taking piano lessons. She and Morgan play computer games together. Both children are good at the games.

Josh smiles as Adrienne enters the kitchen dressed for work. She looks very professional in her work outfit, feminine without flaunting it. Her long brown hair seemed appropriate and contrasted with her naturally tan skin. She is happy as creative director for Biggs and Whittaker Advertising, the Florida branch of one of Chicago's many advertising firms. She pours herself a cup of coffee and checks the children on the move.

"Morgan, don't forget you have drama club rehearsal after school today. Lauren, who are you walking home with?"

"Sara. Mom, may I go to her house for a while after school?"

"If you finish homework first. Call me at the office and let me know when you go."

"Dad, I'm gonna buy Wolverine number one today from some kid at school for three dollars, it's all I need, and I'll have the entire series."

Josh is unable to resist teasing. Great! I didn't know you were in the Cub Scouts.

Adrienne moaned.

To Morgan, this is serious stuff, "Dad," he complains.

Lauren must have her say, "He's not in the Cub Scouts, Dad. It's a comic book."

Morgan raises the corner of his upper lip in a little sneer at Lauren. Josh wonders where he learned to do that. Josh's father had the same lip curl. Maybe it is genetic and skipped a generation?

"Okay, everyone, I need to go. We're presenting a proposal for a new advertising campaign for Universal Studios today. I can't be late," Adrienne announced.

Adrienne kisses everyone goodbye and heads out of the kitchen door to the garage. Josh checks the time and picks up a cup of coffee. He takes a sip and then gathers the two children, herding them to the car. He drives them to their middle school, a short distance from home.

Josh turns on the radio in the car for his drive to the university lab. After twice being cut out by lane-changing drivers, the annoyance causes him to think about yelling obscenities at the errant individuals. While a graphic gesture also comes to mind, he doesn't use it since it evokes much hostility in the South.

"Hey, Siri, play the Heart Sutra mantra."

Quickly the mantra chanted by some monks can be heard, "Gate, Gate, Para Gate Parasam Gate Bodhi Svaha!" ("Going, going on beyond, always going on beyond, always becoming Buddha."). He let their voices gradually occupy his mind until he arrived at the university. "Stay in the present. Focus on your driving," he thinks. "It's a form of meditation. Mindful moments and emptiness."

A recent morning conversation with George pops up in Josh's mind as he drives. Josh and George often discuss the state of the world on their morning runs. They did not expect the current president to be elected in 2016. George maintains that despite the man's corrupt reputation, he appeals to a cross-section of insecure Americans. The country is divided more than usual by years of Republican propaganda. Josh believes the new president's election is a backlash, partly against the election of the country's first mixed-race President. Republicans obstruct his administration at every turn for eight years.

George said, "I'm concerned about the country and our relationship with long-term allies. I hope the current president will not be re-elected in 2020. Hopefully, the government institutions can survive the deconstruction of international relations the administration is implementing. This president is too quick to praise the Russian president and his disdain for NATO. The president's threat to leave NATO is causing alarm in Europe regarding American support and reliability."

Josh believes that the government of the U.S. is the people's government. It is supposed to represent all the people. A disenchanted minority of citizens, manipulated by the Republican party, have become hostile to the fundamental democratic principles outlined by the constitution. They are easily motivated to blame immigrants, Democrats, minority groups, and the government for all their grievances. They constantly vote against their best interests, like politics is a game. They do not understand what each political party stands for and whom their elected officials represent. An act of violence or a school shooting only seems to cause them to buy more guns rather than restrict the sale of weapons of war to the public."

Josh acknowledges the replay of the conversation passing through his consciousness and lets it go. The memory was probably instigated by the few bad drivers he encountered—a natural human tendency to blame those rude people who cut him off.

CHAPTER FIVE

....

"Do not think of doors as obstacles to whatever is on the other side. Practice opening them thoughtfully and closing them with care."

The University of Central Florida has never been noted for the splendor of its sprawling campus. But, Josh's lab is not on campus. It is nearby. With the university having about 70,000 students, Josh is glad to be off campus. Parking is not an issue. Josh's lab is a windowless, cramped space filled with equipment. Designed for top-secret work, the area has a main entrance through a security door. Rumor has it that it is where they worked on the mythical "love bugs" so famous in Florida for leaving acid marks on cars they get stuck to in season.

Small video cameras monitor the room. Against one wall is a countertop with chemical testing apparatus and a computer terminal. Nearby are a desk, bookshelves, and an overstuffed sofa in an adjacent alcove.

Dr. Tamara Arroyo, Josh's project associate, is on the phone when Josh enters the lab. She watches him out of the corner of her eye as he walks into the room and over to the rabbit's cage. Tamara's Mediterranean ancestry is apparent in her dark eyes and hair. One could easily see her as Dona Arroyo, raising horses on an old Spanish ranch. She won a few equestrian metals while growing up on the family ranch in Central Florida.

Tamara feels lucky to be a part of this project. She worked as Josh's graduate assistant while he was still teaching. When he receives the grant, she jumps at the chance to continue working with him. It is an excellent opportunity for a new Ph.D.

Removing the cover on the cage, Josh exposes a rabbit wearing a wire harness. The wires are connected to monitors and computers. One monitor simulates the shape of the rabbit. He offers the rabbit some lettuce which it quickly snatches from his hand. "I see you have a good appetite, Omar. Still visible and alive, that's good."

Tamara finishes her phone conversation and joins Josh by the cage.

"Good morning. How was your weekend?"

"Pretty good. Got out for a couple of decent runs. Did you do a blood count today?"

"Yes, everything's been taken care of."

"We need to check his vitals often. I think this event is an optical illusion."

"Sounds like he's all business this morning," Tamara observes. "The reports are on your desk. Why don't you have a cup of coffee?"

Josh heads for his office, and Tamara follows him. They ignore the camera mounted on the ceiling, observing them walk across the room.

Arno Cameron leans back in his high-backed, leather executive swivel chair, watching Josh and Tamara walk across the room on one of the monitors in front of him. He purchased the chair himself since the agency wouldn't pay for it. It is his one luxury. The room resembles a TV engineering room with monitors across the wall in front of a console. He has a few projects located at different facilities at other universities to check on. His base is here in the same building as Josh's lab.

The phone buzzes. Arno picks it up. Deborah Newhouse is a friend he has been seeing for the last couple of years. Deborah is an FBI agent he met in Washington, D.C., and began dating when they ended up in Florida. As he speaks to her, he watches Josh take off his jacket and hang it over the camera in his office. The screen goes blank.

"Deb, I'm going to have to go. My favorite scientist just decided to hang his coat in a way that blocks the camera's view. Are we still on for tonight.? Yes? Great! See you then."

"What's with this guy," Arno thinks as he dials Josh's office number. There is no answer.

Josh smiles at Tamara and whispers, "tired of all these cameras, I want to talk to you about a few things." Their conversation is interrupted by the phone ringing. They ignore it and head over to a computer.

"Have you checked the printout yet? Do we know how the spray might have altered the light spectrum on or around this rabbit?"

In a half whisper, Tamara, unsure whether to speak up, picks up a printout next to the computer.

She said, "The program analyzes all of our scans of the rabbit using conventional scanning from ultraviolet to infrared. So far, we can't pin down any section of the light spectrum that is different. We can respray it and see what happens?"

Josh shakes his head negatively, "I'd rather not do that again officially. We're dealing with something illusionary, out of our experience, almost like another frequency we can't conceive. In any event, I want to stop this biological line of research."

Josh looks over his shoulder as Arno enters the room, walks over to the camera, removes Josh's coat, and remarks, "hilarious Josh. Appreciate you not hanging your clothing here."

"Don't knock Arno, just barge right in. We're busy."

"Tammy, it must be 'special' working with such a warm, personable individual. It's so rare to find that in a scientist."

"My name isn't 'Tammy.'"

"Excuse me, Tamara, Dr. Arroyo. Everyone is so friendly today."

"What can we do for you this morning?" Josh mutters over his shoulder.

"Hey, if you'd answer your phone occasionally, I wouldn't have to "barge" in. What is it with you guys today? We've got some people coming from D.C. soon to look at this project. You've made such great progress that they want to 'see' for themselves."

"Only in Washington do they want to see what can't be seen," Josh mutters cynically.

Picking up on Josh's cue, Tamara said, "We're not sure what is going on with the rabbit. It is probably some light refraction that made it appear cloaked. Temporary light refraction off his fur. Unfortunately, it doesn't work in normal lighting."

Josh is not happy about the officials visiting. He turns and walks over to Arno in a more conciliatory tone, "listen, Arno, it's too soon. Phone them, tell them we aren't ready for visitors. Nothing has changed since the last time they were here."

"They've made up their minds. It won't be so bad. Feed the bunny a carrot, spout some scientific mumbo-jumbo, and they'll go away."

Arno questions why Josh is suddenly insecure about discussing the project, "Is there something wrong?"

"I'm supposed to be project director, and no one consults me to see if I'm ready for a visit. We're still working on theories. No real results yet. They will come here expecting some revolutionary breakthrough and be disappointed."

"I don't understand why you're worried. They love this project now. You can name your price. Take it easy. How about some lunch?"

"Another time, sure, no time for lunch now, my friend, got to prepare for visitors!"

Simone Greely walks into the fluorescent-lit room at CIA headquarters, Langley. She is slender, five feet eight inches tall, and attractive. She grew up in Georgetown, a Washington D.C. neighborhood. Both her parents work in government. She knows her way around the capital. She is the sole female African American agent she knows of at Langley. Simone sits across from Virginia Walton in the only other chair in the room. She previously met Walton at a group meeting for female government employees. This women's group has cells in major government circles in the United States and under different names in other governments worldwide. In addition, they are established in many corporations and the media. They aim to change the world from what they perceive as male-dominated to sharing responsibility. "Breaking the glass ceiling."

Simone doesn't take all the rhetoric too seriously; she is in it for the contacts and because she has little choice. It is believed that Virginia Walton is a political appointee of the new administration with direct connections to the oval office. Simone thinks Walton may be more interested in "world domination" with her in charge. Ms. Walton gets down to business quickly once Simone arrives.

"Take a look at this video," Walton said, clicking on the screen of her laptop. "This is a top-secret research project at the University of Central Florida. It appears they found a way to cloak this rabbit. We believe this will have military implications. The current agent there tells me the people doing the research say they can't explain what happened. They can't replicate the experiment. As you can see, the rabbit becomes invisible. I'd like you to work with the current agent and see what else we can learn."

Simone watches the video of the rabbit disappearing and reappearing. It reminds her of a magic trick. "This isn't my area of expertise," she said before being interrupted by Walton.

"Simone, you're going on a special assignment. Tomorrow you'll be going to Orlando, Florida. I know you are waiting for a permanent assignment. This mission came up, so you were recommended. Watching Ms. Walton speak in this lighting made Simone aware of why certain coworkers had nicknamed her "Snow White." Her skin was so pale it had a pearl-like pallor.

"You will be assigned to Arno Cameron, who is there as security for classified projects we are jointly funding at the University of Central Florida and other universities in Florida."

"Does Walton have the authority to give me assignments," Simeone asks herself. She also does not comprehend why she has been picked. Not much she can do about it at this point.

Walton briefed her on the project and its progress recently. Simone listens as she thinks about what she needs to pack for Florida. It might be good to get out of D.C. to a warmer climate. She does not know Arno Cameron. She has the impression from Walton's briefing that she should also note what he is doing regarding the project's security. She will check his agency profile before she leaves for Florida. Once she sees his photo in the file, she thinks she might know why she was chosen.

Simone has a bachelor's degree in criminal justice and a master's in international relations. In addition to English, she is fluent in Mandarin Chinese, which she studied at Peking University in Beijing, China. She is waiting for an assignment to take advantage of her language skills. Something more suitable to her background than security in Florida. It appears certain things take time. As far as she knows, her top-secret security clearance is final. She has been interviewed by the head of the Chinese language section, who is impressed with her reading, writing, and spoken Mandarin. She is told they are expanding the section and want to bring her in as soon as they have the allocations. The supervisor indicates that budgets are being cut to build a fence on the Mexican border. So it might take a little time.

CHAPTER SIX

....

We do not have the power to change the past, but we can shape the future by what we do in the present.

Y ou worry too much. Every restaurant or bar in the city can't be bugged. We never announce where we're going to eat. We drive somewhere," Tamara whispers across the booth. The restaurant and bar are crowded and noisy. Looking around warily, Josh said, "I apologize for the paranoia. With today's technology, nothing is impossible. 'Better safe than sorry.' This place is so loud we should be fine," he stopped talking when the server arrived—waiting until he finishes filling the coffee cups. They order some appetizers. They will not stay for dinner.

"Thanks for your follow-up on the optical illusion theory," Josh said.

"You know me. I'm into everything optical even sunspots." Tamara is joking. However, she is into the scientific aspects of the sun's behavior, including sunspot activity, magnetic fields, polar switches, and terminal events. Stellar astronomy is one of her ongoing interests.

Sipping her black coffee, Tamara reasons with Josh. "I've got a stake in this too. We haven't produced a cloaking device or anything close to it. Why don't we try a couple more experiments and conclude that it is an optical illusion? It can't be replicated.

"That might work. We don't have anything concrete at this point. This administration in Washington scares the hell out of me. This is not the Republican party of old. They are moving to the far right of the political spectrum. They have someone at the helm who cares more about cozy upping to Putin, Kim Jong-Un, and Xi Jinping than running the country. It's obvious who his role models are. He's running the government into the ground, dismantling many departments, and installing political appointees with no credentials in key positions. I don't trust them with any technology we're developing. People working for him have declared their prime mission is to 'deconstruct' the government."

"I was talking to my brother Raoul Jr. about why so many people have what appears to be self-destructive attitudes. Why do they vote for politicians who openly enact laws that favor the establishment? My brother Raoul Jr. said that many people believe their 'freedom' is threatened by a strong central government. Some experts say some people confuse 'autonomy' and 'freedom.' "

"That's an interesting idea. We have 'the freedom' to do many things. There will probably be anarchy if everyone is autonomous, free to govern themselves, with no tradition or structure. We can be a country of biker gangs. I'm not anti-government. I don't like autocratic leaders and totalitarian policies. This administration is destroying the current representative government to replace it with a far more authoritarian one. "

"I understand what you're saying. Truthfully, my family feels the same way."

"I don't want to give these guys more ammunition to use for their anti-democratic agenda."

"There is nothing wrong with what we're doing. Don't get depressed."

"If we refuse to continue, they may be able to take our work and get someone else. Who knows what they'll do?"

"In all due respect Josh, listen to yourself. All that is happening is that they're coming for a visit. Let's play it by ear, maybe we can do a demonstration, but this time nothing happens. It's a fluke. Go home—nothing to see here. Oops, maybe use a different expression. You get the idea?"

"You're right. You realize we may be on the right track with our other experiments. I don't trust this government with too much power," Josh said.

"Especially this current government," Tamara mumbled.

Tamara drank some coffee. "We can't be responsible for what is done with our discoveries. We are scientists, not politicians. Besides, this is not some evil dictatorship out to conquer the world."

"Not yet, but all the signs are there. Our "glorious leader" is doing things detrimental to the country's stability. Sometimes I wonder where the real power is. Who's controlling this president? Maybe Russia? The world is becoming a different place, smaller and nastier."

After a pause and another sip of coffee, Tamara remembers, "Oh, Josh, I almost forgot. I've got to take a few days off for a family reunion. I'll be leaving Wednesday and be back on Monday. My parents want us all to be there."

"No problem. One of these days, I'd like to meet your parents. They seem like interesting people."

"I'm sure you'd get along just fine with them. They are interested in meeting you too. You have a lot in common. They may advise us on how to deal with this grant business. Perhaps be able to help. You, Adrienne, and the children can come to the ranch on one of your trips to your beach place."

"Sure, looking forward to it. It will be a good break from all of this. I'll check on a date with Adrienne."

Josh's eyes lit up, "I have an idea what we can do. It will take a little magic. I'm not sure where we can get all the gear or if we can pull it off. If it works, it will get them off our backs."

"Tell me about it. You'd be surprised about the kind of resources I have."

Seated in his car, Arno is in a cynical mood, "I love this job," he thought as he watched the restaurant where Josh and Tamara were meeting. "I get to watch other people do whatever they're going to do, like have some coffee and snacks after work!" Finally, he watches as Tamara and Josh leave the restaurant and head for their cars.

"It might not be so bad if they had a little affair or something," he thought. "No such luck. They are each driving off to their respective homes." "Whom should I follow tonight," he thinks, looking at an iPad mounted on his dash. The App. shows the GPS tracking devices planted on their vehicles moving away from each other. "It doesn't matter. The last time I followed her, this time, I'll check him out. Ms., my name is Tamara, isn't even dating anyone. How am I supposed to do my job? This is not what I signed up for." Arno laughs at himself,

"You're talking out loud to yourself—time for a break. There is no security threat with either of these people and no threat to them. I'll go home too, and I'll give Debbie a call," he said, this time silently to himself.

CHAPTER SEVEN

....

Every Journey begins with the first step.

Paul and his film editor Walter have worked together for many years. Walter often edits a rough cut of scenes for a film on his own. Then they review the rough cut before fine-cutting the film.

"Let's use Charlene's reaction shot when he say's 'I'm sure he fits...,' okay?"

"Yes, that will work," Walter said, fast-forwarding through the "B" roll to find the shot.

"I need to leave a little early today to pick up my sister Tamara at the airport in Orlando. We'll start from there tomorrow, okay?"

Walter nods his agreement and continues to search for the shot.

Tonight is the big family meeting. Sam, Bill, Annie, Carlos, Raoul Jr., and Paul have been briefed on their parent's latest invention and will be there. Tamara is arriving today.

Raoul Jr. and Carlos use the corporate jet to fly Conrad and Julia Arroyo, Raoul Sr.'s parents, to Florida from Maine for the meeting. Raoul Jr. is the youngest sibling. He lives at the ranch when he is not at MIT teaching programming.

Paul chooses the silver Corvette Z06 to drive to the airport. He collects mainly sports cars. Usually, he tries to keep them in stock condition. His father often talks him into an upgrade. In this case, it is an electric motor like in the RX-7. Faster than the stock Corvette V8. The only issue is no exhaust noise. A silent Corvette attracts more interest than the standard "Vette" rumble. To compensate, they install a high-tech sound system with volume control that simulates idle, acceleration, and exhaust sounds. Paul's brother

Carlos programs the simulation to synchronize with the shifting of gears and car speed. One speaker is under the hood, the others in the hollowed-out mufflers. The combustion engine sound effects do stop the questions. It can always be turned off. Then there is the new paint. In addition to deflecting radar, this paint absorbs solar light to charge the batteries for the electric motor.

It is a quick and pleasant ride to the city. Paul navigates to the arrivals area at Orlando airport, looking for the Delta Airlines doors and Tamara. At the same time as he spots the Delta airline sign, he also sees Tamara waving. Paul pulls up to the curb, gets out, and gives Tamara a big hug. There is no mistaking the family resemblance. Paul and Tamara always got along exceptionally well. Paul tends to be protective of his younger sister.

"So, how's the super sleuth electric 'Vette' running these days," Tamara asks after they put her bags in the trunk and get into the car.

"Just fine, and it beats paying for premium gas. How was your trip here?" Paul said with a knowing smile.

"As usual, only thirty minutes from home to the airport and twenty minutes to make my way to the arrival area and wait for you to pick me up."

Tamara sighed, "Same old, same old. Raoul Sr. doesn't want me followed to the ranch, so we go through this charade that I'm flying to Miami. I could also drive to the ranch."

"I don't mind driving," Paul said, pulling away from the gate.

"Well, I'm dying to know what this urgent family meeting is about."

"It's pretty spectacular," Paul said as he made his way to the Beach Line toll road, aka the Bee Line, that will take them toward the east coast of Florida.

"Come on, you can do better than 'pretty spectacular.' This is Tamara remember? Your baby sister."

Okay. You will not believe this until you see it. They've invented a device that manipulates gravitational fields."

"Wow! And to what end are we manipulating gravit?" she asks, puzzled.

"Probably many things. Raoul Sr. installed the device in a van, and now the van flies. Sam built a two-seater prototype, and it is awesome. He took me for a spin. I wonder if they can install the drive in this car too?"

"Isn't 200 mph fast enough?"

"I'm talking fly, you know, like an airplane."

Tamara stares at Paul in disbelief.

In a moment, she replies, "You know how our parents are about the world not being ready for some of their inventions? I feel they're not going to give this one to the world yet, either."

Paul rolls his eyes, "In this case, I believe there may be a good reason. They have ambitious and unique ideas they want to run by the family tonight. I'll let them explain it all. It's going to take a lot of money. However, they have a way of working that keeps expenses down."

The Corvette speeds down the road in silence as dusk takes hold of the sky. The late afternoon light slowly fades to evening hues. The primordial-looking wetland along the side of the road takes on a golden hue as the sun sets behind them. Suddenly a warning light on the dash beeps through the silence. Paul scans the additional gauges and lights on the dashboard, then turns on the engine and exhaust sound effects. Tamara straightens up in her seat, alerted by the sounds and lights.

Paul laughs, "it's a warning that someone is tracking us with radar. I adjusted the exhaust pitch level volume, so it sounds like we are going slower than we are."

"Why aren't you slowing down? You're doing ninety-five," Tamara said, glancing at the speedometer.

"Raoul Sr. worries that this stealth paint job may attract attention since it makes the car invisible to radar and laser detection systems. When we get hit by the radar, we send a false signal to the radar gun. I can set it for any speed. It's a form of radar reflection. There's our local trooper on the shoulder of the road. Right now, his scope says we're doing seventy-five mph. There is a seventy-mph speed limit here. Any slower, and he'd be suspicious on this road. He won't stop us for five miles over the speed limit."

Tamara grimaces as they whiz past the trooper, who looks up and then stares at his scope, wondering if something is wrong. He doesn't feel like pursuing and pacing the car. It would be a waste of time. He'd wait for a verifiable speeder to show on his radar. He rationalized, "sports cars always appear to be going faster than they might be going. It didn't sound like it was going much over seventy."

Several miles later, Paul slows down in the fading light and exits the highway. The exit ramp takes them to a local road. In a few miles, they arrive at the entrance to the Arroyo ranch and property. Approaching the gate to the ranch, Paul pushes a button on the dashboard, and the big gate swings back. A camera observes the car's progress, sending video and an alert signal to the house that someone is on the way. Over the next few miles driving to the house, they pass cattle grazing at dusk. Tamara wonders why the cattle are not bothered by gators. She remembers that the gators usually don't wander this far from the water. They seem to prefer smaller prey like wild pigs they can surprise on dry land.

Sam is sitting in the large living room of the ranch house when he hears the alert sound coming from the monitor closet near the front door. He checks the monitors and sees Paul's car headed toward the house. Sam is the eldest child in the family. He is also the tallest and in good shape. He played football in college at six feet three inches tall and had professional offers. His interest, at the time, was starting a charter boat business with his first wife, Tara Ann. They soon have several charter fishing boats sailing out of Port Canaveral. They have two children and then break up. It is an amicable divorce. They are still good friends. He is proud of the kids and drives them down to the ranch from Jacksonville whenever possible. Tara Ann brings them to Arroyo family special occasions, including Thanksgiving and Christmas dinners. Neither Sam nor Tara Ann has remarried.

Sam and Tara Ann run the business after the divorce. Sam opens a boatyard and the New Cape Canaveral Yacht Club. He is well known and liked up and down the East coast of Florida. He spends a lot of time with his parents working on their projects. Sam can conceptualize almost anything that needs to be built. He can pre-visualize the shape of a building or ship and then figure out how it should be constructed.

Sam switches on the veranda lights. Night bugs immediately appear in the air near the lights, accompanied by subtle sounds of the distant wetlands. It is a clear night with stars shining brightly everywhere in the sky. He waits to hear the prerecorded sound of Paul's Corvette as it approaches. Paul drives up the long drive to the front of the Spanish-style ranch house. It is large and built around an atrium that houses a garden and pool area. Each of the children has a room on the second floor facing the atrium. The master bedroom and all the common area rooms are on the ground level.

"Come on in! It's great to see you," Sam said, giving his sister a big hug.

"You too, Mr. Hollywood," he said, hugging Paul with the other arm.

"Everyone is here except Sharon. I wish we could trust her more. She isn't keeping good company right now."

Tamara shook her head, "It's not just that, Sam. Our parents think Sharon's politics and conspiracy theories are far removed from their humanist notions. Then there's her job with the administration and support of politicians we consider dangerous. She told mom about babies being eaten in the basement of a pizza place, with no basement. Anyway, she's in Australia right now."

Sam shook his head knowingly, "They are all down by the pool, so why don't you guys join them? The dinner meeting will be at eight p.m. in the big dining room."

Despite its size, the formal dining room at the Arroyo ranch is intimate. The dining table is early mission-style oak. It is twelve feet long and four feet wide. It easily accommodates the extended family on Thanksgiving Day. The room is oak trimmed with built-in cabinets and exposed oak ceiling beams. The room has the warmth only fine wood can give. At one end of the room, a large open hearth with a very authentic-looking fire crackling. While a real wood fire may be built in this hearth, the current firelight is unnatural. In Central Florida, air conditioning is more useful most of the year. Marcella thinks the fire is aesthetically pleasing and that it is comforting to see an open fire in the room, hence the simulation. At the other end of the area, glass panel doors open onto the atrium, where most of the family is gathered, exchanging news, and speculating on what might happen today. Conrad and Julia enjoy conversing with their grandchildren. Tamara is one of their favorites.

Notable is the fact that wives, husbands, and children are absent this evening. They are usually there on holidays and other special occasions. Because of the secretive nature of the meeting, it is a select group.

Sam sits in the living room talking to his sister Annie, who is forty-two years old and the second child. Once a CPA with a large accounting firm in Miami, Annie left that position to handle accounting for her parents and Paul. Annie's husband, Captain Andrew Sun, trained in the Space Program at NASA but is currently an airline pilot. With her husband's international flight schedule, Annie has much time to do the books for the family businesses.

Forty-year-old Bill Arroyo is the third child. He is a lawyer with a practice in Orlando. His accounts include Paul's studio, Raoul Sr., Marcella, Arroyo Aerospace, and siblings. Carlos, age thirty-six, a software engineer and programmer, is the next sibling after Paul. Carlos uses a combination of his skills in developing communications software and internet security. Sharon, who is thirty-five, is the sixth child. Tamara, thirty-two, is the seventh. Number eight, Raoul Jr., is twenty-seven years old.

Marcella, the mother of the family, at sixty-five, shows little signs of aging. She is slender with a mature grace that earns respect from everyone she meets. A graduate of MIT at twenty, she met Raoul while on vacation in Florida. He recently started a small industrial engineering and parts manufacturing company. He is also overseeing the family estate in Florida. Raoul and Marcella were married in 1970.

As the space program grows at the Cape, they are in the right place to bid on specific contracts. Marcella has a highly developed design sense that balances Raoul Sr.'s ability to evolve things conceptually. Together they made an excellent team. They compete with major corporations like Honeywell,

Rockwell, Boeing, and other major suppliers for aerospace contracts. Arroyo Aerospace's specialty is making one-of-a-kind parts for the space shuttle, NASA, and others internationally. More recently, their clients include new NASA space projects and other aerospace firms worldwide.

Marcella sits by the pool, chatting with Tamara, Carlos, Conrad, and Julia. Raoul Sr. is not back from the "garage."

"Carlos, please phone your father and tell him we'll serve dinner in five minutes." Carlos heads for the nearest internal phone.

"Your father will be here in ten minutes," Marcella said.

"How do you know; he won't come sooner or later?" Tamara asks.

Marcella replies matter-of-factly, "If I said ten minutes, he'd come in fifteen. He always waits until the time is up, then heads for where he has to go, so if I want him somewhere, I give him extra time."

Tamara mentions, "Sharon called me to chat. I told her I was going away for the weekend. I hope she doesn't decide to start phoning family members and find out everyone is 'gone' for the weekend."

"I love Sharon dearly; she is a wonderful person but stubborn. I don't think she will understand the nature of what we're going to talk about tonight," Marcella replies. "How is everything going with the project you're working on at UCF?"

"Well, Josh, Dr. Bennett is worried about the project's direction. Like you and Dad, he's concerned about the current administration. As you know, I'm not supposed to talk about the project. We're doing some amazing things manipulating molecular structures, maybe cells too, so they're not visible to the human eye. You would love this project."

"What's he concerned about?"

"He thinks they want to do biological experimenting. Ultimately find ways to cloak humans. He says he won't be involved."

"I don't blame him. Let's see if we can get him here to talk with us. I'll mention this to your father."

Sam appears and announces that dinner is being served. By the time everyone enters the dining room Raoul Sr. arrives as predicted.

Since only part of the family is there for dinner, they are all seated at one end of the table. Marcella and Raoul Sr. sit next to each other at the head of the table, and the rest of the family is on either side. Tamara thinks that seeing Marcella and Raoul Sr. together makes it easy to understand their bond. It seems to Tamara watching that they are people who retain their individuality yet are partners in a way that appears they occupy the same space. She thinks they sometimes communicate telepathically as if two brains are working together to solve a problem. They present an aura of harmony and peace.

Margarita and her husband, Oliver Vargas, serve dinner. The Arroyos met the Vargas in San Jose, Costa Rica, where the Vargas had immigration problems. They once owned a large restaurant in Havana where Oliver was Chef before Fidel took power. They fled to Costa Rica. The Arroyos offer them a job at their three-hundred-acre ranch on the Nicoya Peninsula and help them solve their immigration problems with Costa Rica. They brought the couple back to the U.S. the following year when Cubans were given residency once they landed on U.S. soil. Margarita and Oliver think it is odd that they ended up working for the Arroyos instead of opening a restaurant. They are happy cooking and running the food service for Arroyo Aerospace and the family household. They also cater to Paul's studio when he is shooting. When the family travels to Nicoya, they usually travel with them.

The Arroyos raise cattle and do some farming on the rancho in Costa Rica. In many ways, it feels like an extension of the Florida ranch. On the rancho property, the Arroyos have a modern-style home. It is high enough on the mountain that it has a great view of the Pacific Ocean and the Gulf of Nicoya to the east on a clear day. They have their satellite dish and communications equipment situated so as not to disturb anyone's view. The government allowed them to build a landing strip on the property away from the ocean. One provision is that the government can use it for medical emergencies in the area. The government can remotely turn on the beacon and the radar system. Having the landing strip means the Arroyos can fly the corporate jet there, usually after a stop at the Liberia Airport. They have a staff that runs the ranch and takes care of things while they are gone. It is a family vacation home and get away from everything. Throughout the year, someone in the family often vacations at Arroyo Rancho, Nicoya Peninsula, Costa Rica.

The meal gets started quickly. Everyone has time to have at least one serving of food before the meeting begins. Raoul Sr. clears his throat and starts speaking.

"By now, you know that we have a recent invention we want to introduce. Carlos, Raoul Jr., Marcella, and I have been working on this concept for some time. This is an extraordinary device. It may be as significant one day as the creation of the wheel has been to human technology. A discovery with far-reaching possibilities. This invention allows us to use gravity, magnetic fields, and even the sun as power sources. We employ gravitational fields and use gravity waves to push or pull us in any direction we care to move. We believe we have discovered a means to leave this planet and explore, at the very least, this solar system, if not the entire galaxy, without using rockets of any kind."

"The technique is to superimpose gravitational fields, add them, or subtract them. We draw on that power as a means of propulsion. To facilitate this process, Carlos and Raoul Jr. created algorithms that are super-efficient. They do not require quantum computers but need high-speed computing power and energy. We have designed our Superchips and cooling systems for our computers. "

He pauses for a moment. "This discovery can have practical applications right here on earth. Someday it may be the means of propulsion for passenger airplanes, automobiles, trucks, and other vehicles. It can be adapted to lift objects in the same way a crane or forklift does."

Everyone, except Marcella, pauses eating. Marcella sips her glass of Chablis before she speaks. "The question facing us, as usual, is what we do with our discovery. Shall we give it to the world or our government? What will they do with it? Can you imagine adapting this discovery for military purposes? Will our government or another country use this resource to dominate the world? Perhaps the government will create laws limiting its use or calling for tests to prove the drive is not dangerous. Will they carry worldly politics into outer space? Maybe another ten years will pass before our congress and senate decide who will make money from whatever happens."

Raoul Sr. continues, "Imagine the reaction of the fossil fuel industry if they learn of this technology. Oil, gas, and coal resources are owned by the same one percent that controls the country and, with others, the world. The power we harness is like the wind, ocean waves, or the sun; no one owns it. As the inventors, we must consider being caretakers."

Raoul Sr. looks at each of them as he speaks, "This country has fallen into the hands of conglomerates, politicians, and international interests. Democrats and Republicans, whatever their intentions may be, end up as pawns. There is a clinically diagnosed psychopath in the white house. They were voted in by a minority of naive or malicious citizens with documented help from Russia. Few citizens want to enter public life anymore. Even the most righteous cannot tolerate their entire lives and families being scrutinized. Those at the top of the American caste system are plotting to stay at the top even though they no longer represent the majority. Any outsider will be persecuted until they are disgraced or driven out. We don't want to be a part of this in any way."

"We want to share our work with humanity but not on the terms of our current world," Marcella said. "At this time, we want to launch a private effort to explore the solar system and perhaps beyond. We feel it is the only way to ensure our technology will not be used here on Earth for political reasons, war, or world domination."

Everyone stares at each other in silence as they come to terms with what has been revealed. Sam speaks, "I have had more time to think about this than the rest of you. As crazy as it may sound, we can use this invention to establish ourselves in space. We can begin an exploration of the solar system. Consider the idea of creating a new enterprise. Perhaps we call it the 'International Space Exploration Group.' Once we establish ourselves in space, we will be in a strong position. We will do our best to avoid the political realities of Earth. We may create some new actualities. Our actions over the next ten years can change the course of history on the planet."

Tamara looks stunned. "Do you realize what you're proposing? It takes millions, maybe billions of dollars, to launch a satellite. How are we going to explore the solar system? "

Sam smiled knowingly, "we won't be launching expensive fuel-burning rockets. Once we build a spaceship, it will fly again and again without expensive fuel or any conventional fuel whatsoever for propulsion. The startup cost is going to be high. Not as high as it would be using rockets. Also, we don't have to support the government and all its interest groups. We build the first spaceships in secret here at Arroyo Aerospace."

Bill chimed in, "Okay, let's say you build a spaceship, not that anyone will notice, and you fly into space. What happens, then? Won't the government step in and take over?"

Marcella replies, "once we independently establish our capability, launch our ships, and possibly set up a base in space, things may get difficult for us here on earth. We will have the advantage of our momentum as a private company with no government funding. There may be an effort to appropriate our propulsion system and technology. We will be prepared to deal with that and with whom we share it. We do have friends and sources that we've known for decades that we trust. I believe that they will support us if we need it. They may invest in our efforts financially. However, before we look for the outside investment, we believe it's important that we establish our efforts."

"Will you set up a base in outer space?" Tamara asks.

Raoul Sr. answers, "there are a few options to consider. We can build an orbiting station around the earth, the moon, or maybe on the moon. We can go to Mars. Ultimately, we might find a way to build a space colony at one of the Lagrange points like L5. The biggest challenge is getting the materials we need to build. According to the latest information, Mars appears to have lots of sand, basalt, and minerals, even some water. We have advanced techniques using a wide variety of materials for 3D printing. Construction of our ships will utilize 3D printing technologies."

"There are private companies building rockets and preparing to travel in space, like Ramurt, Musk, Bezos, the Amazon guy, Branson of Virgin Airlines, and others. And yes, we must be able to resist government interference. Governments can't compete with private enterprises moving into space. It's already happening," Raoul Jr. said.

"The thing is, this so revolutionary that if we come out publicly with the gravity drive propulsion system before we establish ourselves, we will be attacked by corporations, the government in this country, and others internationally. Hackers will try to overwhelm our business to steal secrets. One of the reasons we asked you all here is to brainstorm how we might establish ourselves as an International Space Exploration Group. That way, we can work with any country on earth and in space. We believe it won't be smart to announce that we've invented a revolutionary new way to propel ourselves into space, and we're going to build a spaceship, etc. There must be some way we can do it covertly. We plan to disguise our patents. Register certain things separately so that we own them," Marcella said.

Tamara looks around the table, "you are isolated out here. How big would this ship be? What will it look like once you launch it? Will they see it on the radar? Can you come back to earth? Do you need to immediately build a base on the moon or a space station?

"We built a mini prototype to test some ideas. I took Paul for a ride the other night. Now we're designing a full-size prototype we can construct quickly for testing. Based on the prototype's design and successful testing, an even larger ship can be built," Sam said. "The prototype will be one hundred percent functional and be able to go into space."

"This is starting to sound like a science fiction movie," Annie said.

"Interesting you're mentioning that," Paul said. "The other night, Sam gave me a ride in the mini prototype he has named Galaxy Zero. Afterward, we got to talking. We came up with a few ideas. Sam is designing Galaxy

One, a prototype version of Galaxy Two. Galaxy One will be built in a hangar here at Arroyo Aerospace. Galaxy Two will be much larger. It will be more difficult to hide."

Paul sounds excited. "We need a cover story. What about this? I will make a science fiction movie epic or series set sometime in the future when everyone is exploring space. I will write a screenplay that covers everything we are doing. We announce that we will build the spaceship set to scale, an actual size ship. What we say is a set will be Galaxy Two. We claim everything must look as authentic as possible for the film. We'd even bring in navigation experts to install real computers so that we can 'simulate interstellar flight navigation.' Our futuristic spaceship set will be worthy of being an attraction at NASA, Universal Studios, or Disney after the movie is shot. People can walk through it or take a simulated ride in space. The media will think what we're doing is publicity for the movie. Actors and a crew are hired, and we start shooting the film at some point. At the same time, we begin developing a studio theme park out here which will cover construction materials for the ship and other things. The working title for the theme park 'Gate to the Galaxy.'"

"We put together a private placement offering to finance the movie for two hundred million dollars," Sam said. "Bill can make sure it meets SEC guidelines. The offering is pre-sold to only the family and selected investors."

Bill is starting to look interested. "If we're going to have an offering, we should do it properly. I can put together a private placement memorandum, maybe a limited partnership, if that's all you need. Since it's so much money, we may need to register it with the SEC even if family members subscribe to it and if we raise money outside of Florida."

"I am investing in the project and the film myself," Paul stated.

"Sounds like financing is available. Is it possible to pilot a spacecraft with members of our family? We'll need to recruit other people to get involved in this enterprise, won't we?" Tamara asks.

Raoul Sr. answers, "Theoretically, we can pilot Galaxy One, a small spacecraft ourselves. We'll need a larger crew to do anything on a large scale. It will take some time. Once we're ready, we will recruit a team and others. This will be under the banner of the reality theme park concept and Paul's film. In the future, we'll need to establish a base off this planet to secure the technology and construct larger vessels. So, we need a mother ship and a way to transport things. That will be Galaxy Two.

Raoul Sr. continues," I like your idea, Paul. As Sam mentioned, we are designing a prototype. It will have a length of about fifty feet. We can do that unobserved in a hangar. We will use the ship to test the viability of our equipment and fabrication theories. Then see what it takes to travel into space."

"Won't they see us on the radar?" Annie asked.

"We can evade radar," Paul said. "Trust me."

"So, what do we think about the approach that Paul and Sam have put forward?" Marcella asks. "Is anyone opposed to us proceeding with the idea and seeing what it will take?"

The family appears to be in an affirmative frame of mind.

Marcella continues, "One essential thing, we must all tell the same story about what is happening here. Certain family members, especially children, may not understand how vital secrecy is at this time.

"Use the cover story when you talk to your children, relatives, or friends about this meeting," Sam suggests. "When we go home, we tell whomever that Paul is raising money for a new science fiction film project in which the family will invest. We'll start leaking news that Paul will do this epic science fiction series. He'll investigate zoning to open our studio theme park attraction, Gate to The Galaxy. In any event, we will have two distinct projects: the movie project and the theme park. The other is a secret project to build the ships and launch the International Space Exploration Group. All projects are actual endeavors.

"The idea of starting a tourist attraction is important," Paul said. Theme parks are part of this area. The Kennedy Space Center is not too far away, so it will seem natural. I already have zoning for the film studio, including tours and commercial projects. It will help establish the notion that we're making this film. Once we launch a spaceship, the theme park can become a reality and a base to launch and land. We will be public at that point and prepared for any eventuality."

"If this all works, it will allow us to establish ourselves in the space industry, just like the rocket companies out there now. Once established, we will have the momentum and clout to negotiate about other things," Raoul Jr. said.

There is a pause in the conversation. All appear to be fired up about the project. "I want you to know that your father and I, with Paul, have committed to funding the space exploration corporation and project. Your father and I will buy stock in each of your names. If anyone in the family wants to invest individually, they can do that too," Marcella announces.

"One last thing. I'm sure you noticed that Sharon is not here tonight. We will find a way to include her without her awareness. Because of her political connections, we believe it is potentially disastrous for her to know anything about this enterprise. She will know what the public knows, agreed?"

All present agreed with a nod of their head and knowing looks. There are a few moments of silence until the dessert is served. Soon everyone starts asking Sam when they can get a ride in Galaxy Zero. Sam said, "Sure, we can go for a spin." He reminds them that the little ship is bare minimum comfort-wise. "It is mainly to test the drive and basic fabrication. It is not meant to go flying into space."

···

CHAPTER EIGHT

"In Kung Fu your arms move as part of your body. If they move independently, they are worthless."

Adrienne and Josh sit cross-legged on their yoga mats, meditating. She can do an actual lotus position. Josh is not that flexible. While they meditate individually during the week, they sit together on Friday night before bed to start the weekend. They relax and talk about life or other things on their minds. Adrienne senses some stress coming from Josh.

"How's the research project going? she asks.

"Things are getting a little stressful at the lab. I'm talking about it with Tamara."

"Is she having a problem?"

"No, it's not about her. I may need to resign from the project. As you know, it's top secret, so I can't go into too much detail. Thinking about going back to teaching."

"Why do you want to quit., I thought this is an interest you have?"

"Yes, it is. I have concerns about with the direction things are going."

"It's hard to understand when I don't know what you're doing."

"We were asked to do an experiment that is not part of our proposal, which we did. Now they are pushing toward more dangerous and possibly inhumane research. I don't like where things are going."

"I thought this had something to do with metallurgy."

"It does. Let's say things took a biological turn, and I don't want to be involved in something that can come back to haunt me one day."

"Have you talked with Arno? He always seems friendly."

"He's a company man. He minds the store."

"Maybe you should step away if it's bothering you."

"It's not that easy. The university received the grant in my name, my proposal. I don't want to walk away and leave them with research that might fall into the wrong hands. Tamara will be left holding the bag."

"Can't you both resign from the project and return to teaching?"

"That is up to the university. The grant money may be an issue unless the project is complete."

"I'm okay with whatever you decide. Did you hear the president on TV talking about a new powerful secret weapon the country is developing that only he knows about? Do you think it is related?"

"No, I didn't hear that. Who knows? Although things may get rough, we have some ideas for working this out. In a briefing after our security clearances, Arno talked about spying by Russia and others. Mainly by hacking servers, which is why we do not share servers with the university. He said he is worried that there are leaks about defense projects and other research coming from this administration. Many of the top people in the administration did not pass an FBI security check like Tamara, the lab assistant Lin Lu and I went through. Plus, the current president likes to brag to foreign leaders he calls on his cellular phone."

"Arno told you all this?" Adrienne asks.

"Yes, he gave me the impression the entire agency feels compromised. Many agents are suspicious of the administration's political appointees."

Adrienne unfolds her legs, stretches, and slowly stands up from a deep knee posture, lifting her arms and hands above her head. "No worries, I'm sure we can handle it."

Josh closes his eyes for two minutes and listens to his breathing. Meditation always brings him into the present moment. It clears his mind of the chatter that manifests itself there. Even while meditating, thoughts surface that must be acknowledged and let go immediately. Focusing on breathing clears random thoughts quickly. As a scientist, Josh understands the logic of studies done by evolutionary psychologists regarding how the human mind evolved. He recalls a theory about how humans' brains, bodies, and organs work together. An organ like the heart is not just an unfeeling pump. It sends signals to the brain as well as receives them. It is believed that early Greek and Roman doctors and scholars chose the heart as the center of consciousness.

Certain scholars today believe all life begins with two simple mandates; survive and procreate what we call the mind developed in multiple ways outside the brain to service those objectives. The brain might be more of a coordinator than a controller. For example, consider the "fight or flight response. Does the impulse originate in the heart or the brain? Studies have shown the heart to be aware of the danger before the brain. Josh recently read about transplanting a pig's heart into a human. "What kind of signals will this animal's organ send to the brain," he asks himself.

Focused on his breathing Josh clears his mind. He joins Adrienne in bed. In the present moment, they touch, hold each other, make love, and sleep soundly.

CHAPTER NINE

....

"Hell is empty. All the devils are here."
--Shakespeare "The Tempest."

Sunny Saturday mornings in the spring bring people outdoors. Lake Baldwin's running, walking, biking, and skateboarding paths can get crowded on those days. The Bennett family and George enjoy going to the area on the lake near the Gazebo at the foot of New Broad Street. They are gathered near the water, watching Morgan and Lauren take turns operating the remote steering device used to steer their model sailboat on the lake. The ducks in the area do not seem to mind the boat. A few people watch them from the long wooden walkway to the Gazebo. On the roof of the Gazebo, a few large aquatic birds look interested either in the boat or the fishing lines a few people have put out into the lake.

The model was purchased as a Christmas present for the family to build. This is the maiden voyage for the eighteen-inch-long scale model sloop. "You're doing great, guys," Josh said as they sailed the boat past a duck.

"Don't chase the ducks," Adrienne said to both children.

"How are things going at the office," George asks Josh in a hushed voice.

"Same as usual. We have this visit coming up."

"I did some checking about intellectual rights. I'd like to see the agreement you signed. Maybe there is a loophole in the contract."

"No problem, I have a copy at home. I believe I reserve certain intellectual rights."

The small sailboat is getting further out into the lake. Adrienne cautions Lauren to bring it back toward the shore. The model's sails are catching some wind and making it move faster. The same breeze is making the water a bit choppy. The sailboat has a keel that doesn't draft much water. Adrienne is concerned that the little boat will flip over quickly. If it does flip, there is no way to get it back without wading into the water and muddy bottom. Adrienne is not anxious to go into the water. She once saw a strange-looking large fish near the shore, and there is always a risk of snakes and alligators in Florida.

Before speaking again, Josh looks around the area as if someone is listening to them. He almost does a double take when he spots Arno and a woman Josh has not seen before coming down the steps from the street toward them.

"You may think I overreact to certain things. Don't look now, but Arno, the CIA agent assigned to the project, is coming toward us, along with a woman I don't recognize."

Arno and Simone are dressed casually. They appear to be out for a walk. They notice the Bennett family and George by the water and head over that way. Arno waves.

"Hi, everyone. I wondered if we might find you out on such a nice day."

"Good to see you," Josh said. You already know Adrienne and the children, I believe. I don't think you have met my neighbor and friend George in person."

Arno acknowledges Josh's "in person" aside and smiles. George and Arno shake hands. Adrienne waves from the water's edge.

"I'd like you to meet an acquaintance of mine, Simone Greely, who has been transferred to the area from D.C. She's working for the Small Business Administration (SBA), auditing some banks in the area," Arno said.

Josh and George exchange a sideways look as Arno heads down toward Adrienne and the children. Josh follows him, leaving George and Simone on their own.

"So, you're an auditor Simone?" George asks.

"Yes, I'm looking at local banks and the SBA loans they've made," Simone replies.

"You're a friend of Arno's from Washington?"

"Yes, he's been showing me around Orlando. He helped me to find an apartment near Lake Eola. Do you work with Dr. Bennett?"

"No, I'm a lawyer, general practice, and certain types of litigation. Who knows, one of my clients might have an SBA loan, George laughs.

"I won't hold it against you," Simone replies. "You live near Dr. Bennett?"

"Yes, right up the block. We get out for runs in the morning once in a while. Our families are friends. Before my divorce, we used to get together for dinner at each other's homes. Now Adrienne takes pity on me and invites me over occasionally."

"How long have you been divorced?"

"It's been a year or so now. Are you married, engaged, or otherwise attached?" George asks.

"No, it's difficult because I have to travel so much."

"Maybe we can get together for dinner. Happy to show you around the area. Possibly go out for a run if you like running?"

"Sure, that sounds good, and I do like running. The apartment complex has a gym, but it's great to go outside. Seems like good weather and clean air around here."

"Why don't you dial my phone so I get your number, and I'll give you a call next week if that's okay?"

Simone got out her phone. George gave her his number to dial. They walk down to the lake, where Arno is taking a turn controlling the model sloop around the ducks that seem to have taken a liking to the boat.

"This is great, guys I think the ducks like the sailboat," Arno said, laughing.

After a few minutes, Arno gave the controller back to Morgan.

"Okay, good running into you guys. Josh, seriously, don't worry about tomorrow. I'll get them in and out quickly." To Simone, "Got time for some lunch? There's a good Sushi restaurant close by?"

Arno and Simone say their goodbyes and walk away along the path. Josh looks at George. "We come here often. Never saw Arno here before. This is not a chance meeting. How did he know we were here? What's he trying to tell me? It is more than 'don't worry about tomorrow.'"

"She's nice. She said they were friends from Washington."

"I bet she is CIA too. Better watch yourself."

"No worries, I'll find out. Even if she is CIA, she must have a social life. Rest assured, we won't talk about you if I can help."

Thinking about the Arno being there, George said, "It might just be a coincidence. He is showing her around the area. Arno seems friendly. "

"I'm skeptical about coincidences in general," Josh said. "

"Maybe he wanted us to meet the new guy, or he may have been trying to help you relax about the meeting," George said.

Josh stopped thinking about the encounter and watched the children sailing the model sloop.

Simone and Arno stop by Simone's car parked a short distance from the lake.

"What did the lawyer friend have to say," Arno asks.

"It was a social conversation. He asked for my phone number and dinner sometime."

"You should go. See if you can pick up any information on Bennett's frame of mind regarding this grant."

"If I hear anything, I'll let you know," Simone said somewhat dismissively.

"Fine, see you tomorrow," Arno said. He watches Simone get into her car and drive off.

CHAPTER TEN

....

"Now you see it, now you don't."

The entourage from Washington in town for a lab tour includes several people. A two-star General from the Pentagon, two aides in military uniform, Ms. Watson, and an unnamed project evaluator. Joining them are Miriam Cohen, Dean of the University College of Science, Josh, Tamara, and Lin Lu, the graduate lab assistant. Before this day, Josh and Tamara decide on a plan of action. They will cooperate with everyone by giving the tour and answering questions about the project. If their plan to dissuade the visitors regarding the experiment fails, they will decide what else they can do later. Their minds are made up. If all else fails, they will find a way to resign from working on the grant as soon as possible.

After the family meeting at the ranch, Tamara decides to work with the family to achieve their planned goals. She doesn't want to resign from the project and abandon Josh. She discusses with Josh that "any progress they have made in exploring the concept of cloaking is mostly theoretical, except for the incident with the rabbit. Even before the family meeting, the president bragging about the United States having a secret weapon no one knows about is disturbing. Since that announcement, there has been a push for this meeting. Then the notification for sending them a primate to test the spray on. Why all this attention and a tour for the pentagon out of the blue?"

"I'm alarmed by the president's loose lips. This is not a routine visit. I do not want to get into experiments on cloaking biological living organisms, including humans. No one can trust this administration with any potential discovery since it might fall into the hands of foreign adversaries or corporate entities. I remember what I added to the spray concoction. It is not written down anywhere. The only record of the event is the video recorded by one of Arno's cameras in the lab," Josh said.

Josh, Tamara, and Lin Lu arrive at the lab at nine a.m. They put on their lab coats and begin their workday as usual. The windowless lab space always looks the same, with its gray and white walls. Josh insists that most lighting be incandescent and daylight balanced, making the area feel less glary. At ten a.m., the group of visitors enters the lab, where everyone greets them. Arno and Simone stay in the small control room watching the monitors and listening as everyone is introduced.

Josh begins the tour, "Welcome to our lab. We are exploring different ideas regarding the molecular structure of various non-biological materials. This new research is based on theories and ideas developed previously. The grant is being used to further the research and test theories."

Tamara led the group to the rabbit cage, "Here is our infamous disappearing rabbit. And like most magical rabbits, we think we have figured out his magic trick."

The visitors from Washington wait expectantly to see the rabbit disappear. In anticipation, the General and Ms. Walton move forward a fraction of an inch.

Josh continues, "As you may have seen on the experiment video, I spray the rabbit with a watered-down version of one of my experimental formulas for metallic surfaces. The rabbit disappears briefly until I pick him up with a towel to wipe him off. I opened the towel, and he was visible and perfectly normal. We've been checking his vitals for weeks, and he is fine. No more disappearing."

"After some investigation, we have determined that what happens with our bunny is an optical illusion caused by the light refracting off the spray mist on the rabbit. Overhead, where we are standing, you will note we have special daylight incandescent bulbs for the rabbit, and behind the cage, there are florescent fixtures and bright surfaces."

Tamara continues, "We will try replicating this illusion for you now. We may or may not get the same effect. It's difficult to replicate the exact lighting."

In front of the counter, Josh opens the cage, lifts out the rabbit, and pushes the cage aside. He picks up a spray bottle and sprays the rabbit's back lightly. The rabbit remains completely visible. Still holding the rabbit in front of him, he then turns his back to the group and places the rabbit on the counter. When he turns back and steps aside, the back of the rabbit appears transparent, reflecting a little light or shimmering. Everyone watches for several moments as that part of the rabbit seems transparent. Josh moves in front of the counter again, picks up the rabbit, then turns back to the group holding the rabbit, which now shows no transparency. Tamara hands him a towel to dry the rabbit and places him back on the counter. He remains entirely visible.

"So, it seems Mr. Cotton Tail has us all fooled. It's an illusion," Josh offers with a sad smile. "The spray simply refracts the light falling on the counter."

Ms. Walton and the General do not look happy. Ms. Walton shook her head, "well, this whole thing has been a waste of time."

"We're very sorry. We never made any claims. We said we couldn't explain anything and there was nothing to report. Somehow things got blown out of proportion," Josh said.

Tamara asks, would you like to see our high-power electron microscope? It's over here. Lin Lu, our lab assistant, will give you a demonstration." The group follows Tamara and Lin Lu over to the microscope.

In the control booth, Arno fingers a few hairs of his beard. He replays the demonstration and partially disappearing rabbit. He punches up the original video of the rabbit disappearing—the same effect. Something bothers him besides the dusty lens this time. He did not have time to zoom in digitally on the rabbit before Josh moved in front of the counter to pick it up.

The Pentagon General and Ms. Walton asked questions about the timeline, anticipated progress, and project goals. They force some smiles as questions are answered. Soon the visitors leave the lab and the building to return to D.C. Dean Cohen returns to her office with no idea what has transpired.

With the help of a couple of Arroyo family members, including Paul and Raoul Jr., Josh and Tamara set up an illusion worthy of David Copperfield. They employ a high-end miniature holographic projector and a little smoke and mirrors to create the desired effect. It has to not only fool the spectators in front of the rabbit's cage but also deceive the ever-present video camera behind the audience.

At night, cameras in the lab go into a screen saver dormant mode. A motion detector in the room pointed at the door activates the cameras if anyone enters. The entire system of cameras and motion detectors in the lab is wireless. Video is streamed to the control room. Josh uses an App. He borrowed from Carlos Arroyo to hack the system and disable the motion detector remotely when they returned the night before to set up the illusion.

A tiny high-definition holographic projector is mounted above the counter in one of the light fixtures. The projector is remotely controlled by Tamara standing by with her iPhone as if she is taking pictures. The analog part of the magic is Josh appearing to put the rabbit on the counter. His back blocks the view as he places the sleepy rabbit in a pouch inside his lab coat. When he turns back and steps aside, the illusion is complete. What is seen by the audience is a holographic projection of the rabbit shot previously. As a safety precaution, the camera facing the counter and others in the room got a light dust spray to slightly diffuse the images they recorded.

Josh steps in again with the towel holding the actual rabbit to dry off and show the assembled spectators. The plan goes smoothly. The projection device is removed from the fixture later that day, and the bulb is replaced by Tamara feigning to clean up after the demo.

....

CHAPTER ELEVEN

Live in the sunshine, swim the sea, drink the wild air."
– Ralph Waldo Emerson.

Two weeks after the family meeting, Paul distributed a press release about his new motion picture project.

"For Immediate Release"

"A new science fiction epic film "Space Pioneers" written, directed, and produced by Paul Arroyo, is beginning pre-production in Florida."

"Space Pioneers is a journey into the future. It is the first in a series of episodic science fiction films. Space Pioneers is about men and women who leave Earth in 2041 to explore the solar system and the galaxy. They face many adventures on their journey. Pre-production is underway, with shooting scheduled for early 2020 at Arroyo Studios in Florida."

During interviews by the local press, both TV and print, Paul describes the film:

"We are building a full-scale, authentic-looking spaceship as the main set for the film. The spaceship set will be an attraction at the Gate to the Galaxy studio theme park when we are not shooting. This huge set is being constructed adjacent to the film studio here in Brevard County. The set will be built with authentic detail to simulate an actual spaceship."

Having a theme park attraction before a film is released is unique. The news generates some enthusiasm. Based on his previous successes, Paul immediately received offers from two significant distributors and cable and online streamers, including Disney, HBO Max, and Netflix. The cable companies are looking for deals to begin streaming the film at the same time it is released in theaters.

Paul believes that he needs to go about making the film in a completely authentic fashion. He intends to shoot a feature-length film. This entails pre-production, casting, shooting, and postproduction. Arroyo Studios already has a good size green screen studio ready for CGI production. They will add additional equipment and software for this type of film.

He has yet to announce that he is also producing a documentary film about the actual mission that will be released once they launch the real spaceship and establish themselves off the planet. In the meantime, he calls it a behind-the-scenes documentary about the film and theme park.

Tamara arranges for Josh, Adrienne, and family to visit the ranch, which is an easy drive from the Bennett beach condo in Cocoa Beach. Tamara leaves for the ranch on Thursday without anyone noticing. Arno is out of town, having been called to Washington for a meeting. Simone has a few days off. She is having dinner with George that weekend.

Josh let everyone know he is taking a few days off to go to the beach with the family. They often go there on weekends. The towns of Canaveral and Cocoa Beach are only about sixty miles from Orlando. Their beach condo is on the third floor of a Cocoa Beach condominium building with a great view of the dunes, beach, and ocean.

Settled at the beach, Josh sits on the condo balcony drinking green tea while watching the tide come in. The sun sparkles on the ocean as the waves raise the tide on the beach. He enjoys the ocean's smell and the dunes between the building and the beach. He believes that all life sprang from the earth's oceans somehow. Running on the packed sand near the water feels like being close to the primal forces of the planet. He jogs from the condo to the jetty, where the cruise ships come in and out. Once he reaches the rocks in front of the jetty, he turns back. Across the jetty is the air force part of the Cape Canaveral space center. He remembers watching the space shuttle, after it launched from near Titusville, come up into the sky over the cape back in the day when the shuttles were still being used. Particular rockets are visible on their pads before launch by looking across the canal from the jetty. Occasionally a nuclear submarine can be seen heading in or out of the base located near there. Mainly there are cruise ships, fishing boats, and pleasure craft. After finishing his tea, Josh waves at Adrienne and the children on the beach by the water. It is a sunny warm day with only the dunes separating the condo balcony and the beach.

After a morning at the beach, Friday afternoon finds the Bennett's at a restaurant in Port Canaveral. They have a table inside, overlooking the dock and canal. It is around four p.m. and not too crowded. It will become packed inside and outside on the deck facing the water in an hour or so. Usually, a musician or band performs out on the deck. A fishing boat arrives at the docks adjacent to the restaurant. Pelicans and seagulls group nearby, waiting for any spoils they can snag. A huge Disney Cruise ship heads to sea for a few days to the Bahamas or a Caribbean destination. People wave from the boat to the people at the restaurant. Lauren and Morgan wave back too.

"You seem more relaxed than last week," Adrienne comments after everyone's food arrives. Fresh fish sandwiches, fries, and salad for the children. Adrienne and Josh have Bahamian chowder and fresh Florida grouper platters.

"I think so. We managed to calm the waters and can now proceed with the project as usual. No one has bothered us over the last two weeks. I'm interested in research, teaching, and no drama. "

"Are we going to Tamara's ranch tomorrow? Morgan asks."

Adrienne smiles, "Yes, we are going. It's not Tamara's ranch. It's her parent's. She will be there."

Lauren asks, "Do they have horses?"

"Yes, I believe they have horses. Tamara has won prizes for her equestrian or horseback riding skills. They also raise cattle," Adrienne answers.

"Can we ride the horses?"

Josh replies, "We'll see what they have planned when we go there in the morning."

Turning to Adrienne as the children return to eating their sandwiches, Josh mentions, "Tamara tells me her parent's company has some big projects in the works. Her brother Paul is starting a new movie project, and they also have plans for a studio theme park in conjunction with the film. Must be a big place."

"Should be a fun day. Tamara has a big family, doesn't she? Adrienne asks.

"Yes, I believe there are eight siblings. Many are involved in the family business. Her parents are more than ranchers. They have a good size manufacturing company, Arroyo Aerospace, that designs and manufactures certain technical projects for space programs here and abroad. Both parents are inventors and tech-savvy."

"Looking forward to the day. This fish is delicious. How are your sandwiches," Adrienne asks the children as she tries one of Morgan's French fries.

Josh is enjoying the fresh fish. "Nothing like freshly caught fish. I believe the restaurant owner gets the seafood right off the fishing boats. Good to be away from the university, enjoying the sea air and the beach, while we still have one. But let's not go there. It is too nice a day."

....

CHAPTER TWELVE

A first date.

George usually arrives a little early for dinner dates. Rather than wait in the entry area for someone to come, George prefers to be seated. He reads the menu or checks his phone while waiting. He likes this Sichuan restaurant and has been a customer since it opened. The owner and senior chef are friendly. He and George always greet each other. George notices Simone at the entrance and waves to her. She makes her way to the table.

Simone has mixed feelings about meeting George after Arno tells her to see what information she can get from him. Hitting him up for news about Dr. Bennett on the first date is evident and stupid. She wants a nice meal, conversation, and a relaxing evening. George seems interesting, and there is some attraction. She looks forward to this meeting being social, not work.

George stands up to greet Simone. "Hi, good to see you. Thanks for coming. Did you have any trouble finding this place?

"No problem, I used my phone GPS," she said as she sat in the booth across the table from George.

"Are you finding your way around the Orlando area? George asks."

"Yes, it's not too difficult. There are lots of neighborhoods and suburbs."

"Orlando doesn't have a large downtown; neighborhoods are spread out, and then you have the theme parks. I'm told that before Disney arrived, they used to run cattle down Orange Avenue in downtown Orlando. They have excellent Sichuan dishes here. Some are very spicy," George said.

Simone opens her menu and begins to scan the entries. She feels uncomfortable. She isn't exactly sure why. In a few minutes, the server arrives, and they both order their food. Simone speaks to the server in Mandarin, to George's amazement. When the server leaves, George asks, "Where did you learn Chinese?"

"I studied the language in Beijing for two years."

"Great, that must have been quite an experience. I've never been to China."

"Yes, it was amazing. "

"Did you get to see the great wall?"

"Yes, and lots of other historical places. China has a long history."

"So why are you here checking on bad loans for the SBA?"

Simone thinks for a moment and realizes what is bothering her.

Lowering her voice, "George, as I'm sure you may have surmised, I don't work for the SBA. I work for the same 'company' as Arno. There's no reason for the cover. I'm sorry. I am here socially, not working tonight. If this is an issue, I understand."

George is surprised by Simone's declaration. He remembers that he and Josh speculated on her employment. It wasn't on his mind, and he was surprised that she had revealed the truth. It doesn't make any difference to him. He appreciates her telling him up-front.

"Yes, we did wonder about Arno's cover story. Thank you for the heads up. I'm here socially too, so I have no problem with it. Okay?"

"Sure, no problem! Now I can enjoy your company and the food."

The conversation continues. "Are you from Orlando originally?" Simone asks.

"No, I grew up in New York, Long Island. Where are you from?"

"I am from Georgetown, Washington, D.C. Grew up in the nation's capital."

"A native Washingtonian. What is it like being there, growing up in the seat of our national government?"

"After a while, you forget about government, politics, and the party in power. D.C. is like a colony; it doesn't control its destiny."

"You think it should be a State?"

"Maybe, it has a larger population than a couple of the current states, but no representation."

"You still have family there in Georgetown?"

"Yes, my parents, who are retired. They live there. My older brother is a surgeon at Johns Hopkins. He lives near Baltimore."

The server brought the appetizers. Simone has sea cucumber soup. George has hot and sour soup with chicken, tofu, and bamboo sprouts. They order a dish of diced chicken Bao, medium spicy.

George asks, "What is it like living in Beijing?"

"It's a big city, bigger than many around the world. A population of around eighteen million. It's the seat of the Chinese government for the Peoples' Republic of China. Hectic, with lots of traffic and people all the time. Public transportation is excellent. You can take the subway mostly everywhere," Simone said.

"No subways in Orlando. Only buses and Uber."

"Lots of taxis in Beijing. You can call it the equivalent of Uber. You need a mobile phone with a Chinese phone number to call for a ride. You also use your phone to pay via WeChat or another service. Most people use their phones to pay for all kinds of things from groceries to movie tickets."

The conversation continues throughout a good meal. George and Simone appear to enjoy each other's company. Before the evening is over, they decide to see each other again.

CHAPTER THIRTEEN

*"Heaven and Earth complement each other to make rain.
No one can order the rain to fall, yet of their own free will
they share it." --Dao De Jing*

Only a few large ranches remain in Central Florida, including a vast, sixty-thousand-acre ranch in Osceola County. It is rumored to be going up for sale soon for residential and commercial development. The Arroyo property, including Paul's Studio area, is considered large at six-thousand acres. Wildlife management areas border sections of the land. Most of the property faces older local roads. The property's border walls are made of local coquina stone that fits in with the environment. The walls are high enough to stop cattle from roaming onto the roads.

The ride from Cape Canaveral to the Arroyo property is quick. The Bennetts arrive at the ranch around 10:00 a.m. Saturday morning. They stop at the security gate with its discreet "Private Property" sign and cameras. In a few moments, the gate swings open. They drive along a road paved with coquina stone and bordered by large palm trees.

Josh tells the family, "You couldn't get more Florida than this. I researched coquina stone because it forms from dead tiny coquina clams in the shallow waters of coastal Florida over thousands of years.

"You mean like the little shells we see on the beach?" Morgan asks.

"Yes, they accumulate over the years in layers forming submerged deposits. The formations are exposed to air, rain, soil, and vegetation during the last ice age. Ultimately rotting vegetation and soil pick up carbon dioxide and become carbonic acid. This weak acid solution soaks downward and dissolves calcium in the shells, producing calcium carbonate. This turns solid in lower layers, much like how flowstone and stalactites are formed in caves. The shell fragments get "glued" together into a porous type of limestone that the Spanish name coquina, which means "tiny shell."

"Did you two get that?" Adrienne asks in good humor. "The tiny dead shells get smashed together over hundreds of thousands of years and become rocks."

Lauren and Morgan nod affirmatively. Josh laughs.

Josh finds it amazing how big the ranch appears with all the open space. Cattle are grazing here and there. As they drive toward the main house, they pass some parked flatbed trailers with bulldozers. Then they go by an area with some horses who look up from their grazing to see if they know these people.

"Beautiful place," Adrienne said as they approached the ranch house.

Tamara is waiting for them on the veranda of the house. She waves as they drive up and park. Tamara met the Bennett family previously at university functions. Josh and Adrienne open the back of the SUV and retrieve some presents, including flowers, and wine, for the Arroyo family.

"Hi, welcome to the Arroyo Ranch," Tamara said as she greeted them. "Come in. We have some brunch prepared."

They walk up the steps to the veranda and then into the house's foyer, where Marcella, Raoul Sr., and Paul are waiting.

Tamara introduces everyone.

Josh said, "beautiful ranch," as they gave the wine and flowers to Raoul Sr. and Marcella.

"Thank you for the wine and flowers. We're glad you're here. The powder room is over here if you'd like to freshen up. When you are ready," we'll go to the kitchen for some brunch."

The kitchen area is on the atrium side of the house next to the large formal dining area. Windows on one side face the atrium and pool. A big tiger-cut oak table with chairs is at the far end, in front of windows and the garden beyond.

"After we eat, we'll give you a short tour of the ranch, Tamara said.

Looking at Josh, Raoul Sr. offers to show him their manufacturing and lab facilities.

Paul mentions to Adrienne that she is welcome to see the studio area.

"Can we see the horses?" Lauren asks.

"You certainly may, and if you like, maybe go for a ride if your mother approves," Marcella offers.

Lauren is all smiles.

The Arroyos and Bennetts settled down to eat.

Josh comments, "This is a wonderful house. When was it built?"

"My family purchased the land around the turn of the last century. In the 1950s, they built this house. They find Coquina stone quarried near here and use it for the foundations and ground floor walls. Termite proof! You will also find buildings in St. Augustine built entirely of Coquina," said Raoul Sr.

Marcella adds, "Raoul Sr. and I looked for older homes in the St. Augustine area and other local places that were set for rehab or demolition. We found ancient fixtures, wood cabinets, beams, and built-ins."

"The overall feel we want is a colonial Spanish ranch house. We've updated things over the years," Raoul Sr. replies.

"My father's family has quite a history in Florida," Tamara said, smiling. "They date some family back to 1672 and the Castillo de San Marco building in St. Augustine. The family spread out as Florida went from Spanish control to English Control and back to Spanish control before it was annexed in 1819 as a territory by the United States. For a while, there was a French settlement near Jacksonville. There was a period when pirates hid on the barrier island now called Cape Canaveral and on the Indian River. They raid St. Augustine and other places on the coast constantly. It won't surprise me if there isn't a pirate or two in our family history, maybe even buried treasure."

Everyone laughed. Morgan's eyes lit up.

Adrienne noticing Morgan's interest, mentions, "We might have some pirates in our family history too."

Looking at Paul, Marcella said, "Sounds like a movie Paul."

"Yes, maybe. You know the Castillo de San Marco has never been taken by force. The British and pirates sack and burn St. Augustine on occasion. They are never able to take the fort," Paul adds.

"We've been there once. I can easily see why it withheld attacks," Josh said. "The Coquina Stone is porous enough to absorb the impact of the cannon fire of the day. Plus, I think they built the walls around 12 feet thick. Some of the older streets in Orlando and Winter Park have curbs made from Coquina. Rub up against them too hard, and you will damage your tires, wheels, or car."

After brunch, it is decided to divide up for a while. Paul wants to show Adrienne the film studio. Tamara and Marcella get the okay to take the children to see the horses. Josh goes with Raoul Sr. for a short tour of Arroyo Aerospace.

Raoul Sr. and Josh leave the house and walk along a shady footpath that leads from the house to the hangars and work buildings. There are enough trees and vegetation, so you cannot see that area from home. The footpath gently winds its way through some trees and open spaces.

"I don't know how much Tamara told you about our work. We have done much-specialized work for NASA over the years," Raoul Sr. said as they walked.

"She did mention it, but not in much detail," Josh replies.

"Marcella and I both have engineering and technical backgrounds, so we work together on most projects. We have quite a few patents for our inventions. Tamara tells me she is working on a project with you, and you both are not too happy working on currently."

"Yes, hopefully, we've resolved some issues for the time being. We are not comfortable with the direction the project is being pushed toward and what the current government might do with our findings if we proceed with the research."

"We have many misgivings about the current administration. We are concerned about how the culture deals with huge jumps in technology. We're alarmed that there is disharmony with the planet ecologically and with each other. Discord is spreading like a virus. So much angst and blame of the other," Raoul Sr. said.

"I agree," Josh said. "The planet goes through changes over time. Homo sapiens have survived ice ages and other climatic changes. Right now, we are contributing to what appears to be a warming period. Ice is melting from the polar caps in both hemispheres. Human activity is either speeding it up or possibly causing it. The odd weather isn't a coincidence. Many people don't seem to care what happens in the future."

"You have a diverse background between physics and molecular studies. Tamara told us that you have interests in many areas, "Raoul Sr. said.

"Yes, I'm interested in metallurgy from a molecular level. I think about the idea that humans have pretty much developed nonbiological technology. Anytime someone proposes biological kinds of advances, everyone gets nervous. 'Like you're tampering with life.' The research we are doing is secret. I can tell you that I'm interested in how biological substances can alter the molecular structure of metals, stone, and other materials." I've been researching new approaches to MEMS manufacturing.

Raoul Sr. said, "I understand. We have some of the same interests, as you'll see."

"My interests cross a few disciplines," Josh replied. "I feel ideas about human evolution and where we go next, for example, are tied with physics, science, psychology, and philosophy. Science and the social sciences are connected. I question why humanity is easily manipulated into anti-science postures even when science benefits them."

Josh is surprised as they come out from under the trees. There is a small geodesic dome in front of a sizeable hangar-type building. The hangar is the length of a football field and almost as wide. There are other similar hangar-style buildings further away along a runway.

"Wow, it looks like you have a lot of space in these buildings. Do you have an airplane?"

"Yes, we have a corporate jet and a smaller prop plane. This building is our "workshop." The smaller building in front is the original shop, but we ran out of space. We called it the garage. The hangar spaces are technical facilities, labs, manufacturing space, and office areas more than airplane hangars. The buildings give us a way to keep everything under one roof. We have enough land to expand outward rather than up."

They entered the dome-shaped geodesic building in front of the hanger, which houses a reception area and offices. "We don't get too many visitors. When we do, we usually bring them here for a conference before going farther."

Down the hall in the rear of the building, they walk through a door that leads into the hangar building. It did not feel like entering a giant hangar, just more offices and doors with no names.

"Through here is our machine shop," Raoul Sr. said as he opened one of the doors.

"Very high-tech machine shop," Josh comments, noting the computers, various computer-controlled lathes, and other typical machine shop tools.

"Yes, we do ultra-precision work, sometimes one-of-a-kind parts for NASA and others. Much of it is automated. A program is written. The machines are very accurate. We can work with any metal or material. Nowadays, much of what we design is produced with 3D printing technology."

They leave the machine shop and head into the next area, a long, expansive room with 3D printing machines as far as the eye can see. Some of the 3D printers appear to be the size of a bus. The 3D printing shop is enormous and, again, state-of-the-art technology. There is the hum of some of the printers working. This open area and high ceilings feel more like a hangar space.

"This our 3D printing shop," Raoul Sr. said.

Josh looks around for a minute in amazement. He notices a technician at one of the machines further along the line. "You can print from small to substantial projects. "

"Yes, we can print the body parts of an entire automobile, pretty much objects of any size or shape."

"Including metals?"

"These five machines are large 3D metal printers. We have smaller printers too. We print using many diverse materials, including Aluminum, Stainless Steel, Titanium, Inconel 718, Copper, etc. We work with carbon fiber, ceramic, and other proprietary materials we've developed. A wide variety of sources can be prepared for use in 3d printing. We custom-built or modified most of the printers in this room. We either fabricate or order certain parts as we need them. "

Raoul Sr. walks with Josh down the center of the aisle. "We have high-level government clearances, so we get orders from NASA, Major aerospace corporations, and others doing prototypes. Most things get flown out of here since we have the airstrip. Air Fed Ex will pick up and deliver. Most of our orders are picked up by the customers, or we can deliver them. If you look over here, this printer is working on a part for a turbine engine. The part was composed of three different elements before this. With 3D printing, we can do it as one piece."

"This is awesome, and you don't need a big staff to do all this?"

"We have several people working here, depending on what we're doing. 3D printing runs on its own once you get started. Marcella, Sam, Raoul Jr., and I can do a lot independently. Marcella is an excellent programmer. She can write a 3D CAD file in her sleep. I'm not so bad myself."

Josh said, "Well, I'm impressed. I didn't know that 3D printing processes have come so far. You can print just about anything you want using various materials."

"Yes, we're experimenting with different alloys that employ metals and other substances."

"That's an area I'm extremely interested in."

"That's what Tamara tells us. We have something to talk about."

"Let's head over to our research lab." Raoul Sr. led the way back down the long row of printers, a few humming along, printing what appeared to be metallic objects.

Paul drove Adrienne to the studio in a silver-gray 1990 Land Rover, a vehicle not noted for its mechanical reliability. Adrienne notices that Paul presses a button on the dash to start the car. There is no starter noise.

"Is this car electric?" she asks.

"Yes, it is," Paul answers. "We did the conversion at Arroyo Aerospace. Raoul Sr. developed the electric drive train and motors. Each wheel has an independent electric motor. Some after-market and custom shops are using a Tesla system to do this. By the time they are done, you're looking at $250,000 to $350,000, including buying a Tesla."

"Great, very quiet, and I guess it still has the off-road capabilities."

"Sure. Although, we did need to lift the suspension because of the independent electric motors."

"I think Josh will like this concept."

"I suggested my parents open a business in Orlando or Miami to do this custom auto work. They are not interested." There are some other things about the Rover that Paul does not mention. Features that made it difficult to be entirely candid about during the conversion.

Changing the subject, Paul said, "I'm starting a new movie project that's going to be very big and different from what I've done in the past. The screenplay is being written, and since you are in the advertising and public relations business, I wondered if you would give me some feedback and maybe even consider working with us in some capacity. I know you work for a big agency, and that's okay. I want to know whom I'm working with for this project. Up until now, I turned things over to the distributors."

Adrienne was surprised. "Sure, what have you got?"

"We are making a science fiction film that may have sequels or become an episodic series later. The working title is Space Pioneers. At the same time, I've convinced my Arroyo Aerospace family to let us open a modest studio theme park where we will shoot the film. We plan to build a spaceship set to scale and then use it to film the story about exploring the solar system and, ultimately, the galaxy. The studio theme park's name will be Gate to the Galaxy. In the film story, space travel beyond the solar system is an evolutionary step for Homo sapiens. I think people will come to the set and tour the life-size spaceship used in the film. It will be built as if it could fly in space. With all the bells and whistles you might find on a spaceship in the future."

"Wow, a movie and a theme park attraction before the movie is released."

"Yes, by the time the film goes into distribution, we will have built up a large audience. What do you think?"

"Great, it's a big idea. Have you got financing?"

"Yes, I'm financing half of it. Some family members are investing, and possibly certain private investors. Initially, we raised two hundred million dollars in financing. If all goes well, we'll open the theme park while shooting and before the movie is finished. There will be some revenue generated early on. Many people come out this way to go to Kennedy Space Center. We should get some traffic, not to mention all the attendance at Disney and Universal in Orlando. I'm not good at writing press releases or handling publicity. I do not know much about advertising."

"It's good you are considering the public relations and advertising part early and a budget. I can help you get started. In a while, it will require a full-time effort and staff. You can go with an agency like ours or start an in-house agency."

They arrive at Paul's studio building and continue their conversation as Paul gives Adrienne a studio tour. Sets for the current production are up. Adrienne meets Annie, Paul's sister. Also, Stacy O'Brien, Paul's girlfriend. Stacy is there helping Annie go over some of Paul's expenses from the latest film. Stacy tries to get there on weekends when possible.

Adrienne is surprised at the scope of the project Paul describes. She has the feeling that it is just crazy enough to succeed. "I'm familiar with concepts for public relations and advertising for attractions because I work on Disney and Universal accounts and, to some extent, help promote their films. Working on a project like this will be new to me."

Paul said, "it will be new to me too, but I feel you are perfect for the job. "

Adrienne said, "I'd like to think it over for a couple of days and then get back to you. We can decide if I get you started or bring the account into the firm with me as the account executive."

Paul is adamant about wanting to work with Adrienne, someone with whom he has a connection. In this case, her husband, because of Josh's association with his sister Tamara. Adrienne feels that their visit to the ranch is more than being in the "right place, at the right time." Josh going off with Raoul Sr. and her with Paul is more than a coincidence. She is anxious to know what Josh has experienced.

Josh and Raoul Sr. make their way to the tech lab, a combination of computer stations and electronic equipment, including high-power electron microscopes, centrifuges, laser equipment, and many testing setups. Surveying the well-equipped lab, Josh comments, "I think you are better equipped here than my lab at UCF."

"We try to stay state of the art. We're looking at many of the same things you may be interested in. We have some ongoing projects that I'd like to talk to you about. Tamara thinks very highly of you. So, let us know if you get tired of academic life or even have time for freelance work that isn't a conflict."

"That's very kind of you. I certainly will consider it and talk to Adrienne. I'm interested and honored by the offer."

Josh quickly realizes that these very private and entrepreneurial people are recruiting him. He feels honored and intrigued. It will be a different world than the one he is accustomed to. The private sector. A very private, private sector firm, from what he can tell. At the very least, he can do some freelancing here. See how things work out. Possibly barter time to do his research.

Finished checking out the lab, they head to the rear of the building, which houses two airplanes. One is a Cessna Citation, the other a Cessna Sky hawk TD. Next to the open space in the hangar, there are two hydraulic car lifts and gear for doing work on cars or airplanes.

"Looks like you do some work on cars, too," Josh said.

"We do. We've converted several cars to electric with our proprietary drive train, motors, and batteries."

"Great!"

"Started as a hobby with Paul, who owns some classic cars. One thing leads to another, including new ideas and a chance to try them out. We learned to use our 3D printing capabilities to print vehicle bodies and parts."

"Ideas like the electric drives and your storage batteries, I imagine," Josh said.

"Off the record, yes. For example, using solar energy to charge car batteries. Not a new idea. Somehow it never made it onto the current crop of electric cars. I think billionaires like Musk and Ramurt are talented and entrepreneurial. They likely make compromises with the establishment to survive. We don't want to fight that fight right now. Eventually, we want to make these inventions available to everyone."

"I completely agree. How do you do it? Don't you need solar panels on the roof, windows, or something?"

Raoul Sr. smiled that same knowing smile he is known for. "I'll show you sometime. It has to do with the paint and proprietary 3D printing of the main surfaces of the car body. You can park your car in a sunny spot, drive in the sun, and charge the batteries as you go."

"That's revolutionary!"

"Yes, which is why we are keeping it secret now; we have patents on all the formulas for everything. It is difficult for anyone to connect the dots. Looking around the internet, you find ideas and information about solar power. Interesting concepts that never seem to go anywhere. You can imagine the pressure we will be under from the fossil fuel industry if we go public with solar absorbing metallic surfaces."

"Yeah, not very nice people. However, you can make billions," Josh said!

"The fossil fuel industry is part of the establishment. International, and always in control as much as possible of various governments. To a large extent, they have taken control of political parties in this country with their financial contributions to candidates and parties. We make enough money as it is. No need to compromise. Better not to go there right now."

"No worries, I understand and empathize completely."

Raoul Sr. said, "Okay, let's head home and get some lunch. I think everyone should be getting back there around now."

Walking back to the ranch, Josh's mind is overwhelmed with all the technical achievements and possibilities that the Arroyos have created. They do it quietly, under the radar of associated industries and interest groups. It will be a privilege to work with them. He needs to think it over. This is a private company, not a public institution. There is a chance for adventure here and a place to be creative. Not much job security even though they seem like good fair-minded people. He wonders what Adrienne will think of the offer.

Marcella and Tamara bring Lauren and Morgan to the stable close to the main house. Some horses have been brought in from the fenced pasture near the stable. Raoul Jr. is there and helps to saddle up the horses.

Each with a riding helmet, Lauren and Morgan ride on two smaller horses. They are guided by Marcella and Tamara, who lead the group on their horses.

Both children have ridden a few times before, including some riding lessons at a summer camp.

The northeast area of the house is primarily dry this year. Further East, it does get wetter. Morgan enjoys the ride. He is on the lookout for likely places pirates might bury treasure. He wonders what is behind a little clump of trees on the rise nearby. Everything is flat and primarily dry here, with no wetland or big rivers until you go farther east to St. John and Indian Rivers. This area and much of the ranch are slightly higher than further east. A bridle path leading out and around part of the property is fashioned so that the horses stay on the trail based on experience.

Lauren loves horses and horseback riding. Tamara gives her and Morgan some pointers on guiding their horses. Marcella looks at home on her favorite horse. She often travels around the property on horseback. It is her way of relaxing and enjoying the outdoors. In an hour or so, when it gets warmer, they decide to head back toward the house.

Additional guests arrive for lunch at the Arroyo ranch this day. Marcella introduces the new arrivals to Josh, Adrienne, and the children. Marcella likes to include vocations in her introduction to get people to know each other more quickly.

"This is my daughter Annie; she's an accountant and works with Arroyo Aerospace and Paul, keeping the studio running. Her husband, Captain Andrew Sun, is an airline pilot and may be back in town this afternoon. This is our son Bill, who is a lawyer in Orlando. His wife, Elizabeth, is a doctor of Internal Medicine. Morgan and Lauren, this is Richard. He is Bill and Elizabeth's son. He is in tenth grade."

Marcella continues the introductions, "Morgan and Lauren have already met Raoul Jr., who teaches programming at MIT. He's also one of our software and computer experts. This is our son Carlos who is also a programmer and IT specialist. Our eldest son Sam said he is coming over today as well. He isn't here yet."

"Sam's over in Port Canaveral with Andrew checking on some boats. He said they would get here soon," Raoul Jr. mentions.

The buffet lunch includes grilled burgers, chicken, Florida-style crab cakes, potato salad, greens, salad, fresh tomatoes from the garden, luncheon meats, cheeses, rolls, and fresh bread. There is green tea, wine, and soda too. Everyone makes their way over to the table and helps themselves.

With Adrienne and Josh in tow, Marcella leads the way toward a table. "The children did well with the horses. Lauren looks like she might have some equestrian potential."

"Yes, she did well at summer camp and loves horses," Adrienne said.

"We rode out over the pasture toward the east. It's dry right now. Farther east, it can begin to get swampy. We are not too far from the tributaries of the Saint John River."

Paul joins them, and they all make their way over to the table. Between bites, Paul tells Josh that he has been talking to Adrienne about his new movie project. He went on to tell Josh about the project. Annie's husband, Andrew Sun and Sam Arroyo arrive and join the others for lunch.

When lunch is finished, all migrate to the living room, where conversations continue. Paul talks about the plans for the movie and studio theme park. He said, "we hope to be in production by the end of the year. The first step is finishing the screenplay, casting, and building the full-scale spaceship set."

"I think it may take a year to complete the starship set. We can begin filming before the set is complete. While the life-size set is being built, we will shoot at the studio for various scenes. Preproduction is going to take about six months. Probably, this is a two-year project. If all goes well, we can launch, I mean to go into distribution for the film in 2020."

"When do you think you will open the set for tourists? Adrienne asks.

"Once the set is detailed enough for people to feel like they are in a real starship. Probably be awhile, close to the time it is finally complete."

Annie adds, "you can have some big screens set up outside the set so people can watch the shooting."

"Good idea," Paul said.

Adrienne mentions how excellent Paul's 1990 Land Rover restoration and EV conversion looks. Josh expresses his interest. He did not go into any details he learned from Raoul Sr. about the solar charging of the batteries. He'd leave that to Paul or Raoul Sr. to mention if the Rover has that feature.

"I'd love to see your collection of cars," Josh said. "I hear good things about them."

"Happy to give you a tour anytime," Paul said.

After a while, Josh and Adrienne thank Marcella and Raoul Sr. for their hospitality and a great day. Goodbyes are said to all.

Around four p.m., Josh, Adrienne, and the children head back to the beach. It is quiet in the car for several minutes. In the rearview mirror, Josh notices the children dozing off in the back seats.

Lowering his voice so as not to wake them, he asks Adrienne, "So, what do you think of the day?"

"Interesting, Paul offered me a job heading their advertising and public relations for the film and studio theme park. I told him I would help and think about how to proceed after I speak with you."

"Interesting. Raoul Sr. wants me to come and work with them on some projects. I can also do my work. I can even begin part-time. I believe we're both being recruited for Arroyo Aerospace and Arroyo Film Studio. I said I will talk to you and think about it."

"I told Paul I would help him freelance or bring his account into the firm. He only wants to work with someone they believe they can completely trust. Most of their family is involved in their businesses, so maybe we're interesting to them because we're a couple, and you have had a good working relationship with Tamara."

"We can try things out part-time or freelance and see how it goes before we make any big decisions. Let's sleep on it and see what we think."

Adrienne agreed.

After a pause, thinking aloud, Josh said, "There seem to be two tracks they are on. Paul with the movie and park and Marcella and Raoul Sr. with their company. I must tell you," Josh again lowered his voice instinctively, "they have an amazing company with ground-breaking inventions and a state-of-the-art high-tech lab. They are doing things with 3D printing that seem way ahead of the curve. They've made some fantastic discoveries and invented some techniques and procedures that have the potential to make billions, but they are keeping it all in-house and under wraps."

"They are quietly wealthy. Money is no problem. Paul said he made money from his films. He is putting up at least half of two hundred million dollars they are budgeting for the film and studio park."

Josh agrees, "Being a billionaire these days is like being a multi-millionaire twenty-five years ago. You're correct. They are not 'Nuevo riche." And not into doing things solely for the money."

"That's kind of refreshing these days," After a pause, Adrienne said. "What are they 'in it for?"

"I'd say they like being independent and self-reliant. No bosses, no corporate stockholders, and no pressure. They have a good life flying under the radar on which most of the entrepreneur population is visible. Speaking of flying, they have a corporate jet and a smaller prop plane parked in the back of a huge hangar building. You can't see the hangars and manufacturing buildings from the house."

"Doing their own thing. I feel like we must be special for them to want to include us in their corporate family, so to speak," Adrienne said. "Some of their children must be adopted, like Bill Arroyo, who is African American. No one seems to notice."

Just then, Morgan woke up. "Are we home yet?" he asks automatically.

"Not too far now," Josh said.

"I hope we can go back. I think I know where the pirates buried the treasure," Morgan mumbles as he goes back to sleep.

At the Arroyo ranch, it appears the family likes Josh and Adrienne. "Sincere and up-front people," Marcella said.

Sam, arriving late, only got to meet them briefly. He said he "got good vibes from them."

Tamara said, "I thought you would like them. Paul, do you think Adrienne will work with you on the film?"

"I do. She said she wanted to talk to Josh about it. She thinks, at the very least, she can help us get started. She knows what needs to be done."

Raoul Sr. said, "I don't think Josh can resist the chance to have so much tech at his disposal. He may not quit his professor job and the grant. I believe he might work with us part-time."

Marcella asked Tamara, "what will you do if he quits the university and the project?"

"I will quit too and come here and help with this project."

Raoul Sr. said, "one thing you can help us with, Tamara, is getting together all the technical requirements for sustaining life aboard the ship."

"Are you going to let Josh and Adrienne come into this blind? I think they need to know what we are planning at some point very soon," Tamara suggests."

"Of course, if they join us and things go well, we will update them as soon as possible. In the meantime, Bill can draw up some confidential disclosure waivers. Also, a contract for Josh that gives him the rights to anything he invents or discovers with his research," Marcella added. "You will need some contract with Adrienne, Paul. Maybe just the confidential disclosure waiver. We will apologize for the temporary deception."

"I'll see Josh on Monday at the University. Find out what he's thinking, Tamara said."

Sam is quiet, listening to everyone. "We'll need more people to make this happen as time passes. The cover story with the film and park is great. We will need people to work on the highly technical requirements for actual travel in space. Saying we're making things look authentic will only go so far until someone working on developing and installing these features begins to wonder why everything needs to work. You can say it is all part of the "illusion" we are creating or that it will be an educational aspect of the park. That only goes so far. Some people will have to be on a need-to-know basis even though they are part of our team. How do we screen them?"

Listening closely to her eldest son, Marcella said, "It will not be easy. We'll screen people as we go. Everyone we've hired or employed has been checked. We want people who fit in and, ultimately, become part of the mission. You know, going into space. We need to know they will not divulge the true nature of the mission to anyone in any way."

Paul remarks, "Security needs to be tight. On the plus side, if we handle this correctly, we publicize this as if this ship can fly. That it takes off and lands on earth, so any leaks or rumors all sound like advertising or PR hype. I have all kinds of ideas. I agree we need to be careful whom we recruit to be part of the project and who knows the actual mission."

Tamara asks, "How many people are needed to fly and maintain the starship in space? How many people will go on the first mission to wherever we go? When will we launch the ship?"

Sam said, "we are building a prototype, a working model first, to test all aspects of the ship construction and the drive. I've been working on design sketches for Galaxy One. Galaxy Two is the full-size version. The ships should also be able to take off and land from the earth."

Marcella said, "We are looking at an optimal date for any eventuality, including a flight to Mars. That date is October 6th, 2020. Over two years away. Mars will be at its closest point to Earth on that date."

Raoul Jr. smiles, "We'll just have to be careful we don't run into some rocket from NASA, the Chinese, Ramurt Rocket, or Musk of Space X. They are all talking about launching at that time."

Raoul Sr. added, "We have much planning to do about all aspects of this project. It is good to have a target date. Important to remember we do not have the limitations of rocket-propelled ships."

"This is the beginning. All these things will be worked out. As Paul says, we're in preproduction right now," Raoul Sr. said.

The family is enthusiastic about this undertaking. However, the reality of what they propose is beginning to be understood. In their favor is that data about crewed flights are out there from all the previous NASA missions. It is a matter of constructing the ship and making it space worthy.

Sunday morning, Josh and Adrienne wake up excited about the prospects of working with the Arroyos. Josh knows he can continue doing his research in a friendly environment, learn something and contribute to what Raoul Sr. and Marcella are doing. He is sure they have many more resources than he had seen on his brief visit. He can juggle things on his schedule at the university. Even take a leave of absence or put in for a sabbatical.

Adrienne is looking forward to promoting a film and studio park. She has experience with theme parks and looks forward to learning more about the filmmaking process. She needs to discuss with Paul more about bringing the account into the firm or establishing his in-house agency. Lots to think about.

Josh and Adrienne jog together on the beach toward the jetty. Approaching the Atlas rocket launch pads across the jetty, they feel a new connection based on meeting the Arroyos and thinking about Paul's film. They laugh as they exchange looks before turning around and heading south back to the condo.

After breakfast, before heading to the beach, Josh brings the family together in the living room in front of the open doors to the balcony and views the beach and ocean.

"Okay, can we have a short family meditation?" This is a regular weekend event at the Bennett's at home or the beach condo. They sit cross-legged in a circle in front of the doors. Lauren, Morgan, and Adrienne do the full lotus position. They can hear seagulls and the ocean waves washing up on the shore.

"Let's listen to the sounds of the ocean for a few moments, everything else out of our minds." After a minute or two, "Listen to your breathing. If anything else comes into your mind, acknowledge it, then go back to listening to your breathing. I set my timer for ten minutes. When you hear the beep, count backward from ten, and you're done."

Morgan and Lauren have practiced meditation and mindfulness with their parents for most of their lives. They are good at it by now. Josh introduced Adrienne to Buddhist philosophy before they were married. They practice mindfulness in their lives. They both study Buddhist philosophy and have read the sutras. They do not consider themselves Buddhists in a religious context, only philosophically and psychologically. Josh discovers through his research that many Buddhist ideas articulated thousands of years ago align with modern evolutionary psychology. In particular, they concern about how the mind works. The idea of "no self" is beginning to be understood in psychological terms. A "self does not generate head talk." It is all part of an elaborate group of survival mechanisms. Meditation allows one to be aware of thoughts and what they might represent.

After ten minutes, the family goes out to the beach for a while before heading back to Orlando. On the drive, earlier meditation is beneficial as the Beach Line traffic is heavy headed west to Orlando. For Josh, being solely focused on driving is a form of meditation. The sun beginning to set in the Western sky glares through the windshield at certain times as they head west to Orlando. Josh and Adrienne both lower the sun visors to help with the glare.

....

CHAPTER FOURTEEN

"Please Mr. Bear don't throw me in the briar patch!"

Three weeks after visiting the Arroyo ranch and returning to work at the university lab, Josh receives a phone call from Dean Cohen, the head of the department. She schedules a meeting with Josh and Tamara for that day. She does not go into detail about why they are meeting. "Probably something to do with the grant. It's been about a month since the Washington officials' visit," Tamara said. On their way to the meeting, they met Arno, also on his way to the Dean's office.

"Hi, Arno, any idea what this is about?" Josh asks.

Arno shakes his head negatively. "Nothing that I'm aware of at the moment." Before Arno can respond further, they are ushered into the Dean's office. They sit down in chairs in front of her desk. Dean Cohen gives them copies of a document.

"This is an official letter we received from the Pentagon. It is a notice that they are terminating your research project. It states that they believe there has been no positive progress reported. According to the grant terms, they can withdraw funding with 60 days' notice at any time they feel no progress is reported."

Arno reads the letter. "We were not notified about this. I received no correspondence," he said.

Josh reads the letter as a few emotions and ideas pass through his mind. First is a dark feeling of rejection, followed in a moment by a brightness revealing a path forward. This may answer his ambiguity about working full-time with the Arroyos. Subsequent guilt that he and Tamara had unconsciously engineered this happening. Fear is replaced by the notion that this letter is a gift. An inner voice tells him he needs to resist and not look too complacent or happy.

"I don't understand. This grant is supposed to be for two years. We have only been working for six months. Are they basing this on the recent visit? How can they pull funding because they think there isn't enough progress?" Josh said incredulously. There are no reporting deadlines!" Turning to Arno, "Aren't two agencies involved in this, not just the Pentagon?"

Cohen picks up the grant proposal and contract from her desk, "I've been through this with the chief financial officer, and they have several ways out of any grant. In this case, they cite 'no viable progress potential' and 'internal budget cuts.' I believe you have copies of these documents. You are welcome to review it and see if we missed anything."

Arno responds, "I'll check with my people. I believe this is coming from higher up than the Pentagon. The current administration has been doing some odd things. They tend to act unilaterally as if they have a 'Royal Mandate.'"

"They are giving us sixty days' notice. I think it says we have the right to appeal this decision within ten days," Josh said.

"If you have any information we can submit regarding 'progress potential,' that would be something we can use. Based on their visit a few weeks ago, I don't know what you might report," Cohen said.

"We're only six months into the project. We are conducting all the research we proposed at this point. What happens now with the grant canceled? Josh asks.

"The university requests that you wrap things up in the next thirty days. Then do a final report. Regarding your relationship with the university, Professor Bennett, you are tenured, so you return to your department and teach. Dr. Arroyo, we will try to find a teaching slot for you," Cohen said.

"If the grant is canceled, as it says here, there may be issues about who owns the research," Arno comments.

"If I remember correctly," Josh said, "There is only some sort of confidentiality regarding outcomes of the research. We haven't had the opportunity to have any outcomes. We have an intellectual property rights clause because Dr. Arroyo and I previously did the initial research. We used that research in the grant proposal. We are verifying this initial research as specified in the grant proposal."

Arno agrees, "I'll check and see if I can find out what's going on and get back to you as soon as possible."

The meeting ends as quickly as it started.

Leaving the building, Arno said, "Sorry about this. I know this project means a lot to you both. I had no idea anything like this was going on. I'll make some calls and try to find out what's happening. I have a feeling this is, in part, coming from one of the people who visited here three weeks ago."

"Thanks, Arno. I appreciate your looking into this. I don't know how to react. It's disappointing that we will not have a chance to do this research. It will not accomplish anything to be angry. We'll have to wait and see if an appeal is viable."

Arno is sure where the move to cancel the grant started. Ms. Walton was not happy after the visit to the project. No doubt, she talked up the original event with the White House and discovered it was all an illusion. The word illusion stuck in Arno's mind like a clue to something he was missing and could not get a handle on.

There was no warning about the grant termination from anyone in his world. Usually, he would have gotten a "heads up" from the company regarding any changes since there are always security concerns. The project and all computers and data are backed up. There is no notice to ban Professor/Dr. Bennett and Dr. Arroyo from the lab. He is anxious to make some calls as soon as he returns to a secure phone.

Away from Dean Cohen and Arno, Tamara and Josh drop their feigned concerned composures. They exchange knowing looks. Tamara whispers, "What do you think?"

"I don't know what to think except that they are unhappy that we did not create an invisible bunny. They decided the research would go nowhere.

Maybe they are upset that we asked them not to send us more animals for experiments. Hard to know with this administration. From what I hear, the administration has placed political appointees at the Pentagon and certain agencies. The only qualification necessary for these flunkies is loyalty to the king. They might be looking for an excuse to give the grant to someone else or divert the money to some other project like building a fence on our southern border," Josh said.

"If the grant is canceled, I'll go on summer break and work full-time at Arroyo Aerospace. Think about coming back in the fall. I don't know what kind of teaching position she has in mind."

"I've spent a couple of weeks working part-time in the lab at Arroyo Aerospace, and I think we can continue our research there since your parents are okay with it. Raoul Sr. said he has some projects he wants to talk to me about. In some ways, I'm relieved. My heart has not been into working on this project under the current circumstances. I do not want to let them know we are okay with the termination of the grant. I believe we have good karma on this development, 'when one door closes, another door opens," Josh said. "Here, the other door was already open."

"Yes, I understand. Exciting things are coming up at Arroyo Aerospace that I believe you will find interesting. I'm sure Raoul Sr. and Marcella will be speaking to you about these things."

Working with Paul on preliminary ideas, Adrienne has been detailing methods for public relations and advertising the film and studio theme park. I guess we'll spend more time at the ranch this summer," Tamara said. "Marcella told Adrienne that Lauren and Morgan were welcome there and that there would be other family children at the ranch during the summer. It will be fun for Lauren and Morgan. They can get some riding instruction and help on the ranch."

"For now, we'll wait and see what Arno turns up. He did not sound too optimistic," Tamara said.

"No, he didn't. We'll have to act like we are not happy with the termination of the grant. Otherwise, it may raise suspicion that we somehow set it up for some nefarious reason. All we wanted to do was get off the topic of the rabbit, not kill the project. We go along with things for now," Josh said.

"I agree. I think this will work out best if the grant is terminated." Tamara is excited about what they are doing at Arroyo Aerospace and wants to participate fully in the International Space Exploration Group project. She knows her parents and family are anxious to bring Josh in on the mission.

Arno checks with Simone to see if she has received any word about this project being canceled. She said she had not. She starts making calls to see what she can learn. She wonders if she will be recalled to D.C. Arno makes his calls and learns, as he suspects, that the word to drop the grant came from higher up than the Pentagon. Not directly from the CIA, either. There is an effort to divert funds from Pentagon projects to the fence construction on the southern border.

Arno lets out a long sigh. "The Great Wall of China didn't keep invaders out for long. The big fence they are calling a wall will not keep migrating people out. No one studies history anymore," he thought. "Walls and the Roman Army couldn't keep the so-called 'barbarians' out of Italy for very long. Hadrian's wall, built by the Romans in the North of England, didn't do much either. This whole 'wall' thing is a dog whistle to certain groups to gain their support." Arno leaves his office to break the news to Josh and Tamara.

Josh can tell by the look on Arno's face that the news is not good. He tries to mirror Arno's concern. Josh has already made up his mind that the termination of the grant is a good thing.

"Looks like there are several Pentagon projects that have been canceled with the money re-directed to building the fence on the southern border," Arno announces. "One of the president's appointees at the CIA recommended the project be terminated.

Josh took a moment to reply and shook his head negatively, "I heard that this administration is diverting money for the project for which Mexico was guaranteed to pay. I didn't think it would go this far."

Tamara adds, "We're not talking about much money for this project. We invested our time and reputation in it."

Arno said, "Apparently, they did some budget slashing of non-essential military spending. What comes under that title depends on your perspective. It would be best if you had a heavyweight backer and no detractors to survive these maneuvers. Honestly, your recent visitors did not get what they wanted out of their visit."

"Yes, that thought did occur to me, Josh said. "What do we do now?"

Arno shrugs his shoulders, "Well, you have 60 days' notice. You can wrap things up sooner. We need to write some final reports and do a debriefing."

Josh looks around the lab, "Everything we've been working on is on the database. Is there some procedure for saving it in case we can get back to it?"

"I think we treat it like the end of a project. As you said, technically, the research data is yours. You can come up with a final report. I'll use it for the debriefing. The university gets to keep whatever grant money it has received. There is no malfeasance here. The government is withdrawing funding," Arno summarized. "I believe you can apply to some other agency or source for grant money to continue your research since the government withdrew without cause before there was any outcome."

"Sorry, if there is any malfeasance here, it's the government diverting money from scientific research for political purposes," Josh said, sincerely angry.

Tamara said, "That's a good idea, Arno. There are other agencies and institutions that we can try."

Josh calms down. "Thanks for checking into things for us. I know sometimes I've been a pain. I will miss waving to you on these cameras.

"Not so fast. You aren't rid of me yet. I'll need the report and to do a debriefing. No worries, maybe we can grab some lunch or dinner soon."

"Sure, that will be great," Tamara and Josh said almost simultaneously. They got to know Arno in the past six months. They sincerely want to keep in touch. Tamara remembers that on one occasion, during lunch with Arno and a friend of his who works for the FBI, he talked about his growing up in Chicago and his favorite local dishes. Arno has always been friendly. He is professional and into doing his job, even though there is some indication that he is not crazy about this type of "babysitting scientist" work.

Tamara and Josh leave the lab and walk to a restaurant serving submarines, Gyros, and other sandwiches. According to Arno, the Gyros are not as good as those in Chicago, but they are all right. On their own now, it is a chance for Tamara and Josh to talk.

Josh asks, "What do you think?"

"I think we are okay. No grant. It's all about the government, not us. I did notice that the Walton woman and the General did not seem happy when they departed after the demonstration. As Arno said, 'there was no one to defend the project."

"Right, we can wrap up the project for the university in thirty days, then do a final report for Arno within the next thirty days. The cool thing is that our research is ours. We can take it anywhere."

"Yes, I believe we can bring it to Arroyo Aerospace. We're on the university payroll. We don't need special funding. I'm confident we can barter space and resources from Raoul Sr. and Marcella," Tamara said.

"I'll mention what has happened to Raoul Sr. when I come in this weekend. I'll talk to Adrienne about the situation. She will not be worried."

Tamara thinks that now is the time to tell Josh about the Arroyo secret project. She decides she will let Raoul Sr. and Marcella do that when they are all together. She is anxious to see how Josh reacts. He is somewhat unpredictable when it comes to surprises.

Over the next few weeks, Josh and Tamara write a report summarizing their project's efforts consisting of ninety-five percent research. They sit for a debriefing with Arno and Simone, who explain that they still have their top-secret clearances and that they cannot discuss or divulge anything they learned during this time.

"That is pretty much nothing," Josh said.

"I need to go through the motions. I wish you both the best of luck in the future. Will you both return to teaching in the fall?"

"It's an option. I might look at doing some research in the private sector."

Tamara replies, "I don't know what they want me to teach. I'll have to wait and see what happens. How about you, Arno, an empty lab now?"

"There are still a couple of other projects here in Florida. I feel Simone and I will be back in D.C. soon," Arno said.

"Let's keep in touch," Josh said.

They all shook hands and went their ways.

CHAPTER FIFTEEN

•••

Trustworthy people, I trust them. Untrustworthy people I trust them. Trust is a dimension of virtue. Dao De Jing

On your left" is often heard from bicycle riders passing. The weather is sunny and warm. People are out running, walking, biking, skating, skateboarding, and pushing their scooters. Some of the bikes, skateboards, and scooters have electric assist motors. It is Thursday morning. Josh and George jog around Lake Baldwin. Josh questions how someone standing on an electric scooter thinks doing so is exercise. People travel in both directions around the lake. Sometimes it gets crowded, but almost everyone is polite.

"Missed you out here for the last few days," George mentions.

"Yeah, sorry, I've been busy working on some new projects since they cut funding for the grant," Josh said.

"You mentioned they might, so it's final now? George asks.

"Yes, they cut funding. I hear It is diverted to fund building the fence between the U.S. and Mexico.

"God, what a waste of time and money. So, what now?"

"I'll go back to teaching in the fall. No worries."

"Wish I could get the summer off."

"I will be working on some research with an aerospace technology and manufacturing corporation. I'll be busy. I'm heading to see them tomorrow, so I cannot run."

"I won't be here either, headed to South Beach with Simone for the weekend."

"You and Simone hit it off. It's been a month or two now, right?"

"We appear to be on the same wavelength. Did I tell you she told me she works for the CIA?"

"Yes, that was very forthcoming of her."

"She has never tried to get any information from me about you. Now that your funds have been cut off, I wonder if she will get recalled to D.C.? She's waiting for an assignment in the China section. She speaks fluent Mandarin. The opening she was hired to fill has not been appropriated in that department. She's spinning her wheels."

"I think they have projects at other universities unless they got cut too."

"I'll find out this weekend," George replied as they passed some parents jogging with baby carriages along the lake.

Josh watches the toddlers bouncing in squeaky buggies as they are pushed. He wonders what the youngsters are thinking or what the experience of being "jogged" around the lake in a squeaky pram will have on them when they grow up. What will their dreams be like if these experiences remain in their memories? He decides they are young and might not consciously remember any of it.

"What does Simone think about the administration's trade policies with China?" Josh asks.

"She doesn't think this administration or State Department knows how to deal with China. These back-and-forth embargoes hurt both countries. China has many plans. The current U.S. administration is backing out of all kinds of international organizations, leaving the door open for China to step up and be the dominating power. In places like Africa, China is moving into business voids left by this administration's support of fossil fuels."

"Hard to understand why this administration is moving toward nationalist isolation. They are breaking treaties and agreements and even threatening NATO alliances. Doesn't make any sense. I think this guy gets advice from Moscow. He is in over his head, just a TV reality show actor."

"Another morning, 5K," George said as they finished running.

"Have a good weekend. Let's try to get back out on Monday or Tuesday if you want," Josh said as they stopped running and walked off the end of their run.

"You too, sure. I will touch base with you Sunday night. I'll text," George said as they parted.

Josh found Adrienne in the kitchen with the children when he got home from the run. She is driving them to school this morning.

"There are no classes tomorrow because of a teacher's conference, so I am thinking we can head out to the beach tonight," Adrienne said.

"Good, yes. I'd like to meet with the Arroyos this weekend," Josh replies.

"I'm meeting with Paul about his film. I'm working on two proposals. One is that he starts his in-house group, and the other is that I bring him to the agency. I talked to the agency's president, and she said she's okay with whatever I decide to do either way. If I bring him in, I will get the account and if I choose, stay as the agency creative director."

"They didn't think you're working with him outside the agency is a conflict?"

"Not really. I can funnel all the buys through the agency. They will do well. And if there are creative services he needs, we can put them through the agency. This will save Arroyo Studio from having to hire many people."

"Sounds good. We might spend time at the beach and the ranch this summer. Maybe move to the beach if you don't mind the commute?"

"No problem. We need to figure out what these two will be doing. Okay, time to go to school, everyone," Adrienne said.

In what seems to be a single motion, Adrienne sweeps up the lunches, Lauren and Morgan, and is out the door. Josh sits, thinking of nothing except the taste of the Oolong tea he is drinking. Later, he meditates and does some Tai Chi before getting a shower.

Josh does not go into the lab at all today. When the children and Adrienne come home, the family packs and departs for the beach, Josh lets Tamara know the family will be at the beach on Friday for the weekend, and he can meet with her, Raoul Sr., and Marcella. Tamara said she would set the meeting up for Josh and Adrienne to visit the ranch on Friday.

Before Arno leaves for his meeting in D.C., he and Simone meet at the lab, where it is tranquil.

"Professor Bennett and Dr. Arroyo are cleaning up things over the next few weeks. Writing a few more reports and removing personal items," Arno said, walking over toward where the rabbit cage used to be kept.

"Simone asked, "What happened to the rabbit?"

"I think Tamara gave it to a rescue center, Arno said. "It did not look very healthy, as far as I can tell."

"So, it never was really in a cloaked state?"

"That's what they say. Did you ever see the video of the first time he sprayed the rabbit?"

"I wasn't here at the time. Ms. Walton showed me a clip before coming here."

"Let's go up to the office. I'll show you that video and then the demonstration they showed of what happened. I want to get your opinion."

"Sure, something bothering you about the demo?"

"I don't know. The whole presentation is rehearsed, which is okay. I don't blame them with all the pressure."

Arno and Simone walk around the lab checking things and then go to Arno's office and the monitor room.

Arno brings up the first video, which is purely surveillance from one camera. "One thing to consider is that they did not want to do this experiment. Walton sent them the rabbit."

"Okay, we have one wide shot, with time code as they work. Josh comes into the picture with a spray bottle and proceeds to spray a fine mist of liquid which you can see has a translucent quality," Arno pauses the video for a few moments.

"A few seconds later, the rabbit disappears from the video." Arno rewinds the video and scrubs over the rabbit disappearing. "Josh and Tamara stand

there dumbfounded like they do not anticipate anything like this happening.
"

Simone tries to watch the video while listening to Arno's narration. Doing both things is difficult.

"Now, Tamara reaches out and touches the rabbit with both hands to see if it is there. They both stand there, trying to figure out what is going on. After a minute, Josh walks around to the other side of the counter. At that time, the rabbit reappears translucent and then solid. Josh picks it up and wipes it off with a towel."

Simone comments, "they both do look astonished."

"Yes, I believe so. Throughout this shot, we have a clear view of the cage and rabbit before and after. Let's look at the new video."

Arno cues up the recent presentation video.

"The focus looks a little soft," Simone said.

"Yes, I think there is some dust on the lens. I don't see any dust on the lens the day before. I checked the other cameras in the room, and they are all a little dusty too. It happens. Cleaners stir up dust. They don't touch the cameras."

Arno stops and starts the video, scrubbing certain sections and continuing his narration. It is challenging to hear what Josh and Tamara are saying. Arno seems most interested in Josh's actions.

"See anything unusual?"

Simone thinks for a moment. "Nothing unusual. However, there is one thing that is different from the first video. Josh moves the cage aside. The rabbit is not in the cage this time. And Josh blocks our view of the rabbit twice."

"Right, good observation. I can't think of anything that would make a difference because of that. He can't switch rabbits or do anything that makes any sense."

Simone thought about it for a while. "Looks legitimate. It is all an illusion."

"Like Josh said," Arno mumbles.

"Josh is unhappy about the whole 'rabbit' thing and the project's direction. Things go back to normal after the demo. He is upset when the grant gets pulled but doesn't fight it or project much disappointment. He isn't outraged. He isn't fighting to find some way to carry on. He and Tamara accept it quickly. At their debriefing, there are no tears," Arno said.

Simone asks, "Do you think they wanted the project to end? They did their best to keep it going. I believe they asked the dean to file an appeal."

"Let's suppose they want out for some reason; this is the perfect opportunity."

"Why do they want out, Simone asks?

"Maybe the research is showing results, and they want to take the project elsewhere? I don't know. It's just that the demo is too easy. Something is still bothering me."

"Do you want me to debrief Lin Lu, the lab assistant? She's finishing a few things at the lab and getting ready for summer vacation?"

Arno heard Simone speaking. He is a little lost in his thoughts, "Sure, that will be great. While you're at it, try to see if she knows anything we don't." After a pause, "Are you still seeing that lawyer friend of Josh's?"

Simone is not surprised that Arno brings up this subject. She sees George socially and does not think it is any of Arno's business.

"Look, he figured out I work for the same people you do. He's not going to tell me anything about Josh or his plans. He hasn't seen much of Josh because Josh, Adrienne, and the kids are at their beach condo on weekends. George doesn't know anything."

"It doesn't matter anymore. Just checking."

Arno knows that Simone is seeing George, and they spend time together. Getting into the subject isn't relevant at this point.

"Let me know when you debrief Lin Lu. We can then consider the lab and project closed."

"Sure. Let me ask you something. What have your dealings with Ms. Walton been like?

"She is a political appointee with an agenda that is not about national security. Now that this project is done, I will not have any dealings with her," Arno said. "Why do you ask?"

"Part of why she sent me down here was to check on you for some reason and to find out as much as possible about this project. I don't think the White House is the only entity she talks to."

"Any ideas who?

"No idea. Although several people have told me to be careful what I say around her."

"That's good advice," Arno said.

"I suspect I will get called back to D.C. soon. I hear a job is finally opening in the China division. I want to stay clear of her. You are right about an agenda," Simone said.

Thanks for sharing the information. If I hear anything, I'll let you know."

"Thanks," Simone replies.

....

CHAPTER SIXTEEN

"Do what you can, with what you have, where you are." —
Theodore Roosevelt

The children come with Adrienne for her meeting with Paul on Friday morning. Annie and a production assistant give Morgan and Lauren a tour around the studio, where sets are being taken down. Morgan takes pictures of the studio with his mobile phone. A behind-the-scenes tour is a new adventure for the children. They have many questions watching the sets come down. Adrienne reads sections of the screenplay for *Space Pioneers* while she and Paul discuss how Adrienne can work with the studio.

At Arroyo Aerospace, Josh, Tamara, Raoul Sr., and Marcella sit around a conference table in a secure room near the labs.

"The government cut the funding for our research. We are free to move on with other plans," Josh explains.

"You both are welcome to continue your research here," Marcella said.

"Thank you. I have the summer off, so I can spend time here. I am happy to help you with anything you may need," Josh said, speaking to everyone.

Raoul Sr. said, "Yes, we have some projects in the works that we believe will interest you. The projects are top secret. We want you to consider joining our team."

"If you don't mind, I will call Paul and have them head over here so we can talk together," Marcella said as she dialed Paul.

Josh said, "sure." He looks at the three sitting there and wonders what this top-secret conversation might be, especially since Adrienne must also be there.

"They are on their way. Let's head over to the hangar and workshop area to meet them. That will be a good place to start," Marcella said after she finished talking to Paul.

Sam is waiting for them when they arrive. Josh remembers that this part of the hangar is where he saw the corporate jet and the prop plane. The airplanes are gone. Everything else looks the same, including the high ceiling, auto lift, and workshop area, except for a minivan and a small tear-shaped vehicle with pods on the bottom instead of wheels parked near the door.

Marcella opens a folder. "We have a standard confidential disclosure waiver which we appreciate you agreeing to and signing. It's a formality we have all agreed to do. This includes everyone, family, and anyone we work with." Handing two copies to Josh, "one for you and one for Adrienne. There is also a short contract about working with us. You will notice a clause stating that you retain ownership of anything you invent or wish to patent. You retain rights to intellectual property when we work together. We only ask that you allow us to use those things you develop with us. You also will have fair use of our proprietary work in your developmental and research activities."

Josh scans the two-page document, "seems very fair to me. I'll give a copy to Adrienne, although I think she already has a deal memo with Paul."

"This is for Arroyo Aerospace Corporation," Raoul Sr. said as the door to the hangar opened. Paul drives in with Adrienne. Lauren and Morgan are still at the studio with Annie. She is going to drive them over to the ranch for a swim after they have some lunch.

Josh gives Adrienne a copy of the disclosure waiver, explaining that it is routine. They both sign the documents.

Raoul Sr. is a thoughtful, soft-spoken person. He can conceptualize many different concepts and somehow find a way to create what he believes will work. He understands that the risk of failure is only another step toward success. "First, let me say we are pleased you are prepared to work with us. Tamara has always said we should get together and share many ideas."

Raoul Sr. continues, "We are working on a project that recently had an important breakthrough. I'm going to start with a demonstration so that you can begin to understand that while our goals may seem impossible at first, they are achievable."

"Josh, please go with Paul."

"Are we going for a ride somewhere?" Josh thinks as he follows Paul to the minivan.

Josh reaches for the seat belt out of habit and fastens it as they sit in the van.

"Don't worry, it's painless," Paul said as he pushed a button on the dash that silently started the van's drive mechanism.

"Electric drive?" Josh asks.

"Not exactly," Paul said, moving the joystick housed where the shift handle might be for a transmission handle on the floor.

The van slowly lifts to about eight feet off the hangar floor a few seconds later. Paul moves the van forward toward where the others are standing. Josh lowers a window and puts his head out to see if they are really off the floor. About midway toward the group, Paul moves the van sideways while facing forward. Then back to the center, where it again moves forward. Soon, he moved the van in reverse, did a 360-degree turn, and then forward again until the van came close to the group. He softly lands the van on the floor.

Everyone applauds. Adrienne isn't sure if it is real, even though she can see Josh looking out the window. Sitting inside the van, Josh knows this is not an illusion.

Marcella walks with Adrienne over to Galaxy Zero, where Sam is waiting. Both gull-wing doors are up on the small ship.

"Would you like a short ride," Sam asks?

"Okay," Adrienne replies, "I get to ride in the sports car version."

Adrienne got into Galaxy Zero and pulled down the door. The inside looks sparse and functional.

"The seats are comfortable," she said.

"This model doesn't have all the 'bells and whistles it will have since it's a prototype. It does move a lot more gracefully than the van," Sam said.

Galaxy Zero gently floats up and sideways, maneuvering around the empty spaces in the hangar. Adrienne feels a little disoriented by the sideways movement. Otherwise, she is enjoying what she first assumes is a flying car.

Josh watches Galaxy Zero float around the hangar. He is amazed at how effortlessly it quietly moves up, down, and in any direction.

After a few minutes, Sam lands the prototype near the van. He and Adrienne get out of the vehicle and join the others.

Raoul Sr. said, "What you have experienced or watched just now is facilitated by a discovery, an invention that may ultimately change the world's technology. However, we don't feel the world is ready to use it humanely or peacefully. We also believe we should try to create a ready world. We can then share what we have discovered."

Josh's curiosity can no longer be contained, "how is this done?"

"The short answer is that we have created a drive that controls or manipulates gravity and even creates what you might call negative gravity. As you know, relatively speaking, "gravity" is not all that strong. We found a way to superimpose and amplify or reduce gravity fields. We use those fields to create negative or positive control, increasing it, decreasing the pull, or converting it to a push. The unit we built for the van and prototype is quite small," said Marcella. "Raoul Sr., Carlos, and Raoul Jr. can discuss the specifics with you.

Adrienne looks at Josh, then Paul and Tamara, "I just read most of Paul's screenplay. Forgive me if I sound delusional. I'm getting the feeling that your project might be space travel?"

Marcella smiled. She is impressed with Adrienne's ability, analysis, and willingness to take a risk with her intuition. "You are correct," she said. "We want to launch a prototype spaceship and our main ship into space by 2020 or 2021. At that point, we will go public. Until then, all our preparation, work, and building will be done under cover of Paul's film and studio theme park.

The film is real, and so is our adventure. We're sorry we could not fill you in completely earlier. We hope you both will join us."

Josh's head is spinning with so many questions and ideas that he does not know what to say, except to himself, "unreal," and aloud, "wow!"

"Sam's background is in boat and ship design. Together we are drawing up plans for a scale model, a prototype of a larger ship we call Galaxy Two. The prototype, Galaxy One, will be about fifty feet in diameter. It is a little difficult to describe the shape we envision. Perhaps a circular wedge shape or teardrop comes close. In some ways, a supersize version of Galaxy Zero, as Sam calls his sports car prototype. We will use Galaxy One as a test ship for design, life support, and flight. We will 3D print the hull and other parts here at Arroyo Aerospace," Raoul Sr. said.

"There will be larger drives for the new ships than we've built. We thought of using the jet for a test, but its aerodynamics are only for going forward. Our needs are closer to marine design than atmospheric-type aerodynamic requirements," Sam said.

"What materials will you use for the hull?" Josh asks.

"That's where you can be of help, Raoul Sr. said, "we have developed some heat-resistant materials that combine Titanium alloys with other materials. Very lightweight, with heat-resistant qualities, but we need to make them stronger. The hull will have four layers, including cushioning behind the outermost hull section. Two layers inside the outer hull, including a water shell, accommodate electrolysis for separating oxygen from the H2O. Then a final interior layer. We have to consider weight and thickness."

"Looking forward to getting started," Josh said enthusiastically.

Adrienne nodded her approval, "this is very exciting. Where will you go? What will you do in space?"

"We are drawing up plans and a timeline for everything. We may need to establish bases on the moon and Mars, to begin exploring the solar system. These bases will become colonies if we can establish life support and a reason for being there. For example, mining mineral deposits that could be shipped back to earth," Tamara said.

"Ultimately, a real space station can be built at one of the Lagrange Points, L4 or L5. These are places in space with equilibrium and a clear view of the Earth or the Sun. Gravity is in balance. The U.S. already has some probes at L2, which is about a million miles from Earth in the opposite direction of the Sun. They plan to park the new James Webb space telescope at L2. The Earth, Moon, and Sun are behind it, giving a clear view of deep space," explains Raoul Sr. "L1 and L2 are unstable. Without constant adjustments, an object will slip out of balance and head toward the Sun or Earth. L3 is directly opposite the Earth behind the Sun."

Paul remarks, "Anyone remember the Man from Planet X film?" A planet we cannot see because it is hidden there at L3, permanently blocked from being seen from Earth by the Sun. No one admitted they remembered the film.

"We don't know the reaction here on earth if we go public. Will we be allowed to continue, go out into space, and return without big corporations or government interference? We don't know exactly what our government here in the U.S. will be like in the future. It does seem like there is a turn toward an autocratic, even a totalitarian, administration evolving as soon as the next election cycle or in the future. We will need to be prepared for any eventuality. Our drive makes all manner of fossil fuel rockets and electrical means of propulsion obsolete," Tamara said.

"You're correct," Josh answers. "This discovery and invention may well threaten the entire political and economic establishment of the world. You are doing the right thing by keeping it confidential. The timetable gives us about three and a half years until the big launch in late 2020 or early 2021, right? The launch of the Galaxy Two ship?

"Yes, it will be built as if it were the set for my film," Paul said. "Since it is part of the Gateway to the Galaxy theme park, we can posture that it must be as authentic as possible as if we are going to launch it. I'm even thinking that we can go as far as to announce a tentative date for the launch as if it is publicity for the film going into distribution. For now, only an idea. We'll wait awhile."

"How large is it going to be? Even with the gravity drives, won't it be challenging to launch and achieve enough velocity to leave Earth's gravity? Josh asks.

"That's what we'll be testing. We believe this isn't about achieving a phenomenal speed to escape the planet and go into orbit or space. Rockets need a tremendous lift to break through the earth's gravity and achieve orbit speed. It's mostly about lift. We are using gravity in a controlled way. We theorize that we can achieve orbit at any speed. Of course, we need to be at certain high speeds to maintain that orbit. We may need multiple drives for the larger ship. We've got a lot of work to do before we decide on several things. For example, I believe we can use our drives to create artificial gravity on the ships. This may require a separate device or derive its power from the main drive. There is a lot we don't know at this point," Raoul Sr. said, laughing. "We've never built a spaceship before."

Marcella smiled, "I'm sure you have a lot more questions. How do you each feel about what we are proposing? Do you think you want to join us in this endeavor?"

"It's a lot to take in all at once," Adrienne said. I am honored that you want to include us in this fantastical enterprise."

Josh nods his head in approval of what Adrienne is saying. "I am also honored that you want us to be a part of this amazing venture. Based on what Adrienne has said, I believe you can count on our participation."

Raoul Sr. and Marcella step forward, "welcome to the family!" They hug Josh and Adrienne, as do Paul, Sam, and Tamara.

"How about if we head back to the house for some lunch? I'm sure Morgan and Lauren are wondering where you are by this time," Marcella said.

"You may be ahead of me on this. We are not telling the family's children about our actual plans since they are too young to understand our security concerns. We can talk about the movie as much as we want, though."

Josh and Adrienne are the first outsiders recruited to work on the project. They have been carefully chosen for their skills and professions. Also, how they fit in with the others involved. The Arroyos have always tried to build a unique organization, starting with their family. Some of the children in the family are adopted but always treated as if they were biological offspring no different than the others. The times of each baby's adoption are arranged to fit in with when the biological children are not being born. While some of the adopted children are of different ethnic backgrounds, the Arroyo's never explain why this is to the other children. The children never have any questions about it until they get older. Ethnicity and the notion of race are not necessary for the family. Everyone is an Arroyo and an American. Their culture and what they make of it is human. Since meeting Josh and Adrienne, the family intuitively feels empathetic vibes with them.

Josh is still determining why he is enthusiastic about this project and working with the Arroyos. Up until now, he did not think about space travel very much. While he thinks NASA and the space programs are important, he didn't anticipate a human-crewed expedition to the solar system in his lifetime. The Arroyos change all that. He is now part of this fantastic idea that may influence human evolution. He needs to catch up on space travel and the space-time continuum. There is something else. Perhaps unconsciously, he is attracted to being part of a large family. He grew up alone, an only child. His parents are loving and supportive but emotionally distant. He has friends in high school and then loses track of them. Returning from his military service and studying abroad, he made new friends. Ultimately, they all went their ways, with different lifestyles, marriages, and career paths. Then he lost his parents. This unique opportunity is a chance to be part of something that will result in an outcome more significant than the sum of its parts in many respects.

The coming months necessitate the careful recruiting of individuals to complete the project. They will be part of the crew and team who launches the ships into space. The Arroyos do not know exactly how the enterprise they name the International Space Exploration Group will evolve or how quickly they can start exploring other planets. The future holds many alternatives. Those who join the team to examine and possibly establish bases on other planets might not be able to return to Earth. Soon new people need to be recruited who can live off earth indefinitely. They can establish new lives and families away from Earth. There are many ways this project may evolve. Priorities and goals might change. The Arroyos want a group of people who can work together as a team. Individuals who have specialties and are partners in the venture. New working, social and political rules need to evolve for survival in space.

The Arroyos are concerned with the politics that may emerge on earth over time around their efforts. No matter how ideal the situation is, it is human nature to become dissatisfied. Find something or someone to blame for one's current situation. Group participation and morale are a deep concern.

Based on events happening as the year progresses, it becomes clear to everyone involved in the project that the world is becoming more dangerous. Perhaps it is time to leave the planet. Even in the face of the increased intensity of natural disasters like forest fires, massive hurricanes, and other natural disasters in the U.S., the administration withdrew from the Paris Climate Accords. There is no humanistic reason for such an action. In Las Vegas, a gunman with automatic weapons killed fifty-nine people and wounded another five hundred. Nothing is done to stop the mainly unregulated sale of military-grade automatic weapons to individuals. More shootings occur, including some based on racial animosity. White supremacist groups staged marches and riots. International relationships are being destroyed while the administration tries to reach accords with authoritarian regimes in Russia, North Korea, and right-wing autocratic governments like Turkey and Brazil. It looks like the administration is on a path to rip apart and undermine the democratic institutions in the United States. Civil strife undermines the country's strength in a world where other states constantly challenge the strongest nations for that role. Even with imperfections, America is the leader of the "free world." A weakened leader signals vulnerability to those seeking to usurp its power.

Over the summer break from the university, Josh begins working closely with Raoul Sr., Marcella, Tamara, Carlos, Sam, and others on critical aspects of the project. Carlos gives Josh a rundown of the security features in the lab. A separate Virtual Private Network (VPN) channel for the lab connects with a private "dark web." It uses a proprietary browser Carlos and Raoul Jr. developed. They do not stop there. The signal bounces back to another VPN server and a couple more servers.

The research they do online will go through these scrambled connections. Josh agrees he will not do any non-classified activity on the lab computers. He can use another network outside the lab, in the conference room. Josh understands the need for high security.

When the new semester starts in the fall, Josh will continue a light teaching schedule and works at Arroyo Aerospace. He commutes from Orlando or stays at the beach condo. Adrienne can handle a lot of Paul's work remotely. She usually comes to the beach on the weekends with the children.

Josh's interdisciplinary academic background facilitates collaboration with Raoul Sr., Marcella, Sam, Carlos, and Tamara. His study and research complement the experience and practical applications that the Arroyos use to create their inventions.

Raoul Sr. and Marcella always continue studying and researching ideas that interest them. In the outside world, some academics and scientists are caught up in their narrowly defined disciplines. Josh is also able to explore ideas outside his academic specialties. He is intrigued by many diverse theories and research.

Scientists have created anti-matter and even a type of anti-gravity. The problem with anti-matter is that it annihilates matter when it comes in contact. This causes a big flash of energy that is difficult to control. The Arroyos managed to isolate positrons and use them to amplify gravity and manipulate it as a propulsion. They never have a formal theory. They experiment with ideas and resources until they discover something that works. Josh appreciates their accomplishments and process of discovery. He needs time to understand the practical outcomes from a theoretical standpoint.

....

CHAPTER SEVENTEEN

*"Our minds are like mirrors. We need to clean the mirror
often so that dust will not obscure reality."*

By late spring 2018, Galaxy One is almost ready to be flown. It reminds Josh of an aerodynamic teardrop in reverse. The narrow top of the teardrop is the bow of the ship. The exterior color of the hull is a light titanium-gray that looks like rain clouds on a dark day. The prototype has a wide hull and a flattened bottom that grows out of the curved sides of the teardrop. The ship comprises three levels, with the first under the swept-back roof. This first level holds the control center and a separate passenger area. The upper two levels are insulated from the lower third level. The second level includes support resources, servers, computers, navigation, hydrolysis, water, and other life support. It also consists of a small galley, a cubicle with berths for sleeping, a toilet, a shower, and a fully stocked infirmary. The third level houses the drive, cargo bay, and an airlock.

The gravity propulsion system housed on the third level moves the ship in any direction using the ship's thrust and steering controls. These controls have been tested on the early prototypes. Next, they will test controls at considerable altitudes and high speeds. Depending on gravity and electromagnetic fields, thrust and acceleration are generated positively or negatively. Like an ocean wave, Earth's gravity is used to carry the ship into orbit, space, and beyond. Then the system will find other gravity fields like the sun, moon, or other celestial bodies. The drive floats the ship into Earth's orbit and can be regulated for speed. The ship's artificial intelligence program allows the subtle use of magnetic and gravity fields.

Sam Arroyo spends months designing and supervising the hull fabrication, which must meet several criteria. It needs added strength to leave earth and fly in space. The ship and hull must be lightweight. He creates a hybrid cross between a fuselage used for airplanes and the transverse frame used in submarines. In its finished form, the hull will have four layers. The exterior layer must withstand high heat, absorb or deflect radiation and be strong enough to resist small meteor or space debris hits.

Using the formulas designed by the Arroyos, the outer hull absorbs solar and magnetic energy to keep batteries and other electrical assets running. By incorporating hydrogen molecules in the alloy, Josh and Tamara help engineer the hull metal to reflect high- and low-energy gamma rays or cosmic radiation. It is crucial to deflect certain solar eruptions that cause electrical and radiation problems in space. Josh and Tamara work long hours with Raoul Sr., Marcella, and Sam, creating the final alloy for the hull and frame of the ship. Josh is engaged in the project. He feels he is a part of something transformational and vital. He is looking forward to the testing of Galaxy One.

The alloy the team develops is based on technology that combines a ceramic and titanium alloy molecule mixture that is lightweight and can be used in the Arroyo 3D printing processes. The formula eliminates resins that do not respond well in 3D printing. In addition to this formula, the anti-radar stealth paint formula is added. The vessel will be virtually undetectable by conventional radar but not by the human eye. Josh and Tamara resume research on an actual surface cloaking device. They need more time to develop it. They can incorporate light-refracting molecules into the alloy, which helps decrease visibility in the light spectrum that humans perceive. The exterior hull material is, of course, resistant to water.

A special coating is applied to the interior side of the outer hull to make it sticky enough to accept the second layer. This second layer is a powdered, aerated, and hydrated coquina-based formula that dries like Styrofoam and is lightweight. Tests show that this substance helps with radiation and impact from small meteoroids by forming a cushion behind the outer hull.

The third layer of the hull houses micro thin flat containers of water that connect and are housed in sections of the transverse frame. In addition, the space between the second and third layers of the hull contains polyethylene plastic (RFX1) to help shield the interior from cosmic radiation that makes it through the outer hull and second layer. The hull's interior or fourth layer is a less thick layer of the same alloy used for the exterior hull, without the solar absorbing qualities and stealth technology. The 3D printers make large hull sections bonded together on the transverse frame of the ship. The entire thickness of all the hull layers is three inches. The traverse frame is an aluminum and steel alloy developed for maximum strength and lightweight.

The drives are housed in a reinforced and heavily insulated space to contain radiation in the rear of the belly of the ship. Drive housings are firmly attached to the ship's frame and the bottom layer's reinforced deck. Batteries and fuel cells are also housed in this area. An electric turbine engine is installed in the drive compartment area for hydro electrolysis. The gravity drive needs high-voltage electricity to function. An RPS-powered thermo-electric generator supports this requirement. A second smaller auxiliary drive is used for artificial gravity in the ship. The engineering and drive area is shielded from the forward part of the third level that carries cargo and auxiliary supplies. Retractable landing pods are housed in hull compartments under the ship. The cargo area includes an airlock for loading and unloading cargo.

The decks for the first and second levels are an experiment. The space under the floors is charged by an auxiliary gravity drive to provide artificial gravity for levels one and two. It is only possible to fully confirm proper functioning once they are in zero gravity.

The first deck holds the flight control center, eight passengers, and a restroom. The ship has an airlock entrance on the second level. It is equipped with a collapsible and extendable metallic tube that allows docking with another ship in space. Next to the airlock chamber, there is a closet with one astronaut extravehicular mobility unit (EMU) space suit. Raoul Sr., through a NASA friend, learned years ago about surplus EMU suits that are either unused, no longer repairable, or not serviceable. Raoul Sr. makes a deal to buy two suits that are to be destroyed, auctioned, or given to a museum. Over the years, he and Marcella repaired, reconditioned, and upgraded one of the suits with state-of-the-art tech. One EMU suit is now fully functional.

As far as launch and entry suits are concerned, it is believed that their only purpose is protection should the ship lose pressure. This is not a rocket ship blasting off from the Earth to orbit. Based on technology, readily available basic pressure suits are obtained. The helmets are 3d-printed, as are other parts. The suits themselves can be instantly pressurized in the unlikely event the Galaxy One cabin loses pressure at any point.

Sam organizes the ship's construction in an adjacent hangar, where a control center is also being built. This hangar is specially insulated for communications security. Everyone at Arroyo Aerospace is involved in the building effort, with the heavy lifting done by robotic devices powered by gravity drives.

Once the transverse frame is in place, each deck from the bottom up is installed. Raoul Jr. and Sam operate the robotic devices used to lift heavy parts. It is incredible to see them float the large exterior hull panels up to the frame, where they are seamlessly bonded together. After the cushion layer is bonded to the inner side of the hull, the unique water sleeves made from a thin, lightweight aluminum alloy are installed. Sleeves are connected so water can flow throughout the hull. Next, the air pressure and circulation system are installed on all decks. Now the layer of polyethylene plastic (RFX1) is applied. Electrical wiring and all communication lines are installed on top of the RFX1. Once all this is finished, the inner hull layer with removable panels is added.

The forward windows on the first level for the control center are made of aluminum silicate glass and fused silica glass. All windows throughout the ship have three optical quality panes, including an interior pressure pane made of tempered alumino-silicate. This system is required because the pressure inside the vessel is higher than the vacuum of space.

When the hull is finished, a unique glaze of finely powdered glass is applied to the belly of the craft as a precaution against heat and burn-up on re-entry into Earth's atmosphere. The rest of the exterior may also get this treatment if needed. The exterior hull material is believed to withstand re-entry heat since the ship's gravity drive controls the rate of ascent and descent. The vessel can slow, slide, and float into the atmosphere at a significantly reduced speed.

Marcella, Josh, Sam, Tamara, and Raoul Sr. gather, viewing the titanium-gray hull of the nearly finished spacecraft. Raoul Sr. said, "we are almost ready to install the drive and fuel cells. Carlos is installing all the flight and life support programs. There is new software for the drive and space navigation."

"Looks great, built in under a year, what major corporations take years to design," Josh said.

Sam replies, "We didn't have to deal with all the corporate and government levels of bureaucracy, including years of testing. We are taking a calculated risk. "

"Most of the construction supplies we require are from inventory since we work for aerospace industry clients. I'm trying to stock up now for Galaxy Two, "Raoul Sr. explains. "It is four times larger."

"I hope the world buys the movie set story. Galaxy Two is going to look very real," Sam said. "We'll get the frame up as quickly as possible after testing Galaxy One."

Josh asks, "Maybe we can erect a big tent or canopy over the field while the frame and hulls are assembled. For privacy and weather protection."

"Not a bad idea," Marcella said.

"Good cover story," Raoul Sr. said, always ready for a pun. We can quickly build a large hangar that will be sturdy and ensure privacy.

"What will the test flight for Galaxy One consist of?" Josh asks.

"Captain Sun, Annie's husband, Andrew, will be here this weekend to supervise all the preflight checks. Once those are complete, Marcella answers, we can move the ship outside for tests.

"We can fly at night. We're checking all the airline flight schedules for next week for what's flying over or nearby commercially. One tricky thing, not far away, we have Patrick Airforce Base, which is south of Coca Beach. Also, Tyndall Airforce Base up North in the Panhandle. We are near the space center at Cape Canaveral. They have state-of-the-art long-range radar. There's no way to know exactly what either airbase is doing. If our stealth radar deflection works, they will not know we're out there. The first test will be up to a certain altitude, maneuvering, and back down again. Probably do this in the middle of the night. Next up and out over the ocean for more altitude tests," Raoul Sr. proposes.

"Have you tested the stealth radar deflection?" Josh asks as Paul joins them.

"Sure, I test it all the time on the Beach Line and other roads around here," he said jokingly. Technically it's called radar reflection. Our top fighter plans use it to disguise their stealth characteristics. I can even send them back a false speed reading. Maybe we could send them back a fake image?"

Tamara laughed, "A Corvette doing 75 mph? Maybe a flock of birds doing Mach 2?"

Everyone laughs, "Let me think about it, Raoul Sr. said. I'll run it by Carlos. Our radar stealth mode will be enough unless someone sees us. By the way, this ship's speed in the upper atmosphere is many times the speed of sound. Once in space, much faster. We have some technology that we believe can suppress the sonic boom in the lower atmosphere if necessary. It can also be tested."

"That's why we chose the teardrop shape. Aerodynamically ready for high-velocity speed in the atmosphere," Sam said. "Once we leave earth, there's no atmosphere to impede speed. With the gravity accelerator, we can use the push-pull of various bodies in the solar system to move at high speed."

"What about flight suits?" Paul asks.

"We'll have pressure suits onboard." With the cabin pressurized and things going as planned, we shouldn't need them. On the test flight, we will wear them, Raoul Sr. answers. "Once we start going into outer space, we will have some EMU suits for exiting the ship for any reason, like walking on the moon or going outside the vessel for a repair. These EMU suits are costly. During the tests with Galaxy One, we have one reconditioned suit that will be on the ship in case of emergency."

"We start spending any time in orbit, and someone is going to notice," Paul said.

"UFO sighting? We can be careful and avoid flashing by the International Space Station," Marcella said. "All we can do is stay elusive for as long as possible. Sooner or later, someone will see us, but no one believes in UFOs, do they?"

"There's been much publicity about UFOs recently, including government agencies' statements about sightings. They're still 'Unidentified Flying Objects.' It seems if we have alien visitors, they will be high-tech enough to remain unseen," Tamara said. "Someone should study times in history when there were more UFO sightings worldwide. Look at the time of year, economy, and other factors."

"Is our airlock compatible with the International Space Station," Josh asks.?

Yes, it is," answers Raoul Sr. Docking may be a little tricky because of the shape of our ship. We need some extension devices to connect. We have a collapsible version that we are installing."

Carlos came down the steps from the ship's airlock door.

"I believe you can install the drive now, he said. By the way, are we using the name Galaxy One for this ship?

Raoul Sr. answers, "Yes, Galaxy One. When we build the next ship, it will be Galaxy Two."

"Sounds good to me," Paul said. The assembled group agrees.

"One thing I'm curious about is communication. Scrambling voice and other signals at the ground control center is no problem. Can satellites or other receivers pick up our communications here on Earth?" Paul asks.

"We're going to use ultra-high frequencies that even the NSA may not seriously monitor, although they do monitor certain types of high-speed communications worldwide," Carlos explains. "All anyone will hear, if they have a radio telescope dish, is unintelligible screeching. We'll also have conventional communications to communicate and listen to various sources like the military. We have the internet. I've set up an anonymous server on something I am calling the 'Uber' net. It's more remote than the dark web and not nefarious. The server IP address is virtually invisible. Signals bounce off twelve random satellites. We can use this for encrypted, scrambled, two-way air-to-ground communication. It transmits at twice the normal speed of high-speed data programs. It requires a key on either end. The first is to scramble the encrypted data, and the second is to unscramble and decrypt at the receiving box. The encrypted data is scrambled into seven random letter and number blocks. It's an old technique but updated with digital encryption scrambling. They say that every transmitter has a signature. We created randomized fake signatures for our transmitters to cover any tracks."

"Okay, we'll install the drive via the rear airlock hatch. That should take a day or two to secure. Then we'll do a system test as soon as possible," Raoul Sr. said.

Before heading back to the lab with Josh, Tamara takes Marcella aside. "I got a call from Sharon. She is coming to visit "Florida" next week. She's in Washington now. She heard about Paul's film. She has administration business in Tallahassee. When she's finished her business, she wants to stay with me overnight in Orlando and visit here to see family."

"How long does your sister plan to be in Florida?"

"She plans to come to Orlando from Tallahassee on Friday evening and go back to D.C. on Sunday, Tamara replies."

"Well, if you can handle it, have her stay with you and then bring her here to visit here on Saturday afternoon. We'll keep her away from the hangar. You can take her over to see Paul's studio," Marcella suggests.

"Paul says he can only tolerate her for a short time. She always goes off on some far-out political conspiracy or the latest right-wing propaganda," Tamara said.

Marcella nods her agreement. "I'll talk to Paul. We can keep her completely in the dark about family plans. She probably wants to know about the film so she can tell her friends or give Paul some unwanted advice. We can make some lunch on Saturday afternoon. Hopefully, you can keep her occupied."

Tamara sighed, "I'll do my best. I don't want to hear about how wonderful this administration is and how they will make the country wonderful."

Later that day, Raoul Sr., Carlos, Raoul Jr., Sam, and Marcella, using the robot lift device, float the drive onto the ship and secure it to the deck and frame. This version of the drive is much larger than Raoul Sr. installed in the van. They also install the auxiliary drive. The gravity drives for the Galaxy Two spaceship need to be even more significant. There might be two or three of them depending on the ultimate size of the ship and if it will be launched in sections or as one big vessel. For logistical reasons, they will likely launch the entire ship from the earth rather than in sections to be assembled in space.

Adrienne set up an advertising and public relations campaign for the film and the Gate to the Galaxy studio theme park. There are periodic releases about the progress of preproduction for the film. Interviews with Paul Arroyo are scheduled. He talks about the film and how he plans a full-scale model of the spaceship as a set for tourists to visit. The ground where the spacecraft will be built is a football field size concrete pad. The actual full-size ship begins construction as soon as the prototype is tested. Activity is documented and photographed for the behind-the-scenes documentary and publicity. The tourism side of things can start once most of the ship is built and filming of scenes in the vessel are underway.

Sharon arrives at Tamara's Orlando condo for her weekend visit on Friday evening. Blond with green eyes, she is visually the opposite of Tamara. They always got along before Sharon went away to the evangelical university. Tamara becomes worried that Sharon will end up in some conspiracy cult group. Once Sharon gets rested from the flight to Orlando, they decide to go for dinner. Sharon talks about her job with the administration and how she met the president several times. She asks Tamara about Paul's new movie.

Tamara tells her it is a science fiction story about the future exploration of the solar system.

"You know the president started the Space Force," Sharon said. "It will have a base here in Florida."

"Really," Tamara said. She had already heard about the Space Force on the news.

"It became official in December 2019," Sharon said. "I want to tell Paul about that."

"I'm sure he'll be interested to know," Tamara said with a straight face.

The rest of the conversation over dinner is about Sharon and her life in D.C. For Sharon, the city is full of transient people like politicians, lobbyists, and government workers. She tells Tamara she feels insecure living there. She doesn't believe many people of sincere faith are involved in politics.

Saturday afternoon, Tamara and Sharon drive to the ranch for lunch. Marcella is happy to see them. During lunch, they chat and listen to Sharon talk about the administration and her job as an advisor. When they finish lunch, Tamara and Sharon drive to Paul's Studio. Tamara points out the large concrete pad where Paul will build the film's set. Tamara explains that a studio theme park will be built around the spaceship set.

"I'm surprised our parents went for that," Sharon said. They're so private about everything."

"Well, I guess Paul talked them into it. They have always been supportive of his films."

"Yes, I know they backed his first film," Sharon said peevishly.

Paul and his girlfriend Stacy are at the Studio with Annie. Annie is going over the accounts for the studio. Paul and Stacy are looking at sketches for the sets based on the screenplay. The scenes are based on the interior configuration of Galaxy Two. After greetings, everyone sits in the studio lounge and green room area.

"What's the name of the new movie?" Sharon asked.

"Our working title is "Space Pioneers," said Paul. "It takes place sometime in the future when people start to explore the solar system and the galaxy."

"When will you be doing the casting?"

"I think in a month or two. We have inquiries from several agents who have interested clients. Pretty big names."

"I have some friends whom I can recommend," Sharon offers.

"Great."

"Tamara said you will build a big spaceship set and create a theme park about the movie."

"Yes, once the set gets built and we're filming, we will probably be ready to open up for tourists by next year, mid-2019 at the latest."

"I've been telling Tamara about the president's Space Force. Maybe you can mention it in the film. I'm sure the Space Force will be in space in the future."

Stacy did a subtle roll of her eyes that only Paul could see, "So what's this 'Space Force' going to do for now?" Stacy inquires.

"They will have installations at certain Air Force bases, one right here at Patrick, near Satellite Beach. They have a support rescue team for astronaut recovery. Everything will be official by the end of 2019."

"I think Patrick Airforce base probably already has that mission," Stacy said.

"Well, everything will be coordinated through the Space Force in the future."

"Where will the other bases be, and what will they be doing?" Paul asked.

"I think the main headquarters is slated for Huntsville, Alabama, and other bases in Colorado, California, and elsewhere," Sharon replies. It is an official new branch of the military. Who knows, maybe they will look for aliens?"

"With no presence in space," Paul remarks. "Maybe the administration can build a space station for them?"

"More tax dollars for the military," Stacy said.

"Well, anyway, it's for the future of American security in space," Sharon said.

"So, what do you advise the White House on?" Tamara asked, trying to change the subject.

"I advise on the concerns of Christians in the country, moral values, and other issues," Sharon replies.

"Evangelical Christians?" Paul asks.

"Yes, other Christians too." "This president wants to appoint Christian judges in the courts, including the Supreme Court. Hopefully, to uplift the moral values of the country."

Paul almost blurted out that he didn't think the president had any moral values, but he didn't want to start an argument.

"Does the president believe in the separation of church and state?" Paul asks.

"This is a Christian country, founded by Christians," Sharon declares.

"Dubious Christians. I believe many were atheists. In the first thirteen colonies, mostly people who wanted to leave England and Europe," Paul said. "Religions not considered legitimately Christian, like the Quakers and others, came to escape persecution at home. In addition, there were indigenous people here before any Christians arrived. They had their own beliefs."

"And I believe the country's founders were very emphatic about the separation of church and state," Stacy adds.

"We want to uphold Christian values, like ending abortions and keeping marriage only between biological males and females. Democrats are destroying the morals of the country."

Stacy replies, "Speaking of morals, we have a president who was married three times and cheated on all his wives. He's certainly no 'moral' Christian Republican."

Tamara can see where the conversation is going and changes the subject again. "So, Paul, who are some of these 'big names' interested in being in the movie? You can tell us."

Paul laughs. I would if I could. I know right now that the agents who call represent top actors. I can't discuss these inquiries. We haven't finished the script yet. I don't know what the lead parts will be. I can tell you there is solid interest for distribution."

Tamara and Sharon stay at the studio for a couple more hours. Paul shows them the sketches for the "spaceship set." Tamara does an excellent job of steering the conversation away from politics and religion. On the way back to Orlando, Sharon complains about Paul's girlfriend Stacy and the Democratic Congressperson for whom she works. Then she went on about why Paul should find a Christian girlfriend. Sunday morning, she talks Tamara into going to a megachurch service nearby Longwood, Florida. She and Sharon have been there before. After the service, before leaving, Sharon makes sure to say hello to church staff and one of the pastors she knows. She compliments him on his performance with the instrumental group. Tamara takes Sharon to the airport in time for her flight to Washington.

During spring break, Josh, Adrienne, and the children stay at the beach condo. When summer comes, it is planned that Adrienne can commute to Orlando. The children are staying at the beach with Josh. They will go to summer camp programs or be at the ranch with other children. Marcella hires counselors who run an educational summer program for family and friends' children. Many activities, trips to the beach, historic sites, and trips to the Space Center are planned. Even a possible trip to Costa Rica for everyone if there is time.

Adrienne continues working at the advertising agency as a creative director. She handles Paul's account herself. She uses agency talent to help design the public relations and advertising campaign for the film and Gateway to the Galaxy studio theme park.

Once or twice a week, she visits the studio to confer with Paul about the design of advertising and possible press releases they can distribute every month until the opening of the studio theme park. Paul wants to wait until the frame and hull are up for Galaxy Two before attracting too much attention. They can continue to promote the idea that the spaceship set is being constructed as if it is a real spaceship. It will then be used as a set for this film and subsequent films requiring a spacecraft. Once the studio theme park opens, there will be ship tours.

George stops by the house one morning as Adrienne is leaving for work. He laments that he has no one to run with in the morning since Josh is always at the beach. Adrienne said she would let Josh know. She mentions he may be back in Orlando to check things at the university next week. She asks George if he is still seeing Simone. He said he was, but she is back in Washington, D.C. They take turns visiting each other, taking long weekends when possible.

"Are you guys getting serious?" Adrienne asks.

"Things are fine as they are. We enjoy each other's company. We're a couple. I don't think either of us wants or needs anything formalized," George said.

"Whatever works for you is good," Adrienne said as they parted and headed off to her Orlando office.

CHAPTER EIGHTEEN

"The way birthed the one. The one birthed the two, the two birthed the three, and the three birthed ten-thousand things."

Annie's husband, Captain Andrew Sun, arrives at the ranch on the Saturday before Easter on two weeks' vacation leave from the airline company. Andrew is third generation Chinese American from Boston. He currently works as a pilot for a major airline flying internationally. His professional airline pilot captain demeanor quickly instills trust in those he meets. His flying experience is extensive, beginning in NASA's astronaut program before the shuttles stop launching. He has flown fighter jets and stealth bombers in the military. Captain Sun completed helicopter training, including license-qualifying flights. Outside the military, he has experience flying most commercial and private jets. However, the idea of piloting this spaceship makes him slightly anxious. Initially, it occurs to him that the significant difference regarding Galaxy One is the means of propulsion. "Never flown anything with a gravity drive, whatever that is," he said. "Seems a lot safer than being strapped to a rocket."

Beginning with a tour of the ship, Andrew works with Carlos Arroyo checking out all the instruments and flight equipment aboard Galaxy One. Andrew is impressed with the state-of-the-art equipment and construction. The helm of the ship is forward on the upper deck. It is spread across the front of the spacecraft well behind the gracefully sloping triple-panel windows of the area. There are five flight chairs arranged in the command center. Two seats are for the pilot and copilot. Three more seats for additional flight crew with access to the life support system, navigation, communications, and engineering.

"We can take the ship outside on Monday night and complete a system check. Tests include lifting off the ground a foot or two to see what happens," Andrew tells Carlos after a couple of hours of checking controls and monitors.

Carlos is prepared to be Andrew's copilot since he installed all the software and synced the instruments with the drive. Sam, Raoul Jr., and Josh are also booked to assist in the first test flight.

"If all goes well, we can take Galaxy One for a spin," Andrew said. "See how it flies and handles at altitude and speed."

"Sounds like a plan, Captain Sun," Carlos said. "As you can see, the flight console resembles a flight simulator game. In addition to dual joysticks, we have a console that can be used alone or in conjunction with the sticks. The ship can be completely controlled from the console. You also have some pedals on the floor, available if you choose, for thrust and breaking. Breaking the ship to a full stop will default the drive to a neutral status while waiting for a direction."

"Hovers like a helicopter, I imagine."

"Floats in place without all the noise. Our tests using the van encountered no problems hovering," Carlos replies. "I have the feeling this ship is going to handle somewhat differently than an airplane. As you say, it will hover like a helicopter but steadier. You can move in any direction. We use gravity for lift and thrust, so you might say we're floating in the spacetime continuum."

"I agree, different dynamic. I'm anxious to see how sensitive the controller and joystick are with the drive and trust controls—like a big game consul. Going in any direction spontaneously might take some getting used to. There are two sets of controls, so if I have a problem, you can help. The setup reminds me of a flight simulator, and I've been on a few of those."

"We can put a simulator together," Carlos offers.

"No worries, we'll take it one step at a time once we get out there. If it all works, we'll be okay. I notice there are three pods for landing gear."

"Yes, they are programmed to retract at a certain altitude and come down automatically. We can override that and operate them manually if necessary. The pods retract into an airtight compartment. This ship can land on water if necessary. Galaxy One takes off vertically. No wheels are necessary. We wanted something to protect the hull when the ship touched down. We have one emergency button on the far left of your console. Of course, it's got a red protective cover. If we are in the atmosphere and the drive fails, the button will release four parachutes to help us float to the ground. I guess the trick is knowing when to deploy them."

Pointing to one of the screens in front of them, Andrew asks, "Is this a monitor for radar detection?"

"Yes, it shows when we are being tracked by radar. There is a stealth feature built into the hull. If everything is working, we will not show up on radar screens. We can tell when there is radar out there. We can also use radar reflection to send out a simulated radar blip. I've programmed a few things like a large flock of birds or a small plane flying at 200 mph."

"I guess it depends on at what altitude we are flying. We also have another system and screen that detects other aircraft. We'll need to be careful since they won't know we're there unless they see us."

"It's going to be interesting, never flown a UFO before, Captain Sun admits as they continue to check the instruments, screens, and controls.

Easter Sunday, the entire Arroyo family, husbands, and wives with their children, arrive for afternoon dinner. In addition, Raoul Sr.'s parents Conrad and Julia, are visiting from Maine. Raoul Jr. and Carlos flew to Maine to bring them to the ranch. They visit on holidays to catch up with their son, daughter-in-law, and grandchildren. Conrad and Julia look more like an uncle and aunt than grandparents.

The weather is in the seventies and sunny, so adults and children spend some time outdoors. The Bennetts and their children are there too. No one in the family needs an invitation. The only non-attendee is Sharon, who stopped attending Easter Sunday dinner because the Arroyos didn't celebrate Easter as she thought they should. She believes Easter and Christmas should only be observed by what she defines as real Christians.

Divorced, Sharon celebrates Easter with her evangelical friends at the nearest mega-church. In any event, she visited the weekend before.

Josh, Adrienne, Morgan, and Lauren are comfortable being there. By now, Morgan and Lauren know some of the other children. Marcella ensures that Josh and Adrienne are introduced to anyone they have not met yet, including Raoul Sr.'s parents.

"Josh and Adrienne, this is Raoul's father and mother, Conrad and Julia. They are visiting from Maine, Marcella said.

"Good to meet you," Josh said. "How was your trip here?"

"Perfect," said Conrad, "Raoul Jr. is an excellent pilot, and Carlos was the copilot. We got to catch up on life at the ranch."

"It's nice meeting you, Julia said. "We've heard a lot about both of you. We're happy to hear you are working with the family."

"Your contributions to the project are much appreciated," Conrad said.

"Thank you," Josh said while thinking, "I guess he knows about the project." "I'm honored to be a part of it,' Josh said aloud. Marcella mentions to Josh that Conrad taught history, anthropology, and political science at Princeton for many years before retiring to Maine.

"That's quite a combination, Professor Arroyo," Josh replies.

"Thanks," Conrad said, "I've found that these three disciplines are connected in many ways. Observing human evolution helps in understanding trends in history and politics. History is a subjective account of the past. Understanding cultural and political behavior adds an objective reality to history and politics in progress.

"I agree. We need more interdisciplinary scholarship," Josh said."

Julia talks to Adrienne about Maine and how she worked as a correspondent and photographer for several newspapers in the United States and abroad. Adrienne mentions her interest in photography and how she met Josh while standing in front of a photograph by Dorothea Lange at a retrospective exhibit of the "Family of Man." Julia said, "I knew Dorothea and admired her work." Julia speaks fluent French. Adrienne admits that her French is far from fluent. Still, they exchange a few words in that language. Adrienne learns that Conrad grew up in Florida. He left the state for university at a young age. Julia and Conrad met in New York City, where Julia grew up.

Josh and Adrienne are amazed at how young Conrad and Julia appear. At first, Adrienne does not think Julia looks old enough to have known Dorothea Lange. Adrienne, doing a quick mental estimate based on Raoul's age and an assessment of his parent's age, put Conrad and Julia at around eighty. They both look more like fifty.

Josh enjoys the beautiful dinner and afternoon. He and Adrienne have met the immediate Arroyo family, including husbands, wives, and children.

Dinner finished, Conrad and Josh strike up a conversation while sitting on the veranda. Josh is curious about Conrad's interdisciplinary approach to current affairs. He asks Conrad what his views are regarding the political climate in the country.

Conrad said, "I believe this is a critical period in America's history. We emerged as the world leader after World War Two. Nations, empires, and dynasties don't last forever. America replaced the British Empire, which replaced another before it. China has gone through many dynasties. Ascendant nations and forces are trying to gain power at America's expense. They see internal strife as a weakness. It is a difficult time. I suspect the current president will be impeached but not removed from office. He will not want to leave office if he loses the next election. This thought would never have dawned on previous presidents." Conrad voices concern that the country is moving toward becoming an autocratic nation. He said, "all the signs are there if you look at history and the rise of totalitarian leaders. The project must make as much progress as possible before the next election. "

Josh agrees. "Things are looking complicated; the president and the administration are systematically destroying the government along with the checks and balances that keep the United States a democracy. Whatever happens, the internal strife will still be there."

Paul joins the conversation and mentions that Sharon, who works for the administration, recently visited his studio. She tells them about the Space Force and how it will be official late in 2019.

Josh asks everyone the same question: "why do we need a space force that doesn't go into space?"

Conrad said, "likely, it's all for show. A tactic to capture the country's imagination like Kennedy did with the mission to land on the moon. This Space Force has no immediate agenda to go to space. It is a Space Force in waiting and possibly a way for the administration to take control of the space programs in the country. It seems like this administration is systematically consolidating power in the hands of a leader with autocratic tendencies. There are claims that there is an American empire. But it has never had an 'emperor' running it."

Easter Monday evening is clear. Around seventy degrees, a few clouds drift in from the ocean. It is quiet on the runway, only the chirp of crickets and buzz of other insects, along with the usual night sounds. To avoid attracting attention, there are no lights except for the violet-blue running lights of Galaxy One. The soft lamps reveal little of the spaceship's grey titanium color. Andrew, Carlos, Raoul Jr., Josh, and Sam are already aboard. Carlos, Raoul Jr., and Sam have pilots' licenses, with ratings high enough to pilot the corporate jet. It is planned that they will all also be able to pilot Galaxy One.

Raoul Sr., Marcella, Paul, Bill, Annie, and Tamara are in the hangar, which has been upgraded and specially prepared to house and service the vessel. In a secure area, a ground control center monitors Galaxy One. All communications to and from the ship are scrambled. Ground control observes the crew on monitors via cameras inside the ship. There is communication between Galaxy One's team and ground control. Ground Control has exact duplicates of all the flight console equipment. In case of emergency, Galaxy One can be operated remotely.

Inside the ship, Captain Andrew Sun and copilot Carlos Arroyo occupy the front two seats while Sam, Raoul Jr., and Josh each sit at one of the auxiliary control positions. All five crew members wear basic altitude pressure suits but have not put on their helmets since the suits are precautionary. Each helmet is nearby, within easy reach, fastened into a holding niche by their seats. Josh is excited to be there. He is handling communications for the test. Raoul Sr. asked him if he wanted to go on this initial test. Josh did not hesitate, although afterward, when he told Adrienne about it, he got a little anxious. It is reasonably safe—there are no plans to go into outer space. Adrienne is supportive and does not show any apprehension. She asks him to call her when possible. She never imagined her husband being a test pilot or engineer on board an airplane, let alone a spaceship. She does not voice any concerns. She is looking forward to taking a ride on the ship herself one day soon.

Paul and Tamara leave the control room and go outside to watch the lift-off. It is a fantastic moment seeing this craft and the starlit night. Soon it will float into the night air, surrounded by all the stars in the universe. Paul can shoot the lift-off with a small, handheld 8K camera. It is equipped with a unique wide-angle lens with an aperture good for night photography.

"Captain Sun said, "It looks like we are ready to lift a few feet." Using the joystick and slides, he floats the ship up off the runway up to five feet. He hovers for two minutes and gently comes back down—everyone in the ground control room cheers.

"Next, we'll ascend higher, move along the runway, turn around and float back, then land. The landing pads will not be retracted. Everything must be tested carefully before we take the ship up higher."

Captain Sun settles in comfortably in the padded pilot's chair. He instinctively knows how to handle the ship and its game controller-style controls. One big difference between Galaxy One and a conventional jet aircraft is its quietness. The drive makes no sound that is discernible in the cockpit. Galaxy One floats down the runway slowly at about nine mph, then turns, which is more of a spin, in place. Captain Sun allows the ship to float back somewhat faster, slows to a hover, and lands again.

"Very smooth and sensitive thrust controls working fine," he said. "I believe we can take the ship up. What do you guys think? Captain Sun asks his crew.

"Looks good to me," Carlos replies.

"All good," Sam said. Speaking to ground control, "Let's turn on the beacon, so we can be sure to find our way back. We may need runway lights."

"Beacon is on Sam. Ready with the runway lights," Raoul Sr. said. "Usually, the lights come on with the beacon. We are manually overriding the lights."

"I have the coordinates logged in to the navigation system," Carlos said. "We will have no problem finding the runway."

"I don't see any other aircraft on the radar," Raoul Jr. said, checking the screen.

"Moving up to five thousand feet," Captain Sun replies as he eases Galaxy One upward slowly. "I am using minimum power to lift us," he said. "Everyone strapped in their seats?"

Josh fastens his seat belt.

After they reach five thousand feet, they stop and float there like a motionless gray teardrop in the night sky. Landing pods have been retracted automatically. Consulting with ground control, they decide to go up to ten thousand feet. Instead of floating straight up vertically, they fly at an angle, gradually upward as they increase speed, moving eastward toward the Atlantic Ocean. This is an essential test for the ship, including how the stealth radar works. They will pass close to the Space Center at Cape Canaveral, where they can be picked up on the radar.

The ship lifts easily to ten thousand feet, accelerating quickly to five hundred miles per hour. They speed east past Cape Canaveral and out over the Atlantic Ocean. Carlos, Raoul Jr., and Josh pay close attention to their monitors. No sign of anyone detecting their presence. Once they are well out over the ocean, Captain Sun increases the speed to Mach 2. Galaxy One flies silently without any vibrations or problems. The air pressure in the cabin is good, and everything functions as it should. Josh and Sam listen for any sounds from the hull.

"We're doing fine," Captain Sun reports, "solid ship. You did a great job with the design Sam."

"Thanks," Sam is overwhelmed with the initial performance. "Great work by our team, including Josh, Carlos, Tamara, Raoul Jr., Raoul Sr., and Marcella.

"I'd like to do one more test since we're out here. I want to go up to thirty-six thousand feet to test the cabin pressure. Okay?"

After a pause, ground control gave an affirmative response. "Good to go," Carlos said. "It appears our sonic boom suppression is working."

"I don't see anything else out here right now," Sam reports.

"Hold on, this will be a bit dramatic and fast at this speed," Captain Sun said.

"First, I'm going to bring us to a hover, then quickly go vertically, straight up."

The ship comes to a stop, hovering for a short time. Captain Sun floats the ship upward rapidly, like a high-speed elevator moving up in a tall building. Galaxy One instantly rises to thirty-six thousand feet at Mach 3. The g-force pushed the crew into their seats. The team let out one form or another of "wow" or maybe "whew," when they slowed and hovered at thirty-six thousand feet. The pressure in the cabin is acceptable. It adjusts quickly to the higher altitude. The only comparison Josh can make is that it feels like sitting in a speedy car accelerating, only stronger.

"Sorry, I didn't anticipate the instant on Mach 3. We'll learn to slow up the acceleration in the future," Captain Sun said apologetically.

They continue to hover at thirty-six thousand feet. "Radar is showing what looks like a commercial jet at thirty-five thousand feet coming this way from the northeast," Carlos reports.

"I'd say he's descending. Let's head home at twenty-five thousand feet and stay out of its way. It could be headed toward Orlando, Miami, or further inland. There are not that many flights coming south at this time of night. I doubt they see us down here if we aren't showing up on their radar. It could be a domestic or international flight. Virgin or Lufthansa heading to Orlando or Miami. They will continue a glide path and reach a lower altitude. If they are headed to Miami or further south, they will continue southward," Captain Sun said.

They floated down to twenty-five thousand feet and then set the speed to about six hundred miles per hour to head home. Once they approach the coast, they drop altitude again, gradually decreasing the rate on their approach to the runway at the ranch. The runway lights are on. Captain Sun floats Galaxy One back down onto the runway. It is now about one in the morning. Raoul Jr. takes control, floating the spacecraft into the hangar. Once inside the hangar, Carlos opens the airlock hatch, and they all walk down the steps to where they are warmly greeted. Paul and Tamara film the landing, following the ship back into the hangar.

There are champagne toasts celebrating the launch. The ground crew and the flight team sit around the conference table for a brief meeting to discuss the test flight. They will meet again the next day to go into more detail.

Captain Sun begins, "I know it's late. We can go over more details tomorrow. This ship is amazing. It is solid. We did not hear a rattle or a vibration at any time. At one point, I moved it from ten thousand feet to thirty-six thousand feet, and it floated upward as fast as we let it as if it had silent rockets. We could feel the g-force in our seats. We could have easily continued and floated into orbit at eighteen thousand mph."

Raoul Sr. smiled, "For all intents and purposes, gravity as we normally experience is transformed in spacetime as an amplified negative or positive force. We appear to be ready for an upper atmosphere test and perhaps moving into an Earth orbit. After an inspection of the ship, it will not hurt to do a few more tests in the atmosphere before we go into space. There are a tremendous number of satellites, some dead, in low earth orbit. Our radar needs to be able to detect them so we don't run into a satellite or space junk."

Carlos said, "we have integrated an AI system with the radar that can detect objects in our path and change course to avoid them. I downloaded coordinates for thousands of known satellites and the International Space Station."

"We don't need to reach an "escape velocity" to go into orbit. We are like surfers riding a wave, except we control the speed and direction of the wave," Marcella said. "To maintain orbit, we will need to reach high velocity."

"Next, we go beyond Earth's atmosphere to test the life support systems, the artificial gravity in the cabin, and handling of the ship in outer space," Raoul Sr. said.

"Isn't there a good chance Galaxy One may be spotted in orbit?" Josh asks.

Yes, that is a problem. No one will know where we came from. We can float down toward Earth and disappear," Sam said.

"Tamara and I have been working on cloaking metal surfaces. So far, what we have developed merely refracts light. We are looking at a way to charge the molecules electronically in metal surfaces, causing a cloaking effect. This may alter other characteristics of the metal itself. We'll need to do tests. We want to be able to turn this attribute on and off. It will take time to develop our ideas," Josh said.

"Not showing up on the radar is good enough cloaking for now. Although, we need to be careful," Carlos said.

"I hope we can go up in the daylight," Captain Sun said.

"I believe we will do that soon," Sam said. "The fact that we can go up vertically to high altitudes means there is less chance anyone on the ground will spot us. We might also try launching on a cloudy day."

"It's late. We can do some more work tomorrow. How about we meet at noon," Marcella said. After the meeting is over, Josh drives to the beach. On the way, he calls Adrienne and tells her everything is fine; he'd be there soon.

Radar technicians at the space center at Cape Canaveral did not pick up Galaxy One on their scopes. They did note a curious faint silhouette or shadow that appeared to move out to sea. Later the same irregularity appears briefly, then vanishes at low altitudes. These are not blips, nothing identifiable. They speculate it could be a flock of birds or another natural anomaly like a methane bubble. Possibly a sizeable consumer-type drone someone is flying on the beach. It did not pass over the center. They made a note of the glitch in their logs. There are no launches scheduled. No further action is indicated.

A few days later, a traffic analyst at NSA looks over a satellite report of unusual high-frequency noise in Central Florida and off the coast. She listens to the bursts of unintelligible screeching sounds but cannot determine if they are random high-frequency reflections of something else. She listed the incident as unidentified high-frequency radio waves on her report.

Over the next few months, four more tests of Galaxy Ones' performance at high altitudes are conducted to test the integrity of the hull and all systems. These tests are at altitudes from forty thousand to fifty thousand feet, about ten miles above sea level. This height is considered the upper atmosphere. Raoul Sr., Marcella, Josh, Adrienne, Paul, Tamara, and Raoul Jr. joined Captain Sun, Carlos, and Sam at different times. The consensus is that Galaxy One is more comfortable than riding in a commercial jet. All the members of the team become familiar with the controls. Carlos and Sam pilot the ship with no problems. Raoul Sr. and Marcella check the drive monitors and life support systems throughout the spacecraft. Adrienne and Paul hitch a ride one night too.

Josh marvels at how the ship moves effortlessly in any direction. He knows the assent to achieve orbit in space, and the descent back to earth is different than with a rocket, capsule, or space shuttle. Galaxy One does not need to achieve a certain escape velocity to go into orbit, only to stay in orbit close to the earth's atmosphere. The small craft can lock itself into orbit two-hundred-seventy-five miles above the earth's surface. Once a velocity around the globe is established, it can stay in orbit at that distance. Re-entering the atmosphere requires slowing down and floating into the atmosphere at a reduced speed to avoid a fiery re-entry.

The stealth technology built into the hull is working well. No military jets from either of the Florida Airforce bases scramble to intercept a suspected intrusion of unidentified aircraft into U.S. air space. However, the space center radar technicians did continue to notice shadowing on their long-range radar. They bring in a specialist to check on the glitches. The equipment checks out perfectly. Technicians are set up to record the anomaly the next time it happens.

Because these signals appear to be coming from near the Kennedy Space Center, NSA put some additional analysts on the high radio frequency broadcasts. They determine that the signals are artificial, not atmospheric noise. The encrypted, scrambled, and compressed squelches are not intelligible. The NSA has specialists in many different areas. These specialists only research things within their areas of expertise. They do not have a "need to know" what is happening in other departments. Traffic analysts are given "need to know" status and look at unrelated areas for correlating communications. One of these analysts notices that specific internet frequency activity coincides with the radar glitches at Cape Canaveral Space Center. He recommends keeping a watch to see any other coincidental traffic patterns. The analyst searches for reports of any unusual activity in that area. Nothing of interest turns up.

One day while working in the ground control room, Carlos and Tamara also notice the shadows on their monitors. They show them to Raoul Sr. and Marcella, who begin looking into it. There isn't much they can check since the stealth is built into the hull. Perhaps there is a leak somewhere. They start an inspection of the hull. They determine that there is a leak through the glass panels in the cockpit. Josh and Tamara quickly developed a transparent stealth anti-reflective coating based on the cloaking spray and the formula for the stealth technology, which can be applied to the glass. Hopefully, they can have something to test on the next flight.

Sam finishes the design for Galaxy Two. He moves ahead with the building of the larger ship. A high-roof hangar is erected on the concrete slab laid earlier to house Galaxy Two. There are folding doors on either side of the hangar. The structural frame for the spacecraft is in the process of being manufactured. It will be assembled as it becomes available. Equipment is put into place to do the fabricating. In the interest of security, Raoul Sr. hires a particular group of workers to do the construction. They are housed at one of the guest houses. It seems that only Raoul Sr. and Marcella know who they are.

Paul and Adrienne decide they will release information about plans proceeding for the film and that the large set is under construction. The press will only be invited to see it after the frame and the complete hull are in place. The studio plans to release photographs and video of erecting the hangar to house the spaceship set.

CHAPTER NINETEEN

••••••••••••••••••••••••••••••••••••••

"Ten thousand things are backed by the Yin to embrace the Yang. These two forces (Chi) yield to each other to create balance."

The orbiting test of Galaxy One is scheduled for 1:00 a.m. on a Thursday in February 2019. The launch is timed for when the International Space Station is on the other side of the planet. The thought is that they can maintain this separation once in orbit and avoid any contact. Estimates indicate at least twenty thousand satellites in orbit, plus tons of space junk and trash floating around the earth. Galaxy One has a program to take evasive action if any large objects are encountered automatically. The hull has been tested in various ways to see how resistant it is to impact from space particles. For example, hull sections have been tested against projectiles fired at point-blank range. The outer hull material did not sustain a puncture, although it was dented on one occasion.

To protect Galaxy One and the crew, a set of high-intensity weapons-grade lasers are installed in the ship's nose section. These are not thought of as offensive or defensive weapons. They are to be used should the ship encounter an object or projectile that threatens to collide with the ship. Space junk can be destroyed or deflected. Theoretically, the lasers can break up a meteorite or small asteroid. Raoul Sr. and Marcella devised a shield to protect the entire ship's hull once in space. It uses the auxiliary drive like the ship's artificial floor gravity. It can be turned on or off and regulated in intensity as needed. By default, it operates oppositely to the artificial gravity for the floors. It gently creates waves that repel small objects.

The air pressure and air circulation systems are also checked. Air in the ship is scrubbed, pulling out the CO2 and recycling the oxygen. Galaxy One is checked inside and out multiple times. All systems are sound. The only thing missing is a stealth coating for the windows. Josh and Tamara believe they are close to a formula but have yet to test it. They only want to spray the windows with something once they are confident it will work since the spray may be impossible to remove. Replacing the windows would be difficult and costly. They go ahead with the test using some treated window tinting film material like that used for tinting car windows for privacy and sunblock. They treat the film with the test formula that Josh and Tamara have been working on. It is applied to the inside of the glass and can be removed if necessary.

The flight crew for this initial flight into space is composed of Captain Sun, Carlos, Sam, Tamara, and Raoul Jr. Flight suits are to be used for this flight. Once in space, they may remove their helmets if all is going well. The pressurized flight suits have an oxygen supply and communications. Josh, Paul, Marcella, Annie, and Raoul Sr. work in the ground control center. Raoul Sr.'s father, Conrad, joins them to observe in the ground control room during the launch.

The flight crew boards Galaxy One, then floats it onto the runway at 12:30 a.m. for a final preflight countdown. Andrew and Carlos go through the procedure while Sam, Raoul Jr., and Tamara check screens and instruments at their stations.

"Our flight plan is to lift off at 1:00 a.m. and head out to the ocean at Twenty-five thousand feet. Once we clear the coast, we immediately rise to the upper atmosphere. We head out at Mach one and increase speed as we leave the atmosphere and go into orbit. We don't need to accelerate into orbit since the drive will push us away from Earth. We'll slide into orbit. We do need to achieve a high orbital speed around the planet. Once we achieve orbit, we can check systems and see how we're doing," Captain Sun announces as the last of the preflight checks are finished.

"It is partly cloudy with a gentle wind bringing sea air onto the mainland," Josh said, thinking that might be good to prevent anyone on the ground from seeing the ship.

"Okay, looks like your good to go," Raoul Sr. said from the ground control center.

"Liftoff," Captain Sun replies as he floats Galaxy One off the runway and into the night sky. Josh wants to be on Galaxy One, but others need experience. He can follow them from ground control video monitors. He will be on the next flight.

On board, Carlos closely watches the long-range radar screen for signs of air traffic. "We have what appears to be a small plane at nine thousand feet," he reports as they approach the coast.

"Captain Sun replies, "We're already at twenty-five thousand feet, so no worries. Our speed is 525 mph. I'm going to keep moving up in altitude."

"Nothing near us at the moment," Tamara said.

Captain Sun let the ship float up to thirty, then forty, then sixty thousand feet, which is over eleven miles above sea level.

"All systems look good," Sam said.

"Okay, make sure your suits are pressurized and helmets on. We will keep moving up into an orbit, and our speed will increase to 17,150 mph. We will maintain that speed in orbit," said Captain Sun. "We're shadowing the International Space Station (ISS), so we'll need to match its speed."

Carlos notices he is pushing on his harness, beginning to rise a bit in his seat. He checks instruments and turns on the floor gravity. After a slight pause, he and the others settle back into their seats. "Artificial gravity is working well, he comments."

Galaxy One quietly floats into space. About two hundred miles above the earth, Tamara notices a piece of space junk on the monitor. The ship's automatic detection system takes control long enough to move away from what looks like an old rocket.

"Did you see that old rocket?" Tamara asks.

"Yes, the ship's auto-detection radar is working well, moving us away from danger. We also need to be on the lookout for trash from the space station orbiting near it. We're hours behind the ISS in our orbit, so that should not be a problem. Radar isn't showing anything else right now," Sam replies.

On the ground, everyone in the control room is elated. Things are going well, but they are still on the edge of their seats. Their small spaceship is out there in space, functioning in test mode. Every move is an adventure and a risk. They got up there and are doing well. Soon they will need to come back down safely.

Looking out the windows as Galaxy One orbits the Earth, Captain Sun views "the blue marble" as he once dreamed he might when he trained as an astronaut. He lost that opportunity when the space shuttle program was grounded. Here it is, the blue planet, with its clouds, oceans, and land masses. The only world in the solar system known to sustain sentient life or probably any life. From this vantage point, a finite sphere, with signs of life in the form of lights seen in certain areas. Being here in space and looking down is a singular experience. Human territorial boundaries mean nothing from this height. All there is to see is the blue planet.

Tamara watches the lights below. If there is intelligent life somewhere in another solar system, can they observe this tiny planet with its lights ring of satellites and space junk floating around it? They may see the earth and want to visit. They need to find a way to travel great distances between the stars. If there is some intelligent design to the universe, maybe it is to keep civilizations apart. Survival in the universe might be remaining anonymous, separate, and staying in one's backyard.

Sam said, "instruments say it is safe to take off our helmets. I'm going give it a try." He took off the helmet slowly, and all was well. He attached the helmet to its holder. Next, he unfastened his seat belt and stood up. He did not float around. He can walk about the cabin. Soon Carlos and Tamara remove their helmets as well. Captain Sun is the last to remove his helmet.

Ever the Captain of the ship, Andrew asked the others to begin their system checks, life support, and drive. He places the spaceship on an autopilot program for orbiting and starts checking his instruments. A message comes in from ground control.

"Congratulations, everyone! You are good to go for two orbits. You should then begin the autopilot decent program. It will alert you before starting."

"Roger that," Captain Andrew Sun said.

The notion that she is two hundred-fifty miles above the earth, flying in a spaceship, is complex for Tamara to accept as a reality. "Somehow, it feels natural and right. Like I belong here. I can see the planet below as we move into the daylight. The earth rotates every twenty-four hours. The ship will orbit the world in about ninety minutes. "

Sam brings Tamara back from her thoughts when he suggests they check the second level. Tamara gets up from her seat, tentatively wondering if she might float. She finds herself walking normally. She and Sam head down to the second level for the inspection. All is well, but there is less artificial gravity on the second level. As a precaution, Sam decides not to open the hatch to the third level. The instruments show it is pressurized, heated, or air-conditioned like the other two levels. Air circulation priorities change as they move from dark to light. The Galaxy One automatically and slowly rotates so the hull will transfer the heat, store it, and then use it on the dark side of the orbit.

Even though Sam has been up for many flights, he is still checking the ship structurally and listening for any odd sounds coming from the hull or frame. He is applying what he has learned from building this ship to the much larger Galaxy Two construction.

Carlos focuses on checking all his instruments and monitors. Having programmed much of the circuitry, he feels a part of the ship's functioning system. Almost as if he is there in the boards and chips moving around. He checks to see how the hull handles converting sunlight into electricity. The batteries are charging, and all systems are good. Air conditioning replaces the heat needed on the dark side when they move into the sun.

Captain Sun and Carlos will soon let the crew know it is time to return to their stations and prepare for the descent. They must consider the Earth's rotation and the craft's orbiting speed. Each moment is a new experience for all on board. Astronauts study and go through much training before going into space. Except for Captain Sun, this crew is self-taught and learns much as they go along. This ship's user-friendly, advanced nature is a significant factor in facilitating their progress.

On Earth, a satellite-watching club in North Carolina gathers to peer at the night sky through powerful amateur telescopes. Their club meets in a mountain park where the sky is free of ambient light.

"Hey Laura, has a new satellite launch since last week?" Dean asks.

Laura checks some data she has on her laptop. "Nothing listed here. Do you have a position?

"Not yet, it is tiny, like a reflection, and I can't be sure if it is a satellite, could be some space junk floating around. It's going out of range, following the same path as the International Space Station. It seems too big to be something they jettisoned."

"See if it turns up again," Laura said.

NSA set up a watch and alert for new signals coming from Florida. They got an alert around 1:00 a.m. High-frequency signals are picked up coming from orbit as if there is a satellite out there that they don't know about. All they can do is record the sounds for analysis later. NSA is not the only national government agency monitoring these signals coming from what appears to be an unknown satellite or other device circling the globe. Peoples's Republic of China's government sky watchers also notices the signals and movement.

Just before 4:00 a.m. Galaxy One begins its descent back to earth. Speed is slowed, and the drive is used to gently bring the ship back into the atmosphere on a flight path back to Arroyo Aerospace. There is no fiery decent. As far as any observers can tell, whatever had been there disappeared. Galaxy One evades all radar detection on the way back to Florida. The film inside the windows reduces the leak enough so that no shadow is seen on radar screens. The only evidence is data streams occasionally between the craft and ground control. The transmitter and receiver remain unknown.

Since 911, there has been an attempt to have security agencies in the government share information so that possible national threats can be identified. This idea lasted through the previous administration. During the current administration, the process could have been smoother. Security agencies turn self-protective after frequent attacks by the current president and his cabinet. Information like unidentified communications, UFOs, or sporadic radar glitches are not prioritized. By 2018 politics put a stranglehold on information regarding national security as if anything reported might embarrass the current president and administration.

It is still dark when Galaxy One touches down at the ranch. The hangar door opens. Captain Sun floats the ship slowly along and then into the hangar. Once inside the hangar, some heat can be felt coming off the hull from the descent—nothing unexpected after two orbits of the Earth at high speeds. Sam prepares to inspect the hull with his equipment to detect any problems. All on board feel fine. Their vitals recorded during the flight via the suits they wear are expected.

Raoul Sr. and Marcella come aboard to check radiation levels and inspect the ship. Radiation levels from during the orbit appear normal. The hull is excellently protecting the interior from harmful cosmic radiation. Raoul Sr. heads down to the second level. He opens the hatch to the third level. Instruments show oxygen and radiation levels are as expected on the third level. Since the drives are on the third level, several redundant instruments and gauges are on the second level as a backup to the control center dashboard. All the meters read at safe levels.

The team gathers in the conference room. Annie, Raoul Jr., Conrad, Julia, and Adrienne bring breakfast over from the house, joining the others, who are watching a rerun of video of the lift-off, orbiting the earth, and re-entry as seen from the Galaxy One's cameras. There is also video recorded inside the control center.

"This is a momentous achievement," Conrad said, lifting his glass of fresh-squeezed orange juice, "Congratulations!"

Everyone lifts their glasses, and Marcella remarks, "not a mimosa, but it tastes like one. Cheers!"

"What's next?" Andrew asks.

Raoul Sr. put down his now empty glass, "The ship is solid. Our next big test for Galaxy One is a longer flight in space, maybe to the moon and back. This will also allow testing of the drive at higher speeds and how all the support systems function for an extended period. Before we do a longer flight, we'll do additional short flights in and out of the atmosphere beyond Earth's orbit. We have some more work on the ground too. We can be ready for the moon shot by summer."

"It is possible we may have been spotted orbiting the earth. A short pause before the next flight allows them time to forget about the UFO. Carlos, as a precaution, we need to beef up our cyber security here in the hangars and on the ranch in general. Anyone who gets a bead on this location might try hacking into our networks."

Carlos replies, "no problem. We can install some more fail-safe features. When not in use, we shut down all links to the internet. No one goes online from this building or the main hangar. Phones are turned off and left in the conference room in the old office. Maybe we will pull SIM cards too. I'm working on a new dark server for our Uber Net. We are working on putting up our satellite. I believe we can get it into orbit secretly using Galaxy One now that we've tested the ship. This will help with communications between the ship and ground control."

Sam is working on building Galaxy Two," Marcella said. "We are manufacturing parts for the ship's frame."

Sam looks a little tired but content. "We have been fabricating and stockpiling the frame materials and parts. We have enough raw materials to build the entire ship. It will take months to get all the parts manufactured. It would be helpful if we had another super 3D printer. As soon as the transverse frame is constructed, we can add the hull's outer layer as sections go into place. Josh and Tamara are working on possible tweaks for the hull material that increases its strength. We begin work on the next layer when the outer hull is in place. A lot more wiring and plumbing are required this time before the third or interior layer of the hull can be installed."

"How big will Galaxy Two be?" Annie asked.

"We are aiming for a ship four times larger than Galaxy One," said Sam. "We're going from a pleasure yacht to a cruise ship. It will have two drives, each larger than the one in Galaxy One. We are also working on a new drive of a different type. More on that later."

"Is it a 'Warp Drive,'" Paul asked jokingly.

Sam laughed, "we're not there yet, brother. Maybe on Galaxy Five."

Marcella sensing how tired they all might be, said, "I'm sure everyone would like to get on with their day or take a nap," as she adjourned the meeting. "Lots of work to do."

On returning to the beach, Josh asks Adrienne what she thinks of the ship and the test.

"Awesome," she said. "Paul's going to present Galaxy Two as a life-size set for his movie. I think it will attract attention because it is such a beautiful design. No giant rockets attached to the hull."

"If we have any more tests before the trip to the moon, I'll try to get you onboard the Galaxy One again if you like," Josh said.

"Sure, I'd be thrilled. Some wealthy people would pay millions for a seat on Galaxy One, taking them into orbit. Many dollars can be raised."

"I don't think the Arroyo family wants to go public with this until they are securely protected. That will be after the launch of Galaxy Two. I believe

Marcella and Raoul Sr. don't want to do anything to diminish the seriousness of the company going into space.

"Paul has this idea about projecting images of the Galaxy One in the sky for advertising the film. He thinks it may encourage people to ignore any sightings of Galaxy One. It will come off as some publicity stunt for the film. What do you think?"

"I think he should wait until Galaxy Two's outer hull is up and people can see it. We've been lucky not to have someone's iPhone picture of a UFO on social media. No use bringing attention to ourselves right now."

CHAPTER TWENTY

• •

Finding the path.

October 2019, the entire transverse frame for Galaxy Two is in place. The frame expands outward and is more elliptically shaped than Galaxy One. The outer hull is going up as quickly as the hull plates can be printed and attached. The hull plate bonding process leaves no trace. Each plate becomes bonded, with no visible seam, to the next plate to which it is attached. The hull for Galaxy Two is an upgrade from Galaxy One. Josh and Tamara invent a way to include an additional element in the outer hull material formula. This allows the manipulation of light in the visible light spectrum using electromagnetic waves, rendering the ship invisible to the human eye and radar. In combination with stealth technology, it provides the ultimate cloaking device. Cloaking can be turned on or off.

However, Cloaking Galaxy One requires a unique formula sprayed onto the hull. It responds to control electronically. The spray-on coating does not interfere with other stealth technology. This coating is formulated to react at a given frequency. Josh calls it the "blue tooth" coating. This layer is not permanent. It may wear off after a few flights, especially after leaving and re-entering the atmosphere. Josh conducts tests with the coating on other materials to find out how long it lasts and what makes it fade. He even tests it on clothing. He has an idea that they can build a special suit that will be used to cloak an individual. Tamara asked him if he wanted to create a new superhero. They can call him "Super Blue," she said.

Josh replied, "Sounds too much like 'super glue.'" He doesn't follow up on the cloaking suit idea. It may be feasible. Probably dangerous to wear a suit that is electronically charged. Like covering yourself with a body size

154

mobile phone or another device. The focus right now is on the construction of Galaxy Two. No time for experimenting with blue tooth suits.

Conrad is now participating in team meetings. His responsibility is to provide information on current affairs that may be of concern. He reports, "during the fall of 2019, the president's attempt to coerce a foreign country into investigating a likely rival candidate in the other party is turning into a scandal that will lead to his first impeachment. The country is experiencing a growing number of mass shootings. Right-wing, white supremacy groups are active. Hate crimes are on the rise. There is a general atmosphere of disorder and chaos growing nationwide. Corruption of the State Department and the Justice Department are apparent issues. Homeland Security is consumed with building a fence and imprisoning anyone they find in the country illegally. Security agencies like the CIA and NSA are quiet. The administration ignores intelligence agency reports. No one pays attention to odd sightings around the planet or radar glitches.

Galaxy One flew beyond the atmosphere into space four more times. On one trip, a secret cloaked communication satellite is launched into orbit. The ship is now fully cloaked with a coating that activates electronically. No entity has the equipment to track displacement in the spacetime gravity continuum. Cloaked or not, the ship still occupies space, and its movement can disturb objects near its path. The flight crew is aware of this and is careful not to come too close to other things in space or on the ground. After servicing the drive and checking all systems, it is determined that a flight either around or toward the moon is feasible using Galaxy One.

"It's only 238,900 miles away," Captain Sun reports. "Round trip, depending on how many times we go around the moon, less than half a million miles." In anticipation of this trip, Captain Sun studies the Apollo 11 crewed flight to the Moon in 1969, plus the other five human-crewed flights in the Apollo program. Apollo 8 is manned but does not land. The crew agrees to study and emulate the Apollo 8 flight plan. "Apollo flights with limited resources are a fantastic achievement. Compared to Galaxy One technology, the Apollo rockets and computers resemble old four-masted sailing ships. Certainly, if they flew to the moon and back, Galaxy One could do the same, Captain Sun said.

All flights in space utilize ground control centers on Earth for precise navigation. Arrays of large dish antennas are used for communication with spacecraft. The Arroyo ranch has one medium size dish antenna and a radar antenna. These are adequate for orbiting missions. They have limited range and ability to aid in space navigation correction. Galaxy One's self-navigation system is based on the same principles as the sextant, which guided sailors across earth's oceans for many centuries. The navigation system for Galaxy One utilizes small camera telescopes to take precise angle measurements between stars, the earth, the moon, and other celestial bodies for use by the computerized navigation system to plot a course. In an emergency, there is an actual modern sextant on board.

This celestial navigation system is the work of a long-time friend of Captain Sun. They attended the NASA shuttle training program together. Kevin Steiner began working as a navigator and engineer aboard commercial airline flights when the program ended. Over time these jobs became automated, combined, then assigned to the Captain and Copilot. Kevin retires from commercial flying and begins designing automatic navigation programs that replace larger flight crews. With Raoul Sr. and Marcella's permission and the usual confidential disclosure documents, Andrew brings Kevin to work with himself and Carlos. They developed and installed the self-navigation system for the Galaxy One. It is also the prototype navigation system for Galaxy Two and all the other ships to be built. Kevin is sworn to secrecy and paid for his efforts. He is excited about helping to develop an independent space self-navigation system. His one condition is that he gets to go on test flights. "It's a deal," Marcella said. Kevin went on the last test flight before the anticipated moon trip. He subsequently became an integral part of the team.

"The Apollo 8 human-crewed mission to the moon in 1968 is a model for our mission," said Andrew as Raoul Sr., Carlos, Kevin, Tamara, Josh, Marcella, Paul, and Raoul Jr. sit around the conference table in the control center. "Apollo 8 did not land on the moon; it flew lunar orbits a few times and then came back to Earth. Remember, the moon is not a stationary target. It is moving around the Earth."

Carlos shows a diagram illustrating the Apollo 8 trajectory and flight paths to the moon and back. It represents the path of Apollo 8 from the launch, an orbit around Earth, flight to the moon, lunar orbits, and then back to Earth. "This does look like a practical guide for our flight to the moon," Carlos said.

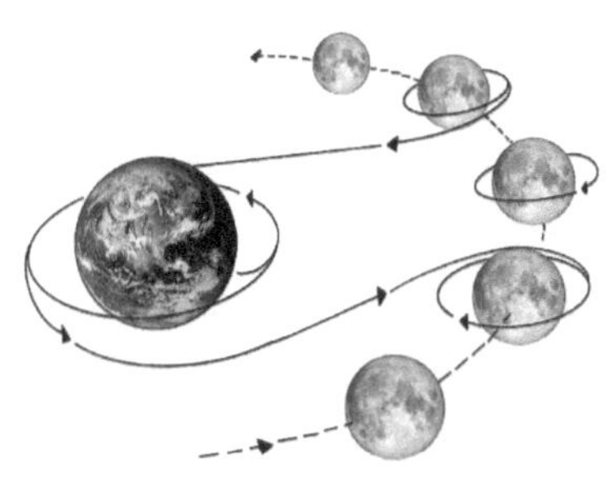

"Apollo 8 broke out of earth orbit at around 25,000 mph. It then coasted to the moon. The average speed was around 4,000 mph. We are not working with rockets. We can make the trip there and back faster. There will need to be speed corrections along the way and again once we encounter the moon's gravity," Sam said.

Carlos agrees, "there are many variables that the flight plan needs to consider. Nothing is static. The earth is moving, and the moon is moving. We can get there faster, but we can't allow the ship to go from 20,000 mph to a screeching halt to orbit around the moon. Newton's first law, 'objects in motion stay in motion.' That's where our autopilot and navigation programs come into play."

"Once Kevin and Carlos's new navigation program is integrated with the autopilot and drive system, we have the best of both worlds. We can program for an auto-programmed flight and self-navigate when necessary," Andrew said. "We do not have ground control to fall back on once we leave earth orbit. Because of security, range, and time considerations, communication with ground control is limited. We have downloaded all the flight data from

Apollo 8's flight. Of course, it is out of date. For us, it's an example of all they considered. After our flight plan is tested on a ground simulator, Kevin and Carlos will upload it to the system based on our flight schedule. As soon as that's done, we'll know how long it will take to make the trip. We can make corrections and changes during the flight manually if necessary."

"Our navigation system and autopilot are based on celestial navigation and gravity in the spacetime continuum because the gravity drive is sensitive to gravity fields. It finds gravity fields to utilize. This is something new. The tie-in with celestial navigation principals allows us to self-navigate anywhere in the solar system," Raoul Sr. added.

"One concern is Space Adaptation Syndrome. Astronauts like Frank Borman got very sick on one of the Apollo flights. Others suffered some discomfort. It is believed that close quarters in the Apollo capsule, about as big as the interior of a standard-size automobile, contributed to this syndrome. There is no issue of cramped space aboard Galaxy One. No weightless floating. There are two levels and space for the off-duty crew to nap on the second level. There is a small galley, a shower, and a toilet," Captain Sun said.

Raoul Sr. said, another concern is passing through the Van Allen Radiation Belt layers that circle the earth. The ship's hull is designed to protect against radiation. Galaxy One passes through the belt at high speed. Possible radiation is not as much as getting a conventional medical x-ray. Additionally, it is planned to fly through thinner portions of the belt. Crew members will wear a personal radiation meter, known as a Dosimeter, to monitor radiation. The ship's instrumentation also passively monitors radiation of all types inside and outside.

Marcella announces, "Crew members for this journey are Captain Andrew Sun, Raoul Arroyo Jr., Carlos Arroyo, Tamara Arroyo, and Josh Bennett." Josh is looking forward to this trip to the moon. Everyone is cross-trained with other crew members. Raoul Jr. trained with Captain Sun on several test flights, so he is an excellent choice to back up the pilot. Josh can split on-duty time with Tamara and Carlos. Sam is staying behind on this flight to assist with ground control. He also is needed to supervise work on Galaxy Two construction.

At the end of the meeting, Captain Sun mentions, "this flight will be more comfortable than your average flight on a commercial airliner. If all goes well, the next flight can include passengers. "

CHAPTER TWENTY-ONE

....

"Look, and it can't be seen.
Listen and it can't be heard.
Reach, and it can't be grasped."

Adrienne and Josh sit close together, feet up, drinking wine on the balcony of the beach condo. They watch the stars and the huge, silver color moon looming in the distance over the ocean. The moon always appears larger and brighter over the ocean, reflecting light on the moving water. Josh remembers being at sea with stars surrounding the ship, giving the moon a special place in the sky.

"Beautiful night," Josh said, "The moon is so bright."

"Did you ever think you would be flying to the moon one day?" Adrienne asks softly as if someone might hear her.

"It never entered my mind," Josh replies. "My father once told his mother that humans will go to the moon. She laughed and said to my father, "Nate, that's impossible. The moon is made of green cheese."

"Well, humans have been going to the moon since 1968, landing on all that cheese and walking around," Adrienne said, laughing.

"We are not landing. Anyway, we only have one space suit. I wish you could go on the flight with us."

"Maybe next time. I'm fine. One of us needs to be here with the children." Outwardly Adrienne isn't worried. A part of her doesn't want to risk Morgan and Lauren losing both parents in case of an accident.

"Too bad I can't tell them what I'm doing. Someday I'll tell them about this adventure," Josh said, looking out at the beach and stars as the waves washed ashore. He is planning a run on the beach tomorrow morning. He loves running by the ocean, doing what he calls a running meditation

160

rather than a traditional "walking meditation." He is fine running on his own. Sometimes he misses the morning runs and conversations with his neighbor George. He wonders how he is doing.

George and Simone spend weekends together in D.C. or Orlando whenever their schedules allow it. This weekend they are in D.C. They decide to go to the Smithsonian American Art Museum. They start their tour looking at the "Folk and Self-Taught Art" exhibit in which Simone is interested. She dabbles in drawing and painting and enjoys this type of art. Afterward, they go to the "Experience American" exhibit with its art from the 1930s, some of it produced under the auspices of the WPA.

They have lunch and decide to visit the "Modern and Contemporary Art Exhibit." There are room size acquisitions, Nam June Paik's "Electronic Superhighway: Continental U.S., Alaska, and Hawaii," which is lit up and quite large. Walking around, they find a recent work by a holographic artist. It is a 3d view of a parrot. One can walk around it and see all sides of the bird. Simone remarks, "this is so lifelike even close it appears solid. No flicker or other giveaway that it is all composed of light. "

"This is amazing," Simone said to George. She brings out her cell phone and snaps a photo. Then she makes a video of the parrot as she walks around the hologram.

"You like this bird," George said, surprised at how much Simone was into this hologram.

"It's amazing. I never knew a hologram could look so real. Even the video doesn't give it away."

They continue their tour of the exhibit and take a walk outside the park. The leaves are starting to turn, and it is a mild autumn day. It occurred to Simone that they were an odd couple, a CIA analyst and a general practice attorney. Even so, she believes they are compatible with their likes and dislikes.

As they walk, George mentions that it is good to be outdoors.

"Are you still running every day?" Simone asks.

"Yes, I'm running on my own. Josh is mostly out of town. He's at the beach a lot now. I'm out there by myself, except when you are there."

"What about his wife and the children?" Simone asks.

"They are at the beach until the summer vacation. I think the children are going to school in Coco Beach now."

Monday, back at work, Simone phones Arno, who is in Florida.

"Hey, how are you?" Arno said, answering the call after checking the caller ID.

"I'm fine. How are things in Orlando?

"Same old same old."

"This past weekend, I visited the Smithsonian Art Museum and saw something that might interest you. Have you been there recently?"

"No, not for a while."

"Well, you should see this when you next come to Washington. It's a hologram of a parrot. I took a photo and did a video. It still looks entirely real on the phone, both the photo and the video."

"I'm not really into parrots or holograms, Simone. Maybe you could put it on social media?"

"Okay funny. This hologram is so good that I thought the parrot was real. From every angle, it looks solid. The projector is set in a recess over the platform on which the bird is projected. As I watch, a crazy thought enters my mind regarding the lab rabbit, remember?

"How could I forget? "

"I'll send you a copy of the video. I had someone here do a spectral analysis of my video to see if they could spot the hologram. They found it quickly. I thought you might want to do a spectral analysis of the lab video. I'll check it if you want to send me a copy."

"It's been a while. I think Josh took a leave of absence. As of August 2019, he's not around, and Tamara left the University. I think she is working at her parents' company in Brevard County.

"George said they are living at the beach, kids going to school there this fall. "

I'll send you a copy of the lab demonstration video. And I'd like to see your parrot video, thanks," Arno said.

"Okay, I'll send you the parrot video."

A short while later, Arno sent Simone the video clip with Josh and the rabbit. An hour later, she replies with a one-word text, "Hologram." Afterward, she sends an e-mail outlining how the switch between the real rabbit and the Hologram may have been done.

Arno remembers Josh's use of the word "illusion." It all makes sense now. At this point, he doesn't care that much. This administration is siphoning off billions of dollars from every department's budget. Much corruption is seeping into the cracks of the government structure. He is expecting a recall to Washington at any time. Still, he'd like to hear from Josh and Tamara about what they were up to with the illusion. Their presentation could easily be justified as a convenient way to explain what happened. A part of him wants to let them know their little "illusion" is finally revealed. Arno decides to ride out to the beach to see Josh and Tamara. First, he will try to contact them.

CHAPTER TWENTY-TWO

"Fly me to the Moon."

No private enterprise has attempted to launch a space vessel from earth to orbit the moon. The first is Arroyo Aerospace and the International Space Exploration Group (ISEG). They feel confident that the mission will be successful. There is a risk that they will be discovered and their long-term goals compromised. The flight of Galaxy One to the moon is necessary to ensure the successful launch of Galaxy Two. Once Galaxy Two is in space, there will be no hiding.

The crew attends a meeting before the scheduled launch. Kevin Steiner explains the programmed navigation to everyone. "There are many possible routes to get to the moon from Earth. Certain flight paths will conserve fuel but take longer. With our type of propulsion, fuel is not an issue. We are working with gravity and the space-time flow of energy. The route we chose is based on the Apollo 8 flight path. Galaxy One will go into Earth Orbit and, after one orbit, will launch to the moon at 25,000 mph. A big difference is that we will maintain that speed until we approach the moon's gravitational field. At this point, the spacecraft will ease back and coast so it can go into a lunar orbit at eighty miles above the surface."

"It will take about fourteen hours to get to the moon. Theoretically, we might be able to go faster. Working with gravity like this is all new. We want to be sure we can slow down, orbit the moon, and not crash into it. It will take about two hours to orbit the moon at 4400 mph. We have programmed three lunar orbits before leaving and heading back to earth. The lunar orbits will be stable at an orbital inclination of fifty degrees. The trip back may be faster depending on our experience getting to the moon."

Andrew added, "We can change the program as we go and self-navigate at any time if needed. As Kevin mentions flying this way is new. We've gained experience on all the test flights. The gravity propulsion drive is sensitive and responsive. We don't know how dealing with the switch from the earth's gravity field to the moon's gravity field will go exactly. Things are programmed based on what we expect."

"So, we're looking at about two days in space?" Josh asks.

"Yes," Carlos said. "We've loaded additional oxygen and water on the ship to accommodate the number of people on board and the length of time of the flight. We can sustain life for three weeks or more with the additional supplies. CO_2 and other gases we humans emit are processed through a carbon scrubbing filtration system, with methane also being expelled from the ship. Whatever is useful will be recycled and combined with the electrolysis system output. This system has worked well in all our flight tests."

Carlos continues, "Average speed getting there is 17,000 mph. We will leave earth at 25,000 mph and reduce speed as we get closer to the moon. If all goes well, we might try pushing the return speed up to 25,000 mph. Then we'll ease into Earth orbit at 18,000 mph before we descend," said Andrew. "Kevin and Carlos have programmed alternate scenarios should we need them."

Josh checks his watch, noting that they will lift off in a few hours. He has already said goodbye to the children and Adrienne. "It's going to be a new moon tonight, so we will see our destination as we lift off." He knows a full moon is not a prerequisite for a trip to the moon, only a good memory. They are allowed to take their company cell phones using them in airplane mode only. He has two cell phones now. He left his phone behind at the beach condo. He transferred his favorite family pictures and videos to the second phone registered to Arroyo Aerospace Inc. His watch is also synced to the second phone. No one has the number besides Adrienne and Arroyo Aerospace. Carlos installed a special VPN App. that obscures the server location and phone number. All calls to and from the ranch are made on the company phone.

Communication with the ground control center during the flight will be limited. Raoul Sr., Marcella, Kevin, Sam, and Paul are staffing the control room. Annie will be in touch with families to give them updates. Adrienne plans to come by ground control often. Bill Arroyo also intends to be there.

"How is everyone feeling? No colds or other ailments currently, I hope?" Marcella inquires.

Josh, Tamara, Andrew, Carlos, and Raoul Jr. all say they feel good and are ready to go. The entire ship has been cleaned and disinfected. Life support checked and rechecked for any issues. Precooked meals, snacks, and beverages are stored in the galley. Paul's mission on this trip is to document the journey. The ship's hull got a second coating of the cloaking spray that Tamara and Josh developed. The cloaking spray has been working well on the test missions. Galaxy Two will not need spraying. It will have the feature incorporated into the metal of the hull.

At 11:00 p.m., the crew got into their flight suits and boarded Galaxy One. This is a significant occasion for Captain Andrew Sun. Since leaving the astronaut program, thoughts of going into space only sometimes entered his mind. Going to the moon is beyond any notion he imagined. Andrew and Annie have been happily married for twenty-five years. Their son is in his final year of medical school at John Hopkins. They cannot tell him about this or any other flights his father is piloting for Arroyo Aerospace. Annie is comfortable with Andrew taking Galaxy One into space. She believes the ship is sound and that Andrew is the best person to Captain the spaceship.

Carlos Arroyo has no fear that Galaxy One will make it to the moon and back to earth. Having written the programming for the ship incorporating all of Kevin's navigational code, he is confident the trip will go well. He studied programming his entire life, ultimately graduating from Stanford with honors. Now at thirty-six, he is a master programmer. The ship can fly itself, given the instruction to do so.

Tamara Arroyo checks all the features of her flight suit. It is not uncomfortable. It seems unnecessary to her since the ship has done so well in tests. She understands the necessity of wearing it. There will be some changes in pressure leaving the atmosphere, so it is better to be safe.

Raoul Jr. quietly contemplated the trip and his responsibilities. He is looking forward to the journey. He is proud to be the designated copilot for this trip. Sam gave him briefings on all the spacecraft's features and the life support system. Raoul Jr. is looking forward to seeing the moon up close.

Josh sits quietly in his flight chair, meditating. His goal is to stay in the present. He will take each step in the flight as it comes. His responsibilities require him to be alert and there in the moment. He and Tamara have control of the ship's systems, radar screens, and communications devices. Carlos is a navigator and flight systems operator. However, there is duplication and overlap at all stations.

Galaxy One floats upward into the night sky and the new moon at midnight. A much more subtle departure than any of the historic Apollo missions. No thundering rockets and fiery lift-off. Nonetheless, dramatic to those on the ship and those observing. After taping the lift-off, Paul returns to the hangar and ground control room. Before Galaxy One is very high in altitude, Raoul Jr. turns on the cloaking. The ship flickers for a moment and disappears into the moonlit night.

Captain Sun watches the instruments as they record the ascent. They will be in orbit 260 miles above the earth in a few minutes. After one orbit, Galaxy One will move toward the moon at 25,000 mph riding Earth's gravity on its voyage around the moon and home again. It is daylight over China as they circle the planet. Josh looks down, wondering if he can see the great wall or Shaolin Temple, but it is cloudy, mainly over China. Galaxy One leaves earth's orbit at 1:45 a.m. on its way to the moon.

First checking internal air pressure and verifying that the control center is okay, Captain Sun announces, "Okay, everyone, it looks like you can remove your helmets."

"Check your dosimeter. The ship's meters show that no significant radiation is getting through the hull," Carlos announces.

"This ship and hull are solid. All systems good," Raoul Jr. said. "Ship's gravity is excellent, a fraction less than the earth, so be careful when you get up from your chairs. The entire ship has artificial gravity now."

Josh looks around the control center. The rest of the crew seems fine, busy checking instruments as reflected moonlight filters through the front window glass. Each crew member is routinely doing their job. Josh is unsure about his feelings or how to react now that they are speeding toward the moon. It is exhilarating to be in space, walking around the ship and not floating around weightless in a tiny capsule as the previous travelers to the moon have done. Space travel is as mundane as an airline flight on earth.

Tamara undoes her seatbelt, stands up, and stretches her arms above her head. She then gently brings her arms down as she bends over to touch her toes. She inhales, moving her hands up her legs and body, her arms and open hands stretching toward the ship's roof. Exhaling her breath, she said, smiling, "I think we are in space now and on our way. It's okay to get up and move around."

Captain Sun turned toward Tamara, "You are right," he said. "We are going to be in space for a couple of days. Let's be comfortable. According to what I'm seeing, the ship and navigation are doing perfectly well on the auto program. Let's confirm our status with ground control. Josh, can you send them a short message saying all is well and that we are on our way?"

"Certainly, will do," Josh said as he typed and sent the message. Looking around toward Raoul Jr., Carlos, and Tamara, "I'm sure your family must be pleased with this moment."

Captain Sun agreed, "this is a momentous occasion. I will turn on the video communication screen so we can see outside. Carlos, please bring up the rear camera so we can see Earth?"

Carlos punches a few keys on his console, and a shot of the blue planet comes up as if in the rear-view mirror of an automobile.

"Few people have seen Earth from this vantage point," Josh remarks. "I believe we have a message streaming in from the ground control center."

The screen changes from the exterior view of the planet to a video of Raoul Sr., Marcella, Sam, Annie, and Adrienne waving. "You're doing a great job; everything looks good from here. We must keep it short. Love you all." The transmission ends.

"Great, Carlos said. That transmission bounced around our little corner of our Uber Net, then off a few communications satellites, including our own. No one will know where it ended up. We still need to be careful. The transmission is a good sign." He switches the monitor back to viewing outside. This time to the forward camera array, which shows the moon in the distance and millions of stars."

"It's been three hours since we launched. At a certain time, we'll slow down to about 18,600 MPH. Then, in four hours, when we get closer to the moon's gravitational field, the program will balance the difference between the earth's and the moon's fields. This will gradually slow us down so we can head to the moon's dark side and do our orbits."

"The Chinese have a satellite in low orbit and a lander on the far side of the moon," Josh said.

Yes," Carlos replies. "If our cloaking holds up, they will never know we are there."

"The Chinese have an aggressive space program. They've had some accidents and bad landings on Mars, but they are not stopping," Tamara remarks. "It seems in the last few years China and countries including Japan, India, and the Arab Emirates, maybe other countries that you do not think of having a space program, have launched satellites. Space is the new frontier."

"Yes," Raoul Jr. said," and they're still using rockets, so out of date!"

The crew all laughed.

"It will be a new ball game once this technology becomes known. We can keep it secret for now. Hopefully, launch Galaxy Two before the world notices this UFO. Once that happens, it will be difficult not to share something, in some way, if we want to survive," Josh said.

"Raoul Sr. and Marcella are aware of this. They will know what to do when the time comes. They want to share the drive with the planet, not just one country. This technology will take humanity into space," Tamara mentions as she walks toward the ship's rear.

"Certain entrepreneurs like Ramurt and Musk have made a big investment in rockets. This invention will hurt their future business," Raoul Jr. said.

"Their rockets will still be needed until the drive becomes available in the marketplace. Then they can adapt their plans and designs to incorporate the new technology," Carlos said. "That will not happen for a long time."

"Once what we're doing becomes public, we'll have to make deals and try to hold on to the rights to the drive. There will be those who will make the argument that it's like patenting the wheel. I'm sure if they had patents when the wheel came along, someone would have claimed it," Tamara said.

"Okay, here's our watch schedule. Every three hours, we can switch around. Raoul Jr. and I will alternate. Tamara, you can relieve Josh for a couple of hours and then Carlos. There are alarms on everything should there be any problems. There are some bunks below if you want to lie down for a nap," Captain Sun announces.

Carlos said, "I'll get up and stretch my legs and then nap in place. I'm too wound up to lie down."

Josh said, "I took a nap before I came in today, so I'm doing okay. Everything appears normal as far as the radar around us shows. No space junk or rocks are flying around here. No other spaceships in our path. Must be a slow traffic day in outer space."

"We're looking good regarding internal or external heat or coldness. The ship's hull is fine. And according to what I can see here, our navigation is perfect. Compensation for the Earth moving and the moon moving is being done automatically, and we are on course. The drive is capable of handling subtle changes in our direction. Rocket ships or space capsules need to fire small bursts for course correction to stay on course," Carlos explained.

Raoul Jr. got up from his flight chair. "I believe we have some breakfast stowed away in the galley fridge. We also have hot water; we can make tea or coffee. Can I get anyone something?"

"Sure, some tea and whatever there is for breakfast. I'm betting it's better than most airline food I've been eating," Captain Sun responds.

"I'll go down with you," Tamara said. Carlos, Josh, can we get you anything?"

"I'll have the same, thanks," Carlos and Josh reply.

Tamara and Raoul Jr. head down to the second level. The steps to the second level spiral down around the shaft, leaving the center open. If they ever encounter weightlessness, there will be room to float down the center part of the shaft using the spiral steps as a handrail.

"All the comforts of home," Tamara said as they walked into the small galley.

In the refrigerator, they find some scrambled egg burritos and other food marked for breakfast, lunch, or dinner with instructions for warming in the microwave oven built into a shielded rack. An electric teapot and coffee maker sit in receptacles that they are latched into. All appliances are housed in secure cabinets. There are cups with lids made of soft plastic for beverages—hot and cold water from a built-in dispenser. Trash goes into closed containers. Tamara, thinking out loud, said, "wouldn't it be nice if commercial airlines had lounges along these lines?"

Carlos replies, "Maybe someday, if they stop being designed as flying tubes with wings, carrying three hundred people."

"Right," said Tamara. "I could never understand exactly why they stuck to that shape."

Six hours into the flight, the auto navigation program gradually reduces the speed of Galaxy One. They are about half of the way to the moon. Total flying time will be under 14 hours to orbit the moon from leaving Florida. In about six more hours, the speed will be gradually reduced again for the approach into lunar orbit. The propulsion system will utilize the moon's gravity field by this point. There are gravitational abnormalities on the moon's far side around giant crater sites, mass concentrations known as 'mascons.' Over several days, these positive gravitational concentrations may affect a spacecraft's orbit around the moon. Kevin did his best to give the autopilot and navigation program enough information to compensate. The captain and the crew planned to be on standby to use self-navigation controls should there be any wobbles in orbit. The danger is considered minimal since Galaxy One will only orbit the moon three times before heading back to Earth.

Finished her breakfast, Tamara relieves Carlos. Raoul Jr. gives Captain Sun a break. Eight hours into the flight, the ship's radar picks up a cloud of space dust directly in their path. There is nothing they can do to avoid the dust. Carlos makes sure the shield is active as they enter the cosmic cloud.

"It sounds like rain. It's minuscule dust particles suspended in space, perhaps orbiting the earth or moon for ages," Carlos said.

There is an intermittent flicker on the ship's hull as they move through the cloud. "Looks like a reaction between the particles and the shield, or it may be the cloaking spray," Raoul Jr. reports.

"Will it damage the hull?" Josh asks.

"It shouldn't do any damage. I believe the shield keeps the grains away or softens their impact. That shouldn't cause a flicker. I do see some fluctuations in the cloaking currents," Carlos said.

After a few minutes, Carlos announces, "We are clear of the cloud. I do not detect any damage. The cloaking of the ship appears to be working. There is still some flickering on sections of the hull. Let's see if it stops. Maybe residual dust on the hull is now traveling with us."

"Do you think the hull is reacting with the electronics built into the cloaking spray?" Josh asks.

"It's possible. The only way to tell is to turn the cloaking off. We can wait a while before we test that theory. Less chance we will be seen. The cloaking is still working," Captain Sun said.

Raoul Jr. suggests, "we can test it on the far side of the moon."

"Yes, we can do that. I wonder if that Chinese rover Chang'e 3 is still working? They were bouncing signals off a couple of satellites to send data and info back to earth," Carlos said. "We also have NASA's Lunar Reconnaissance Orbiter (LRO), which I believe is in an elliptical orbit these days. There are satellites from Japan, India, and others in varying conditions. Some may not be operational."

Privately, Josh is worried about the sparkle and flicker on sections of the hull. He suspects that the grains in the dust cloud might have worn down the coating on the hull. The flicker is either electrical or light reflected off the worn-down layer. He mentions his misgivings to Carlos.

"We can live with the flicker. No one on Earth will be able to see it. Better to keep the cloaking on. The Chinese lander came down to the moon in January of this year. The rover may not be working anymore. I suggest we wait and maybe check the cloaking when we are on the dark side of the moon if the LRO is not passing there simultaneously," Carlos said. "Kevin said he set our orbit to avoid NASA's LRO and other known active satellites. The NASA LRO is taking excellent photos of the lunar surface. It may not notice us in orbit."

"We have about four hours until the next reduction of speed. By that time, we will be about two hours from Lunar Orbit," Captain Sun said. "Stretch your legs. Get a little rest."

Before they launched, Paul gave Tamara and Josh a review of how all the built-in cameras on the ship work and their locations. There is a panel at one of the stations where they can be activated. Tamara oversees the acquisition of the moon's video and stills as they approach and orbit. Paul wonders if the American flag remains there from the Apollo 17 manned landing. He asks them to keep an eye out for it even though they will be at least eighty miles above the surface. Tamara is still determining if their orbit will even cross that area of the moon. The installed cameras are high resolution and telephoto to cover any eventuality.

On Earth, Raoul Sr., Sam, Kevin, and Paul are watching the progress of Galaxy One via signals coded and relayed through earth satellites to servers that are part of Carlos's new "Uber Net." It will be difficult for anyone to know that the signals originated in outer space. Ground control is also receiving tracking information and systems data. They are satisfied with the progress and trajectory of the ship.

Adrienne drives back to the beach after the video of everyone waving to the crew transmission. She is confident in the mission but still on edge. Having your soul mate and father of your children on the way to the moon is not easy to forget. She needs to get some sleep before it is time to get the children ready for school. Morgan is now in 9th grade at Cocoa Beach High School. Lauren is in the eighth grade at the middle school. The following day she drops them both off at school and returns home. She receives a call from Marcella saying, "good morning, and wishing her a good day." This is a prearranged call with a greeting to let Adrienne know all is well.

Adrienne hears Josh's phone vibrating a few times, so she checks it. There were a couple of calls from Arno this morning. A short while later, there is another call from Arno. Adrienne answers it this time.

"Hi, I'm trying to reach Josh Bennett," Arno said.

"Hi, Arno, this is Adrienne. Josh is out of town for a few days. He forgot his phone. Can I give him a message?

"I am just checking with him or Tamara about the grant project. Nothing urgent or official. I don't have a current phone number for Tamara."

"Sorry, I don't have her number. I'll let Josh know when he calls or returns next week."

"Okay, thanks. No rush. I'll give him a call when he returns. Enjoy your time at the beach."

"Thanks."

The moment he hangs up, Arno decides he will not pursue this issue. It isn't official business, and he does not care if they created the "illusion" to get rid of the visitors. They lost the grant. It is over. No time for ego trips. Besides, he has decided that he is leaving the CIA soon. He has an offer to join a law firm in Chicago and an offer to teach at UCF. They are developing some Cyber Security curriculum, and he was interested in that area. Arno thinks he might enjoy interacting with students and academic life. He realizes that teaching is the subject he wants to talk to Josh about.

Adrienne takes a few days off from the agency. She plans to meet with Paul to finalize the latest press releases on the film. Galaxy Two construction is moving along quickly. The frame is in place, and the outer hull gets attached to the frame as sections are bonded together. No pictures of the "set" will go out until the hull is in place. The Gate to the Galaxy studio theme park will not open until late 2020, about a year away. By that time, the ship will have the entire multilayer hull in place, instrumentation installed, and be ready for the drives. When it is finished, Paul will start shooting some scenes for the film inside Galaxy Two. They will claim that it is built using authentic-looking and functional equipment to increase the film's realism. She arrives at the studio, where Annie tells her that Paul is at the ground control center. Adrienne heads over to the hangars. Inside the center, they are waiting for Galaxy One to enter lunar orbit.

"Hi, Adrienne. How are you doing? Marcella asks. "We're about to go into lunar orbit. Good timing. This is a critical maneuver for the navigation system and program." Trajectory data equivalent to what Captain Sun and the others are seeing on the ship came up on the ground control center screens.

On schedule, before the anticipated lunar orbit, the ship slows down to 7500 mph. Looming two hours in the distance is the moon.

Raoul Jr. announces, "the ship is now using the moon's gravity waves for propulsion. Lunar gravity is about one-sixth as strong as earth's gravity. The gradual switch to lunar gravity slows the ship. Programming for switching to an alternate source or balancing between two gravity fields is working as expected. Raoul Sr., Carlos, Kevin, and Marcella installed basic artificial Intelligence assets into the drive programming. The navigation and drive programming are in AI mode currently. We can override the AI if necessary."

Refreshed from his break, Captain Sun returns and is at the helm. Raoul Jr. goes on a break but will return before they go into orbit. It has been twelve hours since leaving earth. Josh is awake after taking a nap. Carlos sleeps in his seat most of the time. Tamara is sleeping in the crew quarters on the second level. She will be paged before they go into orbit.

"There are a lot of old satellites ahead still circling the moon. They are all in stable lunar orbits, so they do not crash onto the surface," Josh noted, checking the radar screen for objects in their path. The auto flight program is configured to avoid them."

"Too bad we can't scoop some of them up for salvage," Captain Sun remarks. That's not what this ship is built for and who knows about ownership or salvage rights."

"Good question," Carlos said. Anyone can claim them if you go by Earth salvage laws since they are in what you might call 'International Space." No boundaries out here. I think it will depend on if they are still functioning. If they are dead, they are space junk."

"Around 25,000 or more satellites are circling the earth. More coming. Elon Musk, Space X is launching 42,000 satellites to beam the internet to earth from space. He started launching in May, Josh said. Plans to have it all up by the end of 2024."

"There are no rules about what anyone can do out here. Some day they will need a giant scoop to fly around the planet and suck up all the space trash so that we can see the stars," Captain Sun said.

The ship slows a bit and makes some adjustments to its trajectory. Carlos announces that they are getting ready to go into lunar orbit. Tamara returns from her nap and joins everyone as they get closer to the moon and orbit. "How's the cloaking doing?" she asks.

"Looks the same, still some flicker. I believe we are still cloaked," Carlos said.

Josh confirms the situation. "All anyone might record are scattered tiny sparkles moving into lunar orbit. We are still a tiny shadow in anyone's view. I'm sure the dust cloud scrubbed some of the coating off the hull. The flicker is an electrical current making jumps where the coating is thin. If we turn the cloaking off, those connections will be broken, possibly resulting in no cloaking."

"I agree," Carlos said. We are about to go into lunar orbit in five minutes."

To achieve the desired lunar orbit, the ship slows and makes some additional adjustments to its trajectory. Each orbit will take about ninety minutes. They are moving at 4400 mph as they float into lunar orbit.

"Lunar orbit achieved," Captain Sun announces. "We're going to get a look at the other side of the moon very soon."

Watching the radar, Josh spots the NASA satellite and the Japanese satellite, each in a different orbit. The NASA satellite is in a polar orbit, whereas Galaxy One is in an elliptical orbit around the middle of the moon.

The side of the moon facing the earth with its craters and dark and light spots turn out to be very different from the far side. It is dark on the moon's near side and bright on the far side. The surface looks much different than the earth-facing side. There are no dark and light patches like you find on the side facing the earth. There appears to be a significant impact area crater near the South Pole-Aitken Basin. This is where the Chinese Lander Chang'e 2 with rover Chang'e 3 put down.

Andrew and Raoul Jr. keep a close watch on the stability of the orbit as they begin the journey around the moon's far side. The ship is in a highly stable orbit, so any fluctuations caused by 'mascons' will be negligible.

Can anyone see Chang'e 3 rover near the south pole?" Tamara asks.

"I've got a high definition, long lens camera looking at that area. I don't see anything. That doesn't mean it's not there or that it can't see us up here. I believe they have another mission headed to the moon at the end of the month," Josh said.

Returning to the near side of the moon Galaxy One begins its second orbit. The auto program navigation and drive are performing flawlessly. The signal from Galaxy One to ground control came back on schedule when the ship started the second orbit. After the third orbit, the next big step will be leaving the lunar orbit and heading back to earth.

Josh keeps the cameras recording video of the lunar surface on both sides of the moon.

Josh said, "looking at the far side is like looking at a different moon. No 'man in the moon' here. A different landscape. There are fewer craters— no change in the grey color of the rocks and soil. Being on the far side, experiencing its unfamiliar terrain from this vantage point, makes me realize what being in outer space is like. We are in our small spaceship orbiting this desolate moon. It's not like being in a submarine underwater, with the ability to come to the surface. Out here in space, the only refuge we have is this ship. There is no place to go except back to Earth. I'm grateful that I'm not claustrophobic."

The second orbit of the moon accomplished, Galaxy one begins the final third orbit. Ninety minutes pass before Galaxy One completes its third look at the moon's far side. Returning toward the near side, the ship accelerates out of the moon's orbit on a path back to earth.

Captain Sun is the first to notice that the acceleration speed does not match their expectations. Carlos quickly confirms the issue. They manually boost the speed, then let the auto program take over again. The drive responds sluggishly and finally gets up to speed as the ship leaves lunar orbit and heads home.

"Wow, what happened there?" Josh asks.

Captain Sun replies, "It appears we were not going to achieve the speed we needed to leave the moon's orbit properly, on a trajectory to send us home. We boosted the speed manually."

Carlos adds, "I think there is a glitch in the drive's programming. It uses gravity waves to push away, a kind of anti-gravity. The moon's gravity is only one-sixth of earth's gravity, so maybe the transforming capability is slow, or the programming is looking for something stronger to pull the ship away. We forced it to decide. In a short time, it will switch over to earth's gravity fields. We can check this later when we get back to earth."

"What would have happened if we hadn't overridden the auto-drive program?" Tamara asks.

"Well, we might not have left lunar orbit, maybe just gone into a fourth orbit at a different height or speed. If we did leave orbit, we would have needed to correct the flight path, which may have required another lunar orbit. We have self-navigation, or we can bring up the auto-drive programming to give us a new trajectory. Luckily, we caught it while it was still within the programmed plan," Captain Sun said.

"Good work Captain Andrew and Carlos, you saved us much possible hassle," Josh said.

"Thanks. Our instrumentation immediately alerted us that there was an issue. Good thing we were ready," Carlos said.

"Looks like we are on track to earth. We will pick up speed soon. We will be ready to go into earth orbit in about thirteen hours. We can relax for a while," the captain said.

"We have a ton of video of both sides of the moon. We can replay some of it if you like," Josh offers.

Everyone wants to see the footage. Josh starts with clips from the first approach into lunar orbit. Looking at it on the screen, it feels faster than it had sitting on the ship. One clip catches a satellite in the view to one side. "This is great footage," Josh said. "No one will ever be able to say we weren't here should that occasion ever arise."

"Raoul Sr. and Marcella will be thrilled to see this footage," Tamara said. "One of these days, we'll get them out in space themselves."

Carlos nods his head, "They probably will enjoy that. Sam wanted them to wait to make sure everything was working well. There is a worry about radiation, but we are not showing any problems. The only glitch we experienced is leaving lunar orbit."

"Speaking of glitches, how's the cloaking doing?" Josh inquires.

"It is still working from what I can tell," Carlos answers. "If the coating is wearing thin, entering Earth's atmosphere will be a test."

Captain Sun said, "We are scheduled for an afternoon touchdown, weather permitting. We can stay in orbit if necessary. If the cloaking is acting up, we will draw some attention. Since cloaking is unreliable, we can disappear into the atmosphere quickly. It might be a good idea to turn off the cloaking before we get to Earth in case it has been picked up by some satellite around the moon or near earth. We are not easy to see. The flickering might draw attention. Think about it."

Carlos said, "you make a good point. If it keeps flickering, we might draw attention to ourselves. It may be a good time to try and reboot it. What do you think, Josh?"

"Good idea. If we've been seen and anyone is still looking, we will become less visible and easy to track. Especially approaching Earth. If we reboot and the cloaking doesn't come back on, we may be spotted close to Earth as we go into orbit."

Tamara said, "Reboot it and see what happens. If it comes back the same way, let's turn it off for a few hours until we get closer to Earth. If someone spotted us, they would look around the moon, not closer to earth."

"I'm okay with that. What do you think, Carlos?" Josh asked.

Checking with Andrew, "Captain?"

"Let's reboot it and see how it goes. This is a good place to test it."

"Good," Carlos said. "Here it goes." He types a reboot command into the system. The cloaking goes off for about five seconds and comes back on again. "No flickering is visible."

"This is good news. We'll keep an eye on it. If anything is tracking us, we have just disappeared again," Josh said.

After screening more moon shots, Josh senses that everyone needs a break. He switches the monitor to a live image of the Earth as they head home. "Returning home to the planet Earth," he thinks. Closing his eyes, he dozes off. Tamara and Raoul Jr. also take a nap. Captain Sun and Carlos rest their eyes, knowing they will receive audio alerts if there is an issue.

"They are on their way home," Marcella tells Adrienne. The tracking information has them on course. It looks like they are slightly behind schedule, leaving lunar orbit for some reason, but no problems."

Carlos sends a short message to ground control that the cloaking is acting up but still working.

Sam adds, "At this point, their safe landing is the most important thing. They are in stealth mode, so radar will not find them. If anyone sees them, they won't have time to figure out what's there. Another unexplained UFO sighting. They will disappear into the atmosphere. The weather is predicted to be cloudy here by the time they arrive."

In China, a technician working in the control center at the Chinese Space Agency notices an odd transmission from Chang'e 3 bouncing off the relay satellite. It is several pictures of something in lunar orbit that seems like it carries a flickering aura or electrical charge. The flickering has an oval shape, almost like an eye blinking. A second transmission shows the same thing again about ninety minutes later and a third time after that. It is then gone. He calls his supervisor to have a look at it. They wait awhile, but there is no other citing. They decide to use the telescope at the observatory to look toward the moon to see if there is anything in lunar orbit that they are unaware of.

NASA downloads pictures taken by The Lunar Reconnaissance Orbiter in the last twenty-four hours. Some shots of a mysterious flickering object that appears to be entering lunar orbit. No one pays much attention to it. They believe it to be some light aberration, maybe some space dust. The flickering eye shape orbits three times and then disappears. The tech person reviewing the pictures decides to send the latest photos up the chain of command with a note about the flickering object.

With its telescope pointed toward the moon, the Chinese observatory scans the view, looking for anomalies like a flickering light. Nothing unusual is detected—no new satellites in lunar orbit. After getting the negative report from the observatory, the supervisor sends the pictures to the photo analysis department for examination.

Awaking from his nap, Raoul Jr. opens one eye to see where he is. He dreamed that a rocket passed them going in the opposite direction. In the dream, he is initially scared, but then he decides it is an Atlas Rocket going to Mars. Not that busy up here yet, he realizes as he scans the instrument panel. About three-quarters of the way home, he notes.

Carlos comes up from the second level with a coffee and a turkey sandwich.

"Everything looks fine," Raoul Jr. said. "How's the sandwich?"

"Very good." "Margarita and Oliver prepared all the food on board."

Andrew, Tamara, and Josh sit at a table outside the galley on the second level, having something to eat. "I'm not sure if this is lunch or dinner, but it tastes good," said Tamara.

Andrew is talking about the spaceship. "It's amazing that we are sitting here eating in comfort. All manned flights up until now have been in cramped quarters, eating out of tubes of paste food or rations. We have real food, a place to sleep, a shower, and a toilet, and we are not floating around the ship."

"It is awe-inspiring. I never dreamed I would fly in space. Let alone with a lot more "leg room" than in first class on a commercial flight on Earth," Josh said.

Tamara said, "What we are doing, you know what Raoul Sr. and Marcella have made real, is beyond imagination. This is a bold step, traveling to the moon."

"Hopefully, any notice of Galaxy One will be written off as some unexplained phenomenon, Andrew said. "As Raoul Sr. says, 'we're only a silhouette or shadow in space.' Things may become complicated if anyone gets a serious track on us."

"I agree. If it gets out that we exist, every country, corporation, and hacker will be looking to get information on us. I don't know how others feel about it, but it may be time to limit flights while Sam gets Galaxy Two finished," Josh said.

Andrew agrees. "You know, it's like the card game blackjack. It would be best to assume the dealer's down card is a ten. We must assume something picked us up while we had the flicker. There are satellites all around us in lunar orbit. We must be careful not to give them more miscellaneous information like a sighting of the ship somewhere on earth."

Thinking like the Captain for a moment, Andrew checks his watch. "We better head upstairs. We are getting close."

Galaxy One slows down from its cruising speed and begins its approach to Earth at 14:00 (2:00 p.m.) EST. Soon it goes into orbit at 260 miles above the earth. It is higher than the international space station and about an hour behind the ISS orbiting position. After one orbit, the ship begins its float down and into the atmosphere. It is at this point that some flicker returns around the hull. When they enter the clouds, Captain Sun turns off the cloaking. Carlos tries rebooting it again. This time it does not reboot. They quickly decide to leave it off as the ship heads home. At 15:15 on a rainy afternoon, Galaxy One arrives at Arroyo Aerospace, then floats into the hangar. They are home. The crew disembarks and has their physical health vitals checked. They are all as healthy as when they departed. There is a short meeting to discuss the flight and record observations. Sam and Raoul Sr. begin a check of all systems on Galaxy One.

One of the astronauts looking out a window on the International Space Station thought she saw lightning in the cloudy upper atmosphere below them. She took pictures of the phenomenon and mentioned it to another astronaut. He believes it is odd-looking lightning. It appears to stop, and they soon forget about it. The first astronaut makes a note of it in her journal.

Raoul Sr. and Sam check the ship and find it in perfect condition. Their scan of the hull finds some space dust adhering to it in a few places.

"Has anyone ever analyzed space dust before?" Sam asked.

"We can scrape some of it off and look at it, Raoul Sr. said.

Marcella sent the crew home after the reports. Adrienne is there to drive Josh home. Sitting in the car, he wonders if he has actually just flown to the moon and returned. Adrienne assures him he is not dreaming.

Josh calls Arno back a few days after getting back from the moon. Arno tells him about the offer he had to teach. They arrange to meet for lunch near UCF.

Josh thinks Arno seems more relaxed. He realizes it is himself who is in a better place away from the grant and all the associated problems. They meet at the Island Fin Poke, a Hawaiian-style restaurant near the UCF main campus.

Arno asked, "How are you doing? I understand you and the family are spending the summer at the beach."

"Yes, Adrienne is working with a film company on a new project. I have a leave of absence from the university. Tamara and I have support from a company to use their facilities to do research. How are you? Did you decide what you are going to do?" Josh asks.

"I have tentatively accepted a teaching position at UCF. They are waiting for the position to be officially open. I'll be an associate program director for the new curriculum in Cyber Security. I spent some time at the agency working on international aspects of this a few years back. Now it's a major problem."

"What made you want to leave the company?" Josh asked quietly after looking around.

"There are many reasons. I've been there for ten years and do not see a future. Only in the movies do you see African American agents rise to prominence and rarely even there," Arno said with a sense of disappointment. "Babysitting grant recipients is not exactly what I see as my career, nothing personal. Over the last few years, the agency and intelligence services have been politicized by far-right politics. Even though I'm moderate, I always try to remain objective regarding my work."

"I understand. I bet you will be an excellent teacher. You have a lot of experience. I understand you're not pleased with all the security stuff around our work. I want you to know that we were relieved when they canceled the grant. The project appeared to be heading in the wrong direction."

"You were upset about the possibility of experiments on more than rabbits?"

"Yes, that, and the administration is so corrupt. We wanted to change the direction of things, so we put together that whole rabbit presentation."

"The illusion," Arno said, smiling.

Josh hesitated for a moment, thinking to himself, he knows something. Let's let him know. "As you may have surmised by now, the demonstration was an illusion. Our intention was not to get the grant canceled, get them off our backs."

"Well, you had me fooled for quite a while. Simone, whom you must know works for the company, thought it was a hologram. We checked a video of the presentation with special equipment, and there it was. It doesn't matter now. Grant is over. I say it was a demonstration to show how the actual event happened. No foul."

Josh looks relieved. "Thanks, appreciate the shade. That was our approach. We couldn't come up with any other explanation except some optical illusion."

"We will be writing the curriculum starting in a few weeks. They say it could take six months. I've never done that before. I haven't officially resigned yet. I will resign if it looks like I will get transferred out of Florida."

"It's a long process, especially if you are developing new courses. I always tried to make my courses more about the students learning than me talking. I looked for ways to get the students involved in the teaching. My theory is that I wasn't teaching I was learning. Student and teacher, we can all learn together, maybe at different levels, still all learning."

"I like that idea," Arno said.

"The only downside to life in academia is internal politics. I've attended several universities and taught at a few. I've met some great administrators and faculty. Great colleagues and learning opportunities but, unfortunately, also some very nasty people. I usually try to stay clear of them and all that political stuff, although it can be difficult when it hunts you down. Beware the person who complains to you about someone else. They are probably complaining about you too."

"I guess it isn't much different from government or the corporate world," Arno said. "We'll see what happens."

The conversation continues over lunch. Both men feel comfortable talking and sharing ideas.

CHAPTER TWENTY-THREE

*"Those who do not learn from the past are doomed
to repeat the same mistakes again."*

Raoul Sr.'s parents, Conrad and Julia Arroyo, visit the ranch often. They like splitting their time between their home in Maine, the family rancho in Costa Rica, and the ranch in Florida. Julia's dark hair, streaked with grey, is shoulder length. Conrad's white beard is close-cropped, and his white hair is tied back in a short ponytail. They are always energetic and happy. Josh enjoys conversations with Conrad. As a historian, Conrad is aware of his inherent subjectivity. He tries to base his awareness on objective reality, a factual, accurate, or false point-of-view. Conrad believes specific trends in the planet's history and human evolution exist. Times of prosperity are followed by disastrous times. So-called enlightenment followed by years of confusion and ignorance. The earth evolves ecologically, which alters the course of human evolution. Human activity alters the planet's ecology. Conrad's observations and subsequent views are based on long-range projections he derives from historical, social, and political trends.

One afternoon Josh and Conrad take a walk around the interior of Galaxy Two, which is fully enclosed now by the outer hull components. They are each wearing a face mask. It is mid, 2020 the COVID Virus is beginning to peak in the U.S. Conrad explains what he believes transpired.

"The world has been hit with a virus that originated in China in late 2019," he said. "This is not the first time a virus has devastated the world. It appears that the Chinese did not release complete information about occurrences of this virus to the international community. They may not have known how fast it spread. China shut down domestic travel in China while allowing foreign travel out of the country. The first significant outbreak happened in Wuhan, China, beginning in late 2019. It is not reported internationally until January 2020. It is unclear where the virus originated. It may have transferred to humans from animals or bad security at a Wuhan lab. It's been reported that the first known case is an individual working at an open food market that sells exotic game animals in Wuhan. The entire city, with a population of eleven million people, and surrounding areas of Wuhan in China are locked down. Social distancing and mask-wearing are mandated everywhere. China refuses to release how many deaths occurred in Wuhan or elsewhere in China."

Josh mentions, "the news of these events in China in December 2019 and January 2020 did not get disseminated to the public by the U.S. administration."

Conrad replies, "For whatever reason, the American administration did not take warnings seriously, and news of the virus is purposefully ignored and suppressed. Reports indicate that intelligence agencies warned the administration in 2018 of dangerous conditions in a lab in Wuhan, China. Possibly a scientist who died of the virus. Nothing is done. All warning signs and procedures to combat infectious diseases spreading are ignored. The administration received an emergency plan from the previous administration on how to handle dangerous virus outbreaks. It is ignored. The U.S. president and his administration did little to combat the spread of the virus this past January when it began spreading in the U.S., thereby creating a pandemic across the country that's killing Americans and others worldwide. The pandemic became a political issue around wearing a protective mask in public places and large gatherings. The failure of the United States to react to the virus in established ways, domestically and globally, may have aided the spread worldwide and the resulting global pandemic. A million people will likely die in the US alone."

"Here we are six months later. The COVID-19 virus is consuming the country. The U.S. now has the highest infection rate in the world. To their credit, the administration took steps to speed up the creation of a vaccine by incentivizing several pharmaceutical firms with pre-orders and billions of dollars. The vaccines cannot be ready until the end of the year at the earliest. I doubt the current administration plans to distribute the vaccine nationally when it is ready," Conrad said.

Josh comments, "there's a presidential election coming on November 3rd. The incumbent president is campaigning without a face mask and tells people that the virus will go away soon. He recommends unproven remedies and discourages any safety measures. He pushes the notion that if enough people get sick and recover, there will be 'herd immunity,' even though he knows the virus is lethal, he downplays its severity. Herd immunity comes from vaccinations. The Centers for Disease Control (CDC) cannot communicate directly with the country about what is happening. The administration uses obvious propaganda techniques to distract people from the pandemic."

Conrad replies, "This behavior is typical of leaders who think of themselves as kings, monarchs, or dictators. You can see the same kind of behavior from the president of Russia. Only their survival matters. This mentality has existed among humans for thousands of years. The country is reeling from the pandemic. Many schools and universities are stopping face-to-face classes and switching to distance learning starting with the spring semester. Hospitals in certain areas are becoming overwhelmed. Many industries are shut down. Where possible, people are working from home, a self-imposed lockdown."

"Yes, Adrienne's firm has everyone working from home. She's working from the beach condo, and Lauren and Morgan are doing what they call 'Launch Ed' classes from home," Josh said. "We are taking every precaution recommended, washing hands, disinfecting, and wearing masks in public."

"We live in dangerous and changing times here in this country and the world," Conrad said. "The experiment of a democracy by and for all the people seems in jeopardy. It reminds me of the growth of totalitarian movements in the 1930s. We know that the founders of this country, as well-intentioned and insightful as they may have been for their day, had a different historical and cultural view of the world. It didn't necessarily occur to them that their notions of freedom included all it does today. Their ideas about freedom and equality were narrow, mostly European concepts. Concepts derived from Roman law that accepts slavery and considers other humans property. The founders ignore the indigenous people who have different ideas about freedom and equality. This country has evolved, and the concepts of personal freedom have evolved. Some say the western notion of personal freedom and equality is based on faulty logic. That they were dreamed up by Europeans who had no idea what equality and freedom meant, their recorded history is about emperors, kings, lords, gods, and hierarchal culture. In the eighteenth century, slavery existed in the world. The founders of the country chose to ignore slavery in the colonies. It has only been about one-hundred-fifty years and a civil war since slavery was abolished in the U.S. We don't have slavery anymore. However, there are still other cultural beliefs that divide the country. Unfortunately, many people are easily manipulated by adversarial nations and dangerous individuals with dreams of power. The human mind is always ready to blame others for their real or perceived problems. Others can exploit this tendency."

Josh agrees, "Sometimes I think humanity is doomed to extinction. Homo sapiens don't seem to be able to adjust to change very well. Maybe we are hard-wired this way."

"There is much debate about those ideas in the social sciences. When you think about it, Homo sapiens in this world are a young species. It may take millions of years for beings to evolve into sentient creatures." Conrad stops as if he has something else to say but changes his mind.

Josh replies, "I thought about a similar idea when we were out in space looking at Earth. It is just this blue sphere in space. From afar, you can't tell if there is intelligent life on the planet. And if there is intelligent life, will they survive long enough to become truly sentient, as you say?"

Conrad is quiet for a moment, "Imagine that light year away in this galaxy. There is a solar system in what used to be known as the Argon constellation. This is a vast constellation that astronomers more recently divided into three separate areas. One solar system has a planet inhabited by a humanoid civilization. It has the same type of atmosphere and conditions as Earth. The Argonites, as I shall call them, survive and evolve over tens of millions of years. The planet is mostly water, with just one mountainous continent that expands toward the north and south poles from the equator. The land mass occupies about one-third of the planet's surface. The entire race of people evolves together. For a while, there are divisions between North, Central, and South. Over time populations unite to share the limited land resources and the generous bounty of the sea. Territorial conflicts end early on. A system of non-authoritarian, participatory interaction prevails, allowing all to live comfortably. The indigenous people can travel anywhere on the continent and be welcome. No one who needs shelter, food, or help is ever turned away. Over the millennia, technology advances. The population grows. Artificial islands are built to accommodate population growth. Ultimately, this civilization faces overpopulation. "

"Exploration of their solar system is undertaken to find another habitable world. The other planets in their solar system are gas or ice. Satellite colonies are constructed to orbit their planet. Starships are developed and built that can go on long journeys. Astronomers look across the galaxy for star systems with planets that might support life. They create large starships that travel at the speed of light carrying a thousand people. Volunteers know it's a one-way trip. They accept that the planet they live on is overpopulated. The ships do not have enough fuel or supplies to return if the faraway planet is already inhabited or not suitable in some other way. Once the starship arrives at the destination, they are on their own. Over time, they send thousands of these ships across the milky way and to other nearby galaxies. Twelve thousand years ago, one ship arrived here on this planet we call Earth. They find a Neolithic humanoid population spread out over the globe. No harm or interference with an indigenous people of a world is permitted. The earth cannot be colonized. A message is sent back to the home planet. It will not arrive there for many light years. No reply is expected. The travelers decide to resupply the ship from the earth. They will refine sea water to refuel the star drive. Accomplishing this requires landing the massive starship on the planet. An uninhabited island far from the nearest land mass is found. Landing the starship on the surface of the earth is problematic. The secondary drives are used to land the ship on the water near the island successfully. One thousand people leave the ship and begin living on the island as the work proceeds. "

"The starship's small landing crafts are used to search for minerals and other resources that can be refined. The ship's technical equipment and medical supplies are transported to the island. After two years, resupplies are ready, and plans are being made to go to another solar system. It is then that they discover that the seawater on earth is harming the hull of the ship, which was damaged entering earth's atmosphere. The sea water is eating away large sections of the hull, creating a kind of rust. Sea water is leaking into the lower levels of the ship. Even lifting the ship off the water does not make it possible for repairs. The high-tech resources needed to make these types of repairs to the hull are not available. Patches cannot withstand the force of light-speed travel."

"Before the ship can be brought to dry land, the island is hit by a category nine hurricane. The ship sinks into the ocean and slides down into the seabed. It cannot be recovered. The Argonites are now marooned on the island, with only two landers for transportation. It is the earth's year of about twelve thousand BCE. Life for the Argonites on the island is crowded but livable. Unlimited food supplies are available from the ocean. They can do some farming. The quality of life is simple. Meetings are held to decide what they might do in the future. They are left with limited technological resources. It is apparent that until technology comes into this world, they have no chance of building a new ship. Creating the technology needed requires resources they do not have. Staying on the island or blending in with the indigenous population is the only alternative."

"Using the landers for excursions around the planet, groups of indigenous people are observed. While having superficial differences in appearance, the indigenous humanoids all share the same DNA. It is comparable to Argonite DNA. It was decided to establish settlements in secluded places high up in the Andes mountains, Central America, the Himalayas, and other places. Mountain living comes naturally to off-world humanoids. It reminds them of their home planet. Some Argonites decide they will find ways to mingle with the earthlings. Others will stay on the island."

"The humanoid features of the Argonites are close to those of the indigenous people on Earth. They disguise different features to blend in with the earth's population. They can pass for Homo sapiens or a related humanoid species. With all the superficial differences between the planet's inhabitants, no one will know if they are from another planet or another continent. One issue is learning the languages spoken by one group or another. The Argonites make recordings of spoken languages to help them learn. At this time, Homo sapiens have no written languages beyond pictorial representations modern archeologists have found on cave walls and mountainsides. Sumerian, the first known pictograph and cuneiform writing language, will not appear until around 3100 BCE in Mesopotamia, and around 1400 to 1200 BCE in Shang Dynasty China."

"Uninhabited areas are sought for settlement. Subtle technological innovation without interfering with the various indigenous cultures is permitted as long as it is not to gain power over the Homo sapiens."

Conrad stops telling his story as some workers come onto the ship. When they are out of hearing range, he continues. He and Josh head out of the ship and hangar on their way back to the lab area.

"As time passes, even though they have a longer life span, many Argonites die from the harsh conditions they face. Others merge with indigenous people who take them in. By mating with earthlings, they lose their identity over the centuries. A small percentage of the surviving Argonites try to remain apart from Homo sapiens. To be among the indigenous people but keep their bloodlines separate. Their goal is that one day if they survive, they can find a way to return to their home planet. Over thousands of years, it becomes genetically impossible to remain separate."

"That's quite a story," Josh said. "Do they ever find a way home?"

"No one knows. I think these people are not even sure who they are anymore. Occasionally, maybe they get the feeling while living through all the chaos, murder, and mayhem on this planet that they are not one hundred percent Homo sapiens."

"I can empathize with them in that regard. I have experienced that notion often. Then I think maybe it's just that some people exhibit such abhorrent behavior. I wish I were not one of them," Josh remarks.

"When the Argonites first got to the planet, they found hunter-gather groups spread out through what is now Europe, Asia, and the American continent. Humans in certain areas like Mesoamerica, Eastern Europe, and other places gather in a few large communities. They appear not to have governments or rulers. In some cases, these cities last for hundreds of years and disappear. There may have been groups of hunter-gatherers who became warriors living off the agriculture of groups who became farmers. Certain experts believe this was when humans evolved into their current hierarchal mindset. The early communal areas disappear. Cities and what we call civilization appear," Conrad said as they returned to the lab. "Some Argonites may have found ways to live in these early communities and cities."

Returning to the lab, Josh learns that specific equipment and materials are in short supply because of the pandemic. Arroyo's have stockpiled assets over the last two years in anticipation that critical metals and other resources needed for the construction of Galaxy Two might be limited. There is enough of most materials to finish the planned projects.

However, there are delays in obtaining the titanium powder needed for the hull formula used on the 3d printers. Arroyo Aerospace's large stockpile is nearly exhausted. Eventually, they get what they need to complete the hull. By the fourth of July 2020, Galaxy Two will have its entire outer hull in place. The inner layers are not a problem, except for delays in receiving the polyethylene plastic (RFX1). This layer must be applied before wiring and air circulation. The last layer of the hull is the interior panels that are ready. They will not be installed until all the wiring, air circulation, and communication lines are in place. Due to the pandemic, there are delays in getting critical parts and materials for life support equipment. The virus is surging throughout the United States and other places worldwide. This slows down the manufacturing and delivery of many goods and services.

After careful analysis, Josh and Tamara determined that the spray coating on the hull of Galaxy One was scrubbed off by the cosmic dust cloud they flew through on the way to the moon. The second application did not adhere well to the first coating on the hull. They did additional hull cleaning until the previous layers were gone entirely. They re-spray the hull with a new cloaking formula, which they believe will bond in a lasting way. Tests show cloaking is working well with no flicker. Even so, it will still be subject to wear. Galaxy Two has the cloaking formula incorporated into the metal alloy of the hull. It is not subject to wear.

The drive navigation program is under review. Additional data is added that corrects issues with gravitational fields from different-size masses. Also, possible aberrations like those emanating from the lunar surface. Two new larger drives are in production for Galaxy Two. Several smaller auxiliary drives that create artificial gravity for the ship and anti-gravity for the hull are also near completion.

Raoul Sr. and Marcella research the possibility of a third drive that uses an alternative power source. Years ago, before they created the gravity drive, they worked on a concept for a nuclear thermal propulsion (NTP) engine. Nuclear thermal propulsion engines use nuclear fission to heat liquid hydrogen, squirting it out the rocket's rear to create thrust. Plutonium atoms split apart inside the core and release heat through fission. This physical process heats the propellant and converts it to a gas, which is expanded through a nozzle to produce thrust. This concept has been around for some time. This method for launching a rocket-propelled spaceship or a crewless rocket from the earth is deemed dangerous because of a possible nuclear explosion or accident. This propulsion system needs to be installed on a ship in space. Once that is done, the ship cannot land on Earth. This type of propulsion for Galaxy Two is deemed impractical.

It is planned to utilize a Radioisotope power system that converts heat from the natural radioactive decay of the isotope Plutonium-238 (used in a ceramic form of plutonium dioxide) into electrical power to operate the computers, science instruments, and other hardware aboard Galaxy Two. NASA missions such as the Curiosity rover on Mars and the New Horizons spacecraft flyby of Pluto and beyond use a Radioisotope power system.

Galaxy One relies on stored electrical power and solar power to recharge storage batteries. The Arroyos install a radioisotope system in Galaxy One as an alternative backup. The Arroyos obtained Plutonium-238 before it stopped being produced in the U.S. and Russia. It is stored in a protected place where it is prevented from decaying. They believe they now have sources for more Plutonium-238 and other nuclear power fuel that is once again being produced in the U.S.

The Chinese Space Agency decides to share their photographs and video footage of the sparkling object in lunar orbit to see if NASA has anything similar from that period. The Chinese are anxious to learn NASA's reaction to the recordings. They want to determine if the U.S. is secretly doing this on the moon. The Chinese speculate it might be a spaceship. If the U.S. has this technology, the Chinese want to learn about it. Their intelligence service and hackers find no traces of any secret program like this by the U.S. government or aerospace industry.

NASA accepts the Chinese material and gives the Chinese Space Agency a copy of what they observed. No one can determine if it is some electrical phenomenon or a UFO. U.S. photographic recognizance specialists at the CIA find that the Chinese photographs and video show a glimmer, a shadowy silhouette on the moon's surface moving along with the image above. The Chinese did not notice these shadows. This phenomenon appears around the moon and disappears there. Officials at NASA place the subject under review. They choose not to release any information to the public. NASA does not wish to be associated with UFO sightings. Astronauts aboard the International Space Station are asked if they have seen any odd sightings. The one incident of possible lightning observed by the astronauts is reported. No one thought to check with NSA or sources at the space center for any odd happenings around this time.

Carlos's new private dark web remains unobserved by security agencies and the internet. All internal communications at the ranch are closed to the outside except for links to Carlos's Uber Net. Only in the corporate office is there a link to the conventional internet. No personal mobile phones are used in secure areas. Carlos is aware that with all their activities, tests, and malfunction of the cloaking in lunar orbit, there must be interest in the unexplained incidents. All he can do now is make sure their systems are as undetectable as possible and secure and that no leaks can compromise the project. While he understands the need for the movie cover story, he cautions Paul to be careful about what he releases to the public. He should ensure the releases have no content that can tie them to unexplained phenomena.

Adrienne sends out press releases routinely about the progress of preproduction for the Space Pioneers film and Gateway to the Galaxy studio theme park. She emphasizes that shooting cannot begin while the pandemic is raging. However, sets and preparations at the studio theme park continue to some extent. Film production is at a virtual standstill around the country because of the pandemic. Theme parks are closed. Media attention is focused on the pandemic and the upcoming presidential election.

CHAPTER TWENTY-FOUR

"Reality is merely an illusion,
albeit a very persistent one." Albert Einstein

Arroyo Aerospace and the ranch are on a partial lockdown during the pandemic. All team members working on the project begin getting tests for the virus. Bill Arroyo's wife, Elizabeth, a doctor, manages to secure test kits administered at the ranch, then sent out for analysis. In addition, quick tests are available. Masks are worn in most situations. Family not living on the ranch keep visits to a minimum and are screened before contact with anyone on the ranch. They also spend a few days in self-quarantine at guest facilities on the ranch. At the pandemic's peak, no one associated with Arroyo Aerospace tested positive for the virus..

Because of lax adherence to the national Centers for Disease Control (CDC), some states have high positive test results, infections, and deaths. It is revealed that the state government may have been underreporting actual cases. Municipal and county governments ignore federal guidelines regarding mask-wearing, social gathering, and distancing. Those people who follow CDC guidelines, practice social distancing, wear masks, wash their hands, and practice safety measures are more able to avoid infection. One significant factor for staying healthy is limiting attendance at large gatherings outside the immediate family. Josh, Adrienne, and the children stay at the beach condo. They practice all the safety measures. Josh or Adrienne does food shopping but little else in public. All goods entering the condo are sanitized. Loren and Morgan are taking particular summer program courses online and working at the ranch when possible. The children are only at the condo or the ranch.

The presidential administration essentially ignores the reality of the pandemic. They claim the virus will end on its own and that life will return to normal. The president privately admits the virus is lethal but denies the severity of it in public. He turns wearing masks and social distancing into being for or against him and the current administration. The president and his staff hold meetings and events where attendees are discouraged from wearing masks. White House staff and supporters at rallies contract the virus and try to keep it quiet. The president does not reveal it when he tests positive for the virus. He remains silent for weeks, including while participating in the presidential debates. He becomes very ill with the COVID virus and tries to hide it until finally he is taken to Walter Reed Hospital. He receives a single eight-gram dose of Regeneron's monoclonal antibody cocktail, called REGN-COV2. This is the highest drug dose being tested in late-stage clinical trials. He also is given seven other drugs, including Remdesivir, Dexamenthasone, Zinc, Vitamin D, Femotidine, Melatonin, and Aspirin. The president receives drugs being tested in clinical trials and not available to the public. When he recovers, he still plays down the severity of the virus. Thousands who cannot get this unique and experimental treatment are dying. Conservative organizations, evangelicals, Republicans, and right-wing media hide the severity of the pandemic.

The interior of Galaxy Two is slowly coming together. Six workers who remain on the ranch living in the guest quarters help construct the frame and hull. They volunteer to stay at the ranch until work is complete or the virus is controlled. Family members, plus Josh and Adrienne, continue working while keeping within safety measures. The pandemic is delaying the finishing of Galaxy Two. However, work continues.

Before the Covid 19 virus pandemic began to sweep the world, Raoul Sr. and Marcella invited Josh, Adrienne, and the children to vacation with them at the ranch in the Nicoya Peninsula in Costa Rica. The trip is scheduled for a couple of weeks in late July 2020. The project has been all-consuming for everyone for the last year, and a break will likely be good. Now it looks like the virus is not only surging in the United States but also on the move in Costa Rica, although not as bad as in the United States. Costa Rican health services work with local communities to take standard precautions and isolate cases.

The family decides it is best not to vacation in Costa Rica. However, because of a close connection with the people living near the Arroyo rancho, Marcella chooses to travel there with medical supplies. The Arroyos gather many masks, disinfectants, and other provisions. Raoul Jr. and Carlos pilot the corporate jet to Costa Rica on the first of August. Sam and Marcella are on the flight with them. The first stop is customs at Liberia International airport. Before proceeding, they show their negative test results from the U.S. Clearance is issued to fly south to their private airstrip at the rancho. Their Citation Latitude can land or take off on 3,580 feet of runway. The Rancho Arroyo airstrip is 4000 feet long and has a beacon and lights. Next to the airstrip is a hangar for the plane and equipment. A small prop plane is housed there. The runway was built with the permission and cooperation of the Costa Rican Government. The license agreement includes the Costa Rican government's emergency use of the airstrip. The Arroyos try to fly in on clear days because of the elevation and mountainous terrain in the area. Today is sunny, even though it is winter and the rainy season there.

The flight to the rancho from Liberia airport takes about forty-five minutes. It can take seven hours on the ground, with a drive up the mountain on a switchback dirt road. There is a road with villages and a school along the top of the mountain. Costa Rica spends a good portion of its national budget on education and healthcare. The schools are well equipped. The Arroyos donate to the local school, including extra computers, enhanced wireless access to the internet, and building a swimming pool for the town near the school.

Everyone in the nearby village knows when the Arroyo's jet lands. Marcella is very popular in the area and well-known to neighbors. Conrad and Julia often stay at the Rancho. In the opposite direction, along the same mountain road, is the entrance to the Arroyo rancho. The folks running the rancho and home are prepared for the Arroyo visit. Clara, who oversees the staff, said masks and other supplies would be appreciated by the local people and at the village school. Locals practice social distancing, wash their hands, and they wear masks. They keep their trips to the regional town at the mountain's base to as few as possible. Villagers have gardens, farm plots, livestock, and chickens, so people usually have basic food supplies.

Residents fashion their cloth masks. They use surgical masks under the cloth masks for trips to the town. So far, they have no infections on the mountain. The city on the main road below has two cases. This town has a small infirmary, so they send patients with symptoms to a hospital in Nicoya city for care. The worse place for infection spread is San Jose, the largest urban area in the country. It is geographically far from Arroyo rancho. The Arroyos' stay for two days and then fly back to Florida.

The pandemic slows the affair between George and Simone as air travel between cities is limited and dangerous due to the possibility of infection. They try to keep in touch by video chatting while planning a possible get-together in Florida. Traveling is difficult because you might carry the virus to whomever you visit. Also, possibly picking up the virus from the person you are visiting. Government employees in D.C. are getting sick because of a lack of policy about social distancing, mask-wearing, and the inability to work from home. Simone cannot work from home for security reasons. She is assigned to a division that needs to use her knowledge of the Chinese language. As a translator, she ran across Chinese inquiries concerning an unidentified phenomenon observed near the moon. Also, the information that NASA shared. The photographic analysis is done in her division at the CIA. There are also reports that the Chinese Space Agency is anxious for information about these occurrences. She searches for any other unusual activity around the moon with no results. Closer to home, she finds a report from the International Space Station of a similar phenomenon near the earth's atmosphere shortly after the moon incidents. Digging deeper, she finds the NSA reports of unusual high-frequency radio signals near the Kennedy Space Center. She cannot find one specific thing linking all these events. She makes notes for future reference.

Sam, with Carlos's and Josh's help, will finish much of the infrastructure of Galaxy Two by September 2020. Most of the interior hull panels are in place. The helm and command center come together under the large glass window across the spaceship's bow. The glass area is comparable to that of Galaxy One on a larger scale. In addition, there are more resources for interstellar navigation. Carlos Arroyo and Kevin Steiner designed an expanded self-navigation system that includes the solar system and known celestial bodies and constellations. A prominent command center feature is a navigation table with built-in screens projecting flight paths.

Galaxy Two's shape differs from Galaxy One since it is about four times larger. Instead of the teardrop shape, it is an elliptical shape, broad in the rear and middle, then tapering into a softly pointed bow. The three-level configuration is the same. The Command Center is on level one. Passenger space is on levels one and two. Galley, Infirmary, and crew quarter levels 1 & 2. Level three is one-third for engineering and the drives—two-thirds for cargo and supplies.

Raoul Sr. and Marcella have two propulsion systems ready for installation, plus two auxiliary drives. They also have a radioisotope system that will furnish electrical power for the entire ship prepared for installation. The drives will not be installed until the power areas of the third level are entirely shielded from the rest of the spacecraft.

Plans for an alternative power plant, possibly nuclear, are still being considered. It is a significant undertaking and requires more resources than

Arroyo Aerospace has available. In addition, there is the issue of obtaining fuel for the power plant. One option is to build a nuclear power plant, then install it without fuel. This will require changing the design of Galaxy Two to accommodate this propulsion device attached to the ship's exterior. Sam is unsure how this can be incorporated into the Galaxy Two's design. The frame must be adapted and strengthened to hold the thrust mechanism. They only need gravity drives to launch and move around the solar system. Finally, he reinforces the ship to accommodate an alternative power plant, should one become available. Rather than trying to build a nuclear drive, they might purchase one after Galaxy Two is launched.

Being the world historian, anthropologist, and political affairs professor, Conrad keeps track of happenings in the country and the world. He is an advisor to Raoul Sr., Marcella, and the team. Understanding the historical and political realities that they face is more important now than ever before. Conrad sees many parallels between world history and what is happening globally today. He finds similar patterns in the world between 1930 and 1945. Based on actions by the Russians, Conrad sees parallels to German expansionism before World War Two. Today there is political unrest, changes in climate, a pandemic, migration, and internal turmoil in the world's major democracies. Unlike pundits and broadcast personalities, Conrad studies human affairs and their long-term impact on the planet. He also keeps track of cultural movements and fringe activities.

In November 2020, a new President is elected in the U.S. The election outcome is clear. The new President wins the popular vote by nearly eight million votes and the electoral college by a wide margin. Swing states that flipped from the Democratic Party to the Republican Party in previous elections convert back to voting for the Democratic presidential candidate
When the outgoing president fails to get reelected in 2020, he intensifies his "Big Lie" rhetoric, stating that he has won the election. He claims, as he did before the vote, that the election has been mysteriously stolen from

him. He and his followers claim fraud and demand recounts. The recounts show the same results. The other candidate is the winner. This type of tactic reminds Conrad of the behavior of past and present autocratic rulers and dictators. These past demagogues did not have the internet and social media to broadcast their self-serving propaganda.

Using social media, conservative media, and rallies during the months after the election, the ex-president, aided by far right-wing Republicans, conspires to overturn the election. He continues to claim that the entire national election is fraudulent and that it has been stolen from him. His supporters believe the "Big Lie" because they are predisposed to believe it. There is no factual proof, only more lies, conspiracy theories, and speculation. The ex-president loses his allegations of fraud in court cases at least sixty times. Still, he persists in causing turmoil and unrest, leading to the final verification of the election in Congress on January 6, 2021. On that day, he holds a well-advertised rally near the capital. Thousands of attendees, including right-wing militia group members, are fired-up by Republican speakers "to fight." Finally, the ex-president urges the mob to march to the Capitol while the electoral election results are certified by the house and senate. He tells them to stop the process at any cost and that he will march with them. The outgoing vice president is legislated to conduct the traditional and mainly ceremonial process.

Based on all the information he has gathered since this president ran for election Conrad is sure that this is a clumsy Coup d' tat attempt by the outgoing president and his right-wing supporters. They try to overturn a legal, constitutional election process by inciting mob violence as a last resort. There is a plan. A last-ditch effort to stall the verification and force the election's outcome to be overturned. It can then be settled in the House of Representatives, where the ex-president's party would have an advantage under the twelfth amendment.

Five people are killed during the attack on the Capitol. Scores of Capital police are injured. The mob overwhelmed the capitol police and broke into the building. There is a clear plan to disrupt the formality of certifying the election so that the previous president can remain in office. Calls to the White House to bring in the National Guard are ignored. The police ultimately repulse the mob. The ex-president's supporters fail to stop the certification of the election. The ex-president leaves office refusing to recognize his duly elected successor. Subsequently, the outgoing president is impeached in the House for his crimes. Not enough Republicans in the Senate vote to convict him of sedition, claiming he is already out of office, having lost the election. Many of these same politicians refuse to acknowledge the new Presidents' victory.

It bothers Conrad that a national election in the United States, for the first time in its history, has come close to being overturned by a wannabe "president for life," corrupt candidate. He believes that even though democracy survives, it has been severely damaged by partisanship and fear. Conrad believes Arroyo Aerospace and the fledgling International Space Exploration Group must take steps to reach their goals before the end of 2024. There are too many disturbing trends in the country and worldwide. They must be prepared to leave Earth.

The new President takes office on January 20th, 2021. He begins fighting the pandemic and enlisting the American people to help. Although the vaccine development did start under the previous administration, there has yet to be a plan at a federal level for mass production and distribution. More vaccines are ordered, and by June of 2021, about half the population in the country is fully vaccinated with the new vaccines developed in 2020. Sixty-two percent of people have a least one shot. By mid-summer 2021, infections and deaths are down significantly because of the mass distribution of the vaccine.

Many individuals are slow to take the vaccine. They are worried by conspiracy theories promoted on social media sites and anti-vaccine rhetoric coming from evangelical Christians and Republican politicians. Right-leaning states threaten the recovery, persuaded into politicizing the vaccine and other health measures. The virus spikes again in late July and August. It spreads among the unvaccinated. Infections and deaths in primarily Republican states, including Texas, Alabama, Mississippi, and Florida, are high.

Marcella does not understand why people are risking death rather than taking steps to gain immunity for themselves and their families. People are fighting about whether their unvaccinated children should wear masks while attending school, even as the number of cases climbs. Certain unvaccinated people refuse to wear masks in public places, on airplanes, or at events claiming that doing so somehow infringes on their freedom of choice. The fact that their actions violate other people's safety does not concern them. The virus is an enemy of all humans, yet a large percentage refuse to fight it in scientifically proven ways. Looking back at the behavior of Homo sapiens as far back as Neolithic times, Conrad recognizes the same kind of contrarian behavior.

Sensing weakness in the American system, foreign Intelligence agencies spread false rumors about American vaccines on social media to disrupt recovery. In addition, simple health protection procedures like wearing protective masks and social distancing are used by right-wing politicians to divide the country for political gain. Misinformation about vaccines, who are getting infected and dying, unproven cures, masks, and mandates are spread on social media sites worldwide.

Unvaccinated people see their families and friends become infected and die. Hospitals in states with large unvaccinated populations become overcrowded and unable to cope with the number of sick people. To stem this new outbreak, there is a major push by the new President and administration in August 2021 using mandates and public pressure that helps vaccinations to go up around the country. By November, the infection rate levels off to some degree. In December 2021, a new virus variant spread, mainly among the unvaccinated population.

Conrad is still determining if anything will be enough to stop what appears to be an inevitable clash between far-right-wing factions and moderate democratic government. Conrad speculates that political forces have purposely created a situation that plays off deep-seated emotions that confuse any form of government as being against individual freedom of choice. There does not appear to be a route toward consensus agreements between these opposed factions.

Like cult members, many supporters of the previous administration and the failed president are convinced that the virus sweeping the world is not authentic or will disappear. Domestic terrorists come out from under their rocks, encouraged by the previous president and Republican members of Congress. During the last presidency, many of these groups, with white supremacy agendas, began harassing minority people. The American caste system comes into full view as unnecessary police violence against minorities continues to seep into the country's consciousness.

Clear signs of the ex-president's megalomania are constantly displayed on his call-ins to propaganda news outlets. The former one-term president urges supporters, insurrectionists, and conspiracy groups to keep things going and to raise money for him. Cult groups and demented people invent narratives about how the government will be overthrown by the military and the previous president "reinstated." Each time their fantasy does not materialize, they move the time frame into the future.

The Arroyos and a large percentage of the world worry that even with the change of administrations in the U.S., the country's future appears to be in jeopardy. The population of the country is divided. Far-right propaganda news and social media pump out a daily stream of lies and misinformation that a large portion of the citizens, for their own reasons, choose to believe. No one can predict the future of the country or the planet. It seems impossible to change the direction of national politics before totalitarian forces cause chaos. These insights worry the Arroyos and their associates. They proceed with their plans with increasing urgency.

Conrad studies current trends. He approaches matters from multiple points of view. Homo sapiens tend to repeat the same patterns in recorded history and perhaps in prehistory. Academics and scholars need help to answer fundamental questions about the behavior of their species at different times. Groups of people can be quickly persuaded to commit atrocities they shunned before. Conrad wants to anticipate a turn of events from current trends. The evidence at his disposal does not support positive outcomes very soon. What looms for the planet are conflict and ecological problems. He hopes that somehow the evolutionary process of humans moving into space will help Homo sapiens resolve some of their issues with each other. To discover their survival as a species is in question.

Josh joined Adrienne, relaxing on the condo balcony. The ocean is dark on this cloudy night. Adrienne is sitting quietly, drinking some wine. Josh sits down next to her.

"Would you like some wine? I have another glass here," Adrienne asks.

She pours some wine for Josh.

"I've been thinking, what will the world be like in the future for Morgan and Lauren," Adrienne said.

"Well, according to Conrad, the prognosis is gloomy but not set in stone."

"I want them to have a good life," Adrienne said. "Here we are working on exploring space with an urgency that seems like a disaster may be imminent."

"I've been thinking about that. If you believe Conrad's stories, some people want to leave the planet for good. I don't think the Arroyos are at that point yet. They want to prepare for any eventuality."

"All the talk of evolution and historical trends may be a waste of time. If time and space are concerned, whatever happens, has already taken place. It is fate now."

"I hope that what we're involved in is part of that future fate. If we are successful, we might encourage worldwide enlightenment about the collective future of Homo sapiens. Can we leap into the future and resolve all the dysfunction accumulated in our world?"?

"I hope so," Adrienne said, sipping her wine. "We need to figure out exactly what is dysfunctional and normal."

CHAPTER TWENTY-FIVE

*"By working with others, we diminish the need
for them to compete with us."*

On a sunny spring day in May 2021, Josh, Paul, and Conrad find themselves outside the huge hangar looking at the gray titanium color hull of the new spaceship. The accordion sliding doors of the hangar have been pulled back, revealing Galaxy Two. No one is wearing a mask since they have all been fully vaccinated and are outdoors. Masks are also not required indoors for regular staff members. Everyone at Arroyo Aerospace works hard to keep their environment clean of the virus. Galaxy Two is almost ready to fly.

"Galaxy Two is much bigger than Galaxy One," Josh said. "Standing here, it is difficult to believe that this large spaceship can launch into space."

Conrad smiled, "Raoul Sr. says it's just a super-size version of Galaxy One, with much more power. He's sure it will fly."

Josh turns to Paul, "When will you start shooting the film," he asks?

"We need to do some casting. There are contracts to be signed with talent if we proceed." Paul answers. "With the delays caused by the pandemic, maybe it's a waste of time to continue with the fiction film idea. The film story is a cover for building the ship. It's built now. It is almost time to launch.

"What about the Theme Park?" Josh asks.

"During the pandemic, all the theme parks shut down. They are starting to open again. We've been putting out press releases that the opening of Gate to the Galaxy theme park is on hold until after the pandemic. We are not getting much attention right now," Paul said. "I'm going to bring the whole thing up at the next meeting."

Paul said, "my sister Sharon is out of a job. She is hinting about helping with the promotion of the theme park."

"Is she buying the 'Big Lie'?" Josh asks.

"She knows he lost. She told me she was at the January sixth rally but didn't go on the march to the capital. Instead, she returned to the White House with a group of advisors and the ex-president's entourage. They watched on TV and knew that he was in the oval office private dining room also watching. He is probably taking calls from his co-conspirators. She claims many people there wanted to call in the National Guard to stop the insurrection, especially since the mob erected a hangman's gallows and is chanting 'kill the vice president. The ex-president wouldn't make the call' The secret service would not take him to the capital to join the mob. He was waiting, hoping that the insurrection would succeed. She believes it was an administration plot aided by certain Republicans, including some in congress. She's disappointed and says she's not a supporter of the ex-president. Not sure who or what she does support, though."

"Times are so weird. The ex-president is acting like he's in some third-world country, waiting to try another coup to get back into power," Josh said.

They begin walking deeper into the hangar toward the side of the ship and steps leading up to the airlock entry to the middle level of the spacecraft. Galaxy Two had multiple airlocks and docking entries. A large docking port for Galaxy One to transfer cargo on the lower level. Another airlock in the bow and an entry on the second level. The ship is one hundred and seventy-five feet (58.33 meters) in length. It is one hundred-twenty feet (36.57 meters) wide in the middle. The overall height is forty feet (12.19 meters). It has an elliptical, nearly round shape.

"Once Galaxy Two goes into space, will we be able to return here and land?" Josh asks.

"Although it has been constructed to stay in space, it should be able to take off and land from the planet's surface. It is possible to construct a larger 'starship' in space in orbit somewhere. Galaxy Two can be the base for that operation. Galaxy One will transport people to Galaxy Two. Raoul Sr. is constructing Galaxy Three. It will be strictly for cargo, about half the size of Galaxy Two," Paul said.

"Maybe there will be a base on Mars or an orbital station around Mars that utilizes raw materials found there," Conrad remarks.

"We will need a large crew and robots to work in the Mars environment," Josh said.

Once inside Galaxy Two, they made their way to the command-and-control center, where Carlos and Kevin worked on the ship's software and navigation installation. The control center occupies about twenty percent of the bow area of level one. Paul sits down in one of the command center's seats. Josh and Conrad soon follow his lead and sit in the comfortable chairs.

"Wow, this looks like a real command center," Paul said jokingly.

"How are you doing with the software installation?" Josh asks.

"Good," Carlos replies. Kevin is doing some testing right now."

"We can simulate certain flight paths and see them on the table monitor," Kevin said. "The most important program will be the launch protocol, getting this ship into earth orbit and beyond."

"I believe the gravity drives are in place and operational, including the auxiliary drives for the ship's interior gravity and the hulls anti-gravity," Josh said.

"Yes," Carlos said. "Everything checks out system-wise. Hopefully, we'll be able to do a test like engaging the propulsion drive to lift the ship a foot or two off the hangar floor. We can't go higher until we take the hangar down or move the ship outside."

"Raoul Sr. is trying to keep the ship away from satellite imaging. We don't want it to show up on Google before we're ready," Carlos said.

"This may be a reason to continue with the film and studio theme park cover story," Paul said. "How much time are we looking at until we launch?"

"Not sure," Carlos answers. "We're still waiting for some important equipment and supplies. We'll get an update from everyone at the meeting tomorrow."

Looking around him, "I just realized we're not wearing masks. Everyone is vaccinated. They even opened it up to teenagers over twelve years," Josh said. "My kids got the first shot."

Paul said, "that's good news. Infections and deaths are going down. There are still a lot of contrary people who refuse shots because they are misinformed or for political reasons. I asked Sharon if she got vaccinated. She said she hadn't yet but planned to do so. She said she wasn't against science. That the vaccine only had 'emergency approval.' I told her everyone here is vaccinated, and we're all just fine."

"Almost sixty percent of the population are vaccinated, with very few getting infected afterward. People all over the world are getting vaccinated and staying healthy. That's enough approval for me. I think wearing a mask in public places is a good idea. There are other things besides COVID that you can catch, like the flu or the common cold. Since people started wearing masks, numbers for the flu and colds have gone down," Josh said. "I believe we want to keep the virus and other things away from this ship and the area here. It might be a good idea if the crew of Galaxy Two quarantines for a week before the launch."

Carlos agrees, "The filtration system on the ship has all the bells and whistles to clean the air once we launch. We need to be careful that none of us gets sick beforehand. The ship will be completely cleaned and sterilized before launching and periodically during flights."

"Okay, maybe we should let Carlos and Kevin focus while we take a look at the rest of the ship," Josh said.

There are steps down to the second level from the command center and an exit to the rear of level one. Paul, Conrad, and Josh leave by the rear door, allowing them to walk toward the ship's stern. The back two-thirds of level one is still empty. All rooms, passenger seats, or other equipment still need to be installed. Some bulkheads and lights are installed on level two. The level three hatch is closed, so they do not go to level three.

The Arroyo Aerospace executive and family meetings are held in the secure conference room. No one is allowed to bring cell phones into this space. Only laptops with no connection to the internet are permitted in the room. Laptops connected to the internal network use "old school" cable connections. No WIFI connections, cameras, and audio disabled.

Raoul Sr. and Marcella worry that ransom hackers looking for likely companies to attack may stumble onto their business. Arroyo Aerospace maintains a presence online. Their website server uses a standalone server with all the protection Carlos can muster. External e-mails are received here and scanned for any viruses. Backups are made, and that link is disconnected from the central server. Nothing about clients or inventory is kept on the server that connects to the internet. Bank accounts and other sensitive information are encrypted and kept on a secure server using Carlos's new Uber network. It is not part of the "dark web." It is an independent internet. Only someone with the proprietary browser software will gain entry. Backups of backups are made to create redundancy. Critical information is transferred to paper in some instances. The precautions go beyond protection from ransom hackers. Raoul Sr. and Marcella are preparing for the day they launch Galaxy Two, and the world learns of their enterprise. Arroyo Aerospace and the International Space Exploration Group will need a communication fortress around them in today's environment.

Marcella begins the meeting, "Good afternoon, everyone. It's been three years since we first discussed going into the space exploration business. Here we are today, having done a lunar orbit with Galaxy One. Galaxy Two is nearing completion. As you know, the virus and resulting pandemic have slowed our progress with Galaxy Two. Our launch date is being re-calculated."

The seats at the table are full. Key family members and spouses, Kevin Steiner, Josh, and Adrienne, are there. For some reason, Josh's memory flashes back to lunar orbit, the close-up view of the moon, and the approach to the 'blue planet' on the way home. He is amazed that he has been to the moon and is here at this moment in time. Adrienne, like Josh, is comfortable working with the Arroyos. She feels good about being part of this extraordinary team of inventors and entrepreneurs. Adrienne remembers Josh telling her Conrad's story about the Argonites being marooned on Earth in 12,000 BCE. It occurs to her that this story might be true. Discussing the story with Josh, she said, "If true, it answers many questions that come to mind. For example, why do Conrad and Julia seem ageless? Is this family still trying to find a way to move on and leave Earth? Maybe leaving Earth is not a bad idea. Humans do not respect our environment. So many people are mired in superstition, fear, and hostility toward each other. Homo sapiens always look for someone or something to blame for their problems. Every step forward ends up with two steps back. I wonder if the species will become extinct because of its inability to evolve further."

Raoul Sr. said, "As Marcella reports, we are near completion of Galaxy Two. The main drives are in place and should be operational, pending a software check. We have been looking at the possibility of a third interstellar drive that can push the ship toward the speed of light. Sam has designed Galaxy Two so that a third drive may be installed later. However, we are still looking into practical means of propulsion for interstellar travel.

Sam said, "The ship will be swift in the solar system where the gravity fields are strong. Theoretically, an alternative drive may propel the ship beyond the solar system at a velocity moving toward the speed of light. There are many options we are considering. There are gravity fields and other phenomena throughout the universe. Perhaps a hypergravity drive or a way to tap into other universal power sources. Raoul Sr. and Marcella are working on a few ideas that depart from conventional thinking."

Raoul Sr. continues, "we installed a Radioisotope power system (RPS) on Galaxy Two. It will convert heat from the natural radioactive decay of the isotope plutonium-238 (used in a ceramic form of plutonium dioxide) into electrical power to operate environmental services, computers, science instruments, and other hardware aboard the ship. This system is installed in a leakproof radiation part of the drive area on level three. In addition, the unit itself is clad to prevent leakage. There is ventilation directly to the exterior. We have also installed this system on Galaxy One. These systems do not require refueling for at least ten years. We will still have the solar energy system. The Radioisotope Thermoelectric Generator, RPS system will complement the solar power and be available where the sun is not so bright."

"Don't ask where we got the Plutonium - 238," Marcella advised. Note that NASA has used this type of system in the past, and the U.S. government is making fresh batches these days to power Mars projects like the Perseverance Rover."

Carlos said, "Kevin will update us on the self-navigation system we have been testing."

Kevin explains, "The system is a celestial navigation program. It recognizes all objects in the solar system, including the sun, planets, and moons. It can find constellations and stars in the galaxy through external cameras. The artificial intelligence program learns by observation as we travel. It can plot a course anywhere in the solar system. It will offer alternative routes based on distance and time. Once an alternative is selected, the system goes on autopilot. The program can be overridden at any point, and self-navigation can be selected. It also is programmed to find, evaluate, and use gravitational fields in the navigation process. This information is used to set speeds for the drives. We've also fully updated the programs used in Galaxy One."

"It might be worth taking Galaxy One out to test the new navigation system and the other upgrades we have made, " Carlos adds.

Sam outlines the construction schedule. "The pandemic slowed down our schedule for a launch in 2020. We must finish the ship's interior on the first and second levels. All navigation cameras, lasers, and features built into the hull are installed. The command center is ready. I believe the interior fixtures, passenger accommodations, crew cabins, galley, and other resources will be installed in the next couple of months. We will launch soon."

"The ship has windows on the second level on either side of the ship. We feel this will be good for the morale of passengers and crew. The command center can shutter these windows at any time. If all goes well, Galaxy Two will be finished within three months."

"So, we can launch by September 2021," Paul said. I'm deciding what to do about the film and the studio theme park. From what you say we need cover for three more months. Once the interior is finished, do we shoot footage on the ship? As far as the Gate to the Galaxy studio theme park goes, we can start having visitors once Galaxy Two is completed. I don't think letting people see the exterior will be enough. We will need tours of levels one and two. Do we want tourists tracking through the ship during a pandemic? The virus is still out there, predominately infecting the unvaccinated and unmasked. There are many of those types of people in Florida. I believe it is Annie who mentioned setting up large monitor screens outside the ship to show us shooting scenes inside. At this point, we might think about stalling the film's shooting and then dropping the shoot once the ship launches. This depends on how secret the launch remains and if Galaxy Two is coming back to earth after it launches."

Marcella answers. "You make some good points. We have been talking about how the delay changes things and the reality of what we are doing here in 2021. The current government situation is somewhat better. There is still a lot that can happen in the next three years. What are our chances of keeping this project and the launch secret?"

Paul said, "It is in the news that the government has acknowledged that many sightings of UFOs or other phenomena are not alien spaceships. They admit they don't know what they are. We might be able to fly Galaxy One secretly. Galaxy Two is much larger."

"It looks like we were partially spotted by the Chinese and NASA while in lunar orbit. Some news is circulating online about lights orbiting the moon that was picked up by the Chinese and NASA Satellites. No one knows what they are," Carlos said. "The Airforce is launching a satellite to detect artificial objects in earth orbit. That should not worry us. However, you never know. There are all kinds of stuff up there. Soon the planet will look like Saturn, but with a ring of satellites and junk."

Paul said, "Carlos, you know that program you and Raoul Jr. wrote that sends back false speed information to radar detectors? Why can't we have something that sends out false data to a surveillance satellite? It is probably using some form of radar with some cameras."

Carlos said, "It's possible. Let me think about it. If our stealth and cloaking work, they will not get any data. If they get anything, maybe they will think their equipment is malfunctioning."

"We should focus on our long-term goals and what we are doing at this point," Raoul Sr. said. "To do this, we can decide what it is we want. In the beginning, we thought of possibly living in space and exploring. It is time to be practical and think about our present and future. Galaxy Two is big. I believe we can launch into high orbit and come back to earth again undetected. Landing a ship this big may not be easy. With the cloaking and stealth technology, launching and landing will not differ much from Galaxy One. We will be careful not to bump into anything going up or coming back down. The question then becomes, what next? If we keep Galaxy Two in space, a crew will fly it. Do we park it in orbit? We can land it on the moon or Mars. Our original idea is to set up a base somewhere. This is still possible. It requires more time to gather the resources and equipment. It may mean going public."

"We will use Galaxy Three for cargo. Although, if we don't finish the interior spaces on Galaxy Two, we could use it to lift equipment and supplies to construct something in space or perhaps on Mars," Marcella commented. "That will take time."

Josh listens carefully to what is being discussed. "Raoul Sr. said, "it seems that perhaps the mission can be redefined. Do we keep our activity secret? Is the goal to go into space to explore the solar system and the galaxy? Is it to build a space colony in space or a settlement on a planet like Mars? Once it is decided what the mission is, goals can be set. Building a colony in space or a settlement on Mars will not remain a secret for long. It might make things difficult here on earth. However, we will have a great deal of momentum.

Instead of waiting to be discovered, it may be prudent to consider planning to go public, get ahead of the situation, and proceed with plans."

Sam explains, "At the start, we considered leaving the planet and going somewhere to establish a new colony for humanity. Maybe fly off to another solar system and find a habitable planet. This option is still a possibility. It will take time to prepare for that eventuality. It can be a future goal. Building a settlement on Mars requires moving equipment, robots, and other resources to construct an environment that will sustain life. Let's say two years of moving supplies and setting things up there. A space colony or station at a Lagrange point, like L5, will require years to build. Without earth resources, it will be difficult."

Tamara asks, "What if we have a public goal to build a base on Mars where we store supplies or even manufacture building materials? This can be the first step in going beyond Mars or elsewhere. We will make news when Arroyo Aerospace's International Space Exploration Group is announced and Galaxy Two launches. We need Galaxy Three to transport equipment and supplies to begin building off-planet. We may need to make deals with NASA and others to help them with their projects. We can take our time divulging anything about the propulsion system. It is proprietary technology. We offer to work with others in space exploration where feasible. This will give us time to work on a starship drive. Development of an Interstellar Drive to go beyond the solar system can continue."

"Tamara makes some excellent suggestions. There will be deep pressure from many places," Carlos said. "Governments and others will try to discover the secret of our propulsion drive and other things. We might ultimately need to move off the planet to be safe."

"We can be ready to do that if necessary and have all our ducks in order," Tamara said.

Raoul Jr. is enthusiastic. "Momentum is an important factor for us. It establishes our space exploration group and our technology as an alternative. The rocket guys are developing better reusable rocket propulsion systems.

They can continue doing their thing. An important idea is that we can make the U.S. the undisputed leader in space exploration."

"What if we gave the world what they have been fantasying about for decades? Flying Cars," Paul said. "Seriously, it will be impossible to ignore. There can be a proprietary version of a drive that lifts cars, but not much else. There are several companies with 'flying car' prototypes. All noisy propeller-driven contraptions. This includes personal vehicles and taxis. What do you think?"

Raoul Sr. said, "We can probably figure out something like that. There is a problem. Our technology may be unsafe for use by large numbers of consumers. Something to think about in the future. Moving on, I believe Conrad has an update for us."

"The immediate future depends on if the current government stays in power. They must survive the 2022 midterm elections and keep the presidency for four more years beyond 2024. They must control the house, senate, or both; in 2023. The U.S. may move toward a right-wing authoritarian form of government if the right-wing party totally controls the government. There is already a political civil war that erupted in violence on January 6th. This type of thing can happen again. We should be prepared for any eventuality. Flawed as it may be, the world needs an American democracy to hold back the never-ending assault of totalitarian forces. If you look at history, even the most powerful nations or empires do not last forever. This world may need to go through hundreds and hundreds of years of turmoil to maybe survive in some humane and truly civilized fashion. There is fear on the part of some Americans that, somehow, they will be replaced by the ethnic minorities they have subjugated or dismissed for hundreds of years. It is more likely that Artificial Intelligence (AI) robots will replace them. Perhaps because of this, there is an anti-science backlash out there. Our technology is at risk of being usurped and misused in this environment."

Marcella said, "We have always thought we would someday share our discoveries. I understand the logic of going public before we are found out. It is na ve to think we can continue to go unobserved and unknown once we launch Galaxy Two. Even if Paul uses it as a set for the movie, or we open the Gate to the Galaxy theme park for tourists, and then the ship is gone one day? It will not go unnoticed. Before the pandemic, we planned to hide what we were doing until we launched Galaxy Two. We may be running out of time."

"Suppose we quietly register the International Space Exploration Group and Paul's Gate to The Galaxy theme park. With Paul's movie and the studio theme park still out there, our activities leading up to a launch might not be taken seriously. We move ahead with our plans to launch the ship and set up a base on Mars. We stockpile the necessary equipment, materials, and supplies. Once we go public with either the launch of Galaxy Two or reveal Galaxy One, I believe we will get support from certain financial sources we can trust. We work with the current government and NASA. This will allow us to buy equipment like construction robots that will take us years to build ourselves," Raoul Sr. said. "I continue to be concerned and think we need to keep any form of the drives out of the public domain for the foreseeable future."

Sam is surprised by Raoul Sr.'s proposal. He and Marcella have been adamant about keeping the project secret. "One option is to launch and return Galaxy Two to earth as a test. Keep it secret. We can then take some time to manufacture parts for a larger starship assembled in orbit. Instead of another ship, manufacture the equipment and materials needed for a base on the moon or Mars. In this scenario, it does seem like it will be difficult to continue our project undetected. Not necessarily impossible. Bottom line, I concur that we may better accomplish our goals by going public rather than ending up as some clandestine operation. Once we are outed, I'm certain the media will go ballistic. Adrienne, do you have any opinions on how this can be handled from a public relations standpoint?"

Adrienne is quiet for a moment. Listening to everyone, she can't help thinking about how it might be handled under different scenarios.

"Going public with something this revolutionary will be big news. I agree that it will be easier to handle the press if the corporation and mission are established as we launch Galaxy Two. We can spin the focus toward space exploration. The world press will eventually latch onto trying to find out about the 'secret propulsion drive."

Adrienne continues, "One option is to announce the fact. For example, 'the International Space Exploration Group has launched Galaxy Two (or Galaxy One) into orbit around the earth today.' We film it ourselves. This will come out at the same time as the launch. The launch can be done cloaked or uncloaked."

"Perhaps it is best to send a release a day or two before the launch inviting the media to be there. A skeptical press will not know what to expect. Some might not even show up. Those who do will broadcast this amazing launch. It will go viral. Either way, many people will not believe it."

Marcella follows up on Adrienne's last suggestion. "I think Adrienne's suggestion to invite the press to the launch makes sense and puts us in charge of everything."

Raoul Jr. said, "I worry about the security of the ranch and everyone here after the public finds out. Since Paul announced building the studio theme park, we have constructed fences, but there are no guards. The press and others will start showing up and snooping around. It can get dangerous. It will be difficult to maintain the kind of privacy we now enjoy."

"It is all private property. We need to hire security and put up more fences, no doubt," Sam said.

Josh has a suggestion. "I know someone who might be a good candidate for ramping up security and knows the intelligence community. We can use someone who will go beyond fences and security guards. I believe he's someone who can keep secrets."

"Let's talk to him," Sam said enthusiastically.

"Consider this another way," Tamara said, playing devil's advocate. "We stay private. We launch Galaxy Two cloaked. We start moving supplies up there until we have enough to build a base. What then?"

Josh counters, "The world will see someone or something dropping supplies on the moon or Mars. You can't hide that. It will be a mystery, and there will be a big effort to find who is doing it. Conspiracy theories about alien invasions will begin. Some people will be scared and panicked. Once everyone starts investigating, it won't be long before they find us. As Adrienne suggested, we will be treated as a clandestine organization with some nefarious mission. The only way staying secret works is if we are leaving the planet. Given what it takes to live in space or build a settlement somewhere in this solar system, it seems very difficult to imagine."

Carlos said, "Sam mentioned that we could delay launching Galaxy Two. Explore options with Galaxy One. For example, we might be able to hide supplies on one of Mar's moons without detection. That's a long trip each time. There are moons of other planets that are interesting and might even support life. We are oxygen breathers, so that makes it difficult. If we had an interstellar drive and could go beyond this solar system, we might find another habitable planet somewhere light years away. I don't think we are prepared for that right now."

"Carlos makes a good point. Exploring the Galaxy at this moment is not feasible," Conrad said. "It will take years of preparation and a large starship capable of traveling near the speed of light. When I look at the news of various billionaires building their rockets and all the publicity they get, I think we can go public with the Galaxy Two launch. If handled well, the notion of going public is a realistic option. This will put us in a strong position to do whatever is decided in the future. We have some time, given the present political situation. However, political realities are still in flux. Anything might happen in 2024."

"We need a mission to launch Galaxy Two, Raoul Sr. said. "That mission can be to go to Mars, land at a selected location, and collect soil samples for testing. We are looking for a site to build a base. We announce this as the first mission of Galaxy Two."

Tamara agrees. "Yes, that's good. It's strategically important to have a mission like this. We are not just launching a spaceship; we're going to Mars! This will emphasize going to Mars, not the propulsion system. China, the U.S., and private sector actors like Ramurt and Musk want to go to Mars.

We will get there first. Pick a site we feel has resources and materials we can use to build."

"Mars will not be close to Earth again until December 2022," Carlos said. "That doesn't mean we can't go there in 2021. Perseverance left when Mars was close to Earth, and it took seven months at a speed of 24,600 mph to get there. Our propulsion system can cut the distance, pick up some extra speed and get there faster. Kevin and I will test some scenarios for getting to Mars and back with the navigational system and the wave fields. For example, we might get a boost from Jupiter if we navigate in that direction, then use its wave field to push us toward Mars."

Tamara said, "We are joining the ranks of corporations and nations exploring space. We keep our means of propulsion proprietary for as long as possible. We contract with NASA and others to work with them. Working with others diminishes the need for them to compete with us. We build our resources and never lose sight of our goal to explore beyond this solar system."

"Raoul Sr. knows many people at NASA, including the current Administrator. Possibly, we can talk to him before launching Galaxy Two. Take him for a ride in Galaxy One. Once we go public, we begin exploring the solar system and perhaps establish small preliminary bases on the moon or Mars," Marcella said.

Marcella continues, "There appears to be a consensus about this direction. Let's take a few days to develop ideas and specific plans. We reconvene, consider feasibility, and finalize our goals and course of action. Is that okay with everyone?"

All raised their hands in agreement with Marcella's proposal.

Five days later, the plan is finalized. A Mars trip is planned. Raoul Sr. contacts the current Director of NASA, an ex-astronaut whom Raoul Sr. has known for many years. Raoul Sr. arranges for a secret meeting two weeks before the launch. The conference is set up as a personal meeting with the Arroyos while the official is at NASA in Florida.

The Administrator of NASA reports to the President. One object of the meeting is to make NASA and the President aware of the launch. NASA and the President will not be surprised by public announcements. They will be asked to keep the information confidential until the public event. The International Space Exploration Group (ISEG) will offer to work with NASA as an independent contractor to advance the national interests in the agency's mission and goals. Raoul Sr. will offer to resupply the International Space Station and do other services in space for NASA in trade or at a fraction of the current cost.

In the meantime, Bill Arroyo registers the International Space Exploration Group Corporation with the Secretary of State, Florida. It will be done quietly. If questions arise, Bill will insinuate that it is related to the film and studio theme park. All company names must be registered with the Secretary of State. Internet domain names for the company, park, ships, and film not already reserved can be registered.

Sam and the team continue work to finish Galaxy Two, including the interior spaces, as soon as possible. They believe they can complete systems checks by September 1, 2021.

Adrienne plans to send releases announcing the launch and mission to Mars a few days before the launch. There will be no mention of the means of propulsion or other technical information. The release will go out on Gate to the Galaxy letterhead. It will be thoughtfully worded as an invitation to observe the launch of the International Space Exploration group's spaceship to go to Mars and explore the solar system. The release will include advanced details about the Mars mission.

The launch's press and attendees will be far from Galaxy Two. The launch pad is part of the Gate to the Galaxy theme park, so attendees may assume everything will stay on the ground. The notion that this is an actual launch of a spaceship to Mars is so audacious that it may not be taken seriously. The press will assume this is the beginning of shooting for the film. The entrance to the theme park launch area has been built and set up. Traffic will be funneled in that direction.

August 20th weekend, the NASA senior official is picked up and driven to the ranch for lunch at the Arroyo home with Raoul Sr. and Marcella. The official agrees to the secrecy of their meeting and that he will keep secret the information he is learning. At his discretion, he may inform only the President in advance of the launch on Saturday, September 4th, Labor Day weekend. After lunch Raoul Sr. and the NASA official walk from the ranch to the corporate office.

Once they arrive at the office, Raoul Sr. asks, "would you mind leaving your cell phone here with mine? We have a complete security blackout for the area we are visiting."

"Sure, no problem. You have raised my curiosity."

"Sorry for all the secrecy. I think you will better understand in a few minutes."

They walk to the hangar where Galaxy One is housed.

Raoul Sr. begins, "Over the past four years, we have been working on quite an amazing project. We have been keeping it secret for several reasons. We feel that now is the time to go public. You are the first outsider to see it."

Raoul Sr. opens the side door to the hangar. They walk inside. The official follows Raoul Sr. as he stops in front of Galaxy One. "This is our prototype spaceship. It has flown to the moon and lunar orbit. Please come aboard."

The official needs to find out what he is seeing. Is Raoul Sr. serious or gone mad? "You flew this to the moon and back?" he asked as they walked around to the open airlock. Raoul Jr. is standing at the top of the steps.

"I know it's hard to believe. Follow me, and we can explain.".

Part of the official's mind is still worried about the sanity of Raoul Sr. He has known Raoul Sr. for a long time as a completely sober and serious person. Another part of him, the astronaut part, wants what appears to be fantasy to be confirmed. He follows Raoul Sr. and boards Galaxy One.

"At the helm today are Captain Sun, and copilot Raoul Arroyo Jr. Also, my son Carlos and daughter Tamara will manage the navigation and communications stations. Dr. Josh Bennett is one of our top scientists." Everyone greeted the official, still unsure what was going on.

"Good to meet you, sir," Captain Sun said. I believe I started Astronaut training when you flew in the space shuttle."

"Good to meet you too."

"Sir, the ship has three levels. As you can see, the top level is command and control, also passengers. The second level has a galley, head, and other amenities. The third level houses the drive and cargo space," Raoul Jr. explains.

"This is very realistic looking, but it's difficult to believe it flies," the official remarks.

"Please take a short ride with us," Raoul Sr asks. "I promise it will be completely safe and stress-free. Have a seat here next to me."

The official thinks for a few moments and then decides, "what the hell, this can't be real," he'd go along for the imaginary ride. He sat down in the seat and buckled up the harness. He isn't sure if this is not some elaborate prank. He will play along. He remembers reading about Paul Arroyo's film and Gate to the Galaxy theme park, so maybe this is a publicity stunt.

The doors to the hangar slide back, revealing it is dusk outside. Captain Sun gently raises the ship and floats out of the hangar onto the runway. The official feels the ship move out of the hangar without a sound. He can see the path on the monitors.

"We are going to lift off the runway," Captain Sun reports. The ship floats up high enough that the entire ranch below is seen on the monitors.

"Is this real?" asks the official, whose heart was beating faster.

"It is genuine," Raoul Sr. claims. "We have invented a drive that makes this all possible. There are no rockets. We can go back down or take a short ride if you like."

"A ride sounds great. Maybe that will convince me to accept all this."

"We will move up to a higher altitude and head east toward the coast and the Space Center. You do not need a pressure suit. You will feel no pressure or rapid acceleration, although the ship can move at very high speeds," Carlos explains.

The ship moves up to 25,000 feet and quickly flies by the space center, which comes up on the monitors as they pass out over the ocean.

"Sir, if you want to get up and look out the windows, we are over the ocean at 25,000 feet. I've turned around so you can see the coast and the Space Center," Captain Sun said.

By this time, the official is beginning to accept this fantastic reality. He remembers seeing reports of anomalous activity near the center. He wonders," have aliens from one of the many UFO sightings reported to NASA abducted me? This is not imaginary. I am here with Raoul Sr. and the others. It is not some hi-tech theme park ride." He stands up and walks to a window where he can see the space coast.

"Raoul, this is amazing. I don't know what is powering this ship, but you are right to keep it top secret. It will change everything we know about space flight. And you say you flew to the moon, to lunar orbit? When was that, the official inquires?"

"Late last year, Raoul Sr. said. "We can show you some of the videos we shot. We can float into earth's orbit now. Again, you will not need a suit and no floating around the ship. We have artificial gravity. This ship is a prototype, and we have built a second ship, much larger, which is what we will launch and go public with on Saturday, September 4th."

"I'm thinking that this means of propulsion and all your innovations might be considered a national security secret," the NASA official stated.

"As a private sector entity, everything we have invented is patented. We intend to keep it proprietary and secret. The government will not have control of it. We are American citizens, so we have come to you before we launch. Arroyo Aerospace's International Space Exploration Group will conduct the launch. We want to work closely with you, NASA, and this administration in whatever we do," Raoul Sr. answers. "We only ask that you wait until just before we launch to tell the President or anyone else."

"I don't think that will be a problem, Raoul. I'm ready for the earth's orbit. Let's go and see the new ship when we return."

"Please take your seats," Captain Sun requests before moving up to earth orbit. Soon they are in orbit at 260 miles above the earth. The NASA official with Josh and Raoul Sr. watches the monitors.

"How come no one has ever noticed Galaxy One flying around?" asked the official.

"Well, that's a proprietary secret right now. You can call it stealth technology. We may have been noticed. I don't know if you saw the Chinese and NASA reports of some strange lights in lunar orbit, possibly other reports of these same lights not so long ago. That is us," Josh confesses.

"Yes, I did see those reports. No one has any explanations for what it might be."

Galaxy One orbited the earth one full time and then headed back down to the surface.

At the ranch, Raoul Sr., Captain Sun, and Josh drive the official to the hangar to see and tour Galaxy Two.

They are joined by Marcella, Sam, Paul, Carlos, and Bill on the now fitted-out ship.

"Sam is our head engineer and lead designer of both ships. Galaxy Two will lift off and land from the earth. As you experienced with Galaxy One, launching is smooth and without the kind of g-force necessary with rocket propulsion vehicles," Raoul Sr. said.

"Have you taken this ship into space as well?" the administrator asked.

"We have tested the drives, and the power is there. We have not gone into space yet with Galaxy Two."

"So, this whole thing about a theme park and a movie is a cover for building this spaceship?" the official asked.

"We are still making the film, but it will be non-fiction instead of fiction," Paul said. "The Gate to the Galaxy theme park will function as a center for the International Space Exploration Group activities."

Raoul Sr. said, "We had no choice about using the cover story given the revolutionary nature of our inventions. We want this technology to be used for peaceful purposes and the exploration of our solar system. Going public before everything is ready may have made us prime targets for all sorts of operators. We hope that our government will respect our approach."

"I will do my best to make that happen. This administration is not like the last one. I think the President will see the reality of peaceful exploration of space. You must know that the military-industrial consortium is extremely powerful. Once they start to understand the potential of this technology, they will assert themselves in any way possible to gain access to it. You may be under constant pressure to acquiesce to their demands," the official warns

"We are aware of this and will gently resist for as long as possible. We hope that working with NASA under this administration, hopefully for the next seven years, will give us some time. If the house and senate can also stay in the hands of the President, that will be good too," Marcella said.

"Whatever party controls the congress and senate, individual members will be under pressure from lobbyists and others to gain access to the technology," the official said. "We need campaign reform and curbs on lobbyists. Unfortunately, this is the way it is currently."

"We have plans to go commercial with some of our technology so that it puts us in a position to stay within the system. The International Space Exploration Group and Arroyo Aerospace Inc have financial support to do some lobbying, if necessary," Marcella said.

"The good news is that your company is based in the United States. It will be hailed as a major achievement for the country," the official said. He looked around the command center, "amazing what you have done. I agree with your principles and believe you are making the right decisions. I want to be here on September 4th when you launch this ship. I think the President will approve of my being here. It will symbolize that NASA approval and cooperation are available without any strings. It shows administration support and that we are not in the dark about your project. Thank you for bringing me in."

Raoul Sr. and Marcella looked at each other and nodded to Sam, who was in accord. Raoul Sr. said, "Your being here for the launch will be an honor. Welcome aboard, sir. We would also like to offer our services in the future to help accomplish NASA's goals, for example, building a base on the moon."

When the tour of Galaxy Two is finished, Raoul Jr. drives the official back to the Space Center. On the way, the official asks, "does this car fly too?"

Raoul Jr. replies, "we're working on it, sir."

The administrator smiles. He begins thinking about how to break this news to the President and be taken seriously.

Back in late July, Josh got in touch with Arno. "How is the new job at UCF going?" he asks.

Arno said, "I've been working with the department to write curriculum as temporary adjunct faculty. I'm not officially hired full-time because of the pandemic. I resigned from my other job."

"Something has come up that may interest you from an employment point-of-view. I can't discuss it on the phone. If you can meet, I'll fill you in," Josh said.

After a moment of surprise, "Sure, why not?"

"Will you be able to come out to Brevard County for the meeting? I can have you picked up if you like."

Arno said he did not mind driving there. Josh arranged the meeting in the Arroyo Aerospace front office a week later. Depending on how the meeting goes, they will move on from there.

Arno knows that Josh and Tamara are working with Arroyo Aerospace. He is looking forward to seeing the place and hearing about this position. He figures it must have something to do with Arroyo Aerospace. He knows they are a private corporation working with NASA, other government agencies, and public corporations. They do top clearance project work for the aerospace industry. He learned about them when Tamara got her security clearance.

A week later, Arno drove to the gate of the Arroyo Aerospace property. He identifies himself and is given directions to go directly to the Arroyo Aerospace front office. On the road to the office, he passes a big sign and the entrance to Gate to the Galaxy Studio Theme Park. Looking down that road, he can see the outside of the large hangar in which Galaxy Two is being built. The hangar doors are closed. He parks in front of the small geodesic domed front office building with the sizeable hangar-type building directly behind it. Once inside, he introduces himself to Annie, sitting up front waiting for his arrival.

"Hi," Annie said. "Thank you for wearing a mask. We are all vaccinated here. If you are, too, you can choose not to wear a mask. I will let Josh know you are here."

Arno removes his mask, "Good, I'm vaccinated."

Josh came into the room to greet him.

"Glad you can be here. Any problem finding the place?"

"No, I followed your directions from the toll road exit."

"We're going to go into a secure conference room to talk. Would you mind leaving your mobile phone here? Annie will put it into the safe, and you can come back with us to the conference room. My phone is already in there."

"No problem," Arno said. He gave his phone to Annie, who put it into the safe, with Josh's phone and a couple of others. They all headed to the conference room where Sam was waiting.

"This is Sam Arroyo. Sam, Arno Cameron. You met Annie up front. She is also an Arroyo family member. Everyone sat down.

"Sam is vice president of Arroyo Aerospace, so I wanted you to meet him. Annie has other responsibilities. I've asked her to sit in on the meeting. I've been telling Sam about your background, legal credentials, and our connection at UCF. Sam has a couple of questions."

"Josh mentioned that you resigned from the CIA to work in academia. Are you happy with that decision?"

"There seems to be no real future at the agency. My background is in law and international studies. I haven't been assigned to anything in those areas for ten years. While working on various assignments, I began learning about cybersecurity and related subjects. When UCF contacted me about a new program they are planning, I thought it might be a better fit. I am looking forward to teaching. This is supposed to happen this fall. I've been working part-time on the curriculum with the course director. I'm waiting for the contract. Now I've been told there may be some budget cuts."

"I understand, thanks," Sam said.

Josh said, "I'm going to give you an idea of what we are doing here, okay? Would you mind signing a confidential disclosure waiver?"

Arno said, "sure, no problem."

Annie opened a folder and gave the document to Arno. He scanned it and signed it. She signed as a witness.

"After leaving UCF, I started working on various projects with Sam, Tamara, and others. All the projects are proprietary and secret. Very soon, the outcomes of the projects will become public. We are worried about maintaining secrecy and controlling the extraordinary proprietary work. We believe that intelligence agencies from governments at home and internationally will try to gain access. We are looking for someone who understands these agencies, the law, cyber security, internal and external security, and international politics. Is this something that might interest you?" Josh asks.

Arno thought for a moment. He was curious. "I do have experience in these areas. I'd like to know a little more about these projects' scope and outcomes. Also, what will my position be?

Sam said, "You will be an executive member of the new corporation being formed under the auspices of Arroyo Aerospace and the International Space Exploration Group. With your participation, we can figure out a title and salary."

"Thanks, I'm not worried about titles. I have a feeling the salary will be fair. Tell me more."

"This is why we ask you to sign a confidential disclosure waiver."

"No problem, something I would recommend."

Josh outlines the mission and project to Arno, who sits quietly, trying to absorb and believe what he hears. Even though he knows the Arroyo Aerospace connection to NASA, he wasn't expecting to hear about space launches to Mars. Josh explains that they need to protect their work from being stolen. Going public requires more insight into what intelligence agencies, foreign and domestic, might do to infiltrate the company. Employees who are screened and given top-level security clearance will be hired. Additionally, we must secure the entire property. Arno listens while Josh talks.

Making sure he understands everything, "this new company will explore the solar system using spaceships with super advanced proprietary technology that doesn't require rockets. Is that correct?"

"That's correct," Josh answers.

"Up until now, this has been kept completely secret. You plan to go public very soon. Does the government know about it?"

"As of now, the government does not know anything. We are in touch with NASA at a high level. NASA and the President will become aware of us just before we launch our new ship. We will show them a prototype we have been testing extensively for about a year while we built the larger ship," Sam explains.

"It's interesting. When I went to DC to get debriefed, Simone Greely, Josh, you may remember her, came in to see me during the debriefing. She asked about Josh and Tamara. I told her I didn't know much, except you were both on leave from the university. I said I thought you were doing research with a private corporation. That you and the family were living at the beach in Cape Canaveral. Simone told me they had some unidentified communications signals from outer space back to Florida near the Space

Center that NSA had picked up. Other curious happenings the Chinese and NASA are interested in. I just listened."

"Why do you think she's connecting these things to Tamara and me? Josh asks.

"I don't know Simone that well. She tends to latch on to unexplained issues or odd facts. In this case, maybe a name like Arroyo Aerospace and you and Tamara's connection with them? Sometimes she figures out how to connect the dots," Arno said.

Sam and Josh exchanged glances. "Thanks for letting us know. "We have taken many precautions. It isn't easy to stay completely under the radar without leaving clues. Once we go public, some mysteries will be solved."

"If you think you might be interested, we can show you the prototype ship and the second ship after some lunch," Josh said.

"Interested and curious to hear more," Arno replies.

Lunch is finished. They walk to the hangar where Galaxy One is housed. Raoul Jr. joins them as they tour the ship. Video clips of the flight to the moon are screened. At one point, while Arno is aboard, they float the vessel outside the hangar and up and down the runway to give him a tangible experience. Arno is impressed and convinced that this is all for real.

"Can't believe I'm in a UFO. This revolutionary invention can change the balance of power in global politics. The world is going to react in many ways. When do you plan to go public?"

"Saturday, September 4th, Labor Day Weekend. We plan to launch the International Space Exploration Group and Galaxy Two in front of the invited press. We are not going to talk about or explain the drive system. At most, we will say it is a proprietary system," Josh replies.

Raoul Sr. and Marcella join them in the command center. Josh introduces them as the founders of Arroyo Aerospace and the International Space Exploration Group.

"Good to meet you both," Arno said.

"What do you think of our plans, Mr. Cameron?" Raoul Sr. asks.

"Please call me Arno. It's a lot to take in all at once. I'm overwhelmed as I believe the world will be when you go public. Many people will not believe it is real, even after they see the ship launch. Rest assured. There will be many offers to invest in your enterprise. I hope you have taken measures to secure all systems throughout your business and personal life. I am assuming that beyond letting NASA know about this before the launch, no one in the government knows anything about it. Some federal agencies get jealous about what they consider to be their turf, especially the military. You can develop proprietary equipment and resources as a private-sector business. This is your technology, as I'm sure you are aware,"

"How do you feel about working with us?" Marcella asks.

"This is an inspiring project and certainly the place to be. I usually don't make quick decisions on career moves. What you are doing is something special and historical. I want to be part of making history. Josh and Sam gave me an overview of where I might fit in. It seems like there is a lot to do before September 4th. The first thing I will offer to do is speak to the persons who set up your cyber security, which I think is probably very high-tech. I'm getting ahead of things. Yes, I want to work with you," Arno said firmly.

"We will draw up the contract. When will you be able to start?" Marcella asks.

"I have been on a holding pattern with UCF about teaching this fall. They have had some budget cuts. There has been no commitment. I will let them know I've had another offer," Arno said. "I can then start immediately."

"I'll call Bill Arroyo, our corporate lawyer, and you can work out all the details. He has a secure Orlando office and handles all Arroyo Aerospace legal work. I'll have him call you and schedule a meeting in the next few days. Hopefully, you will get started the first week in August if that works for you," Marcella said.

"Sounds like a plan," Arno replies.

Josh drives Arno back to his car. On the way, Arno thanks him for the recommendation. "I realize this is a family business, and ordinarily, I might be concerned about it. Somehow, they make me feel like I'll be part of that family. Very different from the government and other institutions I've been associated with."

"That's true. They took Adrienne, the kids, and me in and made us part of the family. Marcella and Raoul have eight children, some of whom are adopted. Almost all are involved in the business in some way. I've never had bad vibes from any of them. It's like we've known each other all our lives. I trust them completely, and I believe they trust me."

"Trust is necessary for an enterprise like this. I think anyone in their right mind would want to be involved in something as dynamic as an outer space exploration company. I assume that more people will be hired soon. It will be important to screen them and do deep background checks."

"They have their sources for checks, but not on a large scale." There is no human resources department, only Annie. You will be a big part of the screening process for future employees."

"One thing I want to mention is that your friend George is still seeing Simone Greely. Be careful what you tell George because his association with her compromises him."

"George knows she works for the CIA. He is a lawyer and knows about privileged information. I do not discuss anything about what we are doing with him. Confidentiality agreements bind me. I do agree that he may be compromised in some way. I don't see him much since I've mostly been living at the beach."

"I understand. I no longer have a direct connection with the agency. Because of his relationship with Simone, I suggest we don't tell George I am working with Arroyo Aerospace."

"No problem, good idea."

On his drive back to Orlando, Arno thinks about his new job and what he has just experienced. "This space exploration company and travel in space is a leap into the future." He felt fate got him here to this moment and this opportunity to be part of something much larger than the sum of its parts. "Teaching will have to wait." He believes he can profoundly contribute to this endeavor by helping to protect valuable secrets beyond numbers. "This propulsion system is in its way as momentous as the 'atom bomb' was when it was revealed. It changed the world. The difference now is that this is not a destructive invention. Potentially it can be weaponized, which is a good reason for all the secrecy. The Arroyos know this and have some initial protection as a private sector entity. Amazingly, they have kept this a secret for so long. How did they manage to fly to the moon and not be seen? They must understand what it will mean when they go public. I'm sure I'll be busy."

CHAPTER TWENTY-SIX

"Which amendment is it that says we have the right to be stupid?"

Running barefoot ahead of their parents' young children, they giggle and splash water on the wet sand. Soon the tide will stop moving higher on the beach. The water will be still for a short time, then reverse for the next six hours. It is early evening, and the sun is setting in the west behind the buildings on the beach. Adrienne and Josh are sitting on their shaded balcony, drinking tea. They speak quietly even though they are secure that no one nearby can overhear their conversation.

"Do you think our lives will change after the public launch?" Adrienne asks.

"No question, a lot depends on the reaction to this giant step in the evolution of space travel and other considerations. Manipulating gravity is a major development in human command of the environment. I think every country will want to have access to the technology. Some may consider it a threat, a shift in the balance of power in the world. Some will try to build weapons around these abilities. Then there are those super-powerful individuals who control commerce these days. For example, the oil industry built its fortunes on oil consumption. They still have oil to sell."

"I mean our personal lives as part of the International Space Exploration Group (ISEG)."

"You're working to give us all as low a profile as possible to protect our privacy and keep individual names out of the news. But you may have more name recognition. It's good we're emphasizing the 'space exploration' ambitions of the group and the company. Including ISEG's plans to work with NASA. The push will be to frame the propulsion system for space exploration."

"We're not planning team interviews, only press releases and statements. I worry about how people will react to the idea of spaceships that fly without rockets. You know the media; they will try to track down anyone associated with the company. I'm concerned about the children."

"I am as well. It will be increasingly difficult to remain anonymous," Josh said. "Our names are not Arroyo. However, you are the spokesperson for the company. I'm a bit concerned about that. You know we hired Arno Cameron. He's moving quickly to increase security and privacy for everyone. Carlos has built an amazing system for cyber security. I believe the corporation connection with NASA, as a private sector business, provides a safe harbor. Sooner or later, the government will push to get hold of the technology for 'national security,' and military purposes like the 'Space Force," so they can patrol space. Of more immediate concern, I think the company will have to fight off foreign attempts to steal the technology. Only Arroyo Aerospace knows exactly how the drive propulsion works. We should not be in the line of fire there."

"I'm going to close a couple of my social media accounts. My family will have to understand," Adrienne said.

"I have some media accounts that I peruse. I don't post very often," Josh said.

"There's a lot of politics and misinformation on most sites. Even if the public accepts what we're doing, the Russian trolls will be out in force, spreading misinformation to create fear in the U.S.

"Conrad says it is difficult to reverse historical trends. The trend currently appears to be to the right. The laws they are trying to pass will limit voting for everyone, even allowing certain people to overturn elections. This can lead to an authoritarian government and, ultimately, a dictatorship in this country. If that happens, Conrad thinks they will just come and take the technology."

Adrienne sat in silence for a few minutes, "School starts soon. I thought we should move back to the house in Baldwin Park so the children could go to the district high school there. Now I think they should go to school here at Coco Beach."

"Yes, it may be safer for the children to go to school locally, or we may want to consider a private school. In Orlando, some more media contacts and neighbors tend to ask questions. George is okay, but Arno says his CIA girlfriend Simone may have an agenda. "

"You told me George and Simone are a couple."

"Arno told me they got through the pandemic together. Off the record, she speaks Mandarin Chinese and works in the Chinese section. Arno warns that, as far as we're concerned, this compromises George because he might divulge information to Simone. Arno thinks like a chess player, several moves ahead in various scenarios."

"Should I be concerned about my higher visibility as spokesperson and press liaison for all three companies?"

"I'm sure Arno will provide you with a high level of security. Living here at the beach is a good idea for the time being."

"Are you planning to go into space with the new ship?"

"I've been thinking about it. It depends on what happens. We can talk about it once the mission is finalized. One of the priorities will be to test for minerals. We can get top geologists to go on the trip who will analyze rocks and soil."

"I'm wondering if it will be for a long period if you do go. The trip to lunar orbit was worrisome. I had to adjust to being married to an astronaut."

"Speaking of Astronaut, we are getting some actual EVA and EMU suits designed for walks on the moon or Mars. Not saying that will be me out there. It's part of the notion of building some bases on other planets. Marcella and Raoul Sr. negotiated a deal with the same company designing them for NASA. These suits are uniquely able to deal with toxic soil on Mars."

Adrienne sighed, "knowing that does not make me feel more secure." She laughs, "I hope you don't ask us to move to Mars before the children finish high school."

Josh laughs, too, "Don't worry, I won't do that. I don't think there will be a habitable place for families on Mars for a while. I'd rather find a planet with breathable air."

"Then all we'd have to deal with is indigenous life forms or alien bacteria."

"I suppose so. The universe seems designed to keep any sentient life that may exist far apart. It appears we're stuck with this solar system. Humans can't even keep the earth healthy. The climate is getting more unpredictable. We are going through a pandemic caused by a virus from who knows where. We invent a vaccine that works against it, and half the people refuse to take it. I wonder what they would have done if they had been around for smallpox or polio. Many would not even be alive if their ancestors had not taken vaccines. George Washington insisted that his troops be vaccinated for smallpox way back then. Now people say getting vaccinated violates their freedom. Which amendment says we have the right to be stupid?"

During the first week of August, Arno met with Carlos, who filled him in on the communications and internet systems.

"You've done an amazing job with these systems. They are way ahead of the curve compared to anything I'm aware of at any of the intelligence agencies worldwide," Arno said. "NSA may pick up some of the scrambled high-frequency signals. I doubt they will be able to decipher them. And you built your dark web?"

"Yes," Carlos said matter-of-factly. "We use it for internal communications. Even those are encrypted."

"Great. You have firewalls everywhere, too, I imagine."

"We built an internal communications fortress."

"We need to talk about hiring people. I suggest we find someplace nearby to do preliminary screening interviews for prospects before bringing anyone here."

"Good idea. We can do preliminary screenings in Coco Beach or Orlando. Once applicants are screened, we can use the Arroyo Aerospace front office for likely prospects. We don't want people showing up here without an appointment."

Arno is impressed with the secure bubble that protects Arroyo Aerospace and now the International Space Exploration Group. In the short time Arno had worked with Arroyo Aerospace, he felt he was part of a team with a righteous purpose. He feels his mission is to protect the corporation from being infiltrated by any entity that might try to do harm or steal its secrets. He believed it was part of his responsibility to find ways to protect the staff. Finishing his conversation with Carlos, he notes that anyone interviewed must show proof of a COVID-19 vaccination. Not getting a vaccination by now might be a reason for immediate disqualification.

Three weeks before the first launch of Galaxy Two, Marcella and Raoul Sr. sat with Josh, Sam, Tamara, Conrad, Carlos, and Arno in the ultra-secure conference room. They finalized that this launch would be the first expedition to Mars. Conrad regularly attends many meetings, even though he doesn't always say much. Josh thinks of him as a history and political consultant. Carlos is there for communications and technical information.

"Josh, we hope you and Sam will negotiate the final deal with NASA. Raoul Sr. and I began talks with top officials after their visit," Marcella said. "We feel that a confidential alliance with NASA can be strategic and give us access to resources it will otherwise take a long time to acquire."

Josh appreciates his being selected with Sam to finalize the negotiations. He feels this will preclude him from going on this first flight of Galaxy Two. He does not have a problem with that. There will be subsequent opportunities to go to Mars.

"Originally, we made plans to be entirely independent of government or outside its influence. It became clear that this would not be completely possible. Working with NASA gives us cover, and we can help them achieve some of Their goals. For example, their project to put humans on the moon once again. Certain other countries and corporate entities are making plans to go into space. Their goals are to establish a presence on the moon and Mars. By teaming with NASA, we make the U.S. the winner of that race by default," Raoul Sr. said.

"This will bring prestige to the current administration and perhaps help them stay in control of the government past 2022 and 2024," Conrad said. "Based on historical trends, there are moves toward autocratic governments in this country and other countries. Anything can happen if right-wing elements gain control of this national government again. The last administration tried to destroy the civil service component of government and international treaties. Professional civil servants bring permanency to the government. There are movements at work behind the politicians. These forces have been around since before the Second World War. This is how aristocracies are formed. Today they tend to call them oligarchies. Since 1945 the U.S. has risen to become the world's leading nation. They say American dominance is now being challenged by other nations, mainly China. Dominate nations or empires are always going through cycles in their existence. The Russians have been working overtime since Putin took power to weaken the United States internally and as a world power. Putin has dreams of creating an empire in eastern Europe. He can't do it without China."

"We are hoping for at least four more years of relative stability to achieve our goal of exploring this solar system," Marcella said. "We want to build a starship during that time with a propulsion system capable of exploring the galaxy."

Josh looks around the table, thinking about how far the project has come since he joined the company. "What is it that we want from NASA as far as resources go?" he asked.

Raoul Sr. said, "For this first trip, we are looking for additional equipment for working on Mars, data, recognizance photographs of possible landing sites, and I believe we can use two volunteer astronauts to go out onto the surface. We are completing a prototype for a minimal lander for the surface that will operate with our drive. It has a roof and doors to protect passengers from radiation and dust. It is not pressurized, so passengers must wear suits while sitting inside. It holds up to four astronauts and some tools and has a cargo area. It will be launched from the cargo bay. This model is intended to be used on the planet. If necessary, it can be launched into space or from low orbit. The next version will be a pressurized lander and utility vehicle."

"We can share samples of the soil and rocks we collect with NASA for their research," Marcella said.

"Under development are robotic devices that will work in the Martian environment. One of the first things we can do is build shelters to sustain human life. Doing this on the surface is a huge task. One thing that may make it easier is finding a cave or access to subterranean spaces where we can create an environmental bubble. A place to build a shelter for human habitation," Raoul Sr. said.

"To accommodate the new activity and the workforce, our buildings here are being expanded," Marcella said. "Arno has been busy creating a process for interviewing and hiring additional personnel. He's doing a great job."

"Thanks. These are exciting times. Happy to be a part of it," Arno said.

CHAPTER TWENTY-SEVEN

"Humanity follows the earth.;
Earth follows the universe.
The universe follows the way;
The way follows only itself."

Galaxy Two is prepped and ready for flight. Earlier in the day, before the press begins to arrive, Captain Sun and most of the team board the ship and float it out to the launch center, where it now sits on its retractable landing pods. In the gray dawn light, Galaxy Two looks like it has arrived from a distant star. Inside the spacecraft, breakfast is served in the second-level galley.

"It's amazing how effortlessly this large vessel rises and moves. At the same time, it is capable of incredible speeds," Tamara said.

Raoul Sr. said, "the ship's captain is very good at controlling the lift and trust of these ships."

"Thank you," Captain Sun replies. "The entire flight control system responds well to manual operation. I have variable assent options. I can select a height and ascent speed or manually control these options."

"Does it feel different than Galaxy One?" Josh asks.

"Well, it's a lot bigger. So far, not much difference in control."

"The media will start to arrive in a few hours," Adrienne announced. "The briefing will be short."

Looking at Marcella and Raoul Sr., Tamara said, "Don't worry, you'll do fine."

With a resigned sigh, Marcella and Raoul Sr. smile in unison. Marcella said, "we don't have a problem speaking in public. Only an aversion to publicity. We realize that this time it is necessary."

Neither Marcella nor Raoul Sr. wants to be at the podium. At first, they try to get Sam and Tamara to be the spokespersons for the event. They are eventually persuaded that it is essential for them to be there as the founders of Arroyo Aerospace.

"What happens after lift-off?" Paul asks.

Sam replies, "We orbit around the earth for a few days and test all systems. This ship is much larger than Galaxy One. I want to be sure there are no glitches."

Raoul Jr. said, "we'll have some time for the crew to learn about the ship and how it handles. Additional crew and team will join us before we go to Mars."

Galaxy Two's crew consists of Captain Andrew Sun, the pilot. Raoul Arroyo Jr., Copilot, Kevin Steiner, Navigator, Carlos Arroyo Communications, Tamara Arroyo, expedition coordinator, two volunteer astronauts, Lt. Tony Capella and Lt. Patricia Sloan, on loan from NASA. Both astronauts can assist in the command center. NASA astronauts will be the first humans to walk on Mars. This is part of the deal Josh negotiated with NASA. It will bring prestige to the space agency and the United States.

Josh said, "this is a historical journey. I believe all of us are going to Mars. We will be with you in spirit even if not physically on board."

Adrienne knew Josh had some interest in being on this first trip to Mars. However, he was happy about staying behind this time. There is a lot for him to do here. She and Josh both know he will likely be on the second trip.

After breakfast, all non-flight crew members leave the ship. The crew does the systems checks and prepares for the launch.

Later that morning, the visitors arrive at the Gate to the Galaxy launch center. Some distance from the ship, in an area set up for the press and spectators, are local and national media representatives. It is not a large group. Only one national network has its local affiliate present. There is skepticism among the media about this event. Many sources speculate this is all a huge publicity stunt for Paul Arroyo's new film, Space Pioneers. Now that they are standing in front of the spaceship, even the skeptics must admit that the spacecraft looks like something that should be flying in space. News camera operators take shots panning along the windows midway up the hull. They shoot close-ups of the upper level with its huge dark glass windows extending back into the hull. A skeptical reporter tells another correspondent, "something this big cannot launch into space even if it has rockets or some fusion drive hidden somewhere. We're too close to the launch pad for a real lift-off. This is nothing more than an elaborate film set."

A podium with the International Space Exploration Group logo on the front is set up on a platform facing the assembled media. An American flag hanging from a pole stands on one side near the back of the stage. Recording the event are stationary cameras and a roving cameraperson working for Gate to the Galaxy theme park. Arno and two plain-clothed security persons are in place by the stage. Adrienne, Raoul Sr., Marcella, Bill, and two officials from NASA enter and wait on the stage near the flag. Adrienne walks to the podium.

"Thank you for being here today. I am Adrienne Bennett, spokesperson for the International Space Exploration Group. After years of planning, tests, and preparation, we are ready to launch Galaxy Two starship into space. Please welcome the founders of Arroyo Aerospace and the International Space Exploration Group, Marcella and Raoul Arroyo Sr. "

Marcella and Raoul Sr. walk to the podium. Marcella speaks first.

"Today, the International Space Exploration Group is launching Galaxy Two spaceship into orbit around the Earth. Private sector citizens of the planet Earth with allegiance to the planet are about to begin exploring our solar system. Even so, we are working closely with NASA and sharing the adventure with the world. Our first expedition will be to Mars. International scientists are scheduled to join us on this trip."

The assembled media stood by, unsure how to react to what Marcella was saying in a heartfelt voice.

"I think she believes what she's saying," whispers one doubting reporter to another.

"Isn't that the head of NASA on the stage?" said the other reporter.

Raoul Sr. speaks next. "You may wonder if this is Galaxy Two; where is Galaxy One? Please look behind us, and you will see Galaxy One come into view."

Galaxy One quietly floats into view some distance behind the stage, rising to about seventy feet in the air. It makes no sound. It simply appears. On board Galaxy One, Sam, Josh, and Paul handle the controls. While only about one-fourth the size of Galaxy Two, it is still an impressive sight. To all appearances a likely UFO. Sam uses the stealth cloaking device until they are near, then floats up from behind the stage facade. The communal gasp from the assembled press and spectators is loud. Cameras zoom in for shots of the ship. Many startled people start to move away. After the initial shock of a floating spaceship settles in, Marcella continues. "Our ships are not propelled by rockets. We have developed a proprietary means of propulsion that employs natural universal forces."

Raoul Sr. follows up, "Galaxy One, the ship behind us, has gone into earth and lunar orbit on test flights. If you look at the large screen to your left, you will see a video recorded from Galaxy One recently in earth orbit and later lunar orbit. Today Galaxy Two is launching into a high earth orbit in preparation for a pioneering trip to Mars. On board are two NASA astronauts who will be the first humans to walk on the surface of Mars."

The confused reporters are not sure what to do or think. They still have trouble accepting what they can see before their eyes, let alone the idea that Galaxy Two will lift off the ground, float into the sky and ultimately go into high earth orbit.

"You will not hear any rockets. Only the sound of the ship moving up through the air and into space," Raoul Sr. said.

"First, Galaxy Two will move from the ground to about fifty feet in the air," Marcella announces as the large spaceship rises off the ground effortlessly. Once again, the communal gasp is heard as the large ship hovers, re-tracking its landing pads.

When Galaxy One appears, the local network affiliate starts feeding its recording signal to its nearby satellite truck. The event is quickly picked up on national television networks and cable news channels. International cable networks linked, broadcast, and rebroadcasted the scene to other affiliates. Images of Galaxy One and Galaxy Two go super viral on social media sites. Within minutes the event becomes a worldwide spectacle. News network reporters and anchors watching the video are still talking about an "alleged launching of a spaceship to Mars." Many claim it cannot be confirmed. No spaceship can launch without rockets. Within seconds trolls and faux experts are united, arguing that "this is all an elaborate hoax."

"We will launch now. We have flight clearance via NASA. The ship will float up and in an easterly direction as it moves through the atmosphere and into space," Raoul Sr. said.

Pointing to the large monitor next to the stage, "You will be able to see a view from the ship on this monitor. We are also providing a feed for broadcast."

Galaxy Two begins its silent assent into the sky and toward the Atlantic Ocean as Galaxy One did secretly many times. Now the world is watching. Even though it is available, no stealth features or cloaking are used by Galaxy Two during the launch. At a certain height, the ship increases its speed, gains altitude, growing smaller in the sky. There is no rocket plume to follow as the spaceship gains altitude.

The crew monitors all the controls as Galaxy Two rises higher in the atmosphere. The team is pleased with the smooth launch. As the ship rises, it sends back a reverse view of the earth from the ship. This image appears on the stage monitors. Soon spectators can see a view of the Florida coast, the space center, and the ocean. The picture changes to a high-altitude view of the area and a stunning picture of the blue planet Earth. Galaxy Two achieves earth orbit, two-hundred and seventy-five miles (443 km) above the world. The ship is clear of the currently estimated thirty thousand satellites and space junk in orbit.

Adrienne takes the podium as Raoul Sr. and Marcella leave the stage. "I'm sure you have many questions. Please review the press release and information in the packets you receive. We will have more information for you very soon. At this time, Galaxy Two is in Earth orbit and will be doing tests and checking equipment before its pioneering flight to Mars. We are cooperating with NASA on this mission. We will keep you posted. We will also supply footage of the lift-off and Galaxy One's trip to lunar orbit to news outlets. If you are wondering about the status of the Space Pioneers film, Paul Arroyo is still producing the film as a documentary rather than a fiction film. In the next few weeks, we will announce plans for a limited number of media and others to take short flights on Galaxy One. Once again, thank you for being here."

Galaxy One moves away from the area as quickly and quietly as it appeared while most eyes are fixed on the launch of Galaxy Two. There are shouted questions of all kinds from reporters that still need to be answered. News commentators worldwide are now covering the story of the mysterious launch of a private spaceship destined to travel to Mars. To keep speculation at a minimum, Adrienne has a series of press releases and videos from the International Space Exploration Group (ISEG) ready to go immediately. They focus on plans to work with NASA, conduct space exploration in the solar system, and establish bases on the Moon and Mars to aid future human travel in space.

Initially, there was no reaction from the current crop of corporate entities using rockets to go into space. The first to congratulate the International Space Exploration Group and Arroyo Aerospace is the founder of Ramurt Rocket. He said his company would continue using conventional rockets to go into space. He hopes that, eventually, this new technology can be shared. Space X sent congratulations with similar comments. They are followed by others who congratulated the International Space Exploration Group as the new player in the "space race." NASA releases a statement congratulating ISEG and confirming NASA's support and cooperation.

Many countries applaud the new technology and claim they are anxious to work with ISEG on future projects. The Chinese government immediately realized it was Galaxy One that they tracked in Lunar Orbit. They begin efforts to contact NASA and ISEG about working together and purchasing technology. China emphasizes that cost is no issue. At the same time, Chinese domestic media expresses doubt regarding the event and speculates that it is all part of a U.S. propaganda movie.

Russian hackers immediately begin trying to hack Arroyo Aerospace but are coming up empty-handed. At one point, their systems crashed while trying to use "brute force" attacks to get into the Arroyo system. Carlos and Raoul Jr. created an automatic cyber-security App, which goes after the attacker's servers in retaliation for blatant hacking attempts. The App. latches on to alien code and moves to disrupt and destroy all data on the attacker's systems. In any event, hacking Arroyo Aerospace leads to a dead end.

The possible military applications of this new propulsion technology are discussed privately at the Pentagon and in military circles in other countries. Behind the scenes, in many international government circles, there is a discussion on how they might obtain this technology for military purposes. In the U.S., a quiet movement by the military/industrial establishment begins to look for a way to gain access to the new technology through government sources.

A week later, after systems tests are conducted on board Galaxy Two in earth orbit, the trip to Mars is confirmed. All systems are working well. A team of international scientists, geologists, Martian experts, NASA experts, astronauts, and others are transported by Galaxy One to Galaxy Two in orbit. All aboard are vaccinated, tested, and have spent time in quarantine before being transported to Galaxy Two. A pressurized link is secured between the two spaceships and the additional passengers board with their equipment.

Paul Arroyo joins the crew to direct the filming of the Mars journey. Other supplies and equipment are also brought on board for the trip.

Press releases and videos of the crew and passengers on board the ship are released to the media. Adrienne convenes a press conference confirming the trip to Mars is ready to begin. She announces periodic broadcasts from the ship and Mars once they arrive. NASA and major networks around the world will facilitate these efforts.

Currently, the orbits of Earth and Mars around the sun are at their most distant points. Earth and Mars will be in conjunction in October 2021. Mars is nearly behind the Sun, opposite Earth at launch.

Kevin's navigational plan is for the ship to use the earth and the sun's gravity to bring the ship to high-speed velocity behind the earth's orbit around the sun, gradually sliding toward Mars's solar orbit. Galaxy Two will intercept Mars as it orbits closer to Earth. The entire trip there and into orbit around Mars is estimated at thirty-eight days. They plan to spend fourteen days on Mars on this first trip and then return to Earth. Galaxy Two will arrive there during Martian autumn in the northern hemisphere and spring in the southern regions. Galaxy Two requires less time to return to Earth since the orbits of the planets will be closer. Initial flight speeds may be increased depending on performance tests.

"Well, my friends, we are about to begin an adventure. A first in human history. A human journey to another planet. Homo sapiens in space. Now there's a title for a film Paul," Captain Sun said.

"Good, I might just use that one," Paul replies as he directs the camera operator filming everyone at their stations.

The final systems check and a navigation lock by Kevin Steiner and Captain Sun are complete. Galaxy Two launches on its journey to Mars. The launch to Mars is broadcast internationally across the globe. Many countries not that friendly with the U.S. carry the launch, stressing that the International Space Exploration Group, a private corporation, is doing it.

Life aboard Galaxy Two settles in quickly. The ship moves through space silently. The crew and team are excited by the fantastic views of the earth and of the solar system. Orbiting Earth four times, Galaxy Two accelerates to 67,000 mph while Earth continues in the opposite direction at the same speed. Higher speeds are anticipated as solar gravity is utilized in sideways maneuvers moving toward Mars's solar orbit.

The ship is comfortable, more like a cruise ship than what everyone imagined a spaceship to be like. Galaxy Two has all the features of Galaxy One, with many upgrades. The meteorite and dust protection on the hull is more substantial. The idea is to protect the hull on Mars and the journey. Mars is notorious for dust storms. The dust on Mars is abrasive and might do some damage in extreme situations.

Galaxy Two is large and can accommodate many more passengers than are aboard for this maiden voyage. The gym and lounges offer places to exercise and relax. One can catch up on delayed news from the earth and call family back on earth.

The flight crew is on standby as the autopilot and auto navigation systems guide the ship. This gives the crew time to check on the performance of all ship systems. Galaxy Two can sustain life based on the current supplies and a small number of passengers for two years or more if necessary. The propulsion system only requires power to turn it on and sustain the manipulation of gravity waves. Like a surfer riding a wave, once the gravity wave is engaged, it is a free ride, provided you can stay balanced.

On earth, there is hope among many sources that this epic adventure by humans will bring the inhabitants of the planet closer. Conrad believes that this type of event has the potential to change history for America and the world.

....

CHAPTER TWENTY-EIGHT

"We have landed. Please remain seated until the unfasten your seat belt seat light comes on, and we have reached the terminal."

The first International Space Exploration Group (ISEG) public launch was amazingly successful. It is September 2021, and Galaxy Two is on its way to Mars. Since the launch of Galaxy Two, there has been public admiration, support, and international acclaim for ISEG and the trip to Mars. Behind the scenes, there emerges pressure from several sources to share the propulsion drive used by ISEG with the U.S. government and competitors in the space race. NASA let the government and the aerospace industry know they are not in control of ISEG or Arroyo Aerospace Inc, simply cooperating with private sector corporations.

Josh is the primary coordinator with NASA. It is the main reason he did not go on the first trip to Mars. Adrienne took over public relations for ISEG and handled affairs for Paul's film company.

Paul Arroyo receives criticism for promoting the fiction film and theme park to cover the space project. Adrienne spun the subject around to the fact that there will be a film about the first human trip to Mars. Paul and a film crew are onboard Galaxy Two filming the flight. Space Pioneers has become a documentary instead of a fiction film. Actual people are going to Mars instead of actors pretending. In addition, there is the reality of Gate to the Galaxy theme park. A theme park and launching site with an information center to give the public a chance to learn about the pioneering space explorations that are underway. The information center has exhibits that include displays and videos about ISEG and the most recent footage from current projects. There are also twice-monthly tourist flights on Galaxy One. These flights are instantly popular and booked for a year in advance. There is no charge for admission to the theme park center.

Galaxy Two continues its journey to Mars. It is built to carry eighty passengers and crew with ease. There are only twenty-eight people on this flight. Artificial gravity throughout the ship makes life more normal than ever for weightless travel in old rocket ships or space capsules. Galaxy Two is equipped to sustain the health and welfare of passengers over long journeys. Various size cabins are built on level two, along with lounges, dining areas, a galley, a gym, and other amenities. The crew has quarters on the first level, where there is also a greenhouse with a garden that grows plants to create oxygen and food. Many of these plants are earmarked for possible use in a greenhouse on Mars. The first level includes labs, support resources, and a large airlock for suiting, leaving, and entering the ship.

During the mission, Paul sends back footage for the public broadcast of the ship's first and second levels. Galaxy. Two travel to Mars is featured every night on broadcast and cable outlets. The footage of the solar system, as seen from Galaxy Two's cameras, is different from anything imagined. The sun and stars cast light on the ship and surrounding space uniquely. The ship's cameras record an intangible cosmic presence that offers no resistance to the ship as it speeds through the long night. The journey continues to capture the imagination of people around the planet. Space Pioneer T-shirts and other ISEG Mars Mission paraphernalia seemed everywhere on the internet.

On board, Tamara reviews the mission for the crew. "The mission includes selecting a location on Mars to land Galaxy Two. The landing site requires suitable places to build a base and research center. We plan to look at sites near mountains where there might be caves or a place to carve out a shelter from the high radiation on the surface. Possible sources of water are a priority for the expedition. The south polar region is thought to contain underground water lakes possibly. Northern areas contain frozen water in the soil. Both polar caps appear to have frozen CO_2 and H_2O. Extracting oxygen from Mars's atmosphere, mainly composed of CO_2, is possible."

"Mars is covered with toxic dust that contains iron oxide and other minerals. The southern hemisphere has higher elevations and is where the largest dust storms appear to originate. Rocks contain other minerals and ores that can be refined. No one knows what is near the surface or buried in the mountains. There are inactive volcanos in many places on the planet. It is suspected that sulfur gases are seeping from certain dormant volcano sites. Methane has been detected leaking somewhere in the Jezero crater near the Martian equator where NASA's Perseverance rover is exploring."

Carlos added, "Recently, high amounts of hydrogen neutrons have been detected by astronomers in canyons known as Valles Marineris, tagged the 'Grand Canyon' of Mars. This may indicate water in some form in the 2,500-mile network of canyons located near the Martian equator. If possible, we want to get a closer look at this area of the planet."

On loan from NASA, two trained astronauts, Lieutenant Tony Capella, and Captain Patricia Sloan will do the initial surface reconnaissance outside the ship. Captain Sun, with Raoul Jr. as copilot, are both comfortable at the helm of Galaxy Two. They obtained experience piloting Galaxy One. Kevin Steiner, chief navigator, and Carlos designed and programmed the navigation system of Galaxy Two. In addition to coordinating the mission, Tamara handles communications and can back up Carlos. She also trained to pilot the ship.

Several prominent scientists are on the expedition to advise and collect firsthand data about the planet. In addition to gathering footage for the Mars mission documentary, Paul assists the flight crew. He plans to have one of the astronauts shoot some footage on the surface. Galaxy Two and the utility rover's camera footage will also be available. The cameras in use are all high-definition equipment. Adrienne prearranges live broadcasts of the astronaut's first moments on the surface of Mars. Based on the final positions of Mars and Earth, it will take about fifteen minutes for the signals to reach Earth. The high-definition video is compressed to speed up the transmission. However, it still looks good.

Paul and most other people on board want to go onto the planet's surface. A decision is made for this trip. It is better first to allow the trained astronauts to go onto the surface. In the future, with some training themselves, others will join them. Another factor is that EMU suits are fitted to each person individually. The astronauts already have suits and are experienced in how to wear and use them. In the future, astronauts will be assisted by robots impervious to the Martian environment.

An essential aspect of training for NASA astronauts is learning to walk on the surface of the moon or Mars, where the gravity is less than on earth. The new EMU suits designed for Mars include weighted boots to help keep leg muscles strong. Arroyo Aerospace is researching artificial earth gravity for long-term resident habitats. How long does it take for muscles to atrophy under lower gravity? NASA is conducting studies using astronauts who live weightless for months on the International Space Station. One known preventative measure is constant exercise.

Galaxy Two arrives in Mars orbit on schedule. The team is anxious to see the planet up close. After two days of orbiting Mars and observing landing site possibilities, the crew picks a location with no large boulders or rocks to land safely. Raoul Jr. explains, "we will land at the foot of a mountain in the northern hemisphere near the equator in the Tharsis bulge region. This area is near the western edge of Olympus Mons, which covers an area about the size of Arizona and is the highest known mountain in the solar system. This edge of the mountain has cliffs and a rising elevation. Olympus Mons is a 'shield volcano.' Its peak cannot be seen from the mountain's base because of gentle slopes of ancient slow-flowing lava and the height of the peak."

Captain Sun prepares for landing with less gravity and an extremely thin atmosphere. Visibility is good. The landing procedure is much the same as floating down to the earth's surface. The difference is that Mars has less gravity than Earth, with one percent of the atmosphere. The spacecraft's drives and navigation programs can adjust to different gravity forces. Once a location is selected, Kevin enters the coordinates into the navigation system. Near the surface, Captain Sun maneuvers the ship into the chosen spot and prepares to set the craft down gently. The retractable pods lower when the vessel is fifty feet from the surface. The pods soften the landing and protect the hull. Once on the ground, the ship's weight keeps it in place.

When Galaxy Two finally came to rest on Mars, Captain Sun imitating what he might say after landing an aircraft at an airport on Earth, said, "We have landed. Please remain seated until the unfasten your seat belt light comes on, and we have reached the terminal." For a moment or two, everyone is unsure if he is serious as they wait for the ding of the faint sound of the seatbelt.

"Ding! Just kidding folks, it's fine to move about. Believe it or not, we are sitting on the planet Mars. The first humans to ever land on another planet in the solar system." After some applause, Captain Sun and his crew began the systems check.

Tamara announces, "It is noon where we have landed. A Martian Sol (day) is 24 hours 37 minutes, almost the same as an earth day. The temperature on the surface is minus eighty degrees Fahrenheit (Minus sixty Celsius). We're going to relax for the rest of the Sol. Tomorrow we'll start exploring. The surface does not retain much heat. The temperature may drop to as low as minus 125 Celsius (Minus 195 Fahrenheit) tonight. Galaxy Two will be the warmest thing on the surface. We will heat the ship with our energy system. During the day, the hull absorbs sunlight for solar energy. The sun is weaker here on Mars than on Earth. We can use the available sunlight."

Scenes of the landscape of Mars taken from the ship while orbiting, during and after the landing, and around Galaxy Two are transmitted and seen everywhere on Earth. Sunset on Mars is observed by people sitting about two hundred million miles away in their living rooms.

The sun came up at 6:24 a.m. the next day shining through the misty thin Martian atmosphere. The crew prepares to launch the utility rover for the astronauts to explore the area while collecting soil and rock samples. Tamara and NASA specialists help the astronauts get into their EMU suits. These new heated suits are individually fitted to each astronaut. The suits are designed for mobility and walking on the planet rather than floating in space. In addition, they are made so that the astronauts can get in and out of the suits without touching the outer part of the suit. The EMU suits are housed in a step-in closet in the cargo bay to facilitate this feature. Each astronaut wears an inner body suit that handles life support and other technical elements. Vitals are sent back to the ship for constant monitoring.

Astronauts Tony and Patricia are ready to be the first humans to walk on Mars and explore the Martian surface. There is an EMU suit check before the astronauts board the Mars utility rover and float it into the cargo hold airlock. Tamara is their primary contact while they are on the surface. This first excursion is set to last four hours. Oxygen supplies carried in the suits last for up to six hours. The suit's heating system is good for about six hours.

Tony and Patricia trained for spacewalks and movement in zero gravity in space. Also, for reduced gravity on the surface of the moon or Mars. Their weighted boots help them adjust, but they will still feel much lighter. They learned to drive the rover before leaving Earth. It is easy to handle with a steering mechanism and a joystick. It is built roomy to accommodate astronauts wearing suits. There are a pair of padded skis on the underside for landing.

"It looks like it is about as a clear day as we can expect on Mars," Tamara said. "The temperature is warming up. We have a heat wave! Close to minus fifty Celsius (-58 F) now."

"We're all set," Tony said. "These suits are comfortably warm."

Paul stops shooting in the airlock and moves back into the ship. The airlock doors slide shut.

"Interior door sealed," Tamara reports.

"Okay, we will open the cargo bay airlock so you can float out. Take it slowly," Tamara said. The utility rover protects the occupants from radiation and dust with its roof and doors.

The airlock opens. In a few moments, the rover quietly floats out onto the surface of Mars. All that can be heard is the sound of some wind on the surface. The drive for the rover is tuned to work with the gravity of Mars. The rover has a homing device linked to Galaxy Two. Several built-in cameras cover 360 degrees around the vehicle, including above and below. The video is transmitted back to Galaxy Two. The rover is equipped with Ground Penetrating Radar (GPR) sensors that can be seen on a screen in the rover while sending data collected back to the ship. The GPR equipment can check below the planet's surface for soil strata, water, objects of any kind, and empty spaces.

After some editing by Paul video of the exploration will be sent back to Earth. Carlos handles the first transmission to Earth of video from the rover moving out of the airlock and onto the surface. Live streaming is only sometimes possible because of issues stemming from the position of Mars and Earth. All the footage is archived for later use. Galaxy Two's cameras focus on the lander moving away from the ship. This can be viewed on the large monitors in the command center and elsewhere on Galaxy Two.

The International Space Exploration Group broadcasts to Earth of the Mars landing, and astronauts on the planet's surface have the highest ratings internationally of any televised program previously aired. Paul said, "we can charge Super Bowl rates for advertising if we accept commercials." Paul knows there is no chance they will run commercials.

"We're going to rise to about 15 feet above ground now," Patricia said. "We'll head northeast toward the foot of the mountain area where we saw the crevices and gullies during reconnaissance. We can take a look around there."

"Great," Tamara said.

"Cameras are rolling. Tell us about what you are seeing and experiencing," Paul asks.

"Well, it looks like frozen dust, soil, and rocks of varying sizes. Not much wind right now," Tony said. "Hard to believe we're flying this utility rover over the Martian landscape! The ground looks rusty."

Tamara replied, "Amazing! We're getting excellent footage of the terrain. As you get closer to the mountainside, look for cracks, caves, or openings in the mountain."

"Gullies are running down the mountain here, must have been made by lava at one time. What if we go up higher and see if there is anything?" Patricia asks.

"Okay, there appear to be some ledges."

The rover floats upward slowly as the morning sunlight reflects off the silver-gray hull of the small vehicle. Most of the ledges are small areas where the gullies seem to stop before continuing below. There are fracture lines or fissures in some places. The rover flew low and slow over the ground below the gorges, with the GPR sending data back to Galaxy Two. Soon they turned and began going higher up the face of the cliff. They then began to move horizontally along the front of the mountain.

"We found a flat ledge that looks large enough to land on. We could collect some rock samples. There is also a fissure in the mountain face between some gullies about a meter wide (three feet)," Tony said.

"Looks like plenty of space. Is the ledge solid and stable enough to land on?" Tamara asked. "Try a scan with the GPR," she suggests.

"It should be. It looks like solid rock," Tony said. "There is a boulder sitting at the far end. It's about forty-five feet (13.71 meters) wide and ninety feet (27.43 meters) long. It doesn't look like anything loose above that could fall on us."

"See if you can bring the rover in over a flat spot with room around it that's not too close to the edge. Hover there a foot or so off the ground for a minute."

Tony moved the rover onto the ledge over a flat area close to the mountainside. He brought the rover down to about six inches above the ledge surface. The rover is lightweight but gets heavy with the two astronauts, their suits, and equipment. Everyone waited for a minute while the rover hovered.

"GPR indicates solid rock, no cracks," said the geologist reviewing the data sent back from the rover.

"Let's set the rover down," Tamara said.

Tony brings the rover down softly onto the surface; he is prepared to lift off if there is a problem. After a crunching sound and rising dust, the rover settles down securely.

"Be careful getting out of the vehicle and walking. There can be some moisture frozen on the surface," Tamara warns.

Patricia emerges from one side of the vehicle.

"I can feel the lighter gravity," she said. "The surface is solid. It appears to be dry."

"Congratulations, Patricia, you are the first human to set foot on Mars! Be careful. We don't want you flying around up there."

Tony gets out of the rover next and joins Patricia at the rover's rear.

"Congratulations, Tony, you are the second human to walk on Mars," Tamara announced as everyone clapped!

NASA astronauts Tony and Patricia raise their arms and wave at the billions of people on Earth who will soon see them. "I hope someone is saving me a selfie of this," Patricia said.

"Just hold that position for a minute," Paul asks, shooting remotely from Galaxy Two. He wanted wide shots and close-ups of the couple before he let them go to work. He continues filming as they open the rover's rear compartment lid, removing the tools and containers in which to put samples.

"Don't rush. You have about sixty minutes to spend on the ledge. Then head back toward the ship to check some other spots," Tamara said.

Both astronauts gather rock samples from the surface and chip away rock from the mountain. Tony uses his helmet light and camera to look inside the crevasse. It appears to open wider and possibly go deep inside the mountain. It is like the mountain split there for some reason. He took photos and shot videos. Including his suit, the opening needed to be wider for him to squeeze through. He wants to go deeper inside. Tamara reminds him that any damage to his suit could cost him his life. He turns sideways and carefully moves into the crevice, where he chips some samples from the walls. Without the glare of the exterior light, he confirms that deeper inside the mountain, there is an open space. Before leaving, he chips "ISEG" on the wall next to the entrance. "Even though the coordinates of the site are recorded, this will be confirmation."

"First graffiti on Mars," Carlos quips. "Next time, we need to give them markers and spray paint."

After twenty minutes of collecting samples, they head back to the rover. The radiation-proof container lids are snapped securely and deposited with the tools in the rover's rear. Using a low-pressure container of air mist, they spray each other's gloved hands, boots, and suits to remove some of the Martian soil before getting back into the rover. The air mist floats into the atmosphere like a small alien cloud of oxygen and H2O. The idea is to keep as much Martian dust as possible from getting into the rover. Once they are in the rover, they gently float it off the ledge surface and head toward Galaxy Two. Their time in the rover gave them additional protection from increased radiation as the sun rose in the thin Martian atmosphere.

Patricia and Tony made one more landing on the surface, closer to the ship, where they collected soil and rock samples. There is more dry sand or regolith at this spot than on the cliff. The rover and the EMU suits are equipped with an antimagnetic coating that helps to keep the Martian dust from sticking. As the ground temperature increases, the wind picks up in the area. The sky turns rusty red from the dust rising. To be safe, Tamara asks the astronauts to finish what they are doing and head back to the ship.

Arriving at the ship, the rover passes into the airlock, receiving a complete exterior vacuuming to remove toxic soil and dust. Next, the astronauts step out of the lander and vacuum the interior with handheld hoses. The Martian soil and dust are exhausted out a vent to the surface. Once the rover is cleaned, they float it into the cargo bay. Tony and Patricia unload the containers from the rover, bringing them with them as they step into a sizeable glass-enclosed space. Compressed air hoses are used to further dust off the containers. Before getting out of the EMU suits, they spend time depressurizing.

The specially designed closet allows the astronauts to step out of their EMU suits into a separate area. The suits stay in the first space as a door slid into place to isolate the suits from the astronauts. The suits are then sprayed with a cleaning solution. The EMU suits and boots need to be cleaned to remove Martian soil, which is toxic to humans because of high levels of chlorine and perchlorates. The dust in the atmosphere and on the ground can corrode parts of the space suits.

Five hours after their historic excursion on Mars, the astronauts, now out of the cargo bay area, are safe aboard Galaxy Two. After a shower, they join the rest of the crew for a brief celebration.

The exterior of the rock and soil containers are cleaned again and brought to the lab. The geologists immediately start work cataloging and determining mineral content and other characteristics. The lab has a closed filtration system and door seals to be safe. All team members in the lab wear protective suits and masks. The samples are examined in acrylic enclosers with arm and hand access ports. The idea is not to contaminate the rocks nor expose anyone to the expected high levels of radiation, chlorine, and perchlorates ($ClO4$) contained in the soil. Perchlorates can be an essential source of oxygen but are a chemical hazard to humans. The samples are checked for radiation. The rock samples and soil contain much higher radiation levels than the soil on earth. The rock wall chips from inside the crevasse entrance tested lower for radiation. They appear to be different minerals than on the surface. All samples are stored in radiation-proof containers. The geologists plan to do tests on the rocks and soil now and on the way back to Earth.

Tony asks Tamara, "are we going to stop by the Curiosity or Perseverance sites? We can bring back Perseverance samples for NASA. Curiosity is at the Jezero crater near the equator. It found what appears to be an ancient lakebed."

Tamara said, "we spoke to NASA about this. We can do a flyby if all goes well and we have the time. We don't want to disturb the Perseverance rover's performance. NASA said they would consider it. We'll give them some of the samples we collect. We want to look at the Valles Marineris if we have time and can land nearby. We recorded excellent videos and pictures of the area from orbit. We might check out the Chinese lander if we don't cause an international space incident."

"I don't know, the Chinese are secretive about their space program since they were shut out of the ISS for what they claim are political reasons," said Patricia. "That's why they are building their orbital space capsule, which will have a space telescope."

"We could ask them if they want some photographs of their lander after we fly over. If we don't touch or disturb anything, it's not a big deal," Tamara said.

Tamara didn't mention that the Chinese Space Agency had contacted ISEG shortly after the first public launch. The Chinese are interested in some joint ventures with ISEG. Money is no object, they claim. Josh and Raoul Sr. spoke with them. The door is left open for possible cooperation. Marcella invites Chinese Space Agency members to the U.S. for a trip into orbit on Galaxy One.

The Chinese are not the only people invited for excursions into earth orbit on Galaxy One. U.S. Government officials, foreign officials, and others are also invited. The idea is to build some contacts and demystify the program. Of course, technology remains proprietary and classified. All anyone knows is that the propulsion drive somehow employs gravity.

Adrienne set up a schedule for several tourist flights on Galaxy One while Galaxy Two is on the journey to Mars. Galaxy One carries passengers comfortably seated on the upper and middle levels. The first flight includes the President of the United States, two senators, and two house members equally divided between political parties. The Vice President is scheduled for a different flight since they cannot be on the same flight. Included in the group are two secret service agents. Raoul Sr. and Marcella join the guest list. Adrienne acts as a guide. Internal and external cameras serve as a feed for all media wishing to use the footage. Network and broadcast groups around the world broadcast the morning event. Every U.S. network came to the 'Gate to the Galaxy' launch site to film the lift-off. It seems like they still expect a rocket launch. Instead, Galaxy One gently floats into the morning sky, gaining speed and altitude. Inside the ship, guests are seated securely with safety harnesses. Monitor screens provide them with a view of the assent. Once they moved into earth orbit, Adrienne spoke to the group.

"While in orbit, you can get up from your seats. You will not float around because we have artificial gravity on this ship. There are some refreshments and a restroom on the second level. Please be careful on the stairs leading down to the lower level, as the gravity is not as strong as on earth. You will feel a bit lighter. Looking out the windows, you will have a view of the earth as seen from 265 miles in space. Since we are over one hundred miles above the planet's surface, you all qualify as astronauts. We will make two ninety-minute earth orbits and then return to the Gate to the Galaxy launch site. When we're ready to descend, we will ask everyone to be seated with harness fastened."

Adrienne walks among the passengers, some of whom are insecure about getting out of their seats. She helps the President stand up and walk with her to the command center; the other passengers begin to relax. Adrienne's assistant guides the others to level two if they wish to go there.

The President marvels at the view of the earth through the command center windows as they circled the globe. "This is amazing! You folks have done a great job. I'm amazed how comfortable it feels aboard the ship coming up and going into orbit." Adrienne introduces the President to Raoul Jr., Sam, and Arno working in the command center.

"How will the ride be when we return to earth?" the President asks.

"No difference. We will float down from orbit. We control the speed of the descent. We will gently reduce speed so that we float down through the atmosphere," Raoul Jr., who is at the helm, explains.

The footage from Galaxy One's launch and journey into orbit captivated the world almost as much as the launch of Galaxy Two did weeks before. To many, it is like science fiction became a reality. Humans can now fly into space without being blasted there on a rocket. For some people, it is too much to believe. They think it is all a movie, not real. Fake news, even though every media available is freely covering it. Conspiracy trolls pop up instantly from under their rocks, decrepit bridges, and polluted streams.

Adrienne does her best to stay above the conspiracy nonsense on social media, where it grows like poison Ivy. Misinformation about the ISEG and the flight to Mars spread like black mold in damp places. Adrienne and her team do their best to correct false information. Even bizarre claims take on a life of their own. Trolls can make up a story, put it on social media, and a right-wing online broadcaster will repeat it as if it were based in fact. Conspiracy groups absorb misinformation, and baseless accusations, like sponges, absorb water.

When Galaxy One returns to earth with the President, he and the other passengers give a joint press conference about their experience. The event has united members of different political parties in common enthusiasm for the great leap in human technology their trip into space represents. The President, Congressional Representatives, and Senators say they appreciate the cooperation between the International Space Exploration Group and NASA. They say they look forward to a new age. NASA now officially authorizes ISEG.

The President said, "I'm impressed with what these guys have done. Fantastic job. This administration is in total support of the Space Exploration Group mission."

NASA subsequently contracts with ISEG to resupply the International Space Station and to carry astronauts to the Hubble Space Telescope to make repairs or additions if or when necessary. Some modifications are made to Galaxy One cargo bay to accommodate astronauts going on spacewalks to do this work. Flights can also be made to Lagrange point L2 should the new Webb telescope need maintenance.

Raoul Sr., Sam, Marcella, and the team that built the earlier ships finish building Galaxy Three while the first trip to Mars is underway. Designed to be a cargo vessel and to accommodate better working in space, it can also carry satellites and launch them into orbit, much like the NASA space shuttles did at one time. ISEG receives many inquiries from governments internationally and the private sector regarding contracting for satellite launches and other space projects and perhaps retrieving non-functioning satellites. A second Galaxy Three cargo model (Galaxy Four) is planned to accommodate private sector contracts and NASA commitments. Arroyo Aerospace expands its facilities and workforce to facilitate the additional production of ships.

The United Nations and NASA began talks on a program to clean up dormant satellites and space junk in Earth orbit. One consideration is asking Arroyo Aerospace to design a ship that can scoop up the debris. One of the main obstacles facing the UN committee is that certain countries do not want their dead satellites to be salvaged because they were military or secretly spy satellites when they functioned. It may take years for any progress toward a resolution to happen on this topic. The Russians use a missile to destroy one of their dead satellites still in orbit. This causes minor damage to the International Space Station and adds more debris to the ring around the earth.

It is anticipated that Galaxy Three, carrying equipment and supplies, can accompany Galaxy Two on the second trip to Mars. Galaxy Three has accommodations for a crew of astronauts to construct in space, on the moon's surface, or Mars. It is designed to rendezvous with Galaxy One or Two in space. Sam has the idea that the Galaxy ships should be able to link together to form the basis for a space station, if needed, at some point.

In 2021 private rocket companies launched rockets carrying passengers into lower earth orbit. One flight goes sixty-one miles up and back down in about five minutes. No earth orbits. The four passengers in the capsule return to earth with the final drop aided by a parachute attached to the capsule. Another rocket, launched from an airplane, goes up to about fifty miles carrying six passengers. They returned to the earth like the space shuttle by gliding to a landing on land. The goal of these companies is advertised as creating a space tourism industry. A third company launches rockets with astronauts who are returned to earth in a capsule after an earth orbit. Passengers on the flights seem to enjoy the rocket-propelled ride, being weightless in space, and the thrill of it all.

Soon after Galaxy Two's launch, Arno detects an avalanche of hacking attempts on Arroyo Aerospace's website. So far, even the brute force attacks have not penetrated or been damaging. Not that hacking Arroyo Aerospace's leading site can reveal anything about the company beyond the fact that they exist and have a place to leave comments. The same type of site is in place for Arroyo Studios, Paul's Film company. Both sites have isolated servers, state-of-the-art firewalls, and protection.

A website is in place for the International Space Exploration Group Inc. (ISEG). It has a page outlining the corporate mission and videos of the launch. The site includes a contact page where a message may be written. Within two weeks of the launch, there were thousands of messages, and the site automatically stopped accepting any more. The site is heavily protected and isolated on a dedicated server with nothing else. Messages are screened for viruses and malware using a computer for that purpose only.

Incoming phone calls to Arroyo Aerospace, Arroyo Film Studio, and the International Space Exploration Group go to the primary office. Annie answers calls when possible. She logs and reviews the voice messages. There are so many calls that one person can't keep up with them, so ninety-nine percent go to voice mail. An AI program listens to the voice mails, transcribes them in English, or leaves them in the recorded language. This makes it easier for the staff to scan for anything important that needs to be answered.

The original private internet set up by Carlos remains undiscovered and is used for external communication. Carlos adds a second private web to the mix. All traffic is split between the two networks. With all the precautions, redundant firewall protection, scrambling, and other measures, security is still not taken for granted. The original security precautions, including those for mobile phones, are kept in place. Carlos wants to launch a second satellite to help handle traffic from space to earth.

Concerned about terrorists or spies posing as guests on Galaxy One demonstration flights, Arno takes precautions. He institutes a policy of security checks for all guests. Guests are screened for weapons of any kind. The most advanced TSA equipment is obtained and installed at the Gate to the Galaxy launch site. Guest laptops, tablets, cameras, and mobile phones are not permitted on the ship. The ISEG crew at no charge records video and stills of guests.

Arno hires security personnel for the ranch, buildings, and launch site. He interviews and screens mainly retired ex-secret service and FBI personnel for these jobs. They are all plain-clothes internal security. Additional uniformed security people are hired to secure the entrances and access to the entire property. Everyone hired goes through a deep security check. Raoul Sr. and Marcella appreciate the security and know it is necessary, but they want to keep it as lowkey as possible. They meet everyone hired to get to know each of them on a first-name basis.

All staff and employees agree that high security is essential to protect proprietary devices. Corporate espionage is just as insidious as foreign or domestic government intrusion. A more conventional commercial space company like Space X, Blue Origin, Ramurt Rocket, or Virgin Galactica might not need such tight security. Although it is likely that they, too, have high-tech security and protection, Arno insists.

The press, media networks, and social media are entirely different situations. With the launch of Galaxy Two, there has been a considerable increase in attention from the media. Adrienne hires several associates to help with the coordination needed in different areas. Many major news outlets demand interviews and press conferences as if the International Space Exploration Group and Arroyo Aerospace are obligated to respond. Adrienne quickly learned to handle the "mainstream media" and other not-so-mainstream entities. Certain national newspapers that rarely run positive stories are constantly searching for bad news. Hack bureau chiefs and reporters looking to create a scandal with their bylines are sniffing around for stories.

Raoul Sr. and Marcella want to do something other than interviews. Adrienne and Paul became the spokespersons for the entire group of companies. Adrienne gave each of her associates responsibility for specific areas. Each handles inquiries for their areas Adrienne or Paul does weekly press conferences and updates regarding the Mars mission and other activities. Paul and Walter, his editor, do video press releases for the news networks.

A blog and website are set up for the Mars project. Pages on social media sites post updates and links to videos.

Adrienne's public relations plan is to keep a steady stream of press releases and video releases to keep attention focused on the work in space. It is hoped this stream of information satisfies the media and the public's interest for now. In addition, press members are invited to take trips into earth orbit on Galaxy One. Generally, this strategy works to keep positive stories in the media and overcome the shock over this leap in the ability of humanity to travel in space.

During Galaxy Two's sixteen-week round trip to Mars, the response to Galaxy One's orbital flights is overwhelming. Scheduled every two weeks, the flights carry press from around the world, government officials, foreign space agency officials, and others from the current commercial space industry. Arno and his staff believe it is necessary to require complete vaccination against the COVID virus as a prerequisite for boarding Galaxy One. When they sign up for a flight, all are informed that official proof of being vaccinated is required. Masks are worn on most flights.

Wealthy people offer to buy seats on a Galaxy One for a ride into orbit. On certain flights, seats can be purchased in a charity auction. Two seats for each flight are reserved for a lottery that anyone can enter. All proceeds from auctions and lottery flights are donated to a foundation offering scholarships to students wanting to study science. In addition to these flights, regular broadcasts from the Galaxy Two Mars mission manage to normalize the activities of ISEG.

Under tight security, work proceeds in several areas at Arroyo Aerospace. A new lander/rover vehicle is under construction. Raoul Sr. and Marcella negotiate a deal with a technological company in Japan for several different robotic devices specifically built for use on Mars. Josh locates a design project at a well-known university that offers out-of-the-box human habitats for use on Mars. He plans for these habitats to be fabricated to be tested on the surface during the second trip to Mars. These modular box habitats unfold out of the box and are set up quickly. They are constructed of the same materials used on spaceships to protect against radiation and the elements on Mars. Modular spaces can be joined to form larger areas. Habitats are planned to be heated and cooled with solar power and Radioisotope Power System (RPS) from Earth.

Equipment for manufacturing oxygen from CO_2 is found and slated to be tested for supplying oxygen to the habitats. Originally this equipment was intended to manufacture oxygen for rocket fuel. Now the entire effort will be to create oxygen for the habitats. Electricity generation from solar power and other sources is also planned.

The balance of the first trip to Mars is spent surveying sites on the surface for suitable places to build a base. Several more landings are made on the planet, including the South polar region, locations along the equator, and northern hemisphere sites. Possible underground frozen water deposits are found at both poles. Several places where an underground center might be built are located in the north. Likely inactive volcanoes are found and tested to see if there are any emissions. One volcano appears to be leaking minimal amounts of fumes composed of sulfur and other gases. The idea of tapping the core of Mars for heat and energy needs is being investigated. There are significant sandstorms near the Valles Marineris canyons. Captain Sun and the crew do not feel it is safe to land there. The next trip will have a lander capable of getting into the area.

Josh and the team at Arroyo Aerospace study reports from the Mars expedition. In anticipation of going on the second trip to Mars, Josh reviews the soil and rock sample tests sent back to earth from the first trip. Once the samples are back on earth, they will be analyzed. Early reports from the mission indicate several types of minerals have been discovered that can make mining them a commercial possibility and aid in creating habitable environments on the planet.

CHAPTER TWENTY-NINE

*"Rituals are flimsy substitutes for loyalty and trust.
Their prevalence invites chaos." -- Dao De Jing*

It took Sharon Arroyo until mid-2021 to find a new job. She began work as a media coordinator for a large evangelical megachurch near Chicago. She is enthusiastic about her work and happy to be out of Washington. While she looked for work, two of her friends, who also worked for the previous administration, got sick from COVID. One died. Many people she knew were still unemployed. A friend said, "It doesn't help that the previous administration tried to overthrow the duly elected government to keep themselves in power. It doesn't help that the previous president can't just shut up and take a nap. Instead, he continually whines that he won an election which he has not." Sharon, like most former staff, is wise enough to realize he lost and that anything after that is a scam, "a big lie," that he perpetuated beginning as early as 2015.

Sharon attended the January 6th rally and later was in the White House during the riot and insurrection. From then on, she knew she had to get away from this mess. Sharon thinks that the disgraced ex-president will soon be facing criminal charges. She tries to distance herself from the previous administration. Because of the experience she went through involved with the breakup of her first marriage, Sharon had a high aversion to any hint of scandal. She learned it did not matter if you were involved in the wrongdoing. She was associated with the scandal, and it stained all nearby. She enjoyed being the contact person for the administration and felt she had good people skills. She started looking for work in public relations. She could work with Paul doing public relations for the film or theme park. But It appeared he already had an entire staff. She is disappointed about not being hired by her brother Paul.

When Sharon sees the news that Galaxy Two has been launched by the International Space Exploration Group and Arroyo Aerospace in Florida, she cannot understand why she knows nothing about it. At first, she thinks it is a huge publicity stunt by Paul. She changes her mind as the news continues to break with videos about the flight to Mars and Galaxy One taking people into earth orbit. Sharon calls her mother, questioning "why she has not been part of this effort. Why has she not even known about it?"

"Sharon, I'm sorry, your affiliation with the previous administration put you and us in a compromising situation," Marcella said.

"We had to keep the entire project confidential. You appeared to be a strong supporter of that administration, working for them and traveling in those circles. Any hint of our plans would have been difficult for us before we were ready."

At first, Sharon is hurt. Thinking about it, she concludes that her mother is correct. Reluctantly she admits, "I guess you're right. I overlooked many things. My goal was to get conservative judges on the supreme court. I was distracted from what was going on in that administration."

"I'm glad you understand. Where are you working?" Marcella asked.

I'm at a mega-church near Chicago, working as a congregation associate and a media coordinator. It's good, lots of enthusiastic people."

"Let me check and see if I can get you on one of the flights into orbit if that interests you."

"Really? Sure, that would be great. I was hoping to visit around Thanksgiving."

"Good, you're invited for Thanksgiving dinner," Marcella said. "Family who is not on the Mars trip and friends will be here. We are also planning a big family and company dinner in December when everyone returns from Mars. You are welcome to attend that as well."

A few weeks after her conversation with her mother, a woman shows up at Sharon's office at the church. Flashing her ID, she introduces herself as Simone Greely from Washington. Following the September launch of

Galaxy Two, the NSA, received permission to listen to the Arroyo families' phones and conversations. They contact Simone at the CIA because she has been investigating the odd communication signals from that area for over a year. NSA could not get anything useful from the personal phones of the Arroyo family or anyone working there. There were only routine family calls. Business phone calls were mostly incoming calls from salespeople and job seekers. NSA's procedure is to gather as much information as possible and then see if there are any patterns or clues they can exploit. As a courtesy, they share some transcribed personal calls with Simone. Sharon and Marcella said nothing revealing during the call except that Sharon felt hurt that she had not been included and knew nothing about the development of the spaceships.

Sharon isn't sure why a government agent is visiting her. She wonders if it has something to do with her time at the White House.

"How do you like your new job?" Simone asks.

"It's a lot different than my previous job, that's for sure," Sharon replies.

"You did outreach to evangelical groups?"

"Yes, I established liaisons with many groups. My job is to let them know that the administration and president support them. It turns out that we mostly want the congregations supporting the president."

"Mainly, it's about the Supreme Court justices?"

"Yes, that's it. I didn't get involved in anything else. I quit after January 6th."

"Did you contact foreign representatives at the White House?"

"Not really. I reported to the Chief of Staff or someone in his office. My work is with U.S. evangelical groups."

"When you quit, did you go to work with your family?"

Sharon realizes that this is where the conversation has been going all along.

"No. I did want to work with my brother Paul's film studio on a new film he was putting together, but he had already hired people to do publicity and marketing. I approached Paul while I was still working for the administration with some ideas I had about the Space Force."

"Turns out, the movie is not fiction."

"I had no idea. I was astonished and shocked when I saw the news on television."

"I guess you wish you could have been involved," Simone suggests.

"With my job at the White House, I could not be involved. And I'm not really into all that science fiction stuff and traveling to the moon, you know. I'm into heaven, earth, and God. Living life as Jesus wants us to do. I don't even know for sure if we are supposed to go into space. There's a lot to do right here on Earth. I can't find anything in the Bible about traveling to other planets. It's all about what you do in this life here on this planet," Sharon said. After a few moments of silence, Sharon asked, "I'm not sure why you're here. What is it you want?"

"Well, you appear to be the only member of the Arroyo family who is not involved in the family business, so do you have some reason for that? Maybe it was against your religious beliefs?" Simone asked.

Sharon listened to Simone and thought about their conversation. "It is obvious that she is here to get information about the family, the business, and the space program," she thinks.

"Look, I took a different path. My family is good people. They raised all of us to find our vocation. I chose the path I'm on. I know Paul is famous for making films and has done well. My parents are scientists and engineers. They have worked with NASA and the aeronautics industry for a long time. That's about all I can tell you. Unless there's something else, I need to get back to work."

"I understand; thank you for your time. If you ever wish to get in touch," Simone said, here's my card. "Enjoy your Thanksgiving holiday."

Simone heads to O'Hare Airport. She has plans to meet George in Orlando. She also wants to talk with Arno, who she recently learned works for Arroyo Aerospace and ISEG.

Considering Simone's visit and the Thanksgiving comment, Sharon wants to alert her mother that she thinks someone may have been listening to their recent conversation. But how to do it without using the phone is the question. She decides to text Tamara on Signal App. In D.C., people use Signal to keep conversations private and off the record. Signal encrypts messages end to end. Sharon got Tamara to sign up for the App. so they could speak privately.

Sharon sends a text message to Tamara, "Hi, talked to Mom. I think someone was listening. A woman, Simone Greely, visited me, asking questions. She said she works for the government. Looking forward to seeing you soon."

Thanks to Carlos's dark web system, Tamara receives the message on her iPhone Signal App. even though she is on the Mars expedition. "Looking forward to it as well. Thanks," she replies.

Tamara checks in with Marcella and learns about the conversation. Tamara got in touch with Arno immediately.

"My sister Sharon thinks someone was listening to her conversation with our mother. Marcella said that Sharon called upset about not knowing about the launch. Mother told her it was top secret at that time and her job with the previous administration compromised her. She invited Sharon to Thanksgiving dinner."

"How did Sharon contact you?" Arno asks.

"She sent me a text on my mobile phone using Signal. Just a few words. She also said, 'someone named Simone visited her,' Tamara mentions.

"Could that be the same Simone that worked with you?"

"I suspect it is. I don't know if NSA or someone else can intercept and unscramble 'Signal.' Maybe they aren't listening to your phone, just your mother's. Signal has end-to-end encryption. It hides phone numbers," Arno said.

"Where is your sister located?"

"She's working for a Mega Church in the Chicago suburbs," Tamara replies.

Arno said, "I'll talk to Marcella, and we'll check her phone for any hacks. We will check all our phones for hacks and see if we can scramble calls on them. Maybe Carlos has some ideas. I will remind everyone not to discuss anything personally revealing, talk about the company or business on mobile phones, and avoid social media. It's a pity we have to live like this."

Sharon's duties at the mega-church include visits with the groups that meet at various times during the week. Services are held on Wednesday, Saturday, and Sunday. Many groups meet after services on certain days. The church sponsors men's groups, women's groups, and youth groups. Groups meet around subjects like abortion, vaccination, bible studies, and religious issues. Sharon makes her rounds of meetings on Sunday afternoon after a sermon by one of the ministers emphasizing following Jesus here on earth. She speculates that the subject is not coincidental with all the attention travel in space is getting.

First, she visits a small anti-vaccine group focusing on the COVID-19 vaccine. About fifty-six percent of the population in the U.S. have taken the vaccine by this time. Many are getting third-shot boosters. Ninety-nine percent of people who receive both doses have no adverse reactions. They become ninety-five percent immune to the virus. The current variants of the virus hit mainly the unvaccinated. Sharon got both shots as soon as she was able.

Before the vaccines became available, services at the church went virtual. This mega church already had a network for broadcasting services, so it wasn't difficult to expand that to cover people during the lockdown in Illinois. When services ultimately resumed, attendees are asked to wear masks. People who got vaccinated can choose whether to wear a mask. The unvaccinated are asked to continue wearing a mask to services. The anti-vaxxer individuals object to this request but wear their masks rather than get a COVID shot. Many of these people have friends or relatives who have contracted the virus, gotten sick, and died. Some decide they will get vaccinated, especially if they have elderly family members.

There is an abundance of conspiracy theories and disinformation about the vaccine. Sharon wishes there was some way to explain that science is not the enemy of Christianity. Vaccines save millions of Christian lives. One new conspiracy theory is that this virus came from outer space, and aliens manufacture the vaccine to control humans. There is speculation that the ISEG is connected with the aliens. There are also reports on social media that the astronauts have gotten COVID shots and other vaccinations. "What were they afraid of, asks one woman shaking her finger. Sharon is a neutral observer, so she cannot offer the simple answer that they took precautions to avoid getting infected."

Individuals in these groups believe positive news about the vaccine is fake. The negative information is accurate. Part of the conspiracy is to get everyone vaccinated and tagged with a secret microchip. How a microchip can be incorporated into the vaccine has yet to be determined. That this is 'magical thinking' does not occur to them. Many are predisposed to this type of thought. This group seems to think that flying into space and to other planets can bring back diseases.

Sharon acknowledges conversations by nodding her head occasionally and making notes on her iPad.

A middle-aged man with a bible in his hand tries to make the case that it is his Christian duty to protest vaccines he believes can kill people, even if he does not have any scientific or empirical evidence. A woman agrees with him. She blames autism on vaccines when there is no proof of this claim. There is evidence disputing this notion.

Sharon finds it perplexing why these people ignore how many lives vaccines save. Do they lack critical judgment ability? Many probably have gotten shots for smallpox, polio, measles, pneumonia, and other diseases growing up. Some group members resent that their children must get vaccine shots to go to school. Others are against children wearing masks at school. Ignored is that every year millions of people are kept from getting sick or dying by getting a flu shot. No one wants to acknowledge that ninety-nine percent of new infections of the COVID Virus are unvaccinated people.

A woman in her late thirties emphatically states, "it is all fake news perpetrated by anti-Christian groups." Her favorite propaganda news cable show has confirmed it. Everything infringes on their freedom, even if it means spreading disease. "Respect my choice" is a catchphrase. There is no acknowledgment that their choice can kill others. They base their beliefs on information from right-wing cable news and misinformation they find on social media or online sites.

Making the rounds of other groups checking for news of any kind, she finds the Bible study group obsessed with conspiracy theories about plots to destroy Christianity. Someone is always trying to do away with Christmas. Saying "Happy Holidays" is a plot to diminish Christianity. The new idea is that going to space secretly tells people that heaven doesn't exist. They try to find quotes in the Bible to support their views.

Sharon listens to each group and asks if they need anything for their meetings. She tries to learn their schedule for future events and conferences to publish them in the newsletter or church blog.

Sharon's faith is still strong. Attending these meetings makes her think about why only a few groups are interested in formal Bible study or learning more about religion or Christian philosophy. These are topics in which she can participate. Evangelism was once about spreading the gospel, not closing ranks against imagined enemies.

Many people are in groups to complain about issues not related to religion. Today there is what Sharon calls "weaponized Christianity." A new direction is looking for others to blame and shame. Sharon thinks, whatever happened to simple concepts like "love thy neighbor" and "do unto others as you would have them do unto you? "Are religions supposed to be involved in politics," she asks herself. "Maybe attendance is not as high as it might be because people go to church looking for spiritual support, not political indoctrination."

Sharon is looking forward to Thanksgiving with her family in Florida.

·······································

CHAPTER THIRTY

Return from Mars.

Galaxy Two's return from Mars is international news. The world has been watching the entire trip from the initial launch to the final orbit and return to Florida. The Gateway to the Galaxy press area is packed. In anticipation of a large turnout and for security reasons, Adrienne requests that all press register in advance for the event. All event attendees are asked to wear a mask to help prevent a "spreader event." Galaxy Two's return from Mars is broadcast internationally. The crew and specific team members give virtual interviews from the ship because of the latest virus outbreak. The crew and team are scheduled for medical exams before leaving the facility. It is determined that the team is healthy.

The celebration dinner about the group's achievements is a chance for the Arroyo extended family, associates, staff, Mars team, and friends to come together socially. The veranda and lawn behind the ranch are the perfect locations. Everyone involved in Arroyo Aerospace and the International Space Exploration Group agrees that there will be no shop talk. No discussing the future or flights. Reminiscing about the flight to Mars is the main topic.

Many of the guests have never been on a Galaxy One space flight. The new director of human resources has begun working on scheduling those who hadn't yet been on a Galaxy One flight. There are efforts to get all those working with the Arroyo Aerospace companies and members of their immediate families on Galaxy One flights as a form of orientation. Adrienne works with Arno to schedule team member-only flights.

Sharon Arroyo arrives in Orlando a few days before the dinner. She is staying at Tamara's condo. She and Tamara come to the ranch one evening to spend time with Marcella. Sharon feels estranged from her mother and the rest of the family. She decides to stay off the topic of religion for a few days and hang out with her family. Growing up, she has been close to Tamara and Raoul Jr., who are near her age. She looks up to "big brother" Paul. Thinking about things, she recognizes that after university, she became consumed with some missionary zeal that pushed her family away. She hopes she can get to know everyone again. Maybe get involved with the family and the future. She is on her best behavior, sensing some distance between her and other siblings. "That's okay. I was probably obnoxious for the last six years, especially while working for the last government administration," she admits to herself. She knows Marcella and Raoul Sr. tended to be apolitical while she was growing up and that they are put off by anything extremist or racist. She realizes she drank the "Kool-Aid" brewed by the former administration and went off the deep end on many issues. "No politics for a few days," she promises herself.

Josh, Adrienne, and the children look forward to the festivities at the Arroyo ranch. Attending the dinners, they always feel like part of the family. Marcella and Raoul Sr. adopt the Bennett family. The Arroyo siblings treat the Bennetts like family. Conrad and Julia, Raoul Sr.'s parents, are best friends with Josh and Adrienne. They have been to dinner at the beach condo. Josh spends time talking with Conrad on trips to the Costa Rican rancho. They play long games of Weiqi (Go). Josh enjoys listening to Conrad's spin on history, including when humans began recording it. It is almost as if Conrad or someone he knows has first-hand information about the past. It sounds like a personal account of events and experiences.

Paul and Stacy are there, along with Carlos and his friend Jason. Raoul Jr. and Halista, an astrophysicist he sponsored to work on the project, are there. Bill Arroyo, his wife Elisabeth, and his family are also enjoying the day at the ranch. Sam, his ex-wife, and their children always attend special dinners at the Arroyo ranch. Tamara and her new friend Tony, the astronaut she worked with on the Mars expedition, mingle with the other guests. Annie and Andrew Sun sit talking to Kevin Steiner and his wife, Samantha. Kevin and Samantha plan to travel to visit their son's family after the celebration. Arno and his friend Debbie are at home with the rest of the Arroyo family.

Arno and Debbie attended Thanksgiving dinner at the ranch a few weeks before this day. They enjoyed the dinner. The crew of Galaxy Two, on its way back from Mars, missed the Thanksgiving dinner. Margarita and Oliver prepared a special dinner for the Mars team, frozen on the ship until the day. Margarita and Oliver are responsible for catering the Galaxy Two return celebration dinner and being part of the affair.

December in Florida is usually warm compared to other parts of the country. Dining today is outdoors. The buffet dinner is set up in the dining room. Guests go inside to help themselves to baked ham, roast lamb, and turkey. There are vegetarian dishes, all the trimmings, and traditional side dishes. Outside they join the rest of the guests at long tables set up on the veranda.

Tamara introduces Sharon to Arno before dinner. She mentions that Arno is part of the company and is in charge of security. Also, he knows about Sharon's visitor. Arno and Sharon walk outside a short distance from the house and arriving guests.

"Here are your vaccine cards. You left them at the gate when you arrived with Tamara," Arno said. "How long are you in town for Sharon?

"Until Sunday, Then back to Chicago."

"You work in Chicago?"

"Well, outside Chicago near Schaumburg."

"Tamara told me a woman contacted you; I believe she said her name is Simone Greely?"

"Yes."

"We're not supposed to talk business today, but if you are around tomorrow, do you mind spending a few minutes relating your experience with her?"

"Not at all," Sharon said. "It was strange. I'm staying overnight, so sometime tomorrow morning will be good."

"Great," Arno said as they headed back toward the rest of the guests. "Good to meet you. You are the only member of the Arroyo family I hadn't met. You have a wonderful family. I'm from Chicago originally. How do you like the area?"

Arno and Sharon chat for a while until other guests sweep them up into conversations and festivities.

Arno came by the following day for breakfast. He joins Marcella, Tamara, and Sharon on the patio. Sharon relates her experience with Simone and gives Arno the business card she gave her. Arno snaps a picture with his phone and returns the card to Sharon. He explains that he knows Simone and that her visit feels out of context with her job at the CIA. He tells Sharon that if Simone is in touch again or if she makes any proposition, tell her you need to think about it. Then, via Signal, let Tamara know she's been in touch. Talk about the weather in Chicago and the water rising in Lake Michigan," he said. He gave Sharon a cell phone. "I will get in touch with you on this cell phone. Don't use it for anything else." Sharon agrees.

"I think she was trying to get information about the family from me," Sharon said.

"Yes, I believe you are correct. I'm starting to ask myself, why and for whom?" Arno said.

The celebration afternoon and evening gave all the Arroyo Aerospace family a chance to meet. Josh and Adrienne found it relaxing to socialize, enjoy dinner, and get to know everyone better. Life has been hectic for the last two years. Josh got a chance after dinner to duck out with Paul, Stacy, and Arno to see Paul's collection of cars. They drove over in the restored Land Rover.

Josh said, "Adrienne told me you did some modifications on this car, along with an electric drive. Can it fly?"

Laughing, Paul said, "No, we didn't go that far. It may happen one day." They walk around the hangar housing Paul's car collection. "If we build a city on Mars, I might be able to take a few of these cars. They all have electric motors now," Paul said jokingly.

"I can see you tooling around Mars in an electric Corvette," Josh said.

"With a few modifications," Arno added.

"Inside a big, terraformed Martian air bubble. Unfortunately, I don't think there will be room for private transportation in Mars settlements for a long time. Outside the settlements, travel across the dusty surface between colonies, who knows?"

"Highways or trains inside tubes, sealed from the elements, might be the future unless they can bore tunnels underground," Josh said.

"Sounds like a job for that electric car guy," Paul said. "He has that boring company and wants to go to Mars. Is this a coincidence?"

At the ranch, Adrienne sits with Julia, Marcella, Tamara, Debbie, and Sharon, enjoying a glass of wine after dinner.

"We're scheduled to take some people up in Galaxy One Friday afternoon," Marcella said. "Would you like to go, Sharon?"

"That sounds awesome. Do I need a space suit?"

"Nope," said Tamara, "come as you are."

"Are you going up too?" Sharon asks Tamara.

"Not tomorrow. Adrienne is going, and she will take good care of you," Tamara replied.

"I've been a tour guide on most of these trips. Tomorrow, we have a special guest, Ron Ramurt. He owns a chemical rocket company. He's very famous. You will be in special company."

"I'm not sure I know who that is?"

"No problem, I'll introduce you. Marcella, Raoul Sr., Josh, and Sam will be aboard. As well as Annie's husband, Andrew Sun as the pilot, Raoul Jr., copilot, and two of our new crew members in the command center."

"Should be interesting," Tamara said, smiling and rolling her eyes. "We have become competitors in the space exploration business."

"Let's not talk business today," Marcella said.

"I'll let you know the time. When Ramurt arrives, we'll pick him up. He's flying in at two p.m."

"On a rocket," Sharon said, laughing.

Everyone laughed at Sharon's joke. "Private jet, I believe," Tamara said.

"Around here, nothing would surprise me," Sharon replies.

George and Simone drove to Cocoa Beach the same week the celebration dinner was held. He thinks spending the holiday break over Christmas and New Year at the beach will be relaxing. The weather is good. Their rented condo faces the beach. Simone subtly suggested they might try to get together with Josh and Adrienne if George wants. He tries calling Josh and leaves a message for him on voice mail. "Simone and I are at the beach; let me know if we can get together for a run and meet for lunch?" After Arno told him about Simone contacting Sharon Arroyo, Josh got George's message.

"It's up to you who you socialize with," Arno said. "It is likely that if you go to lunch with them, she will try to get information about the company. Just stick to public knowledge.

"I might go for a run with George and skip lunch. I'll talk to Adrienne. We'll see."

"After the weekend, do you mind if I have your condo checked for bugs?" Arno asked.

"We have an exterminator that comes once per month, part of the condo dues. Just kidding, I know what you mean. Sure, that's a good idea. We do try to avoid talking about anything confidential at home. A few whispered conversations on the balcony a while ago."

"It can't hurt to do a sweep. Since our security is so tight, certain parties may be snooping around for some access. If you meet, listen, and try to remember the conversation."

"No problem, I'm good at listening," Josh replied.

Josh returned George's call, and they arranged to meet on the beach behind Ron Jon's Surf Shop on Saturday morning while the tide is out and there is packed sand to run on. It is a sunny morning, with a temperature of seventy degrees.

"Hey, good to see you, man," George said, greeting Josh.

"Same here."

"We haven't been out for a run for a while. You are mostly living over here now."

"Yeah, closer to work. How about if we head north to the Jetty."

"Sure, the tide is out. It's still early, not too hot yet, and not too many people."

After crossing the low sand dunes, they started an easy jog north close to the water.

"How's Adrienne? I saw her once or twice in Baldwin.

"She's fine. Busy at work as usual."

"I saw Adrienne on TV when they launched that spaceship and again when it returned. She's the press liaison for the International Space Exploration Group, right?"

"Yes, that's her big account."

"She came across as very professional. The whole thing blew my mind when that huge ship quietly lifted and then went into orbit," George said. "Have you ever been up in one of those ships?"

"Yes, I have. It's an amazing experience. You see the planet and realize how small it is compared to the solar system and the universe. So many groups and countries are all arguing over turf and culture. None of it makes any sense from up there."

"You're working with them now?"

"Yes, it keeps me busy. How are you doing? How's life treating you these days?" Josh asked, purposely changing the subject.

"Business is about the same as always. I've been dating Simone for about two years now. She got transferred back to Washington shortly after you left UCF. It was rough commuting to DC during the worst of the pandemic. But we kept going. I thought about moving to the D.C. area. I'd have to start a new practice or get a position in a law firm there. It would be a big hassle to move."

"Once the vaccine came out, they dropped many travel restrictions, right?" Josh asks.

"Yes, but Florida is surging again because of all the new cases involving the unvaccinated, the delta, and omicron variants. You have whole counties up north in "The Bend," where only about twenty percent of the locals have gotten vaccinated. Now they are all getting the virus."

"Adrienne, the kids, and I all got vaccinated as soon as it was available, and we were eligible. We got the boosters recently."

"Yes, I did too. No side effects, sore arm, and a little tired for a couple of days."

"Florida has the ex-president's, far more sinister, 'mini me' governor, banning mandates, masks, tests, and not pushing the vaccine. He is putting lives in danger."

"It's been nuts since January 6th. I did not imagine an attempt by the Republican party to overthrow a completely legal presidential election and an elected president. But that's what happened. I watched the mob attack the capital on television. I thought maybe it was one of those apocalyptic movies. I checked the other channel. No such luck," George said.

"Scary stuff, the ex-president was watching it on TV, refusing to allow the National Guard to step in and stop it."

"Republicans are still working on stealing the next election from the voters. This is an ongoing project. There are a bunch of Republicans who support this criminal, too," said Josh. "Hopefully, the bipartisan congressional committee you mentioned investigating the coup attempt will get it done before the midterm elections. The whole thing was planned."

"I hope they pull all the criminal stuff together so this guy can't run again. I also hope the Democrats hold on to the house and senate in 2022. It will be a big help in slowing down this far-right wing slide," George said, checking his sports watch and finding his heart rate was up.

"It doesn't look good for the Democrats; they have had trouble getting legislation past because of certain senators who claim to be Democrats holding things up. Meanwhile, the Republicans are doing dog whistle politics with fake issues like 'Critical Race Theory."

"There are no public secondary schools in the country where critical race theory is taught. I think it's a law school course. The Republicans are again exploiting fear of the 'other,' George said.

The sun climbed higher, burning away the clouds that floated in the sky nearby as they jogged up the beach. The sunlight shimmers on the gentle waves creating silver highlights on the water. Josh and George pass morning sunbathers and swimmers in the ocean. Kids run into the sea while their parents usually take longer, splashing themselves with seawater before proceeding deeper. The tide moves the ocean closer as they wade deeper into the water. A few optimistic surfers wait in the ocean far from the beach for a large wave they might ride.

"Seems like you made the right choice getting out of that grant."

"If you remember, I didn't have a choice. The government canceled the grant."

"I understand. I mean, you and Tamara are finding support for your research.

"Yes. We've been working on some new ideas, keeping busy."

"One of these days, maybe you can get me a ride up to orbit?"

Josh nodded affirmatively, "Sure, I'll check on it. They are only making a couple of these trips a month. Seats are booked up for a year. There's a lottery, and they hold a couple of seats open for charity or other purposes."

George sighed, "These rocket companies will charge $250,000 to $450,000 for a ride into space. There's even a balloon company with a floating lounge that goes up 19 miles above the earth for $150,000 per person. That's not even into the upper atmosphere."

"They all seem to forget that chemical rockets have been known to blow up!"

"With no rockets, how do these Space Exploration Group ships fly?"

"That's a good question, George. If I understood how it all works, and I do not, and I told you, I'd have to kill you. Seriously, it's a proprietary propulsion system, top secret. There are only a couple of people who understand it."

George laughed, "okay, forget I asked."

Men and women fishing lined the wooden walkway facing the jetty channel. Josh and George approach the rocks between the beach and the jetty walkway. They can see rockets across the channel on their pads at Cape Canaveral. A nuclear submarine with a crew on deck is passing into the channel from the ocean. Cruise ships also use this passage to come and go from Port Canaveral. Josh and George climb onto the rocks to better view the submarine. Sailors are on the deck, and a flag is flying from the conning tower. A few minutes later, Josh and George climb down from the rocks and head south back down the beach toward where they started.

"I looked up Arroyo Technologies, thinking it may be a good investment. I found out they are a private corporation."

"Yes, very private. The International Space Exploration Group is also a private corporation. I doubt that either company will go public very soon."

"The stock of rocket companies like Space X and Ramurt Rocket has taken a hit. They don't seem to be slowed up. Still building larger rockets," George said.

"We'll see what happens in the future. There is room for all kinds of enterprise in this area," Josh said.

Thirty minutes later, Josh and George finish their six-kilometer jog and agree that Josh will check with Adrienne about a possible lunch date with George and Simone on Sunday. Sunday morning, Josh sends a text to George saying, "they cannot make lunch on Sunday, but that they were looking forward to another time." The fact is that they were swamped preparing for the next Mars launch. Josh does not want to subject Adrienne and himself to any form of faux conversation with Simone, who he assumes will be fishing for any information she can obtain. Josh is skeptical about some of George's questions while they jog.

Flying on his corporate jet, Ronald Ramurt and his assistant Floyd arrive at Arroyo Aerospace at 2 p.m. Adrienne and Arno meet them. A driver takes them directly to Galaxy One, waiting in front of its hangar. Before they arrived, Ramurt and his assistant were informed that no mobile phones were allowed on the flights. They agree and check their phones with Arno before boarding Galaxy One.

Adrienne introduces them to Raoul Sr. and Marcella, who meet them as they board the ship. They are also introduced to Josh, Sam, and Sharon. Sharon is already in her passenger seat. When the guests are seated, Captain Sun, Raoul Jr., and Carlos come out from the command center and introduce themselves. Sam joins the flight crew when they return forward. Adrienne gives her usual talk about how the flight will go.

Ramurt said, "I've seen some photos and video of Galaxy Two's trip to Mars. This ship is a space yacht compared to the larger Galaxy Two,"

Adrienne replies. "It is comfortable. However, this 'yacht' has been to the moon and back."

"Are you planning on going to Mars again soon?" Ramurt asks.

"Yes, we are working on plans for the next trip," Raoul Sr., seated next to Ramurt on one side, answers.

Adrienne leaves them and takes a seat next to Sharon. Captain Sun announces that they will launch in a minute. He directs everyone's attention to the monitors in the passenger area for a view of the launch.

Sharon whispers to Adrienne, "He sounds like an airline captain. I thought he was announcing that we could watch an emergency demonstration. "

Adrienne smiles, "Yes, he's got that mature airline captain voice that he unconsciously slips into on lift-off. Sometimes I believe he does it for fun."

Galaxy One quietly floats off the runway in front of the hangar and rapidly rises to high altitude. At fifty thousand feet, they are out over the Atlantic Ocean. Looking west toward the coast, they can see Cape Canaveral.

"That's one of our rockets down there," Ramurt said.

"It's great that you can land the boosters and reuse them," Raoul Sr. said.

The ship moves up to orbit at two-hundred-sixty miles above the planet's surface. Galaxy one is orbiting at 20,000 MPH.

"No g-force," Ramurt said in genuine amazement.

Captain Sun announces, "We will do two earth orbits before we go back down to the surface. The fasten your seat belt sign is off. You are welcome to get up and move around the ship."

Adrienne explains, "you will not float. We have artificial gravity on the ship. It is not quite as strong as on earth gravity."

Sharon checks to see if there is a seat belt light. There is not.

Adrienne got up and went to where Ramurt and the others were seated. "Would you like a tour of the ship? You can look out the windows. We will be passing over China soon. Also, on level two, there are refreshments and restrooms. Be careful on the circular steps going down to level two."

Ramurt is not accustomed to being overwhelmed by technology, which he lives with all the time. He is impressed by innovation. "This ship and propulsion system our extraordinary," he said. "Really sweet. I've got to admit this is beyond anything imaginable with current technology. It is revolutionary. My compliments."

"Thank you," Raoul Sr. and Marcella reply. Josh leads the way on the tour of the ship. Sharon and Adrienne follow along too.

On the second level, they can see a view of the earth as they circle the globe.

"Initially, I was curious as to why you invited me on this trip. After all, I thought, we are competitors. I believe we are not competitors; you are in a different league. Still, I'm curious," Ramurt said.

Marcella said, "we don't want to be competitors. There is room for different technologies. We are interested in cooperation and support."

Josh added, "the International Space Exploration Group is a new enterprise. We are interested, as I believe you are, in establishing a Mars colony. Perhaps there are ways we can work together toward that goal."

"Are you talking about a partnership?" Ramurt asked.

"Not a formal partnership, more of a cooperative enterprise. Maybe even with others with the same goals," Josh said.

"I know you are already working closely with NASA. You picked up one of our contracts. We are behind schedule on our heavy lift vehicle," Ramurt said. There are other companies building rockets. They seem more about tourism than an exploration of the solar system."

Ramurt walks over to the window. Looking down, he said, "there's China. They are your biggest competitors. I hope you have strong security because they have an army of hackers who love to find technological secrets and make them their own."

"So, we hear," Raoul Sr. said. "Very competitive. We do our best to keep security very tight."

"I have said I want to go to Mars in my lifetime. I believed I might be the first. All that matters to me is getting there. We have been working on several concepts and strategies for establishing a base and, ultimately, a colony on Mars. Maybe by working together, we can build a city," Ramurt said. "Let's agree to meet soon and look at ways we might cooperate. I have some technology that I think will be excellent for building Mars habitation and mining operations."

Marcella said, "great, we are ready to meet again when you are ready. We have an amazing opportunity to establish a colony. Perhaps the beginning of an international city on another planet."

Ramurt nodded, "International city, that's an interesting concept, perhaps even an interplanetary city, lots to think about."

After two orbits of Earth, Galaxy One enters the atmosphere and floats back toward the Arroyo Aerospace landing strip. Ramurt joins Raoul Sr.,

Marcella, Josh, Adrienne, Sam, Sharon, Paul, Julia, and Conrad for dinner at the Ranch. They talk about Mars and exploring the solar system in general terms. It was exciting to consider the possibility of space exploration and what it could mean for human evolution. Ramurt talks about the special documentary series they have just finished about their crew that went up into near space. He talks about his joy in being on that trip. He said today had been fantastic but that "the rocket trip was an adrenaline-producing high he will never forget."

Sharon listens to the conversation. She is still overwhelmed by the trip into space and the travel around the earth. Seeing the entire planet from high up inspired her. She wonders if this is how God sees the Earth. Where is God out there in Space? Beyond the Solar System, looking at the entire universe from some other place? Suddenly she knows she wants to go into space. Maybe to Mars someday. Visit and experience life beyond anything she imagines up to this point. She makes it her goal to prepare and find a way to be part of the early groups of people going into space.

After dinner, Ramurt flew back to his home base. He tweets that he has just come back from earth orbit. Some of his followers think he is joking or high until he tweets again that he has been on "The International Space Exploration Group's Galaxy One Space Yacht."

Raoul Sr., Marcella, Josh, Adrienne, Sam, and Paul meet in the secure corporate office.

"How does everyone feel about the meeting with Ramurt?" Marcella asks.

After a few moments, Josh said, "based on what I've read and researched, he's difficult to predict. I do know he is a practical entrepreneur. If he thinks he can benefit, he will act. He knows we have technology that is light-years ahead of his rockets. He has resources that we can use. So, there is room for negotiation and cooperation that will benefit all. Give him some time. We proceed. Perhaps we invite another rocket man here for an earth orbit trip?"

"I agree. We wait and let him make the next call. He does have resources and has put some research into building a Mars colony. Cooperation will save us some time. He benefits by getting a base on Mars sooner than he plans," Sam said.

Josh said, "Ramurt is entrepreneurial. I think he sees an opportunity. I tried to listen to the conversation. He calls Galaxy One a 'yacht.' He mentioned that his rivals are into tourism more than exploration. An idea popped into my mind. He, his rivals, or others might be interested in building a space hotel resort in orbit, about 280 miles above the earth. We will help build it and incorporate some of our technology. They can bring visitors there with their rockets."

"I like the idea. It's been in some classic films. A hotel in space will capture the imagination of the world," Paul added.

"It might not be too difficult if they use rockets to lift pre-assembled modules that can be assembled in space. We can transport astronauts, other equipment, and parts," Sam said. "We will need to increase production to make it happen. Some of the work can be farmed out to the rocket guys."

Adrienne said, "Maybe two or three other rocket builders with deep pockets will be up for a joint venture. While it's being built, we can proceed with the Mars colony. In the future, it can be a departure terminal for Mars."

"Hopefully, they will all want to cooperate in the enterprise. They're all public corporations. A venture with the International Space Exploration Group involved will boost the stock price of any corporation, which is another reason Ramurt will probably want to cooperate with us on the Mars venture. The space hotel might be a publicly funded joint venture," Marcella said. "Before we talk to the other rocket guys, let's give Ramurt a few days to get back to us. We'll see if he's interested in the hotel venture or only Mars before we talk to the others."

"I bet they will jump at the opportunity once it is presented as a viable enterprise and investment. One of the rocket guys has made his fortune in online retail and another in air travel. This will be a dream come true," Paul said. "I want to invest in it myself!"

"We need to understand that these companies compete with each other. They are now fighting over contracts for NASA's Human Landing System to put astronauts on the moon. I'm unsure what they will do when they get to the moon. NASA will figure that out. We can land astronauts on the moon tomorrow. Get them there and back. Our International Space Exploration Group is now the rocket companies' biggest competitor. We can put them out of business. If we get these companies to put their focus on a joint venture, that will be good. Getting them to work together is another story," Josh said.

Raoul Sr. said, "this is all possible. These positive directions will reinforce our position as a private corporate entity. Working with established corporations and individuals makes it more difficult for anyone to single us out. Remember, our mission proceeds as planned, whatever else comes along. Entering 'joint ventures' is a complicated process. We are already cooperating with NASA, which requires keeping our independence balanced with the ongoing partnership. There will need to be contractual relationships built. We will be entering into commercial ventures. We are a private company with a low profile and small organization. If these ventures materialize, we'll need to establish offices away from here to maintain separation and security. We will be entering the mainstream corporate world."

"We are still on course and will launch the second Mars Mission on schedule in the spring of 2022. If any of this business materializes, we will handle it as we go along," Sam said. "If we wanted to be in the hotel business, we could build a space hotel ourselves. I believe it is a much better proposition to be an investor. We are in the space exploration business."

"What if we build an Earth Terminal Station with space hotels and other resources? A consortium owns the station and leases space to others wanting to build hotels. I think there will be bases on the moon eventually so that this facility can be the departure terminal for ships leaving there for the moon. There might be another terminal station in orbit around the moon. Travelers can be shuttled to the surface from the moon's terminal station.," Josh said.

"Building a facility on the moon is slightly less difficult than on Mars. It is still not a human-friendly place. No atmosphere at all. Habitats need to be radiation-proof. On the plus side, there are no windstorms on the moon. If secure habitats can be built, people might want to go there for a vacation," Raoul Jr. speculates.

"Lunar vacation Spa, enjoy an unparalleled view of the planet Earth. Enjoy the low gravity for hikes on the moon's surface," Paul announces. "I'm sure it will happen one of these days."

"Good meeting," Marcella said. If no one has more to say right now, we have lots to work on and think about. Thank you, everyone. I will put together some notes and circulate them. A few more months, and we'll be headed to Mars again."

CHAPTER THIRTY-ONE

*"Who could quietly stand by and let muddy water sit and cleanse itself?
Who could quietly wait to let turmoil wear itself out to bring back life?"*

Before today's executive meeting, Arno did a unique security check of the conference room to ensure conversations would not be picked up from anywhere, including space. The meeting is being held to determine the mission of the second expedition to Mars scheduled for spring 2022. Everyone attending is fully vaccinated, so no masks are required. The room is sanitized and has a high-end anti-virus air purification and scrubbing system. The executive team, including some of the newer members like Captain Sun, Kevin Steiner, Adrienne, Annie, and Arno, were in attendance. The family is growing.

Marcella began, "It is great to see everyone here. Looking back to the beginning of this journey, we've come a long way quickly. I believe we are at a major juncture in our efforts. Now that we've gone public, security is a major concern. Arno Cameron is doing a wonderful job keeping up with things in that area."

"Thank you, Marcella, Arno said. "As of December 1st, we have hired twenty-eight new employees in addition to the sixteen security personnel hired previously to secure the property. The new employees are working in technical and construction areas. Everyone has undergone deep security screenings. This includes a hybrid lie detector screening that relies on additional video and audio analysis. We rejected twelve individuals because they failed the test, or their backgrounds were suspect in some way. Two of these people had ties to foreign governments. Everyone hired has shown documentation that they are vaccinated against the COVID-19 virus. This means that all at Arroyo Aerospace and ISEG have been vaccinated. Working with Carlos, we found that the number of attacks on our public websites has gone ballistic. There's nothing confidential on these sites. All they might be able to do is crash the public site. The Russians have been nonstop trying to hack our systems. We have stopped them, and thanks to the application Carlos and Raoul Jr created, we retaliated in some measure."

Adrienne adds, "ISEG" also has a social media presence now on Facebook and Twitter. We have millions of followers. Our posts are updates on flights or missions. We get lots of questions, which we try to answer if possible. I have two assistants that keep track of social media. This outreach program deals with public information. I believe it helps to mitigate the misinformation before the trolls take it viral."

"Carlos said, "Our secure in-house communication systems appear to have remained undiscovered. We have found no attempts to hack them so far. It's a matter of time, so we have much redundancy built into everything. All internal communication, including private links with the spaceships, continues to go through our system. We have secure communication links with NASA and our external command center. We send videos and other public information to these links, which we monitor. As far as the world knows, these are our communication links. Technical information is never shared publicly. Shipboard communication programs filter what goes out over the public frequencies. This is location information and broadcasts. Depending on the circumstances, video calls between crew and ground can go either way. There is a public ground control and a private ground control. What we're trying to protect is proprietary information regarding technology and activities. We have a new satellite dish here at Arroyo Aerospace that will help with communication in the future."

"The world knows we are traveling in space," Arno said. We've seen some ransom ware criminals try to go after Arroyo Aerospace. We just deleted the site and installed a new one. We mount retaliatory hacks on these criminals, like shutting down their sites and donating their cryptocurrency to charities. Recent information shows that our government agencies have monitored our communications for some time. "

"One of the immediate Arroyo family members, who is not working with the company, was contacted by a known CIA agent shortly after a phone call she made to Marcella. Nothing compromising was discussed. However, the tactic is to gather information to find patterns and vulnerabilities. We must be careful what we say or text on our public mobile phones. We are working on a proprietary application that will scramble mobile phone calls. We can use this for all our phones when we contact each other."

Josh is next to speak to the group. "We have established a working relationship with NASA. For example, the International Space Exploration Group contracted to bring the next supply shipment to the International Space Station using Galaxy One or Galaxy Three. We will also place a satellite in orbit for NASA. These are essentially barter arrangements. In return, NASA will give us additional technology for the next Mars flight. We have a pool of NASA-trained astronauts who have volunteered to go on our Mars flights. There is an ongoing, high level of cooperation with NASA, which gives us quite a bit of "shade." In effect, NASA is sanctioning the International Space Exploration Group. Currently, NASA is not happy with one rocket company because they are behind on their rocket that is supposed to lift large crews and cargo into space for NASA. A major aerospace company is also currently behind with its rocket program. This allows us to work on contracts with NASA to fulfill urgent needs. It is important to note that this also makes us a serious competitor of a few rocket companies."

"Speaking of our next Mars Mission," Raoul Sr. said. "We are preparing Galaxy Three to make the trip to Mars with Galaxy Two. Galaxy Three is ready to launch. Its primary function will be cargo. Galaxy Four is ready to fly. It is an upgraded version of Galaxy One. We are building a special Mars lander that is especially suited for Mars. We thought its name could be Galaxy Mars One. It can be transported to Mars on Galaxy Three. "

"Based on Galaxy Two's first trip to Mars, we have put together a plan to establish a base on Mars," Marcella said. "The plan for the next trip to Mars is to set up a base in the northern hemisphere in an area we determine is suitable. On the first mission, Tamara and the crew found a crevasse that appears to lead into the mountain, where there may be a large cavern or interior space we can explore. This may be an opportunity to build a shelter for the base on Mars. Inside the mountain, there should be less radiation and protection from sandstorms."

"Our ships will house the construction crew while the first shelters are built. We have 'out of the box' shelters that can go up quickly to accommodate people. Most of the construction work will be done by robots. We need to build hangar shelters for equipment and robots," Sam said. We have 3d printers that can be adapted to use local regolith and other resources to build."

Josh continues, "Much has been learned from our first explorations of Mars. We also have what NASA discovered from their previous landings on Mars. We believe we can build using natural elements found on Mars, like Basalt and Andesite. Both materials are abundant since there are so many extinct volcano sites. These resources can also be refined to create other materials. For example, we can get silicon dioxide from Andesite to make glass. We believe Mars has all the natural resources needed to build a base. Oxygen can be manufactured. The first expedition located several sources of water that could be tapped for the base. Solar arrays and wind turbines will be set up to generate electricity."

Tamara said, "There are plans to maintain the health and well-being of our Mars team. In addition to nutritional needs, we plan exercise regimes to keep bones and muscles strong, minimizing atrophy. Physical well-being is important for morale and psychological demands team members will encounter living in an environment like Mars so different than Earth."

Raoul Sr. said, "The second trip to Mars has an important mission. It would be great to leave a small contingent there continuing to work until the third flight to Mars. This all depends on the successful construction of habitats and other resources. Building a habitat inside the mountain itself will be a big step in housing humans on the planet since it will shield them from the elements. We also need to train astronauts how to use robots for building. It may take a third trip to finish habitation modules and establish a base with humans living there. We think we can accomplish establishing a base and initial colony in 2022. This will require two trips to Mars that year."

Marcella added, "We realize this is an ambitious goal. There are many reasons we need to establish this base. One reason is the political situation here in the U.S. and, to some extent, worldwide. We are revolutionizing space travel as we anticipated. There was no choice but to go public with our space program. Thanks in large part to the creative initiative by Adrienne, our public relations persona is currently positive. We know there are already calls to make our technology available to the military and other sources. Conrad will fill in some details."

"Recent history tells us that much of what is being experienced here in the U.S. and other countries worldwide is not new. For example, public reaction to vaccines in the past has been troubled. In 1900 people had to be coerced into getting the smallpox vaccine. Boston city government brought doctors door-to-door to give the vaccine. If you refused, you were fined $5.00 (equivalent to $75 today). The big difference between then and now is that certain politicians are encouraging anti-vaxxer groups and spreading misinformation. Then others don't want to wear masks for any number of reasons. Masks for stopping the spread of disease are not a new idea. They are an ancient custom. There have always been those who didn't like the idea, but during epidemics, almost everyone tried to help get it under control. Here in the U.S., from the very start of this pandemic, politicians, including the country's then-president, turned it into a political issue. In part because they believed the masks symbolized the out-of-control spread of the virus. It was a stain on their administration. They chose to ignore the virus, thereby causing suffering and death."

Conrad continues, "I point this out because it is one symptom of a troubled culture when a large part of the population will not come together to fight a common enemy. Instead, they allow themselves to be manipulated into focusing on 'big lies,' scapegoat minorities, lower caste others, and conspiracy theories about the government. There are many indications that this government can shift from a form of democracy, as we have here in the U.S., to an increasingly autocratic leadership style. Many troubling signs of violence emanate from far-right white supremacy factions. Even if the current party maintains primary control, the other party will try to overturn election results wherever possible, leading to unrest. The real reason the far-right says elections are fraudulent is that more minorities are voting. Cries of 'fraud' are dog whistles for that idea."

"I believe we must be prepared to resist the appropriation of our technology. Establishing a viable base on Mars gives us an edge. I should mention another thing that differs from past examples of this behavior. Of course, gossip and rumor were mongering amongst humans in the past. Never has there been this level of rumor and misinformation spread far and wide so easily and quickly. Social media and the control of cable and broadcast news by a few countries and corporations are at the root of the spread of fear, conspiracy, and disinformation. What goes unnoticed is that all media is conservative in some way. Conglomerates own the media. There are no 'liberal media.' A few media outlets broadcast or print fewer conservative views than others," Conrad said. "All news is subjective in some way. Sometimes if you drop the adjectives, you can discern some facts."

After a few moments, Josh responds, "Are you suggesting that we might need to move the manufacturing and technological efforts to Mars as soon as the end of 2022?"

Conrad said, "I believe we need to be prepared. If there is a change of power, there will be immediate pressure. We need to anticipate and plan how we will react. Even if the current government holds on and gets re-elected in 2024, with majorities in both houses, there will still be much pressure from sources like the military to obtain and use the propulsion technology for their purposes. If our government gets the technology, it will upset the balance of power in the world to the extent that it could start a war. Once the technology is in the U.S. government's control, it won't be long before foreign governments steal it. I must mention that I have sources that believe Russia is about to renew a war it started in 2014 when it invaded Crimea. It could happen this spring."

"Funding for white supremacy groups comes from wealthy individuals who fear losing power and their way of life. They fund groups like the Horizon group and the Federalist Society, which have tried to move the country toward a far-right autocracy for decades. This totalitarian government will be controlled by the upper caste of predominately rich people of European descent. I imagine they will believe it is their privilege to maintain space exploration.

"Nothing is stopping others with chemical rocket propulsion from going to the Moon or Mars and establishing a foothold there," Josh said. "What will it take to build an off-world facility where humans can survive?"

Sam said, "We need to get supplies off this planet. It can take up to four months to make a round trip to Mars. One thing that can be used is a base on the moon, where we can quickly move equipment and resources that will later be moved to Mars. Right now, no one can do what we do. Chemical rockets are expensive, dangerous, and difficult to handle. Their payloads are small compared to the energy it takes to lift them off the earth. The idea is to get what we need off the planet to continue to work and explore. Mars can be mined for the minerals we need. The asteroid belt is another source. We can build modules, fill them with supplies, then take them to the moon. The modules will also serve as habitats. The modules are basic spaceships with minimal propulsion. These modules can be flown into space or assembled there. Later we can string them together and fly them somewhere like Mars or a LaGrange point."

"It is better to be prepared for whatever may happen than to be caught off guard," Marcella said. "If things are peaceful on Earth, there is no problem sharing technology. All of humanity can benefit. If the government here in the United States becomes autocratic, it can use technology to weaponize itself. There will be war, perhaps civil war. It seems like the best thing for us to do at this point is to continue working with NASA and perhaps others. At the same time, we move ahead with a contingency plan of our own. We have three years to do as much as possible. This includes establishing an off-planet base. We can help others to move into space, but we maintain control of our technology. We resist any attempt by any government to weaponize the technology or to create vessels capable of conducting war."

"Our cooperation with NASA, and perhaps certain corporate players in space ventures, will hold off the wolves for a while. You can be sure that at this very moment, the military-industrial establishment in this country and worldwide are seeking ways to obtain this technology. If they were to get their hands on one of the spaceships, they would try to reverse engineer the propulsion system," Josh said.

"The propulsion system is virtually hack-proof, built to self-destruct if tampered with by anyone," Raoul Sr. said. No current physicists I'm aware of understand the principles of how gravity fields can be manipulated, let alone how to use it as a propulsion system. I'm not worried about that. However, it is worrying that a totalitarian government might step in and try to force us to participate in creating war machines. It is better to go full steam ahead with our plans while we can."

Tamara said, "Increasing production, building more ships, and establishing bases will take more money and staff. Where will the revenue come from? Where will we find staff we can trust?"

Marcella said, "We have been offered billions of dollars to help launch satellites and work with other companies interested in exploring space. Some wealthy friends are not part of the right-wing faction who want to invest in our exploration efforts. I don't think financing will be a problem. As far as staff, we need to recruit all kinds of people with many different specialties. They all need to be screened and cleared security-wise."

"With no advertising, hundreds of resumes are coming in each week. These are from all sorts of people, from scientists to construction workers, who want to go to Mars to work. We have been hiring technicians and workers to help build the ships," Arno said. "I suggest hiring a human resource person. We are reviewing all resumes and sorting them for possible future contact. There is a growing base of qualified people."

Josh said, "I spoke with NASA about helping us train 'astronauts' to work in space, on the moon or Mars. They said they would consider doing it. We did not talk about cost. Most of our cooperation with NASA has been barter and mutually rewarding. I believe the current administration at NASA has a go-ahead from the White House to work with ISEG. Working closely with NASA, as an independent contractor, gives us a friend in high places."

"This is a good thing," Marcella responds. "Conrad informs me that many people he and Julia know are interested in living on Mars. They are willing to make a one-way trip there to colonize and live. It doesn't have to be one-way. If someone can't deal with life once they get there, they should be able to leave. At the same time, going with us to Mars cannot be structured on a trial basis or a visit. Let's research this issue and find physically fit people who can begin the colony. Seniors can live on Mars like anyone else. However, Mars offers too many environmental challenges to become a retirement community. Conditions are severe. It will take some effort to screen psychologically equipped individuals who understand the harsh reality of what it will take to live there. Again, they will all need training, have skills and backgrounds that benefit the colony."

"I've heard some specialists saying that humans will not be able to live on Mars for more than a few years. The radiation from the sun and space is too high on a planet with little atmosphere," Josh said. " Also, there are physical problems for humans living in a low-gravity environment. I think we can take steps to protect people while they are on Mars. The Galaxy spaceships are highly resistant to radiation. We can do the same for habitats on Mars."

The meeting continued to discuss timetables and who would handle specific assignments. They looked at ideas for building habitats and colonies that Tamara had been researching. This was a big step for a small group of people.

Josh is enthusiastic. At the same time, he knows the task is a huge one. One big topic to discuss further is where to build the base on Mars or the Moon. No other humans had walked on Mars. U.S. Astronauts walked on the Moon. No one owns these celestial bodies. No one built a permanent facility in either place. Will a base be private property? Will it be a new country since ISEG is an independent entity not funded by a national government? ISEG decided they would welcome visitors to the settlement. They will require a passport and visa from Earth or a base on another planet. The settlement will be an international city. The United Nations Space Law division needs to consider the status of independent colonies on other planets. The UN needs to update its ideas about outer space.

Before the meeting ended, Conrad said, "I want to make sure we are all aware that the president of Russia is trying to reestablish the Russian or Soviet empire. He used the previous U.S. president to try to disrupt the NATO alliance. He has a cadre of Americans who spread misinformation and propaganda for him on television and in politics. He is intent on toppling America from power. Our new alliances cannot include Russian participation. He has gone on record stating that he wants regime change in Ukraine and maybe other previous soviet countries that are part of NATO. There could be war in Europe soon, according to what I'm seeing. What is happening has historically led to worldwide conflicts. However, now there are nuclear weapons that the Russian president has said he can use for a first strike. First strike or second strike, it is mutual destruction."

....

CHAPTER THIRTY-TWO

"Memories and knowledge passed down over generations."

Josh relaxes in his cabin aboard Galaxy Two on his way home from Mars. He is thinking about the experience of traveling to another planet and how he got to this point in his life. He has just finished his daily video chat with Adrienne and the children. The large video wall monitor still shows their faces. The conversation isn't long because of transmission realities between the planets. It reminds him that he misses his wife and family. They are doing well and anxious for him to be home. He will be back in earth orbit in three weeks. It is the Space Exploration Group's (ISEG) second trip to Mars, but it was his first. Looking back, he has many memories of the trip.

One of the things he confirms for himself after having been to the planet is that "the Mars environment is very different from that of Earth. More than for obvious reasons, like the lack of an atmosphere suitable for breathing. It is a lifeless desert. No biological or organic life can be found. Not even some mold where condensing atmosphere moisture collects on the surface. While they did find some caves, there were no little green men or women hiding in them. No remains of past civilizations or fossils. The terrain is hostile to any form of life, including humans. Still, we humans came to Mars intent on establishing a base and a settlement where we can live and explore the planet. What is motivating humans to go into space, especially to such a hostile environment," Josh wonders.

During the months-long trip to and from Mars, Josh and Conrad have several conversations about various topics. On the flight to Mars, they drink tea, sitting by a starlit window as the ship moves toward Mars' orbit. Conrad brought a Chinese tea set with him and several types of Chinese Teas to brew. They did not strictly adhere to a formal tea ritual, although both were familiar with it. Conrad also brought a Weiqi or GO board and stones. They spent time playing the game and drinking tea.

"How much time did you spend in China?" Conrad asks.

"I traveled a little. I lived at Shaolin Temple for a year to study Ch'an Buddhism and some Kung Fu. I didn't become an expert at Kung Fu; I learned the moves more for exercise and meditation. I learned to play Weiqi from a monk living in a small temple near Shaolin in the Songshang mountains," Josh said. "You have traveled quite a bit in China."

"Yes, many times. Nothing recently because of COVID. Julia and I lived in Beijing and traveled around China for a few years. I bought this tea set there; I'm told it is ancient."

Josh smells the freshly brewed red tea like a vintage wine. "Each tea has its aroma depending on the type and where it is grown."
"

"This is Da Hong Pao (Big Red Robe, 大红袍) from Fujian Province, a red tea grown in the Wuyi mountains," Conrad said. "One of my favorites. It has an interesting orchid smell and a sweet aftertaste. I also brought some green tea and some Pu-er (普洱茶) along for this trip."

Josh smells the tea again and tastes it. "Yes, it does, very good. Just the right temperature too." After a few moments, Josh looks out the window at night. "Difficult to imagine drinking Chinese tea on the way to Mars. The tea ritual goes to Mars. Who would have guessed?"

After another sip, Josh said, "Have you traveled to other places around the world?"

"Conrad nods, "Over the years, I've traveled many places. I've had a long life. Being out here beyond Earth has been a dream until now."

"You and Julia don't show your age. If you don't mind, how old are you?" Josh asks.

"As they say in Spain, 'suficientemente viejo," Conrad replies.

"Old enough," Josh said, smiling.

"Do you remember the story I told you about the Argonite people stranded on Earth after their journey from another solar system?" Conrad asks.

"I certainly do remember the story. I've thought of it many times," Josh answers.

"I spoke to Raoul Sr., and he concurs that I tell you something more about that story. You, Adrienne, and your children have become part of our family, so you should know more about our story. It may seem crazy that we believe the story is true. However, we do have evidence. The Arroyo family has a connection to those ancient star travelers. Julia and I are links to that line. We, human descendants, don't live forever or anything like that. We seem to have a longer life span than average humans."

"There is something else. As you know, all human cells have stored memory. We have access to generations of memory stored in our cells and DNA," Conrad said. "The Buddhists think of it as reincarnation. For us, it is more like a recall of certain memories from past generations. Naturally, we only remember our parent's memories from before we are born. Based on several individuals' separate memories, we think the original starship came from the huge constellation Argo Navis (the shape of the mythical ship of Jason and the Argonauts). It is now divided up into several areas, including Carina (keel and hull), Vela (the sails), and Puppis (poop deck). Recently astronomers have found earth-like planets in the Argo constellation ninety light years from Earth. Therefore, we came up with the name "Argonites.""

Josh closed his eyes for a moment, contemplating what Conrad divulged. As fantastical as it might seem, he somehow knew it might be true. Opening his eyes and looking at Conrad, he said, "I tend to believe you. When you originally told me the story, it sounded personal, almost like you have direct knowledge of the events."

"Memories and knowledge passed down over generations. Some information is lost when certain bloodlines end. Around the world, about five hundred spontaneously remember a portion of our histories. No one remembers the same body of knowledge. Although there are similar stories.

People have different vocations and experiences. For example, Raoul Sr. inherits an intuitive ability for engineering and advanced physics skills. Homo sapiens have assimilated the original race of humanoid Argonites. Even so, through conscious selection or the random luck of the gene pool, many of us found each other. Julia and I had more chances that our children would remember because we do. We have two other children besides Raoul Sr. One remembers, and one does not."

"Natural selection," how about Marcella?"

"We have some DNA, gene, and cell tests to find out if there is any trace of the Argonite line. Marcella has some trace genes, but she does not consciously remember anything. Sam, Paul, Tamara, and Raoul Jr. have access to memories mostly from Julia and I. Memories are not always conscious. They can become more vivid and recognizable with age. Skills seem natural and often innovative."

"Will the Mars colony be the new home for those who wish to move on from Earth?"

"There is some talk of this, or possibly Mars can be a terminal or jumping-off place. There is divergent thinking. Many individuals think there is no reason at this point to leave Earth. Others wish to find a way to leave Earth and find another habitable world. There is concern that Homo sapiens are destroying the planet and eventually becoming extinct. It's demoralizing to many of us that people are dying in a pandemic, not for lack of a cure. But because of ignorance and an apparent inability to maintain the idea of community and working together. Even though some anthropologists believe human survival evolved because of the ability to form groups," Conrad said as he poured each of them more tea.

"Earthlings have not outgrown their tendency to form groups and then decide that all other groups are a threat. To blame other groups for problems. This is scary to us. We remember earth's ongoing history with cycles that include genocide and war. There does not appear to be anything that will stop this tendency."

"I'm curious. Do you think Argonite genes or mentality has had any influence on human evolution?"

"Possibly in good and not-so-good ways. Inspired unconscious creative thinking might account for a few geniuses. Over time, others may knowingly decide to manipulate events for sinister purposes. There may be some mutations that have gone unnoticed. There were only a thousand Argonites, so they cannot hugely impact human evolution over the past twelve thousand years."

"The knowledge of how to build this propulsion system, is that something that Raoul Sr. remembered?"

"Not really. Did you ever get an idea, then develop it, start working on it, and it comes to life? That's how Raoul Sr. explains it. He had help from Marcella, making it all work. He says that they are both inspired."

"This is a lot to absorb. I don't feel at all threatened by what you are telling me. I feel a part of it. I share the same thoughts about life. I should have those tests. Maybe I have some of that DNA. Sometimes I feel different than my fellow human beings—not understanding how we can behave the way we do.".

"It wouldn't surprise me if you and Adrienne did,' Conrad said. "I have a good sense of spotting others with links. Homo sapiens absorbed many other humanoid species like the Neanderthals and Denisovans. Not all these other species are currently detectable in human DNA. You must know what you are looking for. We can do a test when we return if you like."

"Okay, I'll talk to Adrienne. I told her the story you first told me. She listened. There must be descendants of ancient Argonites in many places worldwide."

"Yes, there are—very few who know it. Over the years, I've made it part of my mission to find them, visit and keep in touch. China, Eastern, and Western Europe, the Middle East, Africa, Australia, and parts of South America. Twelve thousand years is a long time. Argonites kept moving, trying to avoid wars and plagues. We are checking to see who might want to move to Mars, even if it is a first step."

"Do you think a habitable and comfortable environment on Mars can be built for a large settlement?"

"It is possible. Not easy because the Martian environment is hostile to life. It was the same twelve thousand years ago. The ancients may have visited Mars and not considered settling there. They had limited resources, and after the starship was destroyed, they did not have a way to get to Mars. We'll see how things shape up on this trip."

"How do you feel about the deals we're making with government entities and the rocket guys on earth?"

"Time is needed to build resources. The main thing is to keep the wolves at bay. Cooperation with others provides shelter. The next few years on Earth may be difficult. There is war in Europe. The Russian leader is trying to expand his territory and inflate his ego. He seems to be trying to drag the US and NATO into a war against Russia. His expansion plans are failing. His aggression has brought democratic allies closer together. The U.S. needs to maintain its democracy to keep the world from possibly regressing into a dark age. The constitution should be modified to adapt to the twenty-first century and beyond. Things have changed a lot since 1776. The villains and criminals have found ways to game the system. Democracy is evolving. Certain cultural elements are resisting. The country must survive intact beyond 2024. The government must stay in the hands of professionals who want it to work and adapt. The non-survival of the United States as a democracy can devastate world stability. The ancient Chinese had emperors and feudal rulers. They also had what we might call professionals or intellectuals, what they called sages, to help rulers run the fiefdom or country. In part, Laozi's Dao De Jing was a guide for those in power to follow to preserve their regimes. It was written about twenty-three hundred years ago. The previous administration in the U.S. tried to destroy professional governance and ignore the constitution, laws, rules, and traditions the country runs on. They or the people who backed them are still trying to do so. They fear losing control. Issues like social equality threaten them."

Tamara came into the area and noticed Josh and Conrad by the window. Conrad waves for her to join them. "Have some tea with us. I'll brew a fresh pot,"

Tamara joined them and sat down. "Is grandfather Conrad telling stories?"

"Yes, I am," Conrad said. "Special stories."

"Good, Josh needs to know. He is one of the family. He's helping to make history," Tamara said.

Part of Josh's mind accepts the Argonite story. At first, he thinks about why Conrad is telling him this tale. "Now it makes sense." Another part of his mind rebels against believing in any conspiracy or notion that cannot be proven scientifically or by objective factual reality. "However, it seems that Raoul Sr.'s and Marcella's invention of the gravity propulsion system is beyond the technical expertise of human achievement. Have knowledge, and ancient Argonite intellect inspired it? If what Conrad is saying is true, it is amazing that it has been kept secret all this time. Given the insight into how Homo sapiens behave toward those perceived as 'other,' it will have been important to at least appear to assimilate into local cultures. Thoughts of all the intuitive women and men accused of witchery or wizardry and who were murdered occurred to him. Yet, in some cultures, they are respected as scholars or sages. There may be a connection."

Josh imagines that whatever test they have to identify the DNA is worth looking at if the procedure is based on scientific methods for collecting data. In the past, he speculated that something was different about himself. Even though his training in meditation and Buddhist philosophy guides him toward being non-judgmental, he condemns certain types of humans and their behavior. It is difficult to admit that many Homo sapiens today appear to have aberrant behavior. But maybe that's what humans are.

Josh thinks that "no one knows what Homo sapiens were like sixty thousand years ago. All that remains are bones and a few artifacts. Many scientists believe that Homo sapiens were peaceful hunter-gathers. What was their behavior when they moved out of western Africa sixty or eighty thousand years ago, displacing other humanoid species? Maybe hunter-gatherers are not all that peaceful? Why is it that Homo sapiens are the only humanoid species left on the planet? Have Homo sapiens evolved in the last twenty thousand years? Argonite history on earth might shed some light on the years for which there is no written history. "

Before Josh left Earth for this trip, he and Sam negotiated a deal with corporate partners. Participants include a significant theme park company, an airline company, Ramurt's rocket company, and a major online retailer. They agreed to build the International Earth Terminal Station (ETS) and the first space hotel 285 miles above the earth. The project is structured as a joint venture between ISEG and the other corporations. Ramurt's company will lift some components into orbit while ISEG handles lifting workers, equipment, and materials. Financial investment from all partners in cash and in-kind contribution is required. Several major hotel chains bid on having their name attached to the space hotel and the theme park partner. It is agreed that the hotel is part of the terminal station. Other facilities will be added as the Earth Terminal Station expands. Additional space hotels can be built at the terminal.

Marcella is reluctant to agree with Sharon's request to work for Arroyo Aerospace at the Earth Terminal Station. It is difficult to say no to her daughter. Sharon wants to be part of the family business. Tamara said, "this will be a good opportunity for her sister. Sharon can be the contact for the hotel and ISEG flights to the hotel."

Sharon exhibits less of her evangelical zeal these days. Leaving her job at the mega-church, she came to work in the non-classified offices of Arroyo Aerospace in Florida. Marcella finally agrees to Sharon working for the Earth Terminal Station. Sharon is pleased and looking forward to moving into her office at the terminal when it is ready. She stays at Tamara's apartment in Orlando or the Ranch working in the public office.

CHAPTER THIRTY-THREE

UNOOSA

Arroyo Aerospace will expand significantly in 2022 while the second expedition to Mars is underway. New buildings are erected to house the necessary equipment and resources to manufacture the needed modules and materials for the International Earth Terminal Station (ETS) and hotel. Work is underway constructing two new Galaxy-class spaceships and a new ship for lifting modules into space. This specially equipped ship will lift prefabricated modules into orbit to be assembled into larger structures like the Earth Terminal Station. Later the ship will tow modules to other places, including Mars or Lagrange point L5.

There is constant activity at Gate to the Galaxy launch center. News crews frequently arrive to observe launches and to interview key people. Press and media are sent to the press area near the launch site but often try to gain access to other parts of the complex. Arno does not allow any press beyond the Gateway to the Galaxy grounds. If an interview or briefing is scheduled, it is conducted in the press room located in the Gateway building. Adrienne coordinates all press activity with Arno.

Production at Arroyo Aerospace is automated using robotic technology. However, many new workers are hired. Arno Cameron establishes a screening process that includes deep security checks for all new employees. Since joining Arroyo Aerospace, Arno has become an essential part of the organization, working closely with Raoul Sr., Marcella, Sam, Carlos, Adrienne, Bill, and Josh in each of their areas. He is a respected member of the Arroyo Aerospace corporate family.

Raoul Sr., Sam, and Marcella maintain high security around the drive construction hangar. They have the help of two employees who have worked with them for twenty years. They are, in the Arroyo tradition, considered family members. Five construction specialists are long-time Arroyo Aerospace employees. They have all been involved in building spaceships, starting with Galaxy One.

Because of the production expansion, Arno increases security around the property. Cameras, lights, motion detectors, and barriers are installed anywhere that might be vulnerable to intruders. The hangars and runway receive increased security. Also, the command center hangar and the drive production hangar. The Arroyo ranch received increased security. Paul's Film Studio is integrated into the security system for Arroyo Aerospace, Gate to the Galaxy theme park, the launch area, and the ranch area.

Based on his sources and many attempts to hack into the network, Arno believes some physical intrusion is imminent. These threats might come from a US government agency seeking to infiltrate the facilities and gain intelligence. Foreign actors might try to obtain information. Corporate espionage is a possibility.

It is reasonable, Arno claims, to speculate that the Arroyo Aerospace offices will be a prime target. Also, the hangar where the drives are built. Arno assumes that surveillance satellites and drones are mapping the entire complex. Drone and aircraft activity over the area is observed on many occasions. Anyone can pull the Arroyo Aerospace complex up on Google.

Arno goes on a few trips up to the International Earth Terminal Station while construction is underway. He anticipates that security will be required once the terminal and hotel are complete. He learns from government sources that the United States Space Force is making inquiries about obtaining an Arroyo Aerospace spaceship for their use. Arno suspects the terminal will be a prime target for their "patrols of space." The U.S. military might usurp the international status of the terminal. He makes a note to research agreements regarding the sovereignty of space stations or colonies in space. He laughed at the notion of "Space Law" when he began his research. However, there it is when he "Googled" Space Law. "The United Nations Office for Outer Space Affairs (UNOOSA)." He speculates about the pronunciation of the acronym. Is it "UN OOSA or U NOOSA?" "UN OOSA" seems more likely. These statements were written and discussed over fifty years ago. The Outer Space Treaty was framed in 1967 by a few existing space powers. The opening online page of UNOOSA reads:

"Space law addresses a variety of matters, such as, for example, the preservation of the space and Earth environment, liability for damages caused by space objects, the settlement of disputes, the rescue of astronauts, the sharing of information about potential dangers in outer space, the use of space-related technologies, and international cooperation. A few fundamental principles guide the conduct of space activities, including the notion of space as the province of all humankind, the freedom of exploration and use of outer space by all states without discrimination, and the principle of non-appropriation of outer space."

"The Office provides information and advice, upon request, to governments, non-governmental organizations and the general public on space law in order to promote understanding, acceptance and implementation of the international space law agreements concluded under United Nations auspices."

Arno questions if law school prepared him to understand United Nations agreements. An initial perusal of the agreements indicates it is between various governments and their space agencies. There is an area labeled:

"Space Law Treaties and Principles"

"The Committee on the Peaceful Uses of Outer Space is the forum for the development of international space law. The Committee has concluded five international treaties and five sets of principles on space-related activities."

"These five treaties deal with issues such as the non-appropriation of outer space by any one country, arms control, the freedom of exploration, liability for damage caused by space objects, the safety and rescue of spacecraft and astronauts, the prevention of harmful interference with space activities and the environment, the notification and registration of space activities, scientific investigation, and the exploitation of natural resources in outer space and the settlement of disputes."

"Each of the treaties stresses the notion that outer space, the activities carried out in outer space and whatever benefits might be accrued from outer space should be devoted to enhancing the well-being of all countries and humankind, with an emphasis on promoting international cooperation."

Arno downloads the Compilation Booklet of which he made copies to bring to a meeting that evening. At the meeting Arno said, "at first glance it appears there are treaties, one of which concerns the registration of objects launched into space. These treaties and articles in the booklet all appear to involve registering objects by 'States (countries)'. Since we are launching from the US how do we register as independent corporate entities? These three articles might have relevance:"

"Article I"

"The exploration and use of outer space, including the Moon and other celestial bodies, shall be carried out for the benefit and in the interests of all countries, irrespective of their degree of economic or scientific development, and shall be the province of all mankind."

"Outer space, including the Moon and other celestial bodies, shall be free for exploration and use by all States without discrimination of any kind, on a basis of equality and in accordance with international law, and there shall be free access to all areas of celestial bodies."

"There shall be freedom of scientific investigation in outer space, including the Moon and other celestial bodies, and States shall facilitate and encourage international cooperation in such investigation."

"Article VI"

"States Parties to the Treaty shall bear international responsibility for national activities in outer space, including the Moon and other celestial bodies, whether such activities are carried on by governmental agencies or by non-governmental entities, and for assuring those national activities are carried out in conformity with the provisions set forth in the present Treaty. The activities of non- governmental entities in outer space, including the Moon and other celestial bodies, shall require authorization and continuing supervision by the appropriate State Party to the Treaty."

"When activities are carried on in outer space, including the Moon and other celestial bodies, by an international organization, responsibility for compliance with this Treaty shall be borne both by the international organization and by the States Parties to the Treaty participating in such organization."

"Article VIII"

"A State Party to the Treaty on whose registry an object launched into outer space is carried shall retain jurisdiction and control over such object, and over any personnel thereof, while in outer space or on a celestial body. Ownership of objects launched into outer space, including objects landed or constructed on a celestial body, and of their component parts, is not affected by their presence in outer space or on a celestial body or by their return to the Earth. Such objects or component parts found beyond the limits of the State Party to the Treaty on whose registry they are carried shall be returned to that State Party, which shall, upon request, furnish identifying data prior to their return."

"It appears that UNOOSA never really considered that independent corporate entities apart from state-sanctioned companies might venture into space," Arno said, reading through the compilation booklet.

"It would seem ISEG should take steps to register 'objects,' including spaceships with UNOOSA, as a non-state actor. Since we are registered in the U.S., we may come under US government jurisdiction even in space or on a celestial body like Mars," Arno told Raoul Sr. and Marcella.

Reading along with Arno, Raoul Sr., Marcella, and Bill Arroyo are troubled by the information. Josh and Sam are more pragmatic, suggesting that "we should ignore UNOOSA. Maybe the rocket companies will give us some advice about dealing with the UN," Josh said. "NASA has experience in this area. I will check on it."

"Thank you for researching this, Arno," Marcella said. "It's important that we deal with these realities before they become issues."

"The Space X company has been launching satellites they call "Sky Net." Who did they register this with? Did they require permission from anyone?" Josh asks.

"Good question," replies Arno. "They got permission from the FCC. Article V states, 'a State (country) from whose territory a space object is launched shall be regarded as a participant in a joint launching.' The UN talks a lot about 'outer space. Where does outer space begin?"

Arno continues, "Regarding the Space Force, I learned from reading these treaties that there is a resolution:

"All members shall refrain in their international relations from the threat or use of force against the territorial integrity or political independence of any state, or any manner inconsistent with the purposes of the United Nations."

"So, as long as we establish the terminal as 'International' the Space Force, technically can't use 'force' to take control of the International Earth Terminal Station," Marcella said.

"Especially if they can't get up there," Josh said. The good news is that we have been working with NASA, which has sanctioned all activities, if not officially, by default. I don't know if they have made reports to UNOOSA. We haven't heard anything from the FAA. They recently flagged one of the rocket guys for their rocket ship going off course."

"There is some news that the UN is trying to convene a new committee to review and update these non-binding guidelines. Russia and China want there to be binding treaties instead. A working group plans to meet twice a year in Geneva in 2022 and 2023 to draft new space laws and security rules. Until then, we're on our own," Arno said. "A big part of the concern these days is about all the debris floating around the planet. There are probably 30,000 or more satellites and other things floating around the planet. Every time I read about the number goes up. Soon we'll look like Saturn."

"Arno do you want to attend the meetings of this group studying the guidelines," Raoul Sr. suggests.

"At some point, establishing the terminal as 'international' will need to be looked at in depth. I believe Dubai is an International City. Arno said. "One criterion might be multiple nations having a presence on the station."

After the late meeting, Arno decides to stay at the ranch. The Arroyos invited him to stay at the house any time he wished. He often works late, so he does stay there on occasion.

He goes to his office to drop off the paperwork he used for the meeting. Before leaving his office to walk over to the ranch, he scans all forty-nine security monitors across the property. He speaks with the security team at the main gate. The main entrance is in touch with the six guards who patrol the property in jeeps. Everything is quiet.

Two hours later, around midnight, the ranch perimeter motion detectors and cameras equipped with night vision lenses pick up movement on the Eastern edge of the Arroyo property. Guards at the security center near the main gate begin monitoring these cameras. They determine that six individuals are making their way across the marshy area headed toward dryer ground near the runway near the hangars. They are about half a mile from the security fence that runs the length of the airstrip.

One patrol jeep is already in that area. According to the protocol, they immediately call the security center, who then notify Arno. He tells them to inform the private security company he retained and the Brevard County Sheriff's Office. Then send two jeeps, headlights off, with four guards to the area between the intruders and the hangars. "The intruders may be armed," he tells the guard at the main gate. "Bring weapons and stun guns. Do not confront the intruders unless they try to come over the fence. Turn on the electric grid for the fences. I'm on my way there now. Send two guards to the ranch house."

Still dressed, he puts on his shoes and grabs a service revolver, his phone, his iPad tablet, and a flashlight. He alerts Raoul Sr. and Marcella to secure the house. He will reach Raoul Sr. by phone if necessary. Raoul Jr. is awake and goes along with Arno. They enable the ranch alarm system once they clear the motion detectors on the house's perimeter.

The security team has been drilled on how to react to an intrusion. They have lethal weapons available but aim to apprehend the intruders and turn them over to the county sheriffs. Arno does not want the security team to get into gun battles with anyone.

The private security company is tasked with patrolling the roads around the property and providing personal protection for people like Josh and Adrienne, Sam, Carlos, Tamara, Paul, Bill, and others who constantly come and go from the property. One of Arno's former coworkers started the company to provide personal security like the Secret Service does for government people. The staff is mainly retired Secret Service, FBI, and CIA employees.

When Arno came to Arroyo Aerospace, his first goal was securing the huge property without making it look like a military installation. Security remains low visibility wherever possible. The area to the east of the main house, hangars, and runway is vulnerable because they are exposed to pastureland, marshes, and water that is part of the Saint John River tributaries. It cannot be fenced off or patrolled well. Sam Arroyo occasionally uses his airboat to come close to the ranch from the Saint John tributaries.

Cameras and motion detectors are installed strategically around the property under Arno's direction. Until now, sensors and cameras have only gotten tripped by animals like wild hogs. The fence near the runway has been electrified but is not turned on unless there is an alert. Motion detectors now trigger video and audio surveillance systems. All the buildings have sophisticated security systems. These advanced systems can go into a defensive posture. For example, release tear gas in certain areas.

Arno visits the Chief Deputy Sheriff of the Brevard County Sheriff's Department to acquaint him with Arroyo Aerospace and explain the delicate nature of the work being done there. He arranges for the Chief Deputy Sheriff to visit Arroyo Aerospace, where he meets Raoul Sr. and Marcella. Later he got the Chief Deputy Sheriff aboard a Galaxy One guest flight.

When Arno and Raoul Jr. arrive at the runway, the jeeps and guards are parked behind one of the buildings where they can see the runway fence. Arno receives a call from the security center that two intruders have broken off from the other four and appear to be heading toward the house. The guards at the house are alerted. The security company has a vehicle with two men at the main gate. They are sent to the house.

The Sheriff's Department is contacted and informed of the situation. The department reports they have launched a helicopter that will approach the rear of the area where the intruders have been sighted. ETA is less than ten minutes. They also say they alerted the Florida Highway Patrol, who are now on their way.

Arno sends two guards to wait out of sight near a service gate in the runway fence. He and Raoul Jr. watch the approach of the intruders on the iPad. Four of the intruders are about 200 yards from the fence. The other two intruders are nearing the stables not far from the house. The Arroyo Aerospace guards and the private security company guards are alerted about where the two intruders are headed. They prepare to apprehend them. Two Sheriff Deputy cars arrive and join Arno at the runway area.

Florida Highway Patrol cars arrive at the main gate. They are directed to the house and the runway area.

As the intruders approach the runway fence, the police chopper is heard coming toward the area with flood lights on. Soon a voice on a loudspeaker from the police chopper behind them tells the intruders to remain in place. At this time, the Sheriff Deputies move through the gate from the runway side of the fence, weapons drawn. They tell the intruders to drop to the ground—Arno and his security guards back up the Sheriff's Deputies. Several long moments pass before all four intruders drop to the ground. It is almost as if they had been waiting for orders from someone unseen about what they should do next.

Before the two intruders at the stables can flee, they are apprehended by the Arroyo Aerospace guards and the Security company guards. They will be turned over to the Highway Patrol.

The police chopper lands. The four intruders are arrested for trespassing, attempted burglary, and possession of weapons. Once they are secured, the other two intruders are brought to the runway area to await transportation to a branch of the Brevard Sheriff's Department.

Arno gets a close look at the intruders. He takes some photographs of them as they are arrested. They do not appear to be ordinary thieves or criminals. None of the intruders carry any identification. They are wearing communication equipment and have mobile phones. In their backpacks, they are carrying cameras and tools for breaking into buildings.

Before turning over the two intruders apprehended at the stables to the Sheriff, the Arroyo Aerospace guard manages to secure their mobile phones. He holds on to them to give to Arno. Later the Sheriff's Deputies confiscate the rest of the intruder's equipment.

The excitement ends with all the trespassers being taken away by the Sheriffs. Arno is told where they will be held until they can get a judge to arraign them, which might be in the morning. The guards have orders to check the property East of the runway for anything the intruders leave behind. Arno thanked everyone before returning to his office with the two mobile phones his guards confiscated from the intruders. He plans to go to the county sheriff's office in the morning.

Raoul Jr. said I'll explain everything to Raoul Sr. and Marcella when I get back to the house."

"Fine, thanks. I'll give them a call to check in with them." The call finds that they are both calm. Marcella said, "she planned to set up a meeting for tomorrow afternoon."

The mobile phones are password protected. Arno tries a few combinations of typical numbers that people like to use, like 1, 2, 3, and 4. Finally, one phone clears with "9, 8, 7, 6." Checking settings, he finds the owner's name. He then checks recent phone calls. There were several from the same number earlier that evening. The area code is 703, which covers northern Virginia. He recognizes the area code since there are several government offices in that area, including the Department of Defense and the CIA.

Messages from that evening appear to be times and meeting places. Earlier that day, there was an outgoing message with what appeared to be a bank account number and routing information. Checking through more messages and e-mails, Arno decides that this person is not a government employee. Not CIA. He notices the 703 area code calls. He plans to do some further checking tomorrow. At 3:00 AM, before returning to the house, he receives a call from Lieutenant Parker, who works for the Chief Deputy Sheriff.

"The chief asked me to call you. The judge came in about twenty minutes ago to arraign these guys. Before the judge arrived and the defendants made any calls, a lawyer arrived who said he represented them. They all made bail and are released pending a hearing. Strangely, this judge shows up in the middle of the night. He usually always waits until morning. The chief said you are welcome to come in whenever you want to review what we have on their identities. You can also sign the complaint."

"Where was the lawyer from?"

"Miami, according to his card."

"How much was the bail?"

"It was a hundred thousand for each of them," Lt. Parker said. "We couldn't find a criminal record for any of them when we ran their prints."

"Okay, thank you and the Chief. I'll be over sometime tomorrow," Arno said.

Feeling exhausted, Arno heads back to the ranch house. As he walks under the stars, his mind begins drifting toward sleep. Unexpectedly a recent phone call conversation came to mind. At first, he ignored the calls, but he finally answered. It is Simone Greely. He is driving along highway 528 back to Orlando and is a little bored. All his calls are transferred to a burner phone linked to a burner satellite. Arno is always concerned about spyware being placed on mobile phones.

"Hi Simone," Arno said, taking the call on the car speaker system.

"You're a hard man to reach."

"Yes, I guess I am. What's up?"

"I understand you are working for Arroyo Aerospace now."

"Yes, you are still with the same company, right?"

"Well, yes. Aside from that, there are some things I'd like to discuss with you, but we can't do it on the phone. We can meet in Orlando if you like."

"I'm swamped, Simone. What is this about?"

"Security," "Is this a secure line?"

"Yes, it is. I understand you spent some time in Chicago recently. It sounds like you are fishing around for information for some reason."

"Just following orders. It would be best if you kept security tight around Arroyo Aerospace. It might be some Russians snooping around. We have information about a certain political appointee from the previous administration. She may have been a Russian Mole. I have a source that thinks Arroyo Aerospace is going to get hit. She's involved."

" Thank you. I want to hear more. I can't meet right now. I'm on Signal if you want to send me a note anytime."

"I understand. If I get more information, I'll be in touch."

Arno did not receive any communication from her after that conversation. Thinking about the call, he realizes she had been trying to warn him about the attempted break-in tonight.

Approaching the ranch house, he pulls out his mobile phone from his pocket. Opening contacts., he finds Greely, Simone. There are two 703 numbers listed for her. The first one is a work number. The second is mobile.

He opens recent calls on the intruder's phone and then scrolls back, looking for either of those numbers. He soon finds the second number from the last time Simone called him. There is another area code 703 number not linked to Simone.

His last thought, as he finally lay down to get a few hours of sleep, is, "you think she would know better than to use her phone to communicate with this guy unless she had no reason to hide it? He is her contact."

CHAPTER THIRTY-FOUR

Explorers New Discoveries.

Everyone on the Arroyo team feels they must remain aware of social, political, and other realities as they continue to move into space. Before the second expedition leaves for Mars, Conrad summarizes the current situation. "While great leaps for humanity are about to happen in outer space, Earth is experiencing political unrest globally and surges of Covid-19 variants. Unvaccinated people are getting ill and dying. To some extent, this persuades more people to get vaccinated. The Omicron variant emerged globally in late 2021. The spread of the virus in the U.S. appears to be slowing as we prepare to journey to Mars. The world is teetering on the brink of another world war. The Russian dictator president is attempting to annex Ukraine by invading and bombing cities. He has made criminal attacks on civilian targets, killing hundreds of children. He has ordered cities to be bombed into rubble. The invading Russian military, aided by mercenaries, is committing war crimes. Ukraine is fighting bravely and, against all odds, is managing to slow the substantial Russian invasion long enough for sanctions and other steps against Russia to take hold. The conflict brings Europe and the United States closer and reinforces the NATO alliance. The Ukrainians have received arms and supplies from NATO counties, including the U.S. They appear to be resisting the invasion and, in some respects defeating the Russians. Cease-fire talks are currently underway, I believe. But they will not go anywhere," Conrad said. Ukraine is being bombed relentlessly under the orders of the Russian dictator. But the Ukrainian people continue to resist and sometimes push back the Russians.

Marcella said, "We had a top-secret meeting with the President of the United States. We agreed to secretly fly supplies into Ukraine to help them with their war of resistance. Galaxy Four has made several clandestine trips to Ukraine with much-needed supplies. The cloaking of the ship performs perfectly. It has become the best-kept secret of the President's administration. Even the Ukrainians are not aware of how the supplies are delivered."

"Here in the U.S., the Democratic majority in Congress formed a nominally bipartisan committee to investigate the January 6th, 2021, insurrection at the capital in Washington D.C. Republicans still loyal to the disgraced ex-president have been trying to obstruct the progress of the committee. The committee is making progress and continues working. Public hearings are being held in June. It appears the ex-president's plot to overturn the election had deep support of certain individuals and others on the far-right."

"The reality of climate change and severe weather is finally beginning to be noticed. The planet is suffering ecologically from severe neglect by human populations. There are fire storms, floods, and extreme weather in the form of high heat and drought. There was massive rainfall on a two-mile-high Greenland mountain where it had never been known to rain. Rising ocean temperatures and increased atmospheric gases like methane and carbon dioxide. Pollution caused by burning fossil fuels is poisoning the air in countries and cities—raising temperatures in northern and southern arctic regions. Efforts to deal with climate change are continually met with resistance globally.

"War, genocide, poverty, petulance, and crime cause millions of people to attempt migration to find someplace where they can survive. All these things existed in the past but not in a world where a global economy and the internet exist. What might happen on Earth in 2022 and beyond appears unpredictable. Sabre rattling by China, Russia, North Korea, and other authoritarian countries threatens the world's stability."

Based on Conrad's assessments, Arroyo Aerospace is gradually moving some of its production to other locations. All gravity drive manufacturing is scheduled to be transferred from the Arroyo Aerospace Florida facility to the new space factory when it is ready. Research and development of future versions of the drive continue to be a priority.

The second International Space Exploration Group (ISEG) trip to Mars begins in April 2022. There are two ships on this trip, Galaxy Two and Galaxy Three. Captain Sun, with Kevin Steiner, pilots Galaxy Two. Raoul Jr. and a newly trained navigator, Cary Brown, pilots Galaxy Three. The flight plans are identical for both ships. They fly in formation. Each vessel has newly trained additional flight personnel in the command control center. Tamara, Josh, Carlos, Paul, and Stacy are also aboard Galaxy Two for this mission. Conrad and Julia join the team on Galaxy Two as guests and research associates. Technical support personnel and additional NASA astronauts, including Tony and Patricia, are on board for their second trip to Mars.

Before returning to Earth, Galaxy Three is scheduled for a trip into the asteroid belt between Mars and Jupiter. The exploratory mission includes finding asteroids that can be mined or transported back to Mars if small enough. The trip includes visits to asteroids previously mapped by astronomers and NASA. Asteroids of interest are those composed of minerals, water, ice, or metals that can be mined for use on Mars.

Once the ships arrive on Mars, they will serve as bases for everyone while habitats safe for living are built. Laser equipment and explosives will be used to carve out the opening to a space in the mountain discovered on the first trip. The entrance will be enlarged, framed, and an airlock chamber will be installed if the cave or cavern is large enough. The cavern's interior should have lower radiation than the planet's surface. If there is space inside the cavern and conditions are favorable, it might be possible to construct a biosphere there.

Galaxy Two's additional crew members include astronauts, scientists, architects, and engineers. If a sustainable human habitat is constructed before the ships return to Earth, a group of astronaut builders will remain on Mars until Galaxy Two returns to Mars in six months.

Galaxy Three has a complement of seven crew members, including pilot Raoul Jr. and copilot/navigator Cary Brown. Galaxy Three is loaded with building equipment and supplies. A warehouse and shelters are planned to store cargo carried by both ships.

The cargo on Galaxy Three includes a four-passenger pressurized utility lander custom designed for transportation and construction on Mars. It has a high-energy laser device capable of carving rock and is equipped with retractable robotic arms for moving objects. It has two airlocks holding EMU suits so passengers can go onto the planet's surface. Sam named it the Mars Galaxy Mini. The cargo bay stores equipment and supplies. The drive is strong enough to lift materials and supplies and fly them to other locations. The Mars Galaxy Mini lander is about one-quarter the size of Galaxy One. It has only two levels. The upper level is for control and passengers. The lower level is for cargo and the drive. Raoul Jr., his copilot navigator, and an engineer trained using the lander before leaving Earth.

Galaxy Two arrives in Mars orbit a few hours before Galaxy Three. The second ship decelerated enough to give Galaxy Two room to settle into orbit. The ships are in communication throughout the journey to Mars. The main reason for delaying Galaxy Three's arrival is to give Galaxy Two time to release a small weather and communication satellite into Mars orbit. This satellite is custom-built to detect sandstorms coming from the southern hemisphere of Mars northward. It also aids communication and relays back to earth or nearby. Astronauts Tony and Patricia guide the satellite from the cargo airlock into orbit. Once they return to the ship, the satellite is booted up, spreading solar panels to supplement the internal radioisotope power system. Galaxy Two floats into a slightly higher orbit after that.

Galaxy Three came into orbit nearby Galaxy Two once Captain Sun gave the go-ahead. The plan is for both ships to land at a preselected site. This is the exact location visited on the first trip. The area is at the foot of the mountain range, where astronauts Tony and Patricia found the entrance to the mountain cave. The ground below the cliff is flat, suitable for the secure landing of both ships, with room to construct shelters. The first shelter is planned to be a large hangar that deflects radiation and maintains an earth atmosphere. They will erect solar arrays for power grids to supplement the plutonium-238 generators. Another essential resource is the equipment to create oxygen from available resources on Mars.

Galaxy Two touches down first. Galaxy Three follows, landing one hundred feet away. Galaxy Three then floats to within fifteen feet of Galaxy Two. A tubular reinforced collapsible bridge is extended from one of its airlock chamber to an airlock chamber on Galaxy Two. Both ships are now joined with a breathable air passageway. This tube is designed to connect ships in outer space or on Mars. Everyone on both ships wears lightweight pressure and radiation protection suits on the trip and while on Mars. The comfortable suits, designed to be worn under exterior suits or clothing, monitor vitals and radiation. As soon as the link is secure, the crew of Galaxy Three joins those in Galaxy Two for a short landing celebration. Photographs and videos of the landing and gathering are sent back to Earth and seen worldwide.

The first thing to leave Galaxy Three's cargo bay after landing is the Mars Galaxy Mini utility lander capable of sustaining life, flying astronauts around Mars, or moving cargo. Raoul Jr. made some recognizance flights around the area to test the utility vehicle's performance. Astronauts using robotic construction devices take a week to build the hangar shelter/habitat from available prefab parts and local materials. Once the large airlock is installed, the balance of cargo from Galaxy Three is unloaded.

The older, non-pressurized lander flew up to the cliff where it landed on the first trip. The entrance is enlarged using a high-intensity laser. Inside the mountain, they discover a vast cavern. Power lines run up to the cliff so lights can be set up inside the cavern. Preliminary exploration reveals that this is a considerable space that goes in three directions. The floor is flat near the cliff entrance. It then slopes slightly downward as it goes deeper into the mountain. The roof of the cavern is high. There is a steep slope parallel to the face of the mountain that goes up higher. The smooth walls of the cavern look like lava flows formed them. Radiation levels inside the cavern are low. The enlarged entrance is framed for an airlock chamber to the cavern to seal it off from the exterior.

Five days after Galaxy Three is unloaded, it floats off with its original crew plus Josh on a mission to the asteroid belt. One of the reasons for launching the satellite into Mars orbit is to allow continuous communication between Galaxy Three and Galaxy Two on Mars. At high speed, including acceleration and deceleration, the ship's time for the round trip to the edge of the asteroid belt is estimated at six days.

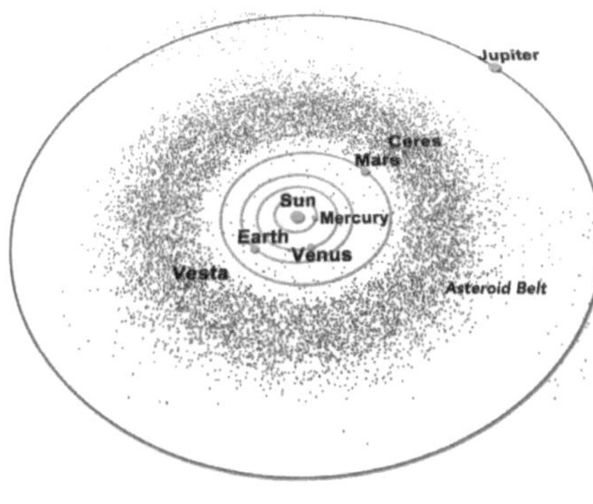

StarDate.org/JRM

Galaxy three arrives at the asteroid belt without incident. Mars and Jupiter's orbits are in line now. However, their size in the sky resembles viewing them from the earth's rotation. The asteroids look like giant rocks floating in the dark when viewed from the ship. A short way into the Belt, an asteroid is spotted that looks mainly composed of a frozen liquid. Spectral analysis shows it is frozen water. The asteroid is big enough for Galaxy Three to land. Using a robotic device equipped with a laser, astronauts cut two manageable size chunks of ice from the surface. These blocks are loaded into the cargo bay cold storage section. Afterward, they continue searching for certain asteroids previously discovered by astronomers. One of the first well-known asteroids they see is Ceres. It's large enough to be considered a dwarf planet. At 580 miles (940 km) in diameter, it is the largest known object in the asteroid belt. The second largest asteroid is Vesta, also considered a dwarf planet with a core of nickel and Iron.

Raoul Jr. and Cary put Galaxy Three into orbit around Ceres. The dwarf planet rotates every nine hours. It revolves around the sun every 4.61 earth years. The shape and density of Ceres indicate a rocky core surrounded by a thick ice mantle. Water vapor has been detected coming from Ceres when it is closer to the sun.

"This little planet is so small it won't take long for us to orbit," Cary said.

"It doesn't have much gravity either, less than the moon," Raoul Jr. said.

Paul brought the cameras online that recorded the first close-up video of Ceres. The monitors show the bright spots, Cerealia Facula and Vinalia Faculae, that the U.S. space probe "Dawn" observed in the Occator crater. Astronomers on Earth will be thrilled to see this footage. ISEG will make sure they get copies of the video.

Based on her previous Wikipedia research notes, Cary says, "They think the bright spots are highly reflective salts left behind when briny water from an underground reservoir moved upward and evaporated. The water oozes from fractures left behind when the crater formed 20 million years ago. The salty regions have not been darkened by micrometeorite impacts, indicating that the bright spots formed in the last 2 million years. Because the bright spots contain salt compounds with water that has not dehydrated, the briny water may have percolated upward in the last few hundred years. This suggests that the salty liquid water underneath the crater is not frozen and might be percolating from underground."

"There's a volcano, too," Josh said. "It only erupts every fifty million years. They detected an exosphere, a temporary atmosphere with water vapor, back in 2014. There might be an underground ocean."

Thomas, one of the astronauts, remarked, "It might be possible to mine some of the water or other minerals and transport them back to Mars someday."

Barry, another astronaut who worked on the ice asteroid, asks, "will we go down to the surface?"

Raoul Jr. replies, "I'll check with Mars. We may not need to if we can get enough information from orbit."

Josh said, "According to maps of the asteroid belt compiled over the years by astronomers, this area contains several interesting asteroids. Spectrographic analysis by astronomers has shown them to contain various metals, mostly nickel and iron. One of the largest objects in the asteroid belt, about the size of the state of Massachusetts, is a rare asteroid that is thought to possibly contain metals like copper, cobalt, silver, and platinum. This asteroid, first discovered in 1852 and named "16 Psyche," measures 226 km (140 miles) across."

In consultation with Galaxy Two on Mars, it is decided that Galaxy Three will not land on Ceres. Instead, they will orbit and attempt a landing on "16 Psyche" if they can find a suitable flat landing site. Once on the surface, they will gather rock samples.

After shooting footage of Ceres and conducting a spectrographic survey, Galaxy Three leaves Ceres and moves on to find 16 Psyche. Once there, Galaxy Three orbits the 16 Psyche asteroid for six hours, examining the terrain. Different surface color areas are spotted that indicate certain possible metallic or mineral elements. Eventually, a flat area is found where they can land. This time a robotic lander is sent to the surface. It uses a laser device to carve samples out of the rocky asteroid. It also drills holes into the rock to collect samples. After a few trips, the robot collects many samples and brings them back to the ship. Galaxy Three moves to another area on the asteroid, where a crater appears to offer a landing site. There are different surface colors at this location. Astronauts use the robotic lander to gather more samples. Galaxy Three spends thirty hours collecting samples on 16 Psyche, then heads back to Mars. Maps and charts are made of areas of the asteroid belt where they navigated.

Galaxy Two and Three will soon return to Earth. After systems checks and maintenance, the ships are scheduled to return to Mars in December 2022. The plan is to bring settlers who will live on Mars to do construction for up to one year. After one year, depending on individual health, they might be able to stay longer. Because of the low gravity on Mars, high radiation, and the mental stress of living in a hostile environment, long-term employment on the planet is yet to be envisioned. Tests and studies of the first year will be examined before more extended stays are approved.

Tamara and six crew members and astronauts decided to remain on Mars until the third expedition returns in December 2022. Before the return to earth, the second expedition to Mars manages to build safe habitats and a warehouse on the surface. They also set up a biosphere with an airlock inside the mountain cavern. All the construction materials and parts came with them from Earth. Importantly, kitchen and bathroom equipment is included in the geodesic dome-shaped biosphere package.

There is enough oxygen to keep the biosphere supplied for one year. Additional tanks of breathable air came from Earth on the second trip for use in the habitats. The biosphere and the habitats receive power from an external power station on the surface generated by solar arrays and the radioisotope power modules. Initial water supplies were transported from the earth. Galaxy Three made several trips to the North Pole of Mars to collect ice for the base. Almost all known water on Mars exists as ice, though it also exists in small quantities as vapor in the atmosphere. Scrubbing the atmosphere for water and oxygen is possible.

The team intends to produce oxygen on Mars to replenish the supply tanks. NASA's Perseverance MOXIE first tested this equipment to pull oxygen out of the Martian atmosphere, which is 96% Carbon Dioxide (CO_2). The surface habitats and biosphere use a scaled-up version of the MOXIE device. This device employs heat and electrical currents to split CO_2 molecules into Oxygen (O) and Carbon Monoxide (CO). Oxygen atoms quickly combine into O_2 molecules, the air humans breathe. Nitrogen and Argon pulled from the Martian atmosphere are mixed with pure oxygen to create a breathable atmosphere for humans. CO_2 scrubbers are used in all environments. The CO_2 is scrubbed and disposed of into the Martian atmosphere.

A lighting system in the biosphere simulates sunlight color temperatures throughout the day. Because of the reduced radiation inside the cavern, the

Mars team will live in the biosphere. It also provides a haven for emergencies like sandstorms on the surface. Additional exploration of the cavern is planned. The interior of the cavern may become a sealed-off space. It might be able to maintain a breathable earth atmosphere. The cavern will be explored for other openings in the mountain to the exterior.

The Mars base has adequate life support, including water for one year. Plus what they can produce on the planet. One of their missions is to prepare accommodations for residents. Tamara coordinates activities and maintains contact with command control on earth. She documents all actions by the team. Four team members are astronauts who received NASA training; each has a specialty that will be helpful while on Mars. Mark Cunningham has a background in geology and mining. Karen Kelly Engineering and four years with the U.S. Army Corps of Engineers. Michael Westin also has an engineering background and a tour of duty with the Army Corps of Engineers. Roberto Gonzalez studied architecture and helped design the out-of-the-box Mars habitat modules. Astronauts First Lieutenant Tony Capella and Captain Patricia Sloan stay on the planet, adding their experience to the team.

Another goal is to continue to build habitats on the surface. Maintaining the oxygen-producing process is necessary. Using the Mars Galaxy Mini lander, two astronauts flew north to the polar region to continue transporting ice back to the base. Another expedition to Valles Marineris is made using the lander. A flyover survey of a few canyons indicates frozen subsurface water in some canyons. Future exploration is anticipated.

An experimental project is underway using 3D printers and robots to produce hard glass building material. They will use Martian sand silica (silicon dioxide) and other ingredients from rocks and Martian sources. These ingredients will be used to print blocks or be poured into forms to construct a building of any shape. One issue is creating the form or mold to hold the thick liquid glass while it dries. Martian regolith is used to make forms for blocks. Metal forms are needed for large slabs.

Mark began producing glass block material for the 3d printer. He adjusts the formula while testing the solution in scaled-down sand molds. A big project will be setting up the equipment for pouring the glass into metal forms. Roberto wants to use large metallic forms to hold the liquid glass in place until it dries. Framing forms are needed for doors, window spaces, and floor supports. One of the immediate outcomes of using liquid glass is a translucent material for building the airlock entrance into the mountain. The liquid glass is poured into forms creating large slabs of glass eighteen inches thick. This allows diffused light to enter the cavern. The glass adheres to the rocks, fusing behind the removable metal frames on either side. The glass provides sunlight and acts as a filter for ultraviolet radiation.

Many things, like building foundations and anchoring structures into the Martian soil, remain to be researched. The out-of-the-box habitats are difficult to anchor to the rock surface. Habitat floors, walls, and roofs help to deflect radiation. Mark begins looking for rocks that absorb less radiation than the regolith on the surface. The cavern might be where basalt and volcanic rock might be found, providing building materials for exterior use. There are many ancient volcanoes on Mars where volcanic rock materials can be procured.

When the airlock entrance to the cavern is complete, the same construction method is used to erect an enclosed lift in front of the cliff entrance to the cavern. With the reduced gravity on Mars, the lift does not require an elaborate motor mechanism. The lift enclosure extends from the ground to a height slightly above the entrance to the cavern. It shelters this part of the cliff and entrance. The significant size lift moves people and equipment up and down from the ground to the cavern entrance. The enclosure is built from glass blocks and slabs anchored to the mountain. Ultimately a twenty-foot wide by forty-two-foot-deep facade in front of the mountain and access to the cavern is constructed. The enclosure's roof is glass, allowing the skylight to filter through to the interior.

Communication between the Mars base and Galaxy Two and Three continue after the ships leave Mars to return to Earth. This initial communication between the Mars base and the spaceships is relayed to ISEG's command on Earth. When the ships arrive back on Earth, secure video and voice communication continues directly via the Mars satellite.

Tamara reports twice daily to Arroyo Aerospace and the International Space Exploration Group about activities, progress, supplies, general morale, and the team's health. All team members have the training and know that being on Mars with no way home until a ship arrives from Earth might foster anxiety. Supplies are more than adequate, but the environment is highly hostile--more life-threatening than winter in Antarctica before global warming. Instead of blizzards, massive sandstorms stop any activity on the surface. Luckily, the satellite in Mars orbit provides information about sandstorms moving toward the base. The entire team knows how important it is to their survival to work as a group and respect each other in every way. Their code of behavior is similar to the Buddhist "Six Principals of Reverent Harmony," used by Chán Buddhist monks living together in monasteries. Group meetings are held daily to discuss all aspects of work and living on Mars. Keeping busy keeps morale high.

It takes several weeks to allow the oxygen production to outpace the crew's needs and habitats on the surface. A second oxygen production machine and CO2 scrubber are set up for the biosphere in the mountain cavern. With adequate oxygen and CO2 scrubbers working in the biosphere, the team members feel secure not wearing full EMU suits inside the biosphere. The mountain shields them from radiation, wind, and sand. A small exercise facility is set up in the cavern biosphere with treadmills, stationary bicycles, elliptical devices, and weights brought to the planet for that purpose. Once the biosphere is secure, all team members exercise daily to keep their muscles and bones healthy as possible while living in the reduced gravity of Mars. Tamara volunteered to lead Tai Chi exercises.

There are two airlocks for the biosphere. One is in the front facing the entrance into the mountain. The main airlock to the biosphere provides space to house EMU suits. The biosphere glass windows allow light from the cavern entrance to be seen. This provides a sense of day and night. The second airlock chamber is on the far side of the biosphere facing the cavern's interior.

The sizeable exterior airlock chamber sealing off the entrance to the cavern is large enough to bring in equipment and the small Mars utility vehicle. There are tubes to expel scrubbed CO_2 from the biosphere into the Mars atmosphere rather than into the cavern. All human waste is flushed into a holding tank for recycling.

The habitats on the surface provide adequate protection and a view of the planet. The extensive habitat module that houses the labs and equipment storage requires surface suiting to protect the team from the corrosive dust and soil brought in by the equipment or robots working outside.

Six weeks into their stay, the team decides to explore other parts of the cavern. The non-pressurized utility lander is available. However, they will first see what things look like on foot. Tamara, Mark, and Michael are selected to walk deeper into the mountain. They will wear lightweight EMU suits. Their suits have two hours of air supply and supplemental heat. It is cold in the cavern, about nineteen degrees Fahrenheit (-7.22 Celsius). It is much cooler on the surface outside the cavern, especially during the night. Michael believes the heated biosphere is warming up the cavern in this area. This close to the equator, surface temperatures are milder in winter, averaging -81 degrees Fahrenheit (-63 C). Temperatures can get as high as 70 degrees Fahrenheit (21 C) during the day in the summer.

Each person carries bright flashlights or lanterns, tools, and boxes. They intend to spend about forty-five minutes exploring and then head back to the biosphere. They speculate that even though the gravity is less intense on Mars, going slightly uphill on the way back may take longer than heading down the mildly sloping floor of the cavern.

The other team members, including Tony, Patricia, Roberto, and Karen, stay behind in the biosphere, working on projects and as backups. Everyone communicates through their helmet headsets, monitored by Roberto and

Karen. Lights shining brightly, the group heads away from the biosphere into the cavern's darkness.

"The floor here is leveling off. The ceiling is still high," Michael said, pointing his light upward toward the space's roof.

"If we were on earth, I'd be looking for dead things on the floor or bats on the roof. Here there is only some dust blown in from the surface," Tamara said. "No stalactites because there doesn't seem to have been any water dripping. Although many scientists believe there was water on the planet at one time."

"Yeah, luckily, not too much dust. The further in we go, the less dust there is. It's not as toxic either, according to my dosimeter," Mark said. "It looks like this entire space is part of some ancient lava flow that occurred when this mountain was formed. I don't detect any drafts of air. There don't appear to be any other entrances besides the one we use. Like the mountain split there for some reason."

Tamara asked, "Do you think certain areas can be mined for the minerals we need?"

"Probably," Mark said. I'm working on analyzing samples. Josh Bennett took some examples back to earth, so we'll see what he turns up—hoping to get some more pieces from deeper inside. There could be veins of other minerals, even some metals available. I brought a laser to cut some rocks as we go along."

Aided by Tamara, Mark got samples from veins in the walls or floor of the cavern where there is a shift in color or other exciting indications. The grotto is getting wider as they move deeper into the darkness.

"This looks like some iron along here," Mark said. A few other metals might have come up from the molten core when the mountains here were formed. Probably nickel."

"Hold on, stop where you are!" Michael shouts. "Shine your lights ahead, down, and to the right and left."

About fifteen feet ahead, there is an abrupt end to the floor of the cavern. A large space where part of the cavern walls drops off and curves away. Cautiously they move forward. Soon they find that they are standing on the edge of a cliff, looking down into a deep canyon below. This canyon extends in both directions. The rift curves on one side into the mountain. Shining their lights down into the canyon, they see rock formations and some flat outcrops. Even with three lights pointed in one place, it was challenging to see very much.

"Look there, do you see some reflection of our lights way down there? Shine your lights over here," Tamara said.

With all the lights focused in one place, some reflection appears to bounce back. It is impossible to tell what it is. They discover what may be a reflective surface. It isn't easy to determine what is there in the dark and so distant.

"Wow," Tamara exclaims. "This is like looking down into a mini-Grand Canyon on Earth in the dark! We need to find a way down there. How long have we been out here?"

"About forty minutes," Michael said.

"We don't have time to explore further right now. Shine your lights wherever I point my camera," Tamara asks as she records video of the area below."

"This canyon looks like it's roughly 500 feet wide, and the drop is at least several hundred feet to the first plateau," Mark said. "There is more of this cavern on the other side of this rift. I see some outcropping of rocks under here. It looks like a dangerous path down."

"The only way we get down there is with the lander utility vehicle unless someone likes the idea of rappelling hundreds of feet down in the dark," Tamara said. "In any event, we need ropes and safety equipment. Let's head back and see what we can figure out."

"I don't think we have the equipment and rope for repelling and climbing back out," Mark said, laughing. "Especially in these EMU suits!"

Listening to them from the biosphere, Karen interrupted, "I could suit up and bring the utility vehicle there, also some new supplies of air."

"Thanks, Karen," Tamara said. "We will come back and look at the video first. Make some plans for an excursion into the canyon. Plan it well, so there are no problems. I also want to contact command control to see what they think."

"Okay," Karen said.

Shining his light up toward the cavern roof, Michael asks, "Is it still light outside?"

"Yeah, I think so," Tamara replies.

"The roof appears very high and shaped by a lava flow. This area may have been shaped by a volcano billions of years ago. There's no light coming in from up there. It doesn't appear that any lava came out of the mountain in this area," Michael said.

"It's possible that the lava may have found a different path. Mars doesn't have any tectonic plates like Earth. There might have been a lot of underground movement of lava from the core. This area may have been a backwash of the main lava flows," Mark said.

"Maybe much of this mountain area was underwater billions of years ago," Michael said.

They gather their gear and start the return journey to the Biosphere.

"What do you think the shiny surface is at the bottom?" Tamara asks.

"Let's look at the video first," right now, I have no ideas," Mark said.

A short time after they returned to the biosphere, the team met to view the video Tamara shot.

"Looks like there are several plateaus as you go deeper into the canyon," Roberto said.

"We can float down there in the utility lander," Tamara said. "It holds four people, but I think it will be safer if only three of us go down this time."

"I agree," Mark said. "We need to take some extra gear. Extra oxygen, emergency equipment, and other tools. We don't know the conditions down there."

"The video picks up a little of the reflection we observed. There isn't enough light for decent resolution of what it is," Tamara said.

"Well, I think it could be ice," Mark offers. "Frozen H2O or Frozen CO2. Several studies have predicted underground frozen water lakes close to the poles. Nothing expected in this area or this deep."

"Makes sense," Michael said. "I thought it might be shiny metallic rocks."

"This is an important find, whatever is down there," Tamara said. "It provides us with a glimpse of the crust deeper down."

When the meeting ended, Tamara got in touch with ISEG ground control. She explains to Raoul Sr. and Marcella what they discovered. Raoul Sr. felt it was safe to use the utility lander to float down there. His best guess is that what they saw is likely frozen water. He and Marcella agree that water in the cavern will be a significant discovery. Water is a resource that, if large enough, can facilitate building a more extensive base there. Possibly, creating other biospheres throughout the cavern and being able to construct on the surface.

Josh joins the conversation on his way back to Earth on Galaxy Two, "Hi Tamara, great work! You mention that the cavern extends on the other side of the canyon. Exploring there might be good to see where it goes."

Tamara replied, "Yes, it's difficult to know how large it is."

"The next expedition can bring material to construct a bridge across the canyon, Raoul Sr. said."

"I wonder if there might be another entrance on the other side of the canyon. Suppose there are none, or if we find an entrance, we could seal it. We might be able to do limited terraforming in the interior of the cavern and the canyon. Maybe create an atmosphere there or expand the number of biospheres," Josh said.

Tamara said, "lots of possibilities. It is dark inside the cavern and darker in the canyon. We need a big source of light to explore properly. Something like what we have in the biosphere but stronger and multiple numbers of them. Something that feels like sunlight."

Raoul Sr. replied, "That' 's a good point, Tamara. A light source that shines down into the canyon. Is there anything there you can use until we build something better? It will need to be strong enough to light up extensive areas."

"There is backup lighting for the biosphere. We can adapt that for our purpose. What we have is working well and should be good for at least a year," Tamara said.

"For now, be careful how far you go into the canyon. As you said, there is no light, so returning from below might be difficult. The lander does have headlights. I suggest rigging some lights to hang out over the cliff so you can see them and a radio beacon. The rover has ground penetrating radar (GPR) that will help you get a feel for what is below," Marcella said.

"Let's wait a few days before you enter the canyon. We may be able to think of some things to help with the exploration," Raoul Sr. said. "In the meantime, we will keep this discovery confidential until we have more information. Use the secure channel to send the video."

"Okay, I'll do that," Tamara said. "I'll see what we can come up with here as well."

....

CHAPTER THIRTY-FIVE

"Tiny shadows in the starlit universe."

Galaxy Two and Galaxy Three set down at the Gateway to the Galaxy landing site completing the International Space Exploration Group's second round trip to Mars. The return is seen on live television across the world. News regarding International Space Exploration Group activities on Mars, the flight back, and other ventures like the Earth Terminal Station (ETS) earn high viewer ratings worldwide. Humanity venturing into the solar system and building a base on another planet sparks the imagination of millions of people. Space travel is not a fantasy anymore. Paul Arroyo's film company has three documentary projects in post-production, almost ready for theatrical release. They are sure to be big box-office successes.

Adrienne narrates the return landing of Galaxy Two from the press area. At the press briefing, she announces,

"The International Space Exploration Group ships have returned to Earth after completing their second expedition to Mars. Seven International Space Exploration Group team members, including four NASA astronauts, are working to establish the base on Mars further. We plan to travel back to Mars in December."

"During the time our ships were on Mars, one of them, Galaxy Three, made a trip to the asteroid belt. We will share information and mineral samples from that exploration with NASA and the world scientific community. Additional footage of the asteroid trip is scheduled to air soon."

"When can we interview the ships' crews?" a reporter asks.

"This has been a long journey in space for both these crews. After a few days of quarantine, rest, and debriefing, we will do our best to make crew members available for interviews," Adrienne answers. "There will be several broadcasts directly from Mars during the next few weeks as the team there explores and builds."

"What are the astronauts doing on Mars? Do they have enough supplies to survive there?" another reporter asks.

"They are safe with enough supplies to last for more than a year. We plan to be there again within six months. The team is creating habitats for additional people. Our goal is to create a suitable environment to accommodate up to fifty team members who will stay on Mars for extended periods."

"Who will the new people be going to Mars?"

"That will be determined soon. Many people have volunteered. Those selected will need to have training for survival on Mars. They will have the occupational skills required to establish, maintain, and expand the base for future habitation. Many will be scientists and researchers. We need medical professionals as well."

"We saw in a previous broadcast from Mars that the team has established a biosphere in a cave. Will they be living there?"

"The biosphere is built as a safe harbor for the team if conditions on the surface become hazardous—for example, a major sandstorm. The cavern has far less radiation than on the surface. It provides a home for the team until we are sure that surface habitats can resist the amount of radiation that hits the surface of Mars. This radiation is from the sun, the entire solar system, and beyond. The Martian atmosphere is not thick enough to shield astronauts on the surface. The magnetic field on Mars is feeble and does not shield the planet from solar radiation. We are exploring other aspects of using the cavern as a habitat."

While the press conference proceeds, the crews of both ships prepare for disembarking. Once they leave the ships, they are transported in a vehicle to the control center hangar. The space in the hangar has been expanded to include a medical facility like the one NASA uses. NASA is anxious to participate in conducting these checkups to add to their body of knowledge for future astronauts traveling and working in space. ISEG arranges with NASA for the astronauts and team members to receive a physical and mental health checkup, blood work, and other tests when they have twenty-four hours to readjust to being on Earth. These tests are the same ones conducted by NASA doctors and specialists when astronauts return from space.

Crew members did not have to deal with weightless environments for prolonged periods. However, team members spent months in space and on Mars, so physical issues need to be checked. For example, blood work includes complete blood count, hemoglobin, hematocrit, red blood cell count, red blood cell indices, white blood cell count, differential count, platelet count, blood pressure, EKG tests, and organ functions. Levels of radioactivity are measured. Tests for viruses and bacterial infection, along with physical tests involving coordination, eyesight, and motion, are conducted. Each person is interviewed to assess the psychological impact of space travel on them. In two weeks, all are to be tested again.

Adrienne is anxious to see Josh, but she understands the need for the twenty-four-hour quarantine and tests. She stops by the hangar and waves at Josh and the others through the glass.

Arno talks to Adrienne about the increased security he put in place, including surveillance of the Bennett condo and a bodyguard for her and the children.

"Do you think all this security for us is necessary?" Adrienne asks.

"After the attempted break-in here, these criminals may get desperate," Arno said.

"They know that you and Josh are part of the inner circle. The Arroyo family members living here on the property have protection. You and Josh and some other people are vulnerable. I'm working on tracking down who organized the attempted break-in. They are after information on the propulsion system or even hijacking a ship. There is some evidence that the Russians sponsored it. It seems like they started a new cold war with the world."

"I only do public relations, so they will not get much from me. Josh is deeply involved. Raoul Sr., Marcella, and Sam are the brains behind the propulsion system," Adrienne said.

"Maybe so," Arno said. There are other proprietary aspects that Josh is part of developing. So, he may be a target. "

"I guess you're right."

"We're looking after you both and the children." "My people are virtually invisible most of the time. We can drive the children to school and pick them up. Also, pick you up when you come to the ranch."

During the twenty-four-hour quarantine, Josh reports his experience on the trip to Raoul Sr. and Marcella.

"Traveling to and from Mars has been an excellent experience. It is like being aboard a cruise ship. I worked out every day, mainly on the treadmill, and while we were on the planet. I believe the entire crew spent time exercising. Every spaceship should have a gym. The ship is very quiet in space, moving along at incredible speed. There is little indication of movement until you look out the windows and watch the stars. The spaceship and its occupants are tiny shadows in the starlit universe."

"On the way there, I researched the geology of Mars. I prepared to test the rock and mineral samples we might find there. I went to the surface a few times to collect rocks and soil. I went on the trip to the asteroid belt. On the way back to earth, I analyzed some of what we collected and what we obtained from the asteroid belt. Based on the diverse types of minerals we found in a tiny sample of asteroids, mining there is certainly an option. Since Mars is closer to the asteroid belt than Earth, there are many options for extracting materials we need for building and possibly for export."

"Galaxy Three transported ice samples from an asteroid back to Mars. If we can capture an asteroid like that and bring it to Mars, it will be a game changer for furnishing water and processing it for hydrogen and oxygen. It does appear that we can harvest water from polar regions on Mars. It is a difficult process. While there, we brought some water ice back from the northern polar region. Using a laser, they carved large chunks of ice and loaded them onto Galaxy Three to bring back to the base. I melted a piece of ice and did an analysis. The water is much saltier than fresh water on Earth. Desalination is necessary to make water humans could drink. The water we found is heavier than earth's water. It is not radioactive. However, there are traces of deuterium, also known as a 'heavy hydrogen isotope.' The human body contains deuterium, equivalent to about five grams of heavy water, which is harmless. Higher amounts can cause cell destruction."

"The water must go through a process to turn it from 'heavy water' to 'light water.' Desalination, distillation, or electrolysis will work well. This process is already used for nuclear reactors. Chemical treatment is an option. I set up a distillation process that works well with the desalinated water. Saltwater takes more time to boil than fresh water. It's a jury-rigged system that will collect the steam. We should have a proper system for desalination and distillation. I favor a two-step process to ensure the deuterium is removed and that we are working with "light water." Reverse osmosis and distillation are the most common ways to desalinate water. Reverse osmosis water treatment pushes water through small filters leaving the salt behind. Distillation on a large scale involves boiling water and collecting water vapor during the process," Josh said.

Marcella replies, "Better to be safe. We will check on the best systems for use on Mars and send it there on the next trip."

Raoul Sr. said, "Water is a major factor in creating a permanent base on Mars. Did you check the specimens from the asteroid?"

"Yes, I started tests. The water from the asteroid is not as salty and is closer to fresh water on earth. I'll do some more tests on it. This might be a good source of fresh water. We visited Ceres in the asteroid belt. It might have some salty underground water. The biggest problem is getting the water to Mars. Finding and transporting asteroids of frozen water to the planet is difficult. I don't think there is any liquid water out that far in the solar system, although some scientists think Ceres might have liquid water underground. Maybe Europa and Ganymede are sources of water. Otherwise, I suppose you could build huge insulated and heated tanker ships to transport water in space," Josh said. "Our best bet is to find sources of water on Mars."

Marcella and Raoul Sr. agree. "There are several options on the planet. Water will help to create oxygen for the habitats. We must think of Mars as a sort of spaceship that we make safe for humans to live on. Water is essential for survival there," Marcella said.

"That philosophy can also be used here on Earth," Josh said. "How are things going? I heard an attempt to break in here at the ranch."

"There was," Raoul Sr. said. "Arno's security system proved more than adequate to stop it and apprehend the intruders. This event has put us on alert. I believe some will go to great lengths to steal our technology."

Marcella said, "It appears the world is experiencing another psychopathic megalomanic trying to become an emperor. Speaking about this Russian dictator, someone said, "he's a little man, 5'6" tall, who thinks he's 5'7" tall. I'm sure Conrad will have thoughts about this subject."

"Yes, he has been following events from Galaxy Two on the way back here. If the Russian president and his minions are not stopped soon, Conrad believes there will be a world war, possibly the use of nuclear weapons," Josh tells them. "Hopefully, severe economic sanctions will cause the Russian people to wake up one day and find a new president. The war is one man's effort to secure his legacy. He's unwilling to admit he made a mistake, so he hurls missiles at civilians in a genocidal attempt to wipe out ethnic Ukrainians."

CHAPTER-THIRTY-SIX

....

"The sound of the ocean and the smell of salt water,"

The Mars team builds a lighting system to hang out over the canyon's edge by adapting the backup lighting for the biosphere. It's bright enough to cast a small amount of light into the canyon and serve as a beacon for the lander. A radio beacon is set up with the lights. The team plans to carry portable battery-powered lights. The lander has bright built-in headlights. Raoul Sr. asks Tamara to stay in the biosphere and coordinate activity. Video of the exploration is to be streamed back to the biosphere on the wireless network set up in the cavern. Mark, Michael, and Patricia will travel into the canyon. Roberto, Tony, and Karen will stay behind with Tamara.

Since the small lander is not pressurized, the three persons going into the canyon are wearing their EMU suits. This first trip is scheduled for up to six hours, depending on what they encounter below. Enough oxygen for ten hours is loaded on the lander. The mission is to explore, shoot video, find the reflective surface, and get some rock samples wherever possible. They plan to be cautious and not take additional risks in obtaining specimens. The lander ground penetrating radar (GPR) will scan the canyon floor to see what might be under the surface. An extra camera is installed on the front of the lander to record everything from that angle.

The lander is checked before departure and is in excellent shape. Its batteries are fully charged. The lander is loaded with all the equipment and supplies required for the trip.

Inside the biosphere, there are last-minute checks on gear. Tamara made sure all the communications equipment was working. Giving Patricia the video camera, she said, "Here are some extra flash cards for the camera. Even though you will be streaming the video back to me here in the biosphere, it is good to have a backup. There is a bag full of charged camera batteries in the lander," Tamara said. "The batteries clip onto the back of the camera. You should not have a problem changing batteries with your gloves on."

The team suited up in the airlock, went outside, and boarded the lander. Michael was designated as the driver. Patricia sat in the front seat next to him. Mark sat in the rear seat area with the auxiliary air tanks.

"Radio check," Tamara announced before they lifted off the ground.

"Loud and clear," the three explorers said in unison.

"Wish I was physically going with you," Tamara said. "But I'll be there with you virtually."

"I'm going to float up a few feet and head out. Our guidance system shows plenty of room above," Michael said. "Headlights on, here we go."

The lander lifts off the ground and floats into the cavern. Its bright headlights reveal the cavern floor's dark brown and rust-red colors as they float forward slightly faster than walking speed.

"Even with the lighter gravity, this beats walking," Mark said. They reach the canyon's edge in about twenty minutes and land there. Mark and Michael get out of the lander and turn on all the lights they rigged there. Some light is cast into the canyon. However, the primary purpose is to provide a beacon for coming back up.

"Before you head down into the canyon, do you want to take a quick look at the other side of the cavern?" Tamara asks.

"We can do that," Michael said."

Patricia turns on the video camera attached to the front of the lander. The video begins transmitting back to the biosphere.

Michael and Mark get back into the lander. Michael slowly moves the lander out over the Canyon and heads to the other side. Looking down as they float over the abyss reminds him of the Grand Canyon, where he had once flown in a helicopter down to one of the plateaus in the canyon. This canyon might not be as big or deep, but it is hard to know in the dark."

Reaching the other side, Michael flew the lander in a wide arc so they could see around the cavern. "Seems like an extension of the other side. Very high ceiling and the cavern extends much deeper into the mountain."

"Do you see any light coming in anywhere?" Tamara asks.

"Nothing we can see from here, "Mark said, speaking from the back seat.

Michael said, "We'll head back to the canyon now, with no end to the cavern in sight after five minutes. We'll need to make a special trip to explore this side of the cavern." He turns the lander and heads toward the lights over the canyon.

"You know, we need to come up with a name for this canyon," Patricia said. "Anyone have any ideas?"

"Well, Michael saw it first, so maybe we should call it the 'Michael Westin' canyon. Not only that, but it is also in a western direction inside the cavern," Mark suggests.

"We all discovered it, so let's see what it looks like and then figure out a name," Michael said, clearly not interested in having the canyon bear his name.

"We are going to head down slowly on a slight angle, so the lights illuminate things for us," Michael reports. He tries to keep the lander in the middle between the Canyon walls as they slowly descend, cameras rolling. Visibility is limited to what can be seen in the headlights.

"There are some changing colors in the walls as we go deeper," Mark said.

"Hope there isn't anything living down here," Michael said apprehensively. Everyone, including Tamara, over the communication system laughed.

"Maybe the reflection is a spaceship from an ancient Martian civilization," Tamara said.

"I think I saw that movie," Mark said.

"Communication is still good," Tamara reports. The wireless relay box we set up with the lights is a good idea. How deep are you now?"

"Looks like about 300 feet lower than the floor of the main cavern," Michael said. "Some plateau areas jut out from one side on the far wall. Some look large enough to land on."

"Any sign of the bottom?" Tamara asked.

"The lighting we set up top is not penetrating this far down. I'm turning on the GPR to see what it thinks is below us," Patricia said. "This GPR system is strong. It will show more when we get closer to the canyon's floor. I don't know how well it will penetrate the rock if that's what's down there."

Michael said, "I'm keeping us floating down slowly. According to the gauges, we've got another two hundred feet before we land on the bottom. It is dark down here. Not much light from above getting through."

Patricia looking out the side window, said, "I think we're getting close to the bottom. Let's hover here for a minute."

Michael let the lander hover in place. The headlights illuminate the space in front of them.

"It looks like we are getting close to the floor of the canyon," Michael said, looking out the front window.

"The ground is reflecting light. The surface is grayish in this light," Mark said. "I think it may be ice."

"The GPR is scanning now. Based on what it is showing, it is a deep layer of frozen water," Patricia reports.

"The temperature down here is -28 Celsius (-20 Fahrenheit)," Mark said. "We need to land and get some samples. First, let's try to measure this area."

Michael slowly turns the lander around to see the area behind them. The surface remains flat with a few rocks. They float forward while the GPR continues getting the same readings. Michael floats the lander toward the one canyon wall and then back toward the opposite wall. The canyon remains wide. The GPR readings remain constant. Having made a three-hundred-and-sixty-degree scan, they float the lander toward where they originally started.

"I'm going to find a place to land. The surface is frozen, so we are fine to touch down. Some large boulders are sitting on this stuff. It must be completely frozen deeper down. According to the GPR and what I can see, there is a soil area on this side of the frozen water. It will be safer to land there."

Michael gently lowers the lander onto a flat area until the landing skis touch the rocky surface near the frozen water. Everyone is holding their breath, waiting for something to happen, but all is quiet.

"Anyone for some ice fishing?" Mark asks.

Tamara came online. "Great job, you guys. I think you discovered a large quantity of frozen water down there. Frozen Martian fish for dinner sounds great. I won't get my hopes up, however. Patricia, are you getting any sense of depth for this ice from the GPR?"

"It is at least twenty-four feet deep. That's as far as the GPR penetrates. It is not showing any change in density. It is possible that at some point deeper down, it is liquid".

Mark opens the lander door and slowly gets out, shining his light in front of him. Patricia follows him with the camera and another light.

Mark said, "I believe we are on a frozen lake or river that is now a reservoir of frozen water from billions of years ago when this planet may have had oceans. We'll see how salty it is. Look at the walls. Some marks appear to have been made by the water when it was much higher sometime in the past. If there is or was life on Mars, it might be preserved in this ice or the walls."

Patricia went ahead with her video recording of the area around them. She tries to get some close-ups of the wall in case there are fossils. Mark brings out a laser and tools to carve some blocks of the frozen water.

Michael steps out of the lander and looks up to see if the lights are visible above them. They look like faraway stars in the night sky. He starts collecting rock samples from around the area.

Tamara came online, "It's been about two hours since you left. We planned on one hour at the bottom and then back up. Everyone okay, with that?"

"That's fine," Mark said. I'm using a laser to carve out some chunks of this ice. Should go quickly."

As Mark replies to Tamara, a slight tremor shakes the ground where he is standing. "Did anyone else feel that?"

"Yes, I felt it," Patricia and Michael said.

"Did you feel anything, Tamara?" Mark asks.

"I didn't feel anything. The seismic meter shows a minimal tremor in this area. They are not uncommon. If you feel okay, finish getting those samples and head back up. Collect some rocks, too, if you have time. That will be great," Tamara said.

"I'll get some rocks while Mark finishes," Michael answers. "I don't want another tremor to dislodge something from above. Some big rocks are sitting on the surface here."

"Mars gets these kinds of tremors all the time," Mark said. "Not too many major Mars quakes. No tectonic plates are moving like on Earth. It is a release of energy from the planet's interior. They have recently been documented at 4.3 and lasting for as long as an hour. At this depth, we get to feel them more strongly and quickly. It doesn't look like anything major has hit this canyon for a long time. If there is another tremor, it may be time to go."

"I'd like to take a ride up and down this canyon to see how far this ice goes and also to see what else is here," Michael said. "Once we've lifted off the ground, we might be able to explore a little more if there isn't another tremor."

"That's a good idea Tamara said. "What kind of radiation are you getting down there?"

Patricia answered, "less than above in the cavern. I'm going to set up a couple of flags and a beacon, so we know where we landed for next time."

"Thanks," Tamara said.

Twenty minutes later, Mark said, "I've got several chunks of this ice. We can pack up."

The samples are stowed in containers and placed in the lander's storage compartment. Patricia records a good amount of video footage of the canyon and clips of Mark and Michael picking up samples. Once everyone is aboard the lander, they lift off and head further along the frozen river in the canyon for about ten minutes. This wide trench appears to go much further into the mountain. Michael turns the lander around and heads in the opposite direction, back toward where they first landed. He then flew ten minutes beyond where they first landed to collect samples. The canyon stays wide, and the river of frozen water remains the same.

"Okay, we're heading back up," Michael said as he turned the ship around again.

The lander floats upward toward the lights at the top of the canyon. On the way up, the overhead light illuminates more of the walls. Patricia records a video of several plateaus jutting out from the sides of the canyon. She tries to get shots of the wall colors and what might be water level marks over the millennia.

"If Mars ever had surface water and a thicker atmosphere, there must have been some major event that changed things billions of years ago," she thought. "Something shut down the magnetic field." The vehicle reached the canyon's top, moved onto the cavern floor, and landed. The crew gets out, turns off the lighting then heads back to the biosphere.

There is mutual satisfaction with the outcome of the expedition into the canyon. Mark is anxious to analyze the ice specimens. This is water billions of years old, deep frozen with no expiration date. If there are Martian bacteria in the water, it might signify that there had once been life on Mars. Once they are back in the biosphere, he will store the ice in the deep freeze storage lockers attached to the biosphere.

Tamara sends a secure message back to the ground control center on earth. "Good news, we discovered what appears to be a huge amount of frozen water at the bottom of the canyon. The team is on their way back to the biosphere."

"That's great news," Marcella replies.! "Scientists have speculated on the water below the surface of Mars. No one has ever located it, for sure. This water is much deeper than anyone might have imagined."

On Earth, Josh finishes his twenty-four-hour quarantine feeling fine. He checks out health-wise, as does everyone on the second trip to Mars. Josh is concerned about Conrad and Julia. He is happy to find out they are as healthy as ever. Before heading home, Adrienne and Josh meet with Marcella in the secure conference room.

Marcella has just finished reading Tamara's message about the water. "I have some great news from Tamara. The Mars team discovered a huge reservoir of ice at the bottom of the canyon in the cavern. It appears to be a frozen river. They will test samples as soon as the team returns to the biosphere. They discovered water," Marcella said enthusiastically.

"Wow, that's spectacular news," Josh said. This might change the potential enough to make the Mars base habitable! Interesting, it's at the bottom of a canyon in a cavern. I read an article about the Valles Marineris canyons near the equator. They think there might be water in those canyons. The team sent the Mars lander there and confirmed that possibility after we left."

"I don't think we want to disseminate this discovery to the public for a while," Adrienne said.

"Not right now. We have much thinking to do about utilizing this resource," Marcella said. "At some point, we need to share this information with NASA and the scientific community. After we confirm the test results, I'll set up a company meeting in the next few days. They did quite a bit of exploring. Tamara will be sending a video."

"I brought back specimens from the asteroids and Mars for NASA scientists. I'm sure they will be anxious to analyze them," Josh said. "Mark has enough equipment at the base to start work on the ice samples from the canyon. The water has been frozen for billions of years away from the surface. It might answer whether there was ever any life on Mars. We may need to hire more scientists to work with us there on Mars."

Marcella agrees.

"We will be releasing news about the successful second trip to Mars and the team living and working there," Adrienne said. Paul and his team are editing video press releases showing the Mars trips and some team activities on Mars and in the asteroid belt. People are fascinated by the group on Mars and how they survive. These videos are mini-documentaries. They are trendy, make the news internationally, and are widespread on Tic Tock and other streaming services. We have captured the imagination of the world. We have not released anything about the canyon or the team exploring there."

"Ultimately, we need to release information about the canyon and the discovery of water," Marcella said. It will soon become evident by our actions there that we have assets we are not talking about."

"A good supply of water will help construction efforts. With water, blocks of concrete using regolith sand can be produced quickly," Josh said. "You're correct in assuming a building boom will raise questions about how it is being accomplished."

Raoul Sr. and Conrad join the others. "The discovery of this underground ice reservoir is a game changer. Other water deposits may be buried in the mountain ranges around the planet. The discovery will encourage more exploration and attempts to set up settlements or bases. Once again, we face sharing information and technology," Raoul Sr. said.

Conrad sounds more serious than usual when he states, "I venture that this is equivalent to the discovery of oil or gold in the past on earth. We all know what happened with the gold rush and the oil boom. Once this becomes public, people will get to Mars in any way possible to find the water! During the California gold rush, prospectors boarded schooners and other sailing ships around Cape Horn, a dangerous passage from the Atlantic to the Pacific Ocean and California. I suggest we take our time sharing this discovery with the world."

Josh is thoughtful, "In the words of Sara Vial, "I am the albatross that waits for you at the end of the world. I am the forgotten souls of dead mariners who passed Cape Horn from all the oceans of the earth."

"Getting to Mars is even more difficult than sailing around Cape Horn, which in many ways is good news. Once you arrive on Mars, you must have a place to live. You also can't easily start digging into the mountains or drilling holes. I suppose you can fly over the surface with powerful GPR and try to find the frozen ponds, but that would require the kind of transport only we possess."

Raoul Sr. replies, "bringing more pressure on us to share the drive system."

Marcella said, "For the time being, I suggest we proceed to build the base. We will not talk about the discovery of the ice."

Raoul Sr. said, "Once we analyze the water, we need to design a refining system and use it responsibly. No waste, continuous recycling of what we use."

"I've been working on a two-step refining process based on salty water with possible deuterium isotopes as we found in the surface ice. This ice may not be "heavy" since it has spent a long-time deep underground," said Josh. "We can transport equipment for desalinization and distillation on the next trip. Once we have a better idea of what the chemical composition of this water is, we can make some decisions. The location is at the bottom of a canyon and frozen. There's a lot to think about. We will be dealing with Martian ecology. How do we melt it and transport it?"

"We can talk more about this during our meeting," Marcella said. "I'm sure you want to go home and see your children and get reacclimated to being back on earth."

"Looking forward to it," Josh said. "I think Conrad and Julia are looking forward to some earth time too."

Conrad nodded affirmatively, "It was a wonderful experience going to Mars. Julia and I did not go onto the surface but being there is amazing. Maybe next time," Conrad said, smiling.

A car is waiting to take Josh and Adrienne back to their condo. Reporters waiting at the launch center cannot see through the tinted windows of the cars that frequently come and go from the property since there are often TV reporters and satellite trucks around the entrance. Arno arranges for empty vehicles to arrive and depart as a diversion. This is also a security measure since the break-in.

Adrienne and Josh sit closely in the back seat of the vehicle. They are both happy to touch and be together.

"Traveling to Mars is unlike a business trip to another city," Josh said. "I imagine it is equivalent to the experience of those mariners who sailed across the Atlantic Ocean between Europe and the newly discovered continent centuries ago. Spending time listening to Conrad on the trip made me think of the mythical 'Quest for the Golden Fleece' and Jason and the Argonauts.' I'll tell you more about that later."

"After twenty-four hours of being on earth, I feel like I still have my "sea legs" or, more accurately, "space legs." I have the feeling of traveling in space, almost expecting to see stars out the window," Josh said. "I'm happy to be with you back on earth."

Adrienne said, "I'm glad you're back safe. To use your analogy, I believe the children and I had similar feelings to the wives and children with husbands and fathers away at sea for months facing unknown dangers."

"In case you haven't heard," Adrienne said after a while, "Arno has a bodyguard watching the condo, and we have a driver to take the children to school. Morgan thinks it's cool. Lauren is a little embarrassed. Her classmates asked her if we were rich?"

"What did she tell them?"

"At a loss for an explanation, Lauren said, "she didn't know. Maybe it was because I was on TV a lot."

"That's a good excuse. The break-in is real. You have high exposure as the spokesperson for the International Space Exploration Group. I've tried to keep a low profile. No interviews. We should be careful. Some serious players are out there looking to score some information. I'll think of something to tell the kids."

Whispering to Josh, "Arno said Simone knows something about the break-in attempt."

"Yeah, he warned me to be careful what I tell George," Josh replies. "I trust George, but he could be manipulated or in danger himself. I told him we could get together when I got back from Mars. We'll see if he gets in touch."

"Will you meet with him?"

"Maybe for a run if Arno thinks it's okay. I'm curious to see what George wants to talk about. Last time he wanted us to have lunch with himself and Simone. I declined for several reasons. I will be suspicious if I get a call that they will be at the beach or will I be in Orlando soon."

"Did you meditate and do your Tai Chi on the spaceship?"

"Yes, I did both things every day. I taught a few others some basic Tai Chi exercises. Conrad and Julia are very practiced and good at Tai Chi. They found time to help us smooth out our moves. As I mentioned, I'll tell you some news about Conrad and Julia later. "

The driver waits until they are back inside the condo before leaving. Josh goes out on the balcony to breathe in the ocean air. He is soon joined by Adrienne, who brings two glasses of wine with her.

"You don't get the ocean's sound and saltwater smell on Mars. Earth is home," Josh said. "We evolved from the sea, they say."

Adrienne passed Josh a glass of wine. "Here's to your safe return to Earth and me. The children won't be home from school for a few hours."

"We have some time to ourselves," Josh said, giving Adrienne a kiss and a long hug.

....

CHAPTER THIRTY-SEVEN

"A blue marble."

Weeks have passed since the break-in attempt at Arroyo Aerospace and the ranch house. Arno has not stopped investigating the incident. His contacts at the CIA tell him they believe it was a foreign operation and are looking into it. He has yet to be able to reach Simone Greely. The Brevard Sheriff's department shared the information and names of the men who participated in the incident. Using their fingerprints and photographs taken when they were arrested, Arno finds information about each of them. Four of the men are not U.S. citizens. Two are Columbian mercenaries. One of the Colombians has a green card. It is his mobile phone that Arno recovered and broke into. Two of the men are Russians in the country on expired visitor visas. They all work for a company that provides "security forces for hire," otherwise known as mercenaries. The lawyer for the group obtained a three-month extension for their hearing. Arno cannot find any of the defendants at the addresses they gave the Brevard Sheriff's Department.

Josh receives a call from George a week after returning from Mars. They chat for a while. Thinking about what Arno told him, Josh decides to record the call.

"Did you really go to Mars?" George asks.

"Yes, I did. It's an amazing experience."

George said, "I was out running around the lake this past Sunday. Do you know how you hear snippets of people talking on mobile phones or some guy on a bicycle listening to a right-wing radio station? I noticed these three women ahead of me leisurely strolling along, talking, and laughing. As I get closer and prepare to go around them, one of the women drops back a little and starts ranting as she walks. First, she's on about 'fake news.' Then she starts talking about how everything is fake. 'In this advanced society, they (whomever they are) can conjure up any reality they want, and ordinary people won't know the difference.' So, she doesn't believe anything. Nothing is real. Everything is fake. As I passed by her, I almost asked, 'am I real passing you right now' or am I an illusion, a hallucination conjured up by whatever drugs you're on? Anyway, many people don't believe The International Space Exploration Group flies to Mars. They think it is a science fiction movie."

Josh laughs, "Maybe I'm hallucinating too. As far as I can tell, it is real. I was going to bring back some Mars rocks for friends, but the rocks carry a lot of radiation. There is so much propaganda, misinformation, and political BS out there that you can't blame people for being confused. And that's what certain politicians and the one precentors want. Confused people lose the ability to reason based on facts because they no longer know what is factual. They throw up their arms and surrender. But they need someone to blame for their loss of reality."

"It doesn't help when there are all these real 'fake news" outlets putting out misinformation."

"Yeah, they make people think all the news is questionable."

"I watched Adrienne's press conference and the video of the team on Mars. It's amazing. At the same time, we still have these companies sending people up in rockets for joy rides in the upper atmosphere," George said.

"Expensive joy rides."

"We're just coming to terms with the global pandemic, and now we have war in Europe. A dictator is trying to kill democracy. Sometimes I think the bad guys are taking over much of the world," George said.

"After a pause, George said, I miss our conversations. I was thinking of heading to the beach this weekend. If you're around, we can run."

"Sure, I'll be here. I'm taking a few days off. Are you bringing Simone?"

"I'm on my own right now. She said she would be gone for a month on some mission. I'm not sure when she'll show up."

"Okay, let me know if you make it over here."

Later, Josh calls Arno on a secure line and informs him about the call from George. Arno thinks it sounds innocent enough. He said to let him know if George does show up over the weekend.

Through his contacts at the CIA, Arno is able to find out that Simone is still on the government payroll. She appears to be still working in the Chinese Intelligence division. She is listed as being on assignment. Everything else is classified with access only by the agency director. Why did one of the mercenaries' phones have a call to Simone's phone number? Arno speculated that maybe her involvement was not a company operation. From his experience, Arno knows that things in that world are often layered in additional layers of intrigue. One operation can be a cover for something else on top of some other mission.

Two days later, Josh let Arno know that George had come to the beach for the weekend and that they were set to do a run Saturday morning. Arno tells him to go on the run. They will have some people cover the route. If possible, he will have a surveillance crew get audio and video using one of Arroyo Aerospace's new stealth drones. They are small, quiet, and unable to be detected. This will be a test run for the new device.

Josh and George meet behind Ron Jon's surf shop in Cocoa Beach. They head North up the beach toward the jetty.

"Good to see you," Josh said as they jogged toward the ocean.

"It's been a while," George said.

"I haven't been able to run outside, just the treadmill on the ship."

"No beaches on Mars?"

"Nope, just a lot of radiation-soaked sand and rocks. Radioactive regolith for soil. It's nothing like earth. The only cool thing is, it's only about one-third the gravity, so jogging in a space suit is possible."

"Hey, I got on the list for a ride up to the space hotel when it opens. Adrienne called me and told me she had set it up. Thanks, I'm looking forward to this a lot."

Josh kept his promise to George to get his name on the list for a Galaxy One ride into orbit. Adrienne got him on that list. Arno checked out all the prospective space tourists and noticed George's name. Since the space hotel will open soon, he suggests that Adrienne offer George and a guest a ride to the space station. Josh is unaware of this since he was in space then.

"Great," Josh said. It will be a fantastic experience, I'm sure. It should be even more interesting than the ride up into orbit. How long will you be up there?"

The stealth drone floated above and led them at a comfortable distance. The faces are clear, audio and video are good. Using a remotely controlled digital camera lens on all sides, the stealth drone scans 360 degrees of the beach for suspicious activity. Nothing unusual appears.

"Three days at the space hotel. I read that the hotel has a spa and two different restaurants. I'm looking forward to the views of Earth and beyond. The hotel plans to have an observatory with a good telescope for viewing. Not sure if the observatory will be open when I go."

"You're going by yourself?"

"I've got a reservation for two. I don't know if Simone wants to come. She has been traveling a lot, and I don't get to see her as much. Everything she does is secret."

"I don't see how she will want to miss this opportunity."

"We'll see. I'll talk to her this weekend. Oops, I shouldn't have said that. She said not to tell anyone she was there. She arrived unexpectedly on Thursday."

"Don't worry. I won't tell anyone," Josh whispered as he raised his hand in front of his mouth, "but that doesn't mean no one will find out."

George glanced at him sideways for a moment.

"We have a lot of security around us these days," Josh said.

In a minute, their conversation turns to other subjects.

George said, "I'm sure you are vaccinated as I am."

Josh nodded affirmatively. "Got a booster too."

George continues, "I thought plagues were a thing of the past. Something we read and study about historically. Yet here we are during a never-ending worldwide pandemic. Our lives are changing forever. At the same time, you're flying to Mars. People are ignoring all the advances in science and dying. Around a million people are dead in the U.S. alone. Soon it will be 2023, and people are not getting vaccinated. Not because of medical issues but for political reasons. Medicine has become political?"

Josh could tell when George was on a rant, so he replied briefly. "Hard to believe. It's like humanity is going back to the Middle Ages."

"I have a theory that this plague is created by the indifference of a certain past president and his administration. Not to mention all the enablers of that madman. This whole cycle we're in started with 911. Attacked, the U.S. and part of the world rushed into hyper-paranoia. People in this country gave up the laisser-faire lifestyle we always had. I was young, but remember when you went to the airport with friends or family to see them off at the gate? We waved to them as the plane taxied away. When they return, we are there at the gate to meet them. We meet visiting friends or relatives at the gate. Now we have the restrictions imposed on flying creeping into the rest of our lives. Of course, vaccines and masks are necessary to fight the pandemic, but to many people, it is another restriction of what they believe is their freedom. I don't think they know what freedom is."

"Underlying it all is 'fear. You make a good point. The paranoia since 911 is all about fear. Since the attackers are not American, all foreigners are suspects. And the fear is used to manipulate people."

"People consumed by fear will latch on to anything that they think will protect them somehow. Unfortunately, it is often some snake oil salesman proclaiming to be the only one who can save them."

"There's a larger than normal slide toward authoritarianism, which seems contradictory for people who think they are losing their freedom. They think this political shift will only be for those they blame for their real or imagined losses. It's a trap many previous generations have fallen into. There has always been a fringe element in this country. But lately, all the conspiracy and fear is magnified by social media." Josh said.

Reaching the jetty, they reverse course and head back toward where they began the run.

"I wonder if there is any hope for this planet," George said after a few minutes of silence. "Are we doomed to have wars and kill each other repeatedly?"

"When you're out in space and look at Earth, you realize how small and fragile the planet is in this unimaginably huge universe. 'A blue marble.' If humanity can come to terms with the notion that the planet's resources are finite, they might understand why we must stop being indifferent to self-destructive acts; begin to conserve and restore our environment."

"Have you thought about living in space, away from all the conflict on this planet? I watched the documentary that Paul Arroyo did for the International Space Exploration Group. It shows how they are working on a base and settlement on Mars. Will people live there?"

"Yes. It is a big undertaking and experimental in every way. Mars is not a hospitable environment. Humans can't walk around on the surface without space suits, and some scientists claim humans can't stay on Mars for more than a couple of years because of the radiation. Not to mention what the low gravity does to your body. We'll have to wait and see what develops. Mars is hostile to life as we know it."

When the run is finished, Josh agrees that, if possible, he will meet George at the space station hotel when George goes there.

Arno has the drone follow George back to where he is staying. Listening to the conversation, Arno isn't surprised to find out Simone is there. He debates whether to contact her under these circumstances. She is still working for the company; she may have immunity from anything to do with the attempted break-in. He can keep tabs on her more readily if she thinks she's safe. "Maybe the place to meet her will be on the space station. She is sure to go when George invites her," Arno speculates, "It will not surprise me if she has his phone bugged."

That evening Arno drives to Orlando to have dinner with his friend Debbie Newhouse. He is looking forward to seeing her. She is still working for the FBI and understands how consuming Arno's job is now. Both their schedules are often difficult to coordinate. They try to spend as much time together as they can spare from their work. Most of the time, they avoid talking about their respective jobs. This time Debbie believes she has information that is important for Arno to have immediately.

They meet at Debbie's apartment. Before leaving, Debbie said, "I thought you should know the FBI is investigating the attempted break-in at Arroyo Aerospace. I'm not on the case, but it came to our office."

"I filed a report with them after it happened. I didn't hear anything back."

"You may hear from them soon. They've assigned agents to keep tabs on the ranch and key people at Arroyo Aerospace. They have sources that suspect there may be some kidnap or another break-in plot by the Russians. One of their sources is the CIA," Debbie said.

"Interesting, the Arroyos turned down the Russians several times regarding visits to the terminal and even the tourist ride to earth orbit. The Russians have tried to hack our systems many hundreds of times. Now with all the sanctions over their invasion of Ukraine, they can't even get into the country. "

"The Arroyos do not like the Russian president. Marcella told the Russians to stop trying to hack their systems, and then maybe they could talk. Of course, the Russians deny any connection to the hacking. 'All the hackers live there. We don't know what they do.' Anyway, thanks for letting me know. I think I know who the CIA source might be. I hope to speak to her soon."

"Okay, enough shop talk," Debbie said. I made a reservation at a restaurant on City Walk. I'll drive."

"Great, and thanks for driving," Arno replies. I know it's not Emeril's, which was one of my favorite places. Emeril closed it a while back. Great calamari."

"I think you'll like this place. It will be a surprise."

While Debbie is driving, Arno runs his last conversation with Simone over in his mind. Maybe she did try to warn him about the break-in.

CHAPTER THIRTY-EIGHT

"Knowing balance is called sustainable. Knowing sustainability is called clarity. Benefitting from life is called auspice. Strength comes from the heart."

Galaxy Two and Galaxy Three make the third trip to Mars in December 2022. Travel time is shorter since Mars is closer to Earth. Galaxy Four, primarily a cargo ship, is ready to make the journey if required. Galaxy Four is built to tow modules that can store cargo for transportation in space. Modules with supplies are sent into orbit. They can be attached and moved by Galaxy Four to Mars or other destinations. Sam Arroyo joins this third mission to Mars to oversee various construction projects. He plans to stay until the next ship comes to Mars from Earth. Tamara and the six astronauts are returning to Earth with the third expedition ships. The consensus of ISEG and medical consultants is that the seven-member team must return to Earth. All team members appear to be healthy. However, since humans have never lived on another planet for this amount of time (or anytime at all), it is crucial to check on long-term effects and the overall impact on their health.

Tamara and the other team members who stayed on Mars are in excellent spirits. They have worked on various projects in the cavern and on the surface for six months. They collect a great deal of information and data that can be useful in the future. They build secure facilities for the larger contingent of astronauts and workers to live safely on the planet. An essential part of the third mission is to do more construction in the cavern and to utilize the water resources in the canyon.

Tamara reports that "preliminary ice tests find it briny salt water. Not as much salt in the earth's oceans. More like some briny bays and marsh areas adjacent to the sea. The water could have supported life in the past, but no traces of life or bacteria are found in the ice. Mineral content is similar, not the same, as salt water on earth. The water is to be desalinated and distilled before human consumption. Desalinated only water will be used for building projects and agriculture. "

"Human and other waste continues to be processed to reclaim water that may be used in building and agriculture. Greenhouses are now planned for the surface of the planet. The greenhouses need oxygen, like biosphere habitats. Soil that plants will grow in needs to be created. Hydroponic farming is a possibility. Nothing grows in the Martian regolith since it has no organic matter. There are possible ways to treat and remove the perchlorates in the Martian soil, then mix it with compose to create usable soil. Pulverized volcanic rock mixed with organic matter might be something with which to create soil for growing".

"Extracted ice from the canyon is melted and pumped to the cavern floor level in insulated pipes. Water is then desalinated. Some water will be desalinated and distilled. Processing facilities are built in the cavern near the canyon. We understand that equipment for this purpose is being procured and is part of the third expedition to Mars cargo. "

Stadium lighting fixtures with specially designed solar LED lights that can shift color balance throughout the day are ready. These dawn-to-dusk lamps are to be used throughout the cavern. Bright lights will also be mounted on both sides of the inside edges of the rift to light the canyon below. More lights will be installed in work areas on the canyon floor next to the frozen river. The idea is to create enough light to illuminate regions of the canyon, especially where the ice-melting facilities are built.

Raoul Sr. said generators, solar panels, wind turbines, and RPS units are being transported on Galaxy Three. Additional components for the wind and solar farm, manufactured on Earth, will be shipped to Mars on one of the Galaxy ships when available. In the future, specific equipment will be manufactured on Mars. Research shows that necessary metals can be extracted from deposits in the canyon and other locations on the planet. Metals may also be mined in the asteroid belt. The goal is increased self-sufficiency for the Mars colony."

Sam reports that "the area on the other side of the canyon is a large open space that extends slightly uphill toward the other side of the mountain. An opening has been found on the far side of the mountain. There appear to be no other entrances or cracks in the mountain. A large landing bay area with an airlock is planned to take advantage of this second opening. This will effectively seal off the cavern. The bay will be large enough to allow Galaxy Three or other ships to land and unload cargo. Inside the cavern, a bridge across the canyon is under construction."

"Expedition three is conducting tests for drafts and air currents inside the cavern. No movement of the atmosphere is detected beyond the two known entrances. Initially, temperatures in the cavern are about the same as outside. The interior has warmed up since the first entrance was sealed and the biosphere built. Sealing up the entrance on the far side of the mountain will further limit exterior air from entering the cavern. "

Circulating the interior atmosphere is required based on the amount of human activity in the cavern, including water processing, manufacturing, lighting, and sealed entrances. CO2 will be scrubbed out and exhausted to the surface."

Sam came up with the idea that instead of only circulating the atmosphere, why not scrub and condition it to create a breathable atmosphere?

"The cavern can have air conditioning, heating, and possibly breathable air. With an abundant water supply, a terraforming project inside the cavern might be possible." Requests for additional supplies to facilitate this process are requested from the earth.

"It is estimated that the water supply in the canyon is huge. However, water on Mars cannot be inexhaustible. There is nothing on the planet that can replenish reserves. Conservation of the resource is a priority. All water used is recycled if possible. Solid and liquid waste processed and used appropriately," Sam explains.

Habitat construction on the surface is vital to the base. Sam has plans for several buildings and resources. Workers wear EMU suits on the surface. They spend limited time outside in specially built huts with extra shielding to limit radiation exposure. Robotic devices used to do various parts of the construction are controlled from the huts.

Sites for the solar and wind farms are selected. Solar arrays need to have dust removed regularly. These custom-made solar panels rotate to follow the sun. They can tilt over at night to discard dust. Each panel is made to fold into a cabinet for complete protection.

When the second expedition team returns to Earth in early 2023, they undergo extensive tests. Examiners find "the seven-member team is generally healthy." Tamara finds herself in a weakened state upon returning to earth. She first notices mild fatigue on returning to Earth aboard Galaxy Two. She became exhausted after exercising in the artificial earth gravity on the ship. NASA astronauts with more training for living in low or no-gravity situations feel less fatigued than Tamara. The astronauts are in excellent shape and do vigorous workouts while on Mars. Tests for muscle tone and strength find that "all members of the team who stayed on Mars for six months lost some muscle strength and mass. Some more than others. There is no bone deterioration. Cardiac fitness levels are below where they were before going to Mars. Internal organs are healthy."

Tamara and the others go into a rehabilitation program to restore their bodies as much as possible. The astronauts begin exercise programs to help them regain tone and muscle strength. Rehabilitation is scheduled for six months. Team members are to be examined again at that time.

Doctors agree that six months on Mars with vigorous exercise may prevent long-term damage. New mandatory exercise regimens for all residents staying on the planet for more than two weeks are ordered. Medical professionals and experts in physical fitness develop special equipment and exercise routines. Space Medicine and Fitness became an essential field of medicine for future dwellers and explorers in space.

Heath information from all three Mars expeditions is compared. The study finds that "expedition members who live on the ships with artificial earth gravity do not suffer fatigue or physical deterioration. Only those individuals who live on the planet have problems." Mars data is compared with data from the Earth Terminal Station, astronauts doing construction in space, and those working at the L5 (Lagrange point) space factory. All these locations have artificial gravity close to natural gravity on Earth. "No deterioration of overall health is found on these sites when exercise routines are followed. "

To ensure the health of the third expedition members and Mars residents in the future, the International Space Exploration Group works with space medicine doctors and physical fitness professionals to immediately take steps to ensure wellness for people living on Mars.

A new biosphere, workout facility, and spa are designed for the cavern. Raoul Sr. and Marcella create an artificial earth gravity device for the facility. The hotel will allow residents to work out in earth gravity. All the equipment and supplies required for construction are loaded on Galaxy Four and other requested supplies. Galaxy Four is sent to Mars with the new supplies before the next scheduled expedition date. Current residents on Mars are informed of the situation. They begin vigorous exercise programs with available equipment and improvised procedures. Galaxy Four will stay on Mars before returning to Earth to give residents the use of the ship's earth gravity gym facilities while the new spa facility is built in the cavern. Sam Arroyo decides to return to Earth with Galaxy Four.

CHAPTER THIRTY-NINE

A visit from the Chinese.

Adrienne's press release began, "Two hundred ninety miles above the planet, the initial phase of the international Earth Terminal Station (ETS) is nearing completion. The hotel is in place and operational. The office complex, retail shopping area, passenger, cargo docking bays, and a terminal area for passengers are also finished. It is mid-2024."

"One airline company is planning to bring passengers to the station in a capsule that will also return them to Earth. Inroads in safer rocket technology are being developed including fusion propulsion engines. A rocket company has designed a high altitude, hypersonic space plane that can make the round trip to the terminal from earth. It can launch and land from the ground like a commercial jet liner. Passenger capacity is limited. The International Space Exploration Group (ISEG) offers scheduled flights to the station and is booked five years in advance. "

"One airline company plans to bring passengers to the station in a capsule that will also return them to Earth. Inroads in safer rocket technology are being developed, including fusion propulsion engines. A rocket company has designed a high-altitude, hypersonic space plane that can make the round trip to the terminal from the earth. It can launch and land from the ground like a commercial jetliner. Passenger capacity is limited. The International Space Exploration Group (ISEG) offers scheduled flights to the station and is booked five years in advance. "

When first announced, critics predicted that the International Earth Terminal Station would take ten years to be built and habitable. The consortium built the first phase in fourteen months. ISEG Galaxy spaceships transport workers, supplies, equipment, and materials. Ramurt's rocket company lifts heavy equipment and materials with their latest rockets. Another rocket company flew robotic equipment to orbit using a reusable space shuttle-type ship. Space X joined the consortium and lifted additional resources. Construction equipment is quickly assembled in space. There is a constant flow of prefabricated sections manufactured on earth flown up and assembled in space. Two crews of construction workers rotate from the planet, alternately working for seven days living aboard an ISEG module docked there. Modules have all the amenities of a Galaxy-type ship but are built to go into orbit and become part of the terminal. Once each terminal section is constructed and pressurized, the module becomes part of the structure. The propulsion drive that lifts the module is returned to Earth for reuse.

The Earth Terminal Station (ETS) includes large airlocks for docking and receiving passengers and cargo. The one hundred-twenty-room space hotel occupies sixty-thousand square feet. It cost about one hundred million dollars to build and furnish. Hotel furnishings and equipment are transported to the station using Galaxy ships. This includes food service and other regular hotel supplies. The operator of the space hotel conducts a recruitment drive for staff to work at the hotel. There is a flood of applicants wishing to work at the space hotel. The entire terminal is built to withstand radiation the same way the Galaxy ships are built. Working on the station poses a manageable health risk.

Near the space hotel, private living accommodations are constructed for station workers. Studio apartments and one and two-bedroom units became available for long-term or short-term rental. There is a spa and exercise center in the complex. Arroyo Aerospace and the International Space Exploration Group lease a block of units for corporate use from the consortium.

The second tier of the terminal with docking stations is under development. NASA plans to have a base in the second tier. Additional space can be built in levels below the original two-tier terminal. A central tube connects the rotating wheel-like decks. The entire station has artificial gravity caused by the centrifugal rotation of the station and artificial gravity technology. Above the top tier is an array of solar panels that looks like a multi-blade fan spread out and rotating to face the sun. Energy is generated, used, and stored. Galaxy cargo ships from earth bring up necessary supplies to keep terminal life support functions. Permanent resources for life support are planned so that the terminal will exist like an orbiting spaceship.

Arroyo Aerospace and International Space Exploration Group Inc are the primary tenants of the office complex. The International Earth Terminal Station consortium also has administrative offices there. The other partners plan to have offices in the complex as well. Office and lab space is included for scientific research institutions.

George Gallagher and his guest Simone Greeley visit the space hotel after several delays because of construction priorities. They arrive via the new Galaxy 6-ETS, an upgraded, more extensive version of the original Galaxy One. Galaxy 6-ETS is specially designed for travel from anywhere in the world to the Earth Terminal Station. It can carry up to eighty passengers and cargo. Galaxy 6-ETS has its landing dock at the terminal.

Arno is there when George and Simone arrive. He meets them as they come through security at the airlock. Simone and Arno arrange to meet for lunch. George doesn't seem to mind. He is so overwhelmed by being in outer space that he does not pay much attention to anything else. The trip in Galaxy 6-ETS up to the terminal is an experience he will not soon forget. He plans to see as much of the terminal as possible.

Four additional landing docks accommodate rocket spaceships, space planes, and conventional rocket-propelled transportation. Capsules are handled the same way they are on the International Space Station. There is a shuttle to take rockets that cannot dock directly at the terminal. No rocket fuel of any kind is stored on the space station. First, it is considered too dangerous. Second, there are many kinds of rocket fuels being used. There is no room on the station for storage.

The combination of technical expertise and entrepreneurial investors in the consortium proved successful. New investors scramble to bid on the subsequent phases. The Arroyo Aerospace and ISEG strategy of working with other corporations insulates them from government interference and criticism for keeping their technology proprietary. However, it has not stopped certain countries and interest groups from trying to steal or gain access to technology. Military sources in the U.S. continue to lobby congress to build a spaceship for the United States Space Force.

Conrad reports, "Political conditions in the U.S. are still volatile, even after the Democrats, with massive turnouts of voters, manage to hold on to the Senate and keep the margin close in the House in 2022. Many state legislators try to overturn elections unsuccessfully. It is unclear how the presidential election in 2024 will turn out. We must be prepared for a right-wing administration to gain power. One positive note is that the previous (2016-2020) president cannot be a serious candidate due to criminal proceedings against him for plotting to overthrow the 2020 presidential election. He also faces felony charges and has been found guilty of fraud and sedition. He has declared he will run for president in 2024 and continues fund-raising as if he can make some miraculous comeback. He is collecting money on the pretense that he is running for president or still trying to overturn a nonexistent fraudulent election. He may run independently if he doesn't get the Republican nomination. His much touted "base," like the remnants of the once feared "tea bag party, are losing interest in the disgraced ex-president."

Since returning to earth, Conrad found world affairs chaotic. He said, "Russia's invasion of Ukraine in early 2022 put the world on the brink of a third world war. It is likely that the Russian president will be ultimately forced to withdraw Russian troops from Ukraine even though he held on to parts of the country. His future hold in Russia is becoming dubious. The Russian economy and worldwide status are in ruins. The Russian president has sent hundreds of missiles to bomb civilian targets in Ukraine. The President of the United States worked with NATO organizing a total of 130 countries around the world to oppose the invasion of Ukraine. Russian military setbacks and economic isolation, coupled with the heroic resistance of the Ukrainian people, appear to have stopped the annexation of the country. Because of the Russian president's folly, Russia has lost creditability. The global slide away from democracy the Russian president created and backed is stalled. After Russia makes nuclear threats, China appears to be moving away from supporting the Russian dictator."

"Perhaps as a veiled threat against those exploring outer space and frustrated by not having a real presence, the Russians use hypersonic missiles to destroy their old non-functioning satellites. This causes more space debris. NASA's International Space Station is constantly being hit with space debris and is not considered safe. NASA and other participants plan to abandon it. The Chinese orbiting space station is functional but has been hit twice by space junk. The Chinese are considering vacating it after the last hit. They also have registered complaints about satellites being put into orbit close to the station."

It occurs to Conrad that another world war is in the making. "The same countries continue to threaten military action for various reasons." Conrad tries not to overreact to the constant propaganda and threats from various places. However, he believes that "this type of brinkmanship can escalate into a conflict that will spread. Social media continues to spread misinformation and propaganda." He is consoled by the fact that the space beyond earth's atmosphere is primarily neutral at this time.

Arroyo Aerospace continues building spaceships and developing resources in Florida. For two reasons, one practical and the other precautionary, they develop and launch special space modules into earth orbit. These modules connect in space to form an orbiting manufacturing facility. This space factory begins building new additions to the Earth Terminal Station. These modules become a space factory orbiting earth near the International Earth Terminal Station. The space factory is moved from earth orbit to another location after the main construction work is finished on the Earth Terminal Station. The space factory is parked at Lagrange point L5.

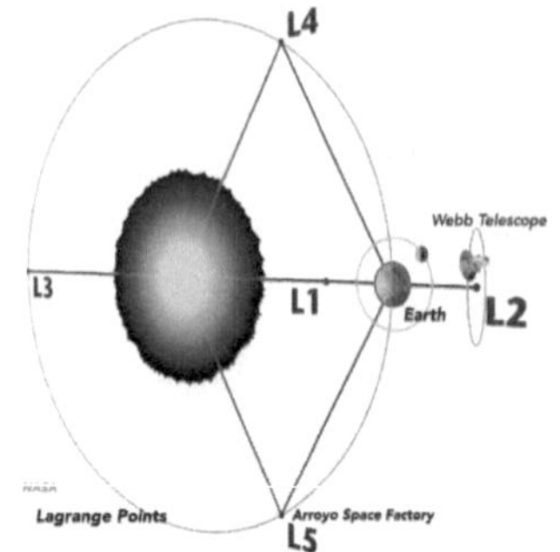

Raoul Jr. explains, "an object parked at this Lagrange point stays in a stable orbit around the Lagrange point with little degradation. If the factory modules at L5 start to move, they pick up speed. This is when the Coriolis effect comes into play. The same type of force causes hurricanes to rotate on the earth. This keeps a structure at these Lagrange points in a stable orbit around the Lagrange point. Gravity is balanced here. There is little need for constant physical adjustment of the factory satellite to keep it from moving toward the sun. The gravity drives in the modules are seldom needed to maintain orbit."

Arroyo Aerospace enters negotiations with New Zealand regarding building facilities in that country. Publicly they talk about launch sites in the southern hemisphere. There are other considerations. In addition to establishing a corporate presence in New Zealand for future expansion, there is the possibility of a complete relocation. In recent months Costa Rica granted Arroyo Aerospace corporate status in the country, and some business is being conducted from the rancho on the Nicoya peninsula. The family visits there often.

Josh, Adrienne, and the children join Conrad and Julia at the rancho in Costa Rica for a few days' respites. The weather is beautiful, and there is no worry about security. A small cottage-style building next to the hangar and runway become the corporate headquarters for Arroyo Aerospace and ISEG in Costa Rica. Carlos upgrades the communications and internet resources to connect with satellite and space links. Relays at the Earth Terminal Station allow ISEG to privately tap into the entire network, including Mars and L5, from Costa Rica or New Zealand.

One day, while Adrienne, Julia, and the children go to the beach, Conrad and Josh drive a Land Rover from the rancho to the office and hangar area. They park beside the hangar. Conrad tells Josh he wants to show him Argonite history archives. They walk to the rear of the hangar. Conrad unlocks a door leading to an area with controls for the airstrip beacon and lights. There is also a small lounge area with a kitchen. Conrad opens a small panel on the room's rear wall that houses an iris recognition device. He places his eye in position, and the back panel of cabinets swings out, revealing a door. He enters a code on the door panel lock and opens the inner door. Josh follows him inside. The door closes behind them.

Josh is no longer shocked by anything the Arroyo family comes up with. However, this level of security here on a forested mountain in Costa Rica piqued his curiosity. They walk along a corridor with sensors that turn on the lights ahead as they progress.

"We are walking inside the mountain," Conrad said. "It may smell a little musty. We do have air conditioning. It has been on a maintenance schedule while I've been gone. Now that we are here, it will freshen things up."

"I can feel some fresh air already."

"You will see a repository, a library, and a museum started by the Argonite star travelers who came to Earth twelve thousand years ago. This is one of three places we know of on the planet."

"They built this twelve thousand years ago?"

"Originally, there was only a cave here on the mountain. They sealed off the cave and carved out space inside the mountain. Over the millennia, more security has been added. Before we built the airstrip and hangar, this was all jungle. Over time we remolded the interior and added all the modern security, air conditioning, and temperature controls."

The corridor ends at a wall with three square doors. Josh wonders if two doors have tigers or death rays behind them. Conrad smiles as if he knows what Josh is thinking.

"No tigers or daggers out of the ceiling. It's more like 'three temple gates.' The difference is that choosing the wrong door will make the correct door impossible to open." Conrad takes what looks like a credit card with a picture of a fish from his pocket and slides it into a slot on the wall next to the first door on the left. There is a beep as the door opens, revealing a large room that looks like something found in a typical museum and library. There are displays, glass cabinets, paintings, and photographs on the walls. Rows of bookshelves line one side of the room.

"Wow, I'm honored to be here."

"This archive holds the history of the Argonites stranded here on earth. You will find artifacts from the original starship, journals, and historical accounts of life on this planet as they found it and lived in it over the centuries. I think there are some works of art as well."

"I hope I can spend some time here studying this history."

"That's one reason I brought you here. You're a scholar. You can research and understand this history. I've spent much time here and can familiarize you with what I learned. I don't know how long I will be around for one reason or another."

"You look healthy to me. Unless you are thinking of going someplace?"

"I don't know what will happen. Many of us want to explore the stars and perhaps find the home planet if it still exists. Records here indicate a means of propulsion that moved the starships at the speed of light or, as they wrote, 'is light.' Raoul Sr. and Marcella are studying these ideas. They have only gone as far as trying to understand the theory."

Conrad gives Josh a tour of the Argonite repository. Before they return to the rancho, he enters Josh into the system so he will have access on his own to the archive. Josh notices, leaving the libraries, that they come out the door on the far right in the entry area. However, inside the archive, there appears to be only one door in or out. Josh tucks one of the two entry cards into his wallet. Later he places the second card in a safe at the rancho. He is looking forward to the many stories he may find here.

Sharon Arroyo began her life on Earth Terminal Station as the management representative for the terminal soon after it was habitable. She adjusts well to life in space and is comfortable in her one-bedroom apartment. Helping the space hotel operators with their grand opening keeps her busy in the beginning. She manages to talk the hotel management into setting aside a small space as a non-denominational chapel. She is happy with her job and has the respect of the hotel management and others coming to the station. Earth Terminal Station is growing. Her office coordinates all docking and supervises traffic control.

Today, Sharon and Arno discussed her planning for a Chinese delegation to visit the station. They are scheduled to arrive in the next twenty-four hours. The Chinese are negotiating with the consortium to build another tier of the station, especially for them. It is still being determined whether the Chinese are willing to integrate with the international terminal community or looking at creating their private national tier. ISEG stresses that the international community aspect of the terminal is essential in all negotiations. The consensus at ISEG is that the Chinese may be serious in their negotiations or looking at options while deciding if they want to build an independent station. There are advantages to being part of the International Earth Terminal Station since it is destined to become a hub for travel to the solar system. The Chinese are building a base near the south pole on the moon's far side. Transporting their astronauts from ETS to the moon can be a lot less expensive than sending them on rockets from China to the moon.

Raoul Sr., Marcella, Josh, and Adrienne plan to be at the terminal to meet with the Chinese delegation. Paul Arroyo and a film crew are getting footage for another documentary at ETS for a few days. He is directing several documentaries based on the ongoing activities of ISEG, Arroyo Aerospace, and the terminal (ETS). His most famous documentary series is about the Mars Expedition.

Arno meets with Simone for lunch while George is touring the terminal. George and Josh plan to meet at some point later. The terminal space hotel has two restaurants. One mainly for breakfast and lunch and another more formal for dinner. Both have beautiful views of Earth and space as the terminal station orbits the planet.

"Good to see you, Simone."

"It's been a while," Simone replied. "Whoever thought we'd meet out here in space."

"Quite a coincidence," Arno said, smiling. "Are you here on business?"

"No, as you already know, I'm here with George Gallagher, a friend of Josh Bennett. I believe Josh snagged a couple of tickets on the Galaxy shuttle for George, who invited me. George is thrilled to be up here, like a kid in a toy store."

"Great! You and George have been a couple for a few years, but you never thanked me for the introduction."

Simone laughs, "is that what you call it?"

"Whatever, it seems to have worked out well. How do you like the Earth Terminal Station?"

"It's an amazing place. Approaching here in the Galaxy shuttle ship, I thought it looked like a giant work of art in space. Amazing construction built by private enterprise in the sky. Even the shuttle is aesthetically designed. Are you spending much time here?"

"I'm here regularly. A special meeting is coming up with a Chinese delegation looking to finance a new tier. I'm sure you already know this. "

"The Chinese are interested in expanding their presence everywhere in space. They built their equivalent to the international space station. They are moving along on the moon base and considering joining the International Space Exploration Group on Mars with a Chinese settlement. However, they will need to invest huge amounts of their national resources. Without the technology that the International Space Exploration Group has, getting to Mars is time-consuming and a huge expense."

"I imagine you must be one of the company experts on China by now."

"Off the record, I can only say you have a good imagination. I work hard and follow orders I don't always agree with. My passion is China. I have my studies and body of knowledge. Maybe I'll write a book or teach one day. Speaking of which, I hear there will be a reception for the Chinese delegation. Any chance of getting George and me in there?

Arno knew where she was going as soon as she mentioned "passion." One of Arno's decision-making methods is to take in all the information available and see what his mind comes up with. No, back and forth with should I do this or say that.

"Let me check. I'm told it would be casual. The discussions and negotiations are behind closed doors. Because I know whom you work for, I'll have to clear it with the Arroyos. There will be clips from this event and the meeting broadcast back to earth. I don't think it should be a problem. If I get the okay, you and George will be there at the reception as guests of Josh or something like that."

"I understand. I'm not here on assignment. Maybe you can ask them to keep me out of the clips if we attend. So, in this case, I can unofficially work with you. I can give you guys a good assessment of who is in this delegation and how serious they are. I'm sure there is at least one spy and one top communist official. High-level space engineers and architects will be included in the delegation. I speak and understand Mandarin."

"Yes, I remember. Beyond what you report to us, are you just adding to your personal knowledge? No report filed on this meeting?"

"As I said, I'm here on holiday. This will be for my eyes only, and you will know everything I know."

"I'll get back to you as soon as possible. If we do this, we can debrief after the event, right?"

"Good idea, no problem," Simone agrees.

"Have things improved at the company under the new administration?"

"There's less outright political stuff going on. Things are less stressful. A lot depends on who gets to be president next. Why are you thinking of coming back?"

"No way! I'm delighted with my situation here. Best time of my life so far. I've been wondering about your telephone calls from a while back. What did you want to talk about?"

"I had information that the Russians were planning to break into Arroyo Aerospace. It was all classified information. I did tell you something was about to happen."

"How did you find out about it?"

"I have a source working with a mercenary company. He has been a mole for us for some time. He's usually a reliable source for both Russian and Chinese operations."

"You had direct contact with this 'mole?'"

"I did. By the time I heard from him, the operation was underway. Before I could do anything, you busted them. Great work! But wait, there's more. This is totally off the record. During the previous administration, several Russian moles infiltrated the government due to lax security or by design. It has been confirmed that one of them is our old friend Virginia Walton!"

"Walton, the 'snow queen,' a Russian mole. No wonder she was so interested in the rabbit," Arno replies. "Where is she now?"

"We're not sure. I've been trying to track her down. She is responsible for the pressure to do biological experiments. There is evidence she is behind the attempted break-in at Arroyo Aerospace. This is all I know at this point."

"Makes sense now why the FBI took more interest in the break-in," Arno said.

"You need to be on high alert. The Russians are desperate to figure out how these spaceships fly. I've been told their scientists are working on anything to do with gravity."

"What about the Chinese?"

"They are working on it too. However, they are proceeding with all their plans using conventional rockets. They have a program. The Russians have nothing except a stagnant economy after they invaded Ukraine."

"Thanks for the information and the attempt to warn me about the break-in," Arno said.

While Arno and Simone are having lunch, George makes his way to the office complex. Before leaving the hotel, he tries out the weightless chamber. Then he jogs on the treadmill in the gym, watching a video of the solar system and stars. He is tempted to try jogging around the terminal next time. Even though the terminal station observes the GMT zone, there is a sunrise or sunset every forty-five minutes. "A morning walk or jog around the terminal might feel like a whole day had passed," George imagines.

At the International Earth Terminal Station front office, he asks if he can get a tour and inquire about renting space. George feels inspired about opening an office at the terminal station. "Surely there is a need for legal counsel at the terminal station. There are no lawyers or law firms here currently." A young man guides him to Sharon Arroyo's office.

"Hi, I'm Sharon Arroyo, Earth Terminal Station manager."

"Good to meet you, Sharon. I'm George Gallagher, an attorney from Orlando, Florida. Also, a friend of Josh Bennett."

"Great, Josh is an integral part of Arroyo Aerospace and ISEG. How do you know Josh?" Sharon asks.

"We've known each other for a few years. We are neighbors in Orlando and often running partners in the morning, at least we were when he was teaching at UCF. He's not in Orlando as much these days. He got me a ride here on Galaxy 6-ETS."

"Yes, I remember hearing him mentioning missing the morning runs in Orlando. Would you like a tour of the complex?"

"Yes. I'll tell you why. I'm interested in opening a law office here at the terminal. I don't think there is one now. As the station grows, there may be a need."

"You make a good point. We don't have a law office at the terminal. With international traffic and various firms opening offices, there will be a need. I can give you a tour of the offices available and show you around the terminal."

"Thank you, that's fantastic."

"You're ahead of the curve; we are getting more inquiries from an assortment of firms about establishing a presence at the terminal. As this place grows, businesses want to be here. We need a doctor and a medical clinic too. The station is a growing city in space."

"Yes. I believe space is international territory. Whatever laws exist seem to be more like guidelines from the UN that members abide by. I believe Space Law is an emerging specialty," George said. "For example, suppose a business is established here at the terminal station. Will it be subject to taxes on Earth? How will a business incorporate in Space? Will the business need an Earth location? The UN appears to link anything in space to a legal entity or country on Earth. At what point does the Earth Terminal Station need to establish itself in an international posture? It's all new territory." Sharon and George chat as she shows him around the office complex and the terminal. George is convinced that he should follow up on establishing a law practice on the station with a corporate and space law specialty.

Marcella, Raoul Sr., Josh, and Adrienne, arrive at the terminal together. The Arroyos and Bennetts' go to their apartments in the terminal apartment complex.

The Chinese delegation arrives at Earth Station Terminal later that day. They first travel to Arroyo Aerospace/ISEG in New Zealand to get there, where they board Galaxy 6-ETS. There are eight members in the delegation, five men and three women. There are also two individuals the Chinese say are security. They are not permitted to carry weapons onboard Galaxy 6-ETS. No weapons of any kind are allowed on the station, either. The delegation has rooms reserved at the terminal space hotel. They plan to rest overnight to allow for jet and space lag before getting a tour and meeting with Arroyo

Aerospace and the International Space Exploration Group. There are two scheduled meetings, one before the reception and another the next day.

Arno let Josh know about Simone and George arriving at the station. Josh mentions that he is aware that they are there. Marcella and Raoul Sr. do not have a problem with George and Simone attending the reception for the Chinese delegation if Arno thinks it is okay.

Paul and his film crew plan to film the reception. There will also be an archival video of the meetings. Stacy has been working as Paul's assistant director, helping coordinate the filming at the station over the past week.

The first round of meetings with the Chinese is formal but friendly. Most Chinese delegation speaks English or understands it enough to respond or use their interpreter. Josh understands and remembers Mandarin enough from his time in China to establish some rapport with members of the delegation.

After Introductions all around, Raoul Sr. begins the meeting, "Welcome to the International Earth Terminal Station. We hope your flight here was comfortable." The Chinese are complimentary about the Galaxy 6-ETS ship and their ride to the station. One of the engineers, a conservatively dressed woman, said, "the ship is truly a marvelous achievement."

With an iPhone in his hand, a younger man shows a picture of the earth he took from a window in Galaxy 6. "Smooth ride," he said.

"How are your accommodations at the space hotel?" asks Marcella.

"A good hotel. I took some time in the weightless chamber," Lee Ming, a middle-aged man in a dark blue suit, said. He continues in English, "It is pleasant to float for a short time. I prefer gravity, feet on the ground.""

Josh replies slowly in Mandarin, "是的，我们大多数人都有同样的感觉 (Yes, most of us feel the same way,). 对不起，我的中文有点生疏. (Sorry my Chinese is rusty,") Josh said noticing that the interpreter is repeating what he says in more fluent Chinese.

"The hotel has morning Xing Qi Tai Chi exercise session for guests with Zhang Yue, a visiting instructor from China, who is quite good," Yang Lu, an engineer, said."

"Yes, I hear he is very popular on the station and gives lessons to others around the terminal. He incorporates Ta Na breathing exercises from Qigong for a healthy immune system. Seems like good practice for space," Josh said."

Getting down to business Lee Ming, the head of the delegation, proceeds to say they are impressed with the International Earth Terminal Station concept and want to explore the possibility of having a level built onto the station for the Peoples' Republic of China (PRC).

Marcella said, "Arroyo Aerospace and the International Earth Terminal Station consortium are happy to welcome the addition of a Chinese tier. Since this is an international space terminal, we can extend diplomatic concessions to the Chinese regarding their area. However, there are specific rules that everyone, corporate and governmental, abides by to which they would need to agree—for example, the station has no uniformed military personnel, weapons, or rocket fuel. You will have your docking ports and other necessary features you might require. "

"We want to have a hotel in the tiered space," Lee Ming said. "I believe tourists and others will be visiting. We will also require docking and storage."

"We can work with you to design the space to your specifications. You are entitled to all the resources other tiers have," Sam Arroyo said.

The delegation engineers have questions regarding the artificial gravity and placement of the tier level on the terminal stack.

Raoul Sr. explains that "their tier goes below the existing tiers and that additional tiers might be built below their tier in the future. The central stack runs through all the tiers and provides access to other tiers. However, they can limit access to their tier by closing their spoke doors. The design of the station and the rotation creates artificial gravity. However, we supplement this artificial gravity so that all space, in each tier at the terminal, has gravity close to that of earth."

They discuss the square footage of each tier and the cost of maintaining living conditions.

Once the basic parameters are tentatively agreed on, initial costs and an agreement outline are discussed. There is talk of an option for a second tier to be built.

The meeting lasts for three hours. It is agreed that they will meet again in two days. No commitment is made. However, the Chinese appear interested in a deal. The meeting adjourns. Everyone is invited to the reception that evening at 19:30 UTC. The Earth Terminal Station uses Universal Coordinated Time (UTC). This is also known as GMT or Greenwich Mean Time.

That evening, Josh and Adrienne arrive at the reception in the hotel at about the same time as George and Simone.

"Hi, good to see you both," George said. "You met Simone briefly some time ago in Baldwin Park."

"Yes," Adrienne said, "happy you are here."

"This is your first time in space. How do you feel?" Josh asks.

"I feel great," George said. "Being up here is like a fantasy. I keep wondering if it's a dream or a movie."

Simone said, "It's wonderful to see you folks again. This station and all you are doing is a fantastic achievement."

"I met Sharon Arroyo at the terminal headquarters while I was touring today. I'm seriously considering opening a law office on the station," George said.

"Wow!" Josh said. "Great idea. I'm sure it will be needed as Earth Terminal Station grows."

"I want to be the first law firm in space. I believe it is an emerging specialty."

As they converse, the room fills up with members of the Chinese delegation, Arroyo Aerospace, and International Space Exploration staff. Raoul Sr., Marcella, and Sam chat with Lee Ming and two other Chinese delegates.

Servers circulate the room with appetizers. Food is set out buffet style and includes both Chinese and Western dishes. Wine and other beverages are served.

Three delegates, two men and a woman, approach Josh, Adrienne, George, and Simone. Everyone introduces themselves.

The female delegate Li Hua, an engineer, introduces herself to Josh in Chinese. She asks him, "how he learned Chinese?"

In some Chinese and some English, Josh tells her he spent some time in Beijing and lived for a year at the Buddhist Monastery Shaolin Temple when he was younger.

"Did you learn Kung Fu," Li Hua asks?

"I learned a little. I became familiar with the Shurangama and other sutras. I learned to meditate."

Josh introduced Li Hua to the others standing there. Simone started a conversation with Li Hua in Mandarin. Simone's Chinese is quite good, and all three delegates appear surprised and impressed. They ask her if she is an interpreter. She tells them she is not officially and studied Mandarin at Peking University. She mentions she is a guest of her friend George, a friend of Josh.

One of the other two people in the group is from the Chinese Space Agency, and the other is a government official. Simone translates some of what they are talking about to Josh, Adrienne, and George as they speak.

Soon they are joined by Raoul Sr., Marcella, and Lee Ming. Lee Ming notices from a distance that a conversation is partly happening in Chinese. He does not participate in the discussion. He begins speaking to Josh, who introduces him to Adrienne, George, and Simone.

Simone and Li Hua continue their conversation. In a while, Li Hua leads Simone off to meet other delegates.

Sharon Arroyo and Arno Cameron are conversing with a delegate about the hotel and security at the terminal. Arno explains that everyone must be vaccinated and take a test for the virus and other issues before coming to the station. The Chinese say they did not mind being tested before boarding the Galaxy 6 shuttle. Testing everywhere is routine in China.

The reception appears to be a success. The food and drink are good, and there is a friendly mingling of all attendees.

After the reception, Arno meets privately with Simone at his office.

"Did you enjoy the reception?" Arno asks.

"Yes, it was a pleasure, and I got to speak Chinese," Simone said.

"Anything interesting?"

"Well, delegate conversation is about their jobs and trip to the station. They all seem to be big on having a base here. They estimate the cost will be much lower than building an independent station on this scale. They don't have the resources to facilitate building anything currently. I did overhear them talking about the artificial gravity here, trying to figure out how the Galaxy ship they came here in flies. One guy from the space agency said that it is a big mystery in China and that they have spent time trying to figure it out to no avail. I got the impression that nothing is available through spying or hacking. Security is too good."

"Do you think they are serious about building a tier?"

"Definitely, very serious. They may want to bargain but know they cannot get much. They want to transfer personnel to their moon base and soon a station on Mars. They can dock here, pick up people and land their rockets on the moon. They will ultimately try to work with ISEG to move people beyond the moon. I'm sure you know that ISEG has the corner on moving around the solar system. Chemical rockets can't compete. Arroyo Aerospace and ISEG are non-governmental entities, so there are no political entanglements. This is a big deal to China and other countries and corporations worldwide."

"Yes, we have a monopoly right now. It is getting tougher to stay out of politics, even in space. All kinds of problems on earth."

"You have remarkable security; NSA has been scratching their heads to catch up with you. Sooner or later, they may get in. No system is bulletproof. Li Hua, the woman I was talking to, asked me many questions about what I do and my connection to Arroyo Aerospace and ISEG. I used our old cover story about working for the SBA. 'I'm a friend of a friend who was invited to visit ETS, and we managed to get invited to the reception.' She spoke excellent English too. I think she is an intelligence agent, maybe MSS (Chinese Ministry of State Security)."

"Was there any recruitment innuendo?" Arno asks.

"Nothing beyond pushing to know how deeply I was involved. She did ask for contact information. I gave her the SBA cover phone number."

"Anything else?"

"This group wants to go home with a good deal. They will try to firm up something at the next meeting."

"Okay, great. Thanks for your insights. Appreciate your working with us," Arno said. He believes the trade-off with Simone is worthwhile. She gains some personal insight into what the Chinese are doing but passes along valuable information to him.

After Simone leaves, Arno phones Marcella and updates her based on what he learned from Simone. Marcella thanks Arno for the information and tells him they have a proposal for the Chinese and are preparing to present and discuss it at the next meeting.

"It appears they are serious. If they move ahead, others will follow. This station can grow quite large," Marcella said. "Hopefully, we can keep it apart from the political life on the planet. The Chinese and other nations having space here will help us maintain the 'International' status of the terminal. It may also ensure no country attacks it or tries to own it."

Overnight the Chinese delegation communicates with Beijing and the Chinese Space Agency. The conference call lasted for two hours, and at one point, they heard from President Xi Jinping, who said he was looking forward to visiting the new Chinese terminal in space one day.

The final meeting begins the next day after lunch at 13:30 UTC. Marcella narrates the presentation, which includes slides and video. The first part shows the steps it takes to build a new tier. They present video footage showing the current facility being constructed. Timelines are discussed.

Finally, the overall budget and payment. All that is required is a signed contract and down payment, and construction can begin.

Each of the Chinese delegates receives a booklet with all the information. In addition, each delegate receives a small box with official International Earth Terminal Station astronaut wings as a gift.

There are questions about the timeline and budget. The budget is reasonable, considering that they are constructing a space station. The plans include the construction of a one-hundred-room hotel with a spa and restaurant. Furnishing is up to the Chinese.

The Chinese tier will have an independently controlled power and air control system. The system is tied into a universal grid that the entire station shares. This grid keeps the power to all areas supplied as required and collects surplus energy when available. Terminal tenants receive power usage bills periodically.

The estimated time it takes to build to completion is under two years if there are no interruptions, like solar flares or other natural or logistical problems on Earth. The Chinese understand that additional tiers will be built on the stack below their level for others. Marcella suggests that one tier should be large enough to accommodate the Chinese mission.

The meeting ended with the Chinese indicating that they thought the government would approve the proposal. The delegation goes back to the hotel. They mention they are looking forward to another night on the station before returning to Earth.

Only some Arroyo Aerospace team can attend the meeting or reception with the Chinese on the Earth Terminal Station. Once the Chinese depart to return to Earth, a secure virtual meeting is called for executives of Arroyo Aerospace and the International Space Exploration Group. Those not there in person will attend virtually. Raoul Sr. and Marcella open the meeting with a report on the Chinese visit and the deal to build them a tier.

"We're not going to make a huge profit building this tier," Marcella said. "The significance of a nation, in this case, China establishing a presence, is important. I believe the European Union and others will follow in the future."

Sam added, "The design of Earth Terminal Station allows for expansion in the form of additional tiers on the stack. The Chinese considered building two tiers. I don't think they will. We emphasized that one tier is more than enough for their mission. Once the deal closes, we can begin production of the tier modules at L5 and on earth. The modules and crews will assemble the tier modules via spokes attached to the stack. Once the initial modules are attached and stable, work crews can continue to attach additional modules in each direction until the circle is complete. Work on the interiors begins when all the modules are in place and the atmosphere is pressurized. I believe the Chinese will want to be involved at that point."

"We have work crews trained and ready to begin construction. They all worked on building the Earth Terminal Station," Marcella said.

Raoul Sr. said, "We have two tiers now. The new tier will be the third. The consortium will see some revenue after this third tier is built. We expect to hear back from the Chinese in the coming week."

"The Chinese pay to build a tier. Do they own that space?" Tamara asked on a secure virtual link from Arroyo Aerospace at the ranch.

"They pay to build the tier. They are leasing the space for that tier from the International Earth Terminal Station consortium," Marcella explains.

"Just curious where the money goes once the Chinese come up with the funds," Tamara asks. "Do they pay in dollars?"

Bill Arroyo answerers, "This is an international trade transaction. China will buy or trade currency to pay us. We have corporate branches in three countries now, the U.S., Costa Rica, and New Zealand. We've invested in banks in these countries and may bank money in any of these places. We also own an international bank created in Switzerland two years ago. I believe we can open a branch bank on Earth Terminal Station anytime. To keep things legal, we need to ensure transactions are in the open and, where necessary, pay appropriate taxes. Certain countries have agreed to a minimum corporate tax. I'm sure we can work things out with China. They can pay the consortium directly. There will be a schedule of payments. The funds will be exchanged. We only need a bank to transfer and hold the money in a legal account. We already have international accounts for the consortium. The accounting firm will figure it all out."

"Our financial situation is excellent," Marcella said. Arroyo Aerospace and ISEG are still privately owned corporations. We are part of the consortium that built the Earth Terminal Station. We are working with NASA, many national and international corporations, and governments to facilitate their efforts in space. By working with them, we have managed to keep control of proprietary technology and make some money. If this China deal goes through, it will give us a genuinely neutral international status. "

Sharon Arroyo reported on the status of the Earth Terminal Station. She talked about the tourist traffic and the success of the space hotel, which has named itself 'The Celestial Hilton' since it is now officially part of the Hilton chain. Disney is interested in building a resort in one of the existing tiers. Trade through the terminal is ongoing, and docking fees are a source of revenue. Sharon mentions that she has an inquiry from a lawyer friend of Josh's about opening a law office on the station. She has also received questions from businesses and corporations about opening offices at the station. She wants to establish a medical clinic at the station.

Adrienne reports on the popularity of ISEG and Paul's documentary films about space exploration and Mars City. According to polls she conducts in the U.S. and internationally, Arroyo Aerospace and the International Space Exploration Group are extremely popular for their neutral posture and space exploration. The Earth Terminal Station is also high on the list of destinations people would like to visit in the future.

CHAPTER FORTY

....

"A stout tree trunk, began in a tiny seed."

The International Space Exploration Group base on Mars is becoming self-sustaining in 2029. Mars City, as it has come to be known, has a population of one hundred and thirty-two people. Residents live in the mountain cavern biospheres and the habitats on the surface. The vast cavern and interior canyon provide shelter and water that is more valuable on Mars than any fossil fuel or mineral resource on Earth. Based on what has been learned from the early residents on Mars, vigorous exercise is crucial for long-term residents. Humans on Mars who do not exercise face muscle, heart, and lung atrophy because of the low gravity on the planet. Human bodies, muscles, internal organs, and bones become weak under lower gravity. A fringe benefit of vigorous exercise regimes is that obesity is rare for Mars City inhabitants.

During the third expedition to the planet, a large gym and spa biosphere facility is built in the cavern. This biosphere is equipped with artificial gravity equivalent to that on Earth. In operation twenty-four hours per sol, it provides residents of Mars City with a place for daily exercise with earth gravity. Mars City residents' health is maintained by regular and vigorous daily exercise in artificial earth gravity. Muscle deterioration is avoided. Heart and organ health is maintained with no bone mass loss. A clinic with a Doctor of Internal medicine and staff is available. All residents receive a physical exam after six months. Residents are encouraged to rotate back to Earth after one year. They may apply for up to another year on Mars, providing their health is good. The International Space Exploration Group (ISEG) is studying ideas to extend artificial earth gravity to residential biospheres or expand it throughout the cavern. No one knows what effect this might have on the mountain itself.

There are six ISEG outposts on the surface of Mars where mining operations are underway. Minerals such as iron, nickel, and deposits of other minerals are beginning to be mined and smelted on the planet. There are deposits of iron ore on or near the surface. Smelting processes for ore on Mars, where conditions are very different from Earth, require new technology. Josh recruits a few of his prior graduate students who believe they are up to the challenge. They look forward to time on Mars developing a new smelting process suitable for this environment.

Ideas emerge using "green steel" methods to strip the oxygen from the ore producing pure iron metal. In this process, hydrogen is used to replace fossil fuels. Hydrogen is not a gas available on Mars. It can be stripped from H2O. It is also found on Mars and in the solar system. Jupiter is composed mainly of hydrogen. ISEG is looking at the possibility of mining hydrogen gas from Jupiter or one of its moons. Hydrogen can be transported in cryogenic tankers or gaseous tube trailers built for use in space. This type of storage is already being considered for hydrogen for rocket propellant. ISEG currently transports hydrogen from Earth to Mars in cryogenic tanker modules. Other resources on Mars include silicon, oxygen, magnesium, and by-products derived from volcanic rocks. All these assets are being studied or used in some way on Mars in 2029.

Mars City develops methods to manufacture and construct safe habitats for humans to live on Mars. These habitats and biospheres allow the expansion of the city. Habitats are built for corporate and national clients who want to be on Mars. Utility lander vehicles are made available for lease by other settlements on the planet. These utility landers are equipped with the Arroyo Aerospace gravity drives suitable for transportation on the planet. Any attempt to gain access to the propulsion system will immediately detonate a controlled minor explosion that will destroy the system and create a virus that destroys related data and navigational programs. Lessees are warned and agree not to try to access the propulsion system. All landers have tracking devices installed and can be destroyed remotely.

Since Mars City is the most established and advanced settlement on Mars, astronauts from other bases like to visit Mars City for a break. The interior of the cavern has been modestly terraformed. While there are still biospheres where residents live, the air in the cavern is scrubbed, circulated, and breathable. Excess CO2 is vented into the Martian atmosphere. As a precaution against radiation and leaks, the cavern's walls are sprayed with a sealant. Airlocks housed in sealed chambers provide decontamination areas where EMU suits are stored and cleaned.

By terraforming the cavern, the risk of earth bacteria becoming established in Mars habitats became real. There is no way to stop it since humans live and breathe in these spaces. Outside the habitats and cavern, the bacteria are not likely to survive in the Martian environment. Working from ISEG headquarters on Earth, Tamara Arroyo makes prevention of the spread of harmful viruses and diseases in Mars City, Earth Terminal Station, and L5 factory station a priority.

Mars City air scrubbers include filters for eliminating harmful bacteria. Terraforming in the cavern provides an environment where bacteria can grow. Even with rigorous screening and sterilization, it is impossible to eliminate all bacteria that might arrive from the Earth with humans, supplies, food, and equipment. Everything imported from Earth is exposed to ultraviolet light to kill as much bacteria as possible on arrival.

Arroyo Aerospace and ISEG have strict guidelines and testing for all travelers coming to Mars City. All future residents are tested. They receive the latest vaccines and spend thirty days in a quarantine facility on earth before coming to Mars. Visitors from other Mars colonies are screened and must show proof of testing and vaccinations before entering Mars City. Visitors who test negatively are still asked to wear auxiliary breathing masks for their visit to Mars City. Surface habitats require EMU suits and the exact testing requirements as the cavern space.

Mars City apparel includes a lightweight pressure suit with built-in warming elements and an auxiliary oxygen supply should levels drop in the cavern. On the surface, EMU suits are necessary. In the cavern, masks are worn by everyone in public places. These hybrid masks can tap into the pressure suits supply of air if necessary. The pressure suits and masks are something everyone wears, even if they add clothing, like a shirt, pants, a coat, or jacket on top. Resident biospheres do not require pressure suits since temperature and oxygen levels are regulated.

Food production is a significant project that helps the colony move toward self-sustaining status. Greenhouse habitat structures are built on the surface for farming. Both hydroponics and hybrid soil are available to grow vegetables in the protected Martian environment. Certain high-protein crops like soybeans are grown in giant biospheres on the surface. Growing soil, they call "New Mars Soil," made up of compost, recycled sewage, conditioned regolith, and volcanic rock makes adequate growing soil. All the people living on Mars are involved in agricultural projects to support food production. One unique crop is a hybrid lettuce that helps prevent bone damage.

Inside the mountain cavern, a garden area is formed near the edge of the canyon bridge. Artificial solar lighting and "New Mars Soil" provide an excellent growing environment for certain crops grown in the terra-formed air of the cavern. Seedling trees imported from Earth are planted in pots and used to create a small park in another area. The trees are all high CO2-absorbing varieties. Because there is a community living in the cavern and visitors from other bases, a public dining and gathering place is created. It is a popular gathering place in the evenings.

Water from the canyon reservoir is the lifeblood of the city. It is not wasted. Galaxy Four successfully moves an ice asteroid from orbit in the asteroid belt to a crater on Mars near the settlement. It is gradually being melted and processed. The water is pumped into insulated reservoir tanks below the surface. This water is available for manufacturing, mining, and building projects.

Wind turbines and solar arrays generate electricity. It is stored in a range of electrochemical storage facilities. This includes chemicals, flow batteries, and capacitors. Surface mechanical storage devices that harness kinetic or gravitational energy are also under development. Surplus electricity generation is converted to hydrogen by electrolysis and stored. Since frigid surface temperatures drain chemical-based electrical storage capacity, areas inside the cavern on the far side of the canyon are used for storage areas.

Under construction is a habitat where an experimental attempt to raise chickens is planned. Chickens will be raised mainly for fresh eggs and some meat. After creating an environment for them, the main issue is feeding the chickens. What is provided to the chickens might also be consumed by humans. Is producing limited quantities of eggs and meat worth the trade-off? The colony still receives food, medicines, and other supplies from Earth. ISEG flights come to the settlement every two months.

In 2021 NASA was under presidential orders to land humans on Mars by 2033. Thanks to help from ISEG, the NASA facility, with twelve staff, is up and running in Jezero Crater by 2027. Jezero Crater is 28 miles (45 kilometers) wide and is located on the western edge of a flat plain called Isidis Planitia, which lies just north of the Martian equator. Under the contract, ISEG provides transportation for NASA to land on Mars. ISEG builds the habitats, to NASA specifications, for the astronauts. NASA astronauts rotate back to earth every three months.

NASA plans to expand its base in the Jezero Crater for research. Scientists claim there was a lake and delta river area at this location billions of years ago. In October of 2021, the Mars Perseverance lander found clay minerals that spilled over into the crater from the delta river areas. This evidence confirms the theory.

The Ramurt rocket company, with ISEG support, lands on Mars after some delays in 2028. They establish a base in the Southern Hemisphere near the equator. Ramurt lands enough supplies to sustain the base for a few months. The crew plans to return to Earth on the same rocket that brought them to Mars. Additional rockets will bring supplies and other people to form a settlement near Valles Marineris canyons.

Closer to Earth, the International Earth Terminal Station (ETS) has expanded over the past five years. The Chinese financed tier is operational. It is used as a station to send astronauts to the Chinese base on the moon's far side. China still has plans for a settlement on Mars. They claim they are using the moon as a training and experimental base for developing habitats for Mars. The Chinese space hotel and restaurant welcome all tourists visiting the terminal station. Other governments and corporations also establish a presence on ETS. The third space hotel and resort are planned to be built by an international theme park corporation. A new fourth tier is needed to accommodate the additional expansion.

Even though it is expensive, tourist travel from Earth to the terminal is constant. Passports and the usual travel documents or procedures are required for travel. Earth Terminal Station requires a visa issued by ETS that ensures health requirements are met. Export licenses from various countries for shipping cargo to interplanetary destinations are necessary. ETS customs agents check baggage coming through the terminal. They regulate cargo between Earth, the terminal station, and ISEG planetary destinations. All travelers are screened before and after arriving at all docks. All individuals visiting the station must show proof of vaccination and immunity to the latest viruses. All visitors are encouraged to wear masks while they visit the station if there are viral outbreaks on earth.

Sharon Arroyo runs the day-to-day operations of Earth Terminal Station. She makes trips back to Earth for meetings and vacations. After a few weeks on earth, she is usually anxious to return to the station. It has been her home for five years. She has friends working on the station and enjoys life in space. The terminal is well protected from radiation and has artificial gravity, so long-term health is not an issue. Regular strenuous exercise is recommended at the terminal station. The Arroyo family and corporation members visit Earth Terminal Station, so she is always in touch socially with the family. Sharon put aside her desire to go to Mars. She likes being closer to Earth. She successfully gets a doctor and medical resources established at the terminal.

Like many other countries, the United States now has a consulate on the station. After negotiations, the U.S. Space Force is permitted to dock at the consulate port. They fly there by conventional rocket-powered planes or shuttles. They have no jurisdiction, military, or police function on the station. Security at the terminal remains private and within the guidelines set by ISEG. Arno Cameron, now an Executive Vice President at Arroyo Aerospace, administers all security concerns for the corporation and ISEG. He works closely with Sharon Arroyo on issues related to ETS. He is at the terminal each month and journeys to the L5 station. New personnel for Arroyo Aerospace, ISEG, L5, and Mars City divisions are carefully chosen and screened. Arno and Carlos Arroyo work to keep communications secure.

Arroyo Aerospace and ISEG establish a private station and manufacturing facility at Lagrange point L5. During any new construction at Earth Terminal Station, the space factory at L5 provides resources and materials to build. Factory modules can be moved to the earth terminal station for construction work. The L5 factory is also used to create a sizeable interstellar starship secretly. Factory modules become part of the starship. Galaxy-class spaceship technology is used to incorporate the modules into the body of a larger vessel. The ship has gravitational propulsion and a fusion reactor built by a U.S. firm. It was transported to space by ISEG. Starship Galaxy-L5 is a well-kept secret. To the outside world, the L5 station is a factory.

Paul Arroyo, with Stacy and others, continues to produce documentary films about space exploration. Several films show the evolution of Mars City. Another is a further exploration of Ceres and other bodies in the asteroid belt. The discovery and mining of precious metals on several asteroids are popular documentaries. The extraordinary feat of moving an ice asteroid to Mars is a popular film. Each of the documentaries is a box office success. A documentary about the pioneering flight to Jupiter's moon Ganymede is planned to be released soon. The films are seen in theaters and streamed on cable TV networks. Paul is restless and looking forward to spending time away from making films. He looks forward to spending time with Stacy on vacation in Costa Rica or off the planet earth. Perhaps, even traveling in space.

Mining operations in the asteroid belt are underway. Further exploration of Ceres found water kept liquid by volcanic activity below the surface. Heated tanker modules are brought to Ceres. The modules are tankers to transport water processed and pumped from Ceres. This water is then transported to Mars or L5. Module water tankers sent to L5 become part of the Galaxy-L5 Starship. A base is being built on Ceres.

The Arroyo Aerospace engineering team led by Raoul Sr. and Marcella believes they are close to inventing a propulsion system to achieve a speed of light flight. This system goes beyond gravitational and electromagnetic waves to the essence of light waves themselves. They believe it is how the Argonite starships were powered thousands of years ago. This notion is reinforced by recent research by Josh Bennett at the Costa Rican Argonite archives.

The "Rosetta Stone" key to understanding the Argonite language is a star map with celestial longitude references and extensive notes. The navigational notes calculate time and distances at the speed of light. With this development, more documents and artifacts found in the Costa Rican archives are identified and translated.

Josh discovers information related to light-speed travel in navigational logs. Another important find is a technical manual with diagrams and drawings of what resembles a propulsion system. The manual refers to "matrix recordings and schematics." After some thought, Conrad remembers containers with small metallic cards stacked in rows in the archives. They ask

Carlos to have a look at the cards. He discovers a type of laser imprinting on the cards. He has no way to read them. Conrad does more searching in the archival storage area. He finds a device that appears related to the cards in that it has a slot where a matrix card can fit.

Carlos takes the device and cards back to Florida. Raoul Sr. and Carlos decide the device must have been used to project a three-dimensional image or hologram imprinted on the card or matrix. They start work learning how to power the device. These discoveries ultimately give Raoul Sr. and Marcella new insights regarding light as a propulsion source.

Reading journals and logs, Josh finds coordinates for islands in the Pacific Ocean ranging from Cocos, 300 miles west of Nicoya Peninsula, Costa Rica, to the Galapagos and Easter islands further to the south. There are coordinates for an island about twenty-five miles Southwest of Cocos that do not appear on modern maps. Conrad and Josh believe the coordinates may be the location of the uninhabited island where the Argonites initially landed. It makes sense that the Argonites would move things they value from this island to the nearest stable environment they can reach, which was here in Costa Rica.

All the Southeast Pacific Islands, including the Galapagos and Easter Islands, were uninhabited by humans until about 1200 CE when the Polynesians came to the Easter Islands. With modern detection equipment and knowing where to look, who knows what might be found in the ocean?

Carlos Arroyo continues to administer all communications for Arroyo Aerospace and ISEG creatively. He spends most of his time at the Florida ranch but flew to Earth Terminal Station, L5, and Mars to set up communications. He especially enjoys setting up a WIFI system for Mars City. Carlos works closely with Raoul Sr., Marcella, Sam, and Kevin Steiner on programming projects.

Tamara recovers from her fatigue and physical problems within a year of her return from Mars. She continues researching ways to make Mars living conditions more practical and comfortable for the residents. She also studies the psychological impact that being away from Earth imposes on humans. She designs a course for prospective residents who want to live on Mars or somewhere in outer space. All new employees, after being hired, who are going to Mars, taking jobs on Earth Terminal Station, or working with ISEG take a short course that Tamara has written.

Tamara works with Josh to improve the cloaking devices used on the spaceships. Since going public, the Galaxy ships have used full cloaking less than before. Carlos designs programs that disguise the hull stealth functions and allows the vessel to be seen on radar. Full cloaking, making the ship invisible to radar and the human eye, is a feature that can be turned on and off.

Raoul Jr. pilots Galaxy ships and works with Carlos on programming for communications and navigation. Captain Sun, Annie, and Kevin Steiner work together, training new pilots and navigators for Galaxy ships now in service. New pilots are needed for the module flights to Earth Terminal Station and L5. The International Space Exploration group provides transportation for clients traveling away from Earth to the terminal station or other destinations.

Adrienne is internationally known as the spokesperson for Arroyo Aerospace and the International Space Exploration Group. Morgan and Lauren are both studying at Cambridge University. Josh and Adrienne purposely keep the children out of the limelight. They believe the children will attract less attention at a foreign university than at a U.S. university. Josh and Adrienne are committed to being on earth as much as possible while the children are in university. Morgan and Lauren have yet to go to Mars. They have spent long weekends on ETS with their parents from time to time.

George Gallagher establishes his Space Law Firm on ETS. He spends half of his time there handling various legal matters for clients. Several corporations take steps, which George facilitates, to incorporate themselves into Earth Terminal Station. This is done through agreements with the ISEG and the consortium, which collect annual franchise fees. George has a good working relationship with Sharon Arroyo at ETS. She asks him to handle legal paperwork for import and export shipments coming through the terminal and from interplanetary outposts. In anticipation of George opening the ETS office, Simone Greely decides to attend law school. After the Chinese move into their new tier at ETS, Simone leaves the CIA and joins George's firm. On behalf of the firm, she begins handling certain legal matters for the Chinese on the station. While not yet a lawyer, she does qualify as a paralegal apprenticing with George's firm. Once she graduates and passes a bar exam somewhere, she will become an associate at the firm.

In a surprise move, Arroyo Aerospace offers its solar energy-gathering paint technology to automobile manufacturers of electric cars and trucks. They made the formula public and released their patent rights. This formula can be applied to any surface to absorb solar radiation and transmit it to storage batteries. Arroyo Aerospace conducts demonstrations for interested parties in Florida using their vehicles. It does not have stealth capabilities. Electric cars will now have an extended range using solar power. Vehicles using the new technology can be charged by solar energy or plugged into the grid for charging. Based on the reputation and status of Arroyo Aerospace, the world takes notice, and one by one, auto manufacturers start applying the process to their most recent electric vehicle models.

Earth Terminal Station currently has three working tiers and a fourth nearing completion. This fourth tier is to be shared by several countries and corporate entities. The European Union, Great Britain, and Japan will have space and docking facilities on the fourth tier. Multi-national corporations involved in future mining and mineral acquisition from the solar system want a presence on the Earth Terminal Station. NASA is scheduled to install a research module in the new tier. The theme park hotel and resort will complete the fourth tier.

At a meeting on L5, Raoul Sr., Marcella, Josh, Sam, Tamara, Arno, Carlos, Raoul Jr., Conrad, and Kevin Steiner meet to discuss plans for a new propulsion system primarily.

Raoul Sr. speaks first. "We have been working for many years to develop propulsion systems that can be used for practical solar and interstellar travel. Our gravity and wave generation drives with navigation tools developed by Kevin and Carlos is at maximum potential. We can move freely in the solar system and perhaps beyond. Interstellar travel requires faster speeds and systems beyond gravity fields.

Recently we obtained a compact nuclear power plant that may be used for propulsion or as a power generator for starship system functioning. Propulsion of this type is not dependent on gravity or electromagnetic impulses. It can move spaceships around the solar system and perhaps beyond at reasonable speeds. When it comes to travel to star systems that are light years away, this means of propulsion still needs to be faster and more efficient of fuel.

To travel beyond this solar system, around the galaxy, and perhaps beyond, we need a propulsion system capable of moving at or near the speed of light and possibly becoming light itself. Traveling beyond the speed of light is difficult to imagine, even for Einstein, who didn't believe it possible. We have no conceptual theories of how light-speed travel might work."

"Our latest propulsion system is based on our experience with gravity, the electromagnetic spectrum, and new information that Josh and Conrad have been gleaning from Argonite archives in Costa Rica. They discovered what we believe is a technical manual for servicing a star drive. Carlos found a way to bring power to the device you see here. When you insert these "matrix cards," as the Argonites call them, into the device, it projects a three-dimensional image of what is on the card."

Carlos activates the device, which already has a matrix card inserted. A three-dimensional image appears above the machine.

"Based on what is in the manuals, this is a representation of the actual drive by which the Argonite ship is propelled," Raoul Sr. said. According to the navigation logs, these ships flew at the speed of light. The only way we can describe it is that this drive transforms the starship into light waves. Navigation systems direct the ship to preprogrammed destinations. The starships can break out of light speed and take advantage of gravitational propulsion once it nears its journey's endpoint."

"We are using the manual, drawings, schematics, and projections to construct the drive. The science behind this propulsion system is currently beyond our complete understanding. We can try to build it based on their specifications and then test it without understanding why or how it works," Sam said.

"How soon do you think you will be able to build and test it?" Josh asked.

Raoul Sr. replies, "we're going to try to build it here on L5. Certain parts will need to be made on Earth. We are still trying to figure out equivalent metals and materials for some of the technical specs in the manuals. They had alloys of perhaps alien metals and other materials we haven't figured out yet. These alloys may be stronger or have other unfamiliar qualities, so we'll need some testing. We're getting close. Again, we have the diagrams, etcetera, but we do not understand conceptually how it is all supposed to work. We may have some trial and error before we create the actual device. Conrad and Josh are still researching the archives for more information. We have some theoretical ideas about the concept."

"There is a big learning curve here, and then we have to figure out how to program navigation and other functional aspects. We aim to have a prototype ready within two or three years," Marcella said. "Until then, we will continue to develop all current resources."

Sam said, "We have grown hugely in the last eleven years. We have accomplished so much. We have managed to survive, retain, and grow our assets. Others interested in colonizing the solar system have not been able to develop a drive like ours. The original reasons for not making it available to everyone on Earth have not changed. There is ongoing chaos on the planet Earth. Maybe it's part of the human DNA, this self-destructive tendency to destroy what has been achieved. To create dark ages that encourage ignorance, malign science, and knowledge. I'm not a historian, but I feel there is a good chance that civilization on earth is continuing a steady turn for the worse. "

Everyone waits for Conrad, sitting there with his eyes closed. He begins speaking with his eyes still closed. "There appear to be many roads to disaster on Earth. The oceans are rising. On the U.S.'s east coast, hurricanes and high tides constantly flood coastal areas. Forrest fires spontaneously ignite, burning millions of acres of land on the West Coast of the U.S. The Midwest, Southwest, and Southeast have unpredictable weather patterns. Earthquakes have been recorded all over the country, primarily where fracking gas has been employed. Several volcanoes have had massive eruptions globally. Extreme weather events continue worldwide.

"China has been hit with heavy rain in certain areas and drought in others. Parts of Asia are contending with torrential downpours. South America is suffering devastating droughts."

"Europe is no better than the rest of the world regarding devastating weather events. Cities like London are experiencing major flooding. Certain leaders still refuse to accept global climate change and the fact that human activity has been brought about or made worse. The planet may be ready to reboot itself."

"In the U.S. and other countries, political movements motivated by ruling class members have sought to throw established democracies into chaos so that they can maintain control. If history is any indication, the next couple of decades may see upheaval and wars until mid-century. The difference is that we have a bastion, not on the planet. Who knows if some despot will decide to aim missiles at Earth Terminal Station or try to invade it for some reason? We've been lucky so far. We have captured the imagination of the world. The entrepreneurs and rocket people out here exploring and establishing settlements have so far respected each other. I believe we have set an example for cooperation beyond the boundaries of Earth. The International Earth Terminal Station has established itself as neutral territory for most countries."

"Outer space is a hostile environment. Humans must band together and support each other. Civilization is not necessarily large groups in big cities. It can be small groups working together in innovative ways to survive. We don't know how long this d tente in outer space will last. If our technology falls into the wrong hands, I'm afraid they will weaponize and start wars on earth and in space. Here in space, earthly politics mean nothing. No one owns the universe as far as we know."

"Reading the Argonite journals, it appears that they thought that intelligent life on certain planets did not survive for many reasons," Conrad continues. "One major cause is the environment naturally turns against the inhabitants. They are unable to cope with the new environment and do not survive. Another problem might be that a more aggressive or assertive species overcome them. Certain species do not evolve and stay primitive.

The Argonites wrote extensively about what they found when they arrived on earth. Their journals detail the movements of Homo sapiens twelve thousand years ago, almost up until recently. They write about groups which ranged from peaceful hunter-gathers and farmers to savage predators."

"Viruses and diseases can decimate a primitive humanoid population. However, the virus will wipe out a group and then die off. Now there is a global population. Huge numbers of people may be wiped out from unchecked disease. People whose parents might never have survived to create the next generation are running around acting like plagues are nothing to worry about. Forget about smallpox or polio. Measles can kill their children, and they are willing to risk it."

"We are the descendants of multiple humanoid species on the planet. Not to mention the Argonites. We may have no choice but to travel beyond this solar system if it appears humans on Earth can't evolve beyond their current place."

Josh said, "Studying the Argonite journals and listening to their stories, it is clear they did not journey in space looking to conquer other civilizations. Once they find Earth has a humanoid population, they plan to leave. They are bound by their culture not to stay. In contrast, Homo sapiens project their warlike tendencies onto the universe. They think aliens are out to conquer Earth! Other species who survive, humanoid or not, probably have no wish to conquer other civilizations. Some may know we're here but choose to stay away. Once they observe the culture on earth, they probably choose to cross the street and look away. If Earth survives with its current tendencies, it may find a universe that rejects it."

Marcella seems a bit sad when she says, "we don't know for sure what might happen on Earth in the next decade. The politics, chaos, and climate change may bring disaster to the planet. Some people want to evolve and save the planet. Others seem to not care about future generations. I dream that somehow humanity survives and matures."

Marcella continues, "We must be prepared to continue the journey the ancient Argonites began twelve thousand years ago. We continue to build a human presence in the solar system. Do our best to foster a cooperative, empathetic, and science-based culture both in space and on earth. We continue to build this new ship and develop a star drive. When things are ready, we can decide how to proceed."

Tamara said, "Here we are, sitting in space at L5, talking about how dire the direction of humanity on planet Earth appears. Do you think we are overlooking how far we have come in so short a time? I say we because whatever traces of alien humanoid cells we may have, we are human. Seventy-five years ago, no one was in space. In 1957 Sputnik was launched. Science has cured a myriad of diseases, and life has been prolonged for masses of people. Technology logarithmically advances every year. No one can deny the cruelty of war or the use of weapons like nuclear bombs. We have managed not to use them since 1945. Homo sapiens have been the dominant species on this planet for a short time. Reading and writing are so new that many indigenous people still have no written language. There must be potential for a species that can learn this quickly."

Arno hesitates to speak but then finds his voice. "I did the DNA tests that Conrad recommends. According to the tests, I might have some Argonite DNA tucked away somewhere. I don't have any memories I can't explain. Humans like me have been subject to some of the worse instincts of Homo sapiens over time. We are only several generations away from slavery in the U.S. There are still caste systems around the world that put darker-skinned people at the bottom. It is easier to classify people by skin color than by some other system like religion, but they do that too. I look around and see the amazing achievements of architects and engineers of all persuasions. I find great works of art in museums. I am not religious, but I feel the spirituality in some religions. I understand the human quest to comprehend how we fit into this universe. I see acts of cruelty at the same time as sincere compassion. I'm not a social scientist or a psychologist. I think about half of humanity is ready to evolve culturally. What we do here in space may be the spark that finally unites humans. I believe it is too soon to make a summary judgment on the long-term survival of Homo sapiens."

"I agree with both Tamara and Arno. What happens in human history is more than the toss of a coin. Resilience and learning by trial and error are human traits. There may be some rough periods ahead. We came from the medieval dark ages and the horrors of the second world war. And we, because everyone is human now, whatever our memories. By being in outer space, we can help to make the road to the future less bumpy. I'm not suggesting we abandon the earth or that all is lost. My task is to make us aware of current trends. It may be that we need to be out here in space to preserve humanity. Evolution has its ups and downs. Conditions in the solar system may cause drastic changes in the environment on earth. Humanity needs to be prepared," Conrad said. "At this time, there is a cyclic struggle between certain countries on Earth to be the dominant culture. Some of the stronger rivals are totalitarian states. They seek to destroy American power worldwide. They encourage internal strife in democracies to make them weaker."

Josh said, "We are a species with intellect and emotions. We allow fear to dominate our emotions. Fear is the harbinger of anger, hate, guilt, judgmental thinking, and blame. A small percentage of people are learning about fear and how they are manipulated and used by those who want to control them. I don't want to abandon earth. I want to help it survive and evolve. What we are doing is hopefully helping the planet imagine the future."

"Raoul Sr. said, "Travel around the galaxy and return to this solar system is possible if we choose. This is what we are working on doing. Mars City is close to being self-sustaining for a limited population. I believe it is becoming possible to travel beyond our solar system and stay in communication with settlements and Earth here. We are at the gate to the galaxy. It may take a few years to open the gates fully. I'm sure they will be opened."

Coming Soon

PART II SILHOUETTES AND SHADOWS.

PART II

Life on Earth becomes dangerous for everyone associated with the International Space Exploration Group and Arroyo Aerospace. Josh, Adrienne, Tamara, Arno, and the Arroyo corporate family must consider where to be in the future.

It is 2037. Climate change on Earth is decimating portions of every continent. Human civilizations continue to fight for dominance of the planet. Europe is once again at war. Nuclear bombs have exploded in Eastern Europe and the Middle East. North and South American countries signed treaties and trade agreements with China to maintain peace between them.

The International Earth Terminal Station completes additional tiers. It is established as an international city. Certain countries on Earth threaten to invade the station or direct missiles there if they are not permitted to have a base on the terminal. A war between Earth and the space colonies seems likely.

Mars City and other Martian settlements have grown. They form a Martian planetary settlement alliance and pledge to work together despite tensions and earthly connections. They resist control by Earth. Mars has become the center for solar system exploration, asteroid belt mining, and travel to other planets. Arroyo Aerospace constructs and tests light-speed star drive at L5. The Space Exploration Group ships travel throughout the solar system. The Arroyo gravity drive remains secret. Unexpected visitors arrive at L5.

James R. Martin

Coming Soon

by James R Martin

ARGO NAVIS ODYSSEY ©

*The story of the Milonian (Argonite) Odyssey
on Earth.*

*Twelve Thousand years of recorded Earth
history previously unknown.*

ARGO NAVIS ODYSSEY

Twelve Thousand Years Ago.

The starship "Velo" moves in space as quickly as light from a solar object moves across the universe. Moving at the speed of light is becoming light for this ship carrying one thousand Milonians. They travel from Milonia, one planet in a vast constellation of Milky way stars known in another part of the galaxy as Argo because the shape of an ancient Greek sailing ship could be imagined from its bright stars.

Milonia's star is at the top of the ship's main mast. The star has twelve planets. Only one world, Milonia, sustains life. The other planets are uninhabitable. Five are too close to the giant star. Six are big rocks or frozen gas. Humanoid-type life evolves on Milonia, a watery world with one large continent. On Milonia and in the universe, water, H_2O, is the key to life emerging on a planet.

I am the Commander of the Velo. This is my journal. Our humanoid-type species evolved from the vast oceans onto the land. Over time, we inhabited a mountainous continent that spreads from the North to the South, covering about a third of the planet. The rest of the world is water—the oceans team with abundant life. The environment forced our ancestors to move onto the land. Our species has evolved on the mountainous terrain of the continent for millions of years.

The humanoid characteristics of Milonians from all parts of the land mass remain the same, with a few exceptions. Skin tone, height, eye color, and hair color vary. Everyone had two legs, arms, heads, facial features, ears, nostrils, mouths, and three eyes. A common language develops over time. Three distinct groups emerge as a civilization establishes itself on Milonia. There are Northern, Central, and Southern cultures on the planet.

The people of our planet never know war. There are no territorial lines anywhere on the continent. Food is abundant in the ocean. Milonians farm the sea and the land. Families are part of groups. Groups are part of communities. Communities are part of continental networks. Trade and barter exist. Early on, groups of families move from Northern to Southern or Central latitudes and from Southern to Northern or Central latitudes, depending on the weather. They learn to work together to survive climate change over millions of years. Time creates an advanced civilization of Milonians that springs from the myriad of small communities on the planet. They are advanced in science, technology, and medicine. There is no government or group of leaders. There are no rich or poor. These words are not in our vocabulary. There is an empathetic culture that celebrates life and health. There is a mentality that wherever one might live on the continent, you are part of the family.

The population on the planet grows to the point where floating cities are built on the ocean. Satellite communities are constructed to orbit the planet. Finally, starships are built that can transport Milonians to other solar systems where they might find uninhabited worlds to populate.

The Milonians aboard the starship Velo sleep while their ship, like a beam of light, moves toward the third planet in a distant solar system. A world our astronomers calculate has an abundance of water and a breathable atmosphere. As far as they could tell from light years away, the planet has no advanced life form. Presuming the world is habitable, there is one caveat regarding resettlement on the new planet. If the earth has a sentient life form or civilization, we will not be able to settle on that planet. We will need to find somewhere else to go. Even though this might be difficult since the starships are built and fueled for a one-way trip. Resources will need to be found to refuel and move on.

While we sleep on our starship streaking across the galaxy, life emerges on the blue planet. Evolution continues until one species, using its primitive intellectual abilities, dominates and absorbs other humanoid competitors. The primitive species spread across the planet over about 200,000 years. Only fully sentient for about 35,000 years before our starship goes into orbit around the planet. As the Captain of the ship, I am among the first to awaken on arrival.

To be continued.

James R. Martin